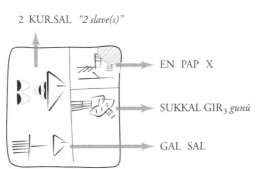

2 KUR.SAL *"2 slave(s)"*

EN PAP X

SUKKAL GIR$_3$ *gunû*

GAL SAL

2 KUR.SAL

EN PAP X

SUKKAL
GIR$_3$ *gunû*

GAL SAL

"2 slave(s)"

"ENPAP-X"

"SUKKALGIR"

"GAL-SAL"

"2 slave(s) (held by) GAL-SAL, (their names are) ENPAP-X and SUKKALGIR"

THE ORIENTAL INSTITUTE
2010-2011 ANNUAL REPORT

The Oriental Institute, Chicago

ISBN-13: 978-1-885923-88-2
ISBN-10: 1-885923-88-0

Editor: Gil J. Stein

Production coordinated by Zuhal Kuru, Publications Office Editorial Assistant

Cover illustration: Tablet with lists of Sumerian conjugations for the verb gub, and the equivalent Akkadian forms, nearly always a form of the verb *i/uzuzzu*, treated at length in CAD U/W, the final volume of the Chicago Assyrian Dictionary (2010). OIM A24186. Clay. Acquired from Crozer Theological Seminary. Old Babylonian(?). Ca. 10.5 x 9.0 cm. Photo by Andrew Dix

The pages that divide the sections of this year's report feature the various stages in the life of the cuneiform script

Printed by United Graphics Incorporated, Mattoon, Illinois

Overleaf: This text appears to identify two named slaves in the possession of a third individual. The sign for "slaves" in fact derives from two distinct signs, one for male (𒅘) and one for female (▷) slave. Typical of proto-cuneiform texts, the inscription does not include a preposition or verb, which would clarify the roles of the participants. This ambiguity is, in part, resolved by tablet format and the organization of information into cases. OIM A2513. Clay. Purchased (Jemdet Nasr?). Ca. 3100 BC. 4.6 x 4.6 x 2.4 cm. After Christopher Woods, "The Earliest Mesopotamian Writing," in Visible Language: Inventions of Writing in the Ancient Middle East and Beyond, *edited by Christopher Woods, p. 39, fig. 2.6 (Oriental Institute Museum Publications 32; Chicago: The Oriental Institute, 2010). Photo by Jean Grant*

CONTENTS

CONTENTS

INTRODUCTION

INTRODUCTION

Gil J. Stein

I am honored to present you with this year's *Oriental Institute Annual Report*. Looking through its various sections, you will see that the past year has been one of extremely important changes within the Oriental Institute — both milestones to celebrate and losses to mourn.

This year, I am sorry to report that we lost four dear members of the Oriental Institute's Visiting Committee — Alan Brodie, Janina Marks, David Kipper, and Marjorie Webster. Early this summer, we were all saddened to hear of the death of Oriental Institute Director Emeritus William Sumner. Bill was an internationally recognized scholar of Iranian archaeology and a Director who quite literally transformed the face of the Oriental Institute. Through his regional surveys of the Marv Dasht Plain around Persepolis, and his pioneering excavations at Malyan, Bill made a lasting contribution to our understanding of the civilizations of highland Iran. As Director of the Oriental Institute, Bill Sumner was one of those rare people who combined sweeping, creative vision with the nuts-and-bolts organizational skills to re-make the Oriental Institute by adding the new wing and undertaking the complete reinstallation of our permanent Museum galleries. Bill Sumner also was the guiding force behind the computerization of the Oriental Institute and the development of our website — now the most frequently visited Internet portal for the civilizations of the ancient Near East. Bill Sumner was the architect of the modern Oriental Institute, and we will miss him.

At the same time, we are proud to celebrate an extraordinary milestone in the completion of the Chicago Assyrian Dictionary (CAD), after an epic scholarly effort that lasted ninety years from inception to the publication in 2010/2011 of the final volume. The Oriental Institute is one of the very few places with the expertise and the intense institutional commitment necessary to undertake an enterprise of this magnitude. Editor-in-Charge Martha Roth and her colleagues deserve our thanks for having brought to fruition the work of her predecessors such as I. J. Gelb, A. Leo Oppenheim, and Erica Reiner. Thanks to the talents of these scholars who worked on the CAD for so many years, the world now has a true encyclopedia of Mesopotamian culture, as seen through the deep richness of the Akkadian language.

This past year has also been a time of momentous changes across the modern Middle East, as the revolutions of the "Arab Spring" overthrew long-standing regimes in Egypt, Tunisia, and Libya. In these upheavals, Egypt was a major focus of our concerns. It was inspiring and reassuring to see crowds in Cairo forming a human chain to surround and protect the Egyptian National Museum from the threat of looting. At the same time, the professionalism and support of the Egyptian Supreme Council of Antiquities made it possible for Epigraphic Survey Director W. Ray Johnson and his colleagues at Chicago House in Luxor to continue their work in complete safety and without interruption at Medinet Habu, Luxor, Karnak, and in the tombs of western Thebes.

Within the Oriental Institute, another major change has been the establishment of the Public Education Department as an independent unit with a broadened and ambitious mission of outreach to several "publics" — the University community, K–12 students, families with children, and the educated lay public. Carole Krucoff and her colleagues have embarked on an impressive variety of new initiatives in docent training, programming for the Kipper

Family Archaeology Discovery Center, new docent tours, outreach to the Latino community, public symposia, websites to help provide high school teachers with curricula for teaching about the Middle East, and the first of what we plan to be a full array of Internet-based adult education courses.

Our Museum also saw major changes with the departure of Chief Curator Geoff Emberling, and the arrival of our new Chief Curator, Jack Green, who comes to us from the Ashmolean Museum at Oxford University. It is a tribute to the abilities of the talented people on the Museum staff that this transition went so smoothly. During the 2010–2011 academic year, the Museum mounted two highly successful special exhibits. Visible Language, guest curated by Christopher Woods, told the fascinating story of the multiple inventions of writing in Mesopotamia, Egypt, the Maya world, and China, while exhibiting — for the first time in the United States — the world's earliest-known examples of writing from the fourth-millennium BC Mesopotamian city of Uruk. Our second special exhibit, Before the Pyramids, curated by Emily Teeter, gave a unique view of the Pre-Dynastic period, when Egypt first coalesced into a unified, centralized state during the fourth millennium BC.

A final major change in the Oriental Institute over the past year has been the implementation of the first stage of the Integrated Database, or IDB. This long-term project aims to connect all the major archives of objects, images, and data records in the Oriental Institute into a single searchable digital resource. We estimate (perhaps over-optimistically!) that it will take us ten years to complete this project. After an extended search process, John Sanders, Scott Branting, Foy Scalf, and others on the IDB committee ended up selecting KE Software's Electronic Museum (EMu), an advanced collections-management software system, as the platform for this ambitious database. This year, we finally began the actual creation of the database. The first data archives to become part of the IDB are the Museum's registry with its hundreds of thousands of objects, and the catalog of the Research Archives. The IDB is a tremendous advance that will transform the way we do research.

During these transformations at the Oriental Institute, our archaeologists have continued their important work of excavations across the Near East, at Edfu (Nadine Moeller), Giza (Mark Lehner), Hamoukar (Clemens Reichel), Kerkenes (Scott Branting), Marj Rabba (Yorke Rowan), Zeidan (Gil Stein), and Zincirli (David Schloen), while Don Whitcomb started a new joint Palestinian-American excavation project at Islamic Jericho-Khirbet al-Mafjar. Our text-based research flourishes as the Demotic Dictionary, under Janet Johnson's editorship, and the Hittite Dictionary, edited by Harry Hoffner and Theo van den Hout, continue their progress. Concurrently, the Persepolis Fortification Archive Project, directed by Matthew Stolper, moves toward completion of its urgent task of recording the texts and seal impressions in this endangered trove of tablets from the Persian empire.

Taken together, this is an extraordinary set of innovative research projects and programs of public outreach. In these times of major transitions, I am proud that the Oriental Institute remains true to the heart of its mission, while at the same time embracing change and seizing the opportunities and challenges it presents.

IN MEMORIAM

Alan Reid Brodie

We are sorry to inform you of the passing of our friend Alan Brodie, age 79, on October 18, 2010, at his home in Chicago. Alan joined the Oriental Institute Visiting Committee in 1997 and volunteered for a number of years prior to joining, becoming a consistent and engaged supporter of Oriental Institute work at Hamoukar in Syria.

Alan was born in Portland, Oregon, and attended Grant High School and Reed College, class of 1951. He then attended the University of Chicago Law School and was admitted to the Illinois Bar in 1954, practicing law at the firm of Bell, Boyd & Lloyd LLP for thirty years. Alan also served in the United States Army. We at the Oriental Institute will miss Alan's quiet wit, his keen curiosity, and his loyal friendship. Please keep him in your memories.

John L. Foster

We regret to announce the death on January 25, 2011, of long-time Oriental Institute research associate John ("Jack") Foster. Jack was a well-known translator of Egyptian literature, especially poetry. Among his books are *Love Songs of the New Kingdom; Echoes of Egyptian Voices*, and *Hymns, Prayers and Songs.* He was professor of English literature at Roosevelt University from 1966 to his retirement in 1994. An active member of both the Society for the Study of Egyptian Antiquities and the American Research Center in Egypt, for the latter, he was the editor of the *Journal of the American Research Center in Egypt* from 1984 to 2001 and a member of the Executive Committee of the Board of Governors from 1986 to 2001. At the time of his death, Jack was preparing a catalog of the Egyptian literary ostraca in the Oriental Institute collection.

Barbara L. Hamann

It is with great sadness that we learned that Barbara L. Hamann, who worked in the Conservation Laboratory from October 22, 1990, to September 5, 1998, passed away in November after losing her battle with cancer. Barbara initially pursued a career in archaeology and was awarded an MA in classical art and archaeology from the University of Michigan, Ann Arbor, but then decided to take a parallel track, that of archaeological conservation. After her graduation with honors from the Institute of Archaeology, University of London, with a degree in archaeological and ethnographic conservation, she spent a year at the Art Institute

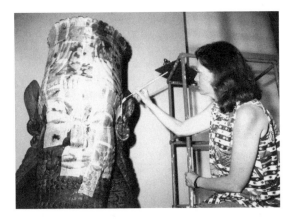

as the Getty Trust Post-Graduate intern before coming to the Oriental Institute as our first assistant conservator.

During Barbara's tenure, she played a key role in the Assyrian relief relocation project. During the years of preparation for the relocation and stabilization of the Museum's large-scale reliefs from Sargon's palace at Khorsabad, she tested and researched products and techniques that would be used in the stabilization of the reliefs. She worked closely with the riggers and framers as the reliefs were moved and placed in steel frames, and spent many hours ensuring that conservation standards and procedures were followed.

Her hard work and dedication to the field was evident from the beginning and she continued to grow as conservation professional throughout her career. When Barbara left in 1998 to broaden her conservation experience, her absence was keenly felt. Her contribution to conservation at the Oriental Institute, and her legacy, is something that will live on in the Institute's memory. Anyone who has worked in the Lab after Barbara's time here recognizes her name, from her countless conservation treatments to her pivotal work on the Khorsabad Assyrian Relief Fragment Project. Her contribution was instrumental in making that undertaking a success. We missed her dry wit and conservation expertise when she left Chicago. We are even more saddened that her life and career were cut so short.

David A. Kipper

Oriental Institute Visiting Committee member Dr. David A. Kipper passed away on December 2, 2011. David, a clinical psychologist and research professor, was a committed supporter of cultural institutions in the Chicago area. In addition to his deep involvement with the Spertus Institute and the Joffrey Ballet, he was a real friend to the Oriental Institute. The generosity of David and his wife Barbara in founding the Kipper Family Archaeology Discovery Center has enriched the lives of many children in the short time since its opening. In the years to come it will continue to inspire school children with the excitement of exploring ancient civilizations. It is hard to think of a more fitting memorial to David. He will be remembered for his intelligence, fairness, warmth, humor, wisdom, and kindness. We will all miss him.

Janina Monkuté Marks

This past year we were greatly saddened by the death of our friend Janina Marks, age 87, on November 13, 2010. Janina had been a member of the Oriental Institute Visiting Committee since 1995, after having been a supporter for the previous twenty years.

Janina had a lifelong love of archaeology and especially art, as reflected not only in her engagement with the Oriental Institute, but also by own work as an artist. She was a nationally and internationally exhibited artist, best known for weaving large tapestries initially of Lithuanian folk themes and subsequently drawing from her American life experience after immigrating to Chicago in 1949. Her participation and support of the Oriental Institute and other art and cultural institutions in Chicago and beyond are a testament to her belief in giving back to her community. Ten years ago, Janina founded the first nonprofit museum, a textile museum, in her native Lithuania — the Janina Monkuté-Marks Museum Gallery in Kėdainiai.

William Sumner, Director Emeritus, Oriental Institute

William M. Sumner, a leading figure in the study of ancient Iran and director of the Oriental Institute at the University of Chicago from 1989 to 1997, died July 7, 2011, in Columbus, Ohio. Sumner, who oversaw a major expansion of the Institute's building, was 82.

Sumner, a resident of Columbus, was a 1952 graduate of the United States Naval Academy. He served in the Navy until 1964, rising to the rank of lieutenant commander.

He developed his interest in archaeology during naval service in the Mediterranean. Visits to ancient sites in Italy and Greece inspired him to pursue a graduate education. While serving in Iran, he developed a keen interest in that country's ancient civilization and he pursued that interest by taking a class taught at Tehran University by Ezat Ngahban, a professor there and a graduate of the University of Chicago.

Sumner resigned from the Navy to pursue graduate work in anthropology. He received his PhD from Pennsylvania in 1972 and was a member of the anthropology faculty at Ohio State from 1971 until he joined the Chicago faculty as professor in the Oriental Institute and in the Department of Near Eastern Languages and Civilizations in 1989.

"Bill Sumner was an outstanding archaeologist and a transformational leader at the Oriental Institute," said Gil Stein, director of the Oriental Institute. "His survey and excavations at the urban center of Malyan in the highlands of Iran made a lasting contribution to our understanding of the Elamite civilization and the deep roots of the Persian empire. He trained an entire generation of archaeologists who went on to become major scholars in their own right in the study of ancient Iran and Anatolia.

"As director of the Oriental Institute, Bill Sumner had the vision, the drive, and the organizational skills to conceptualize and carry out the building of our new wing, and the complete reinstallation of our permanent Museum galleries. Most of all, Bill was a man with tremendous personal integrity, who led by example. His death is a sad loss for our field, and we will miss him very deeply," Stein added.

At the Oriental Institute, Sumner encouraged the use of new technologies to expand the work of archaeologists in the field and in the laboratory.

"He saw the value, and sensed the impending importance of digital communication and publication, and laid the foundations for the next decade of development along these lines in the OI," said Gene Gragg, professor emeritus at the Oriental Institute. Gragg succeeded Sumner as director.

Sumner recognized the value to archaeology and history of the use of computational technologies and scientific instrumentation. "Bill was a visionary, one of the first who understood the ways that digitalization and computational tools could transform the humanistic and social science disciplines," said Martha T. Roth, the Chauncey S. Boucher Distinguished Service Professor of Assyriology in the Oriental Institute and dean of the Humanities Division. "And he was a scholar and person of deep personal and professional integrity."

He also oversaw the initiation of the largest expansion of the Oriental Institute building since it was constructed in 1931. With the help of a federal grant and a $10.1 million campaign, the Institute built a new wing to provide space for the equipment needed for climate control, as well as provide space for proper and climate-controlled artifact and archival storage. The new wing also houses a modern artifact conservation laboratory.

The Oriental Institute Museum also underwent a massive redesign that began under his leadership. That redesign led to a rearrangement of the galleries and an updated presentation of the Museum's art and artifacts from throughout the ancient Middle East.

Sumner's own academic work specialized on ancient Iran. From 1972 until 1978 he directed the University of Pennsylvania's excavations at the site of Tal-i Malyan, ancient Anshan, in the Fars province in western Iran. Sumner oversaw the publication of a series of monographs based on the work of five field seasons of fieldwork there.

The Malyan archaeological project was seminal not only in discovering the highland Elamite city of Anshan, known locally as Malyan, but also in the cycles of nomadism and sedentism in the region of Fars, southern Iran, that operated in the region from at least fifth millennium BC, said Abbas Alizadeh, an Oriental Institute archaeologist who specializes on Iran.

In addition to his work on the Malyan monograph series, Sumner wrote many articles on the development of civilization in ancient Iran.

———————

Marjorie Webster

Most of you are aware that our dear friend Marjorie ("Madge") Webster passed away this past May at her home Santa Barbara, California. Madge grew up in Winnetka, Illinois, and early on developed a deep intellectual interest in archaeology and the ancient world. Madge participated in archaeological excavations in the American Southwest, and shortly after World War II worked as a volunteer on a dig led by Robert Braidwood at Starved Rock, Illinois. This began her close friendship with the Braidwood family and her involvement with the work of the Oriental Institute. Madge was an engaged and loyal member of the Oriental Institute Visiting Committee starting in 1961, and had just marked her fiftieth year of service shortly before her death. Madge was a strong supporter of Bob and Linda Braidwood's Prehistoric Project — first at Jarmo (Iraq) and later in southeast Turkey at Çayonu. After the Braidwoods' death in 2003, Madge was instrumental in establishing the Robert and Linda Braidwood Visiting Scholar program. Madge's lifelong involvement with archaeology was matched by her fascination with antique astronomical instruments and her involvement with the Adler Planetarium, where she and her late husband Roderick were co-curators of the Adler's world-renowned collection of antique astrolabes. We will miss Madge greatly.

———————————

Overleaf: This Old Babylonian letter details a request for money to buy a slave girl; it also includes an ingratiating inquiry into the well-being of the recipient. The tablet exemplifies the physical characteristics of the script in the first half of the second millennium. OIM A22003. Iraq, Ishchali. Clay. Old Babylonian period, 2000–1600 BC. 7.3 x 4.1 x 1.7 cm. After Christopher Woods, "59. Letter," in Visible Language: Inventions of Writing in the Ancient Middle East and Beyond, *edited by Christopher Woods, p. 94, no. 59 (Oriental Institute Museum Publications 32; Chicago: The Oriental Institute, 2010). Photo by Anna Ressman*

CAMEL
CENTER FOR ANCIENT MIDDLE EASTERN LANDSCAPES

http://oi.uchicago.edu/research/camel

Scott Branting

This past year found CAMEL in the midst of several long-term projects focused on making geospatial data of the ancient and modern Near East more widely available and easily accessible. Geospatial data like maps, satellite images, and aerial photographs are critical because through them we can see changing landscapes from ancient to modern times for this important region of the world. From its inception almost a hundred years ago, the Oriental Institute has been actively involved in the collection and analysis of these types of data. CAMEL has accelerated this research trajectory by working extensively on digitally capturing, preserving, and making more accessible maps and images from both the Oriental Institute's collections and other important collections around the world.

A primary focus of work within CAMEL this year has been the preliminary stages of collaboratively digitizing large portions of the map collection held at the W. F. Albright Institute of Archaeological Research in Jerusalem (AIAR). This initiative, made possible by a four-year United States Department of Education, Technological Innovation and Cooperation for Foreign Information Access (TICFIA) grant, will make some of these rare maps available for the first time online to researchers and interested individuals around the world. While undertaking the work of cataloging the collections and producing metadata for each of the maps, I was reminded of how Ray Tindel, the longtime registrar of the Oriental Institute Museum, said that the basement of the Institute was like an archaeological site that he continued to excavate every day. The same could be said of the AIAR map collection, preliminary estimates for which suggested that there would be 230 unique maps to digitize. This past year, in partnership with the excellent AIAR library staff, we have identified 784 map sheets. This is nearly three times what was thought to be there. Each of these 784 maps is now largely cataloged and ready for digitization later this summer. Over the next three years not only will these maps be digitized and georectified, a process by which spatial data are encoded with their real locations on the surface of the earth, but the same process will be undertaken in collaboration with the American Research Center in Egypt (ARCE), the American Institute for Maghrib Studies in Algeria (CEMA), and Chicago House. Important portions of each of these unique collections of maps will be digitally preserved and made available online through CAMEL by 2014.

While working collaboratively on these new sources of maps, CAMEL continued the long process of georectifying the over 1,100 U.S. Declassified Spy Satellite images in the CAMEL collections. As noted last year, over 300 of these images had been sent to Jesse Casana at the University of Arkansas to be georectified in a more automated fashion as part of a National

Endowment for the Humanites grant. The additional images we have set out to rectify our-selves, one at a time and at a fraction of the cost, while we await the outcome of Jesse's proj-ect. Over this past year 156 additional strips of these images were carefully georectified by CAMEL, bringing the total for two years to 261 images. These images, once georectified, are extremely useful to researchers interested in finding traces of ancient Near Eastern settle-ments and landscapes that existed into the twentieth century. They also provide important information on how the modern Middle East has changed over the past fifty years.

In addition to these long-term projects, CAMEL continued to serve the research com-munity both within the Oriental Institute and around the world. Data searches were con-ducted and data made available to researchers from across the United States, Europe, and the Middle East. These requests encompassed a wide range of geospatial data from countries all over the Middle East. The CAMEL laboratory has been busy facilitating research by those at the Institute and also printing out a number of large-format illustrations for the Museum's ongoing program of special exhibits. Finally, CAMEL has also been hosting Arne Wossink, a post-doctoral scholar who graduated from Leiden University. His work at CAMEL, focusing on site detection and preservation in Iraqi Kurdistan, has been funded by a prestigious Rubicon Grant from the Netherlands Organisation for Scientific Research (NWO).

CAMEL continued to partner throughout the year with Wendy Ennes in the Oriental Institute's Public Education Department in order to expand our outreach program among Chicago's public schools. Last year a grant was received from the Chicago Public Schools' Mu-seum Connection Program that allowed us to develop a cross-disciplinary program for sixth-grade students at Claremont Academy. It combined hands-on archaeological excavations in the Kipper Family Archaeology Discovery Center at the Oriental Institute with skills in using Geographic Information Systems (GIS) computer software to analyze spatial distributions of artifacts. The success of this program was recognized this year by the Lloyd A. Fry Founda-tion, which chose to generously fund a two-year follow-on project. The new project, ArcGIS Cross-Curricular Education for Sixth Grade Students Program (ACCESS), will train a group of sixth-grade teachers across three Chicago public schools in these same concepts. We will then work collaboratively with the teachers to design a suite of educational modules that fit their cross-curricular needs while making use of these tools and a variety of geospatial data.

The time and effort of CAMEL's dedicated staff and volunteers are what make CAMEL a success. During most of this year Robert Tate served as associate director. In April, Robert left us to pursue a wonderful opportunity for employment. We certainly wish him the best and thank him for his years of dedicated service. Following his departure, Susan Penacho and Elise MacArthur were elevated from their previous rank of assistant directors to associate directors. Matt Cuda and Meg Swaney served as senior supervisors. Bryan Kraemer continued to serve as database administrator for our growing collections while also working with us as a student assistant. Hannah Loftus, Sami Sweis, Sadie Samuels, and Courtney Jacobson were all student assistants. Xander Piper and Tiana Pyer-Pereira worked with us on the ACCESS project as interns in Public Education, while Haeden Stewart worked on ACCESS as a volun-teer. CAMEL volunteers for this year were Alexander Elwyn, Larry Lissak, Craig Tews, and Peter Fiske. Without their patience and hard work little could be accomplished. In the same way, I would like to thank all those this year who donated financially or in contributions of geospatial data to CAMEL's collections.

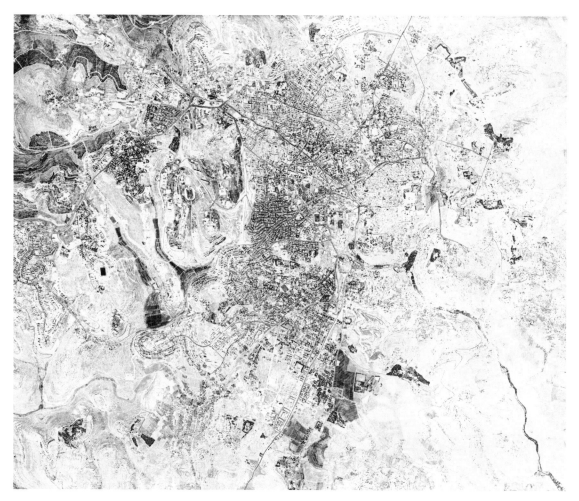

Figure 1. A portion of one of the just over 1,100 U.S. Declassified Spy Satellite images, also called Corona images, from CAMEL's holdings. These images form an important part of the CAMEL archive and offer researchers important clues to now vanished ancient and modern landscapes. This image of Jerusalem was taken in 1970

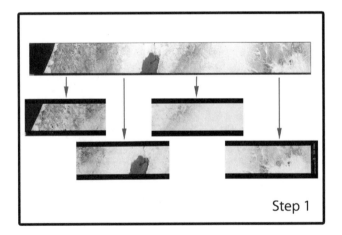

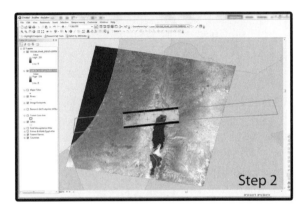

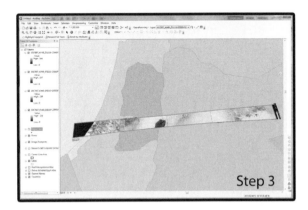

Figure 2. Georectification of the Declassified Spy Satellite images is a three-step process. The digital images are first digitally cut into four separate images so as to minimize distortion along the long image during the rectification process (Step 1). The locations of common points, things like building corners or more permanent landscape features, are then input for both the first image being rectified and an already georectified second image such as this Landsat satellite image. The computer shifts the images so that the points from the first image match the locations found in the second image (Step 2). With each segment in its proper location on the surface of the earth, a footprint for the entire image and each constituent segment is added into the CAMEL database along with the georectified images (Step 3)

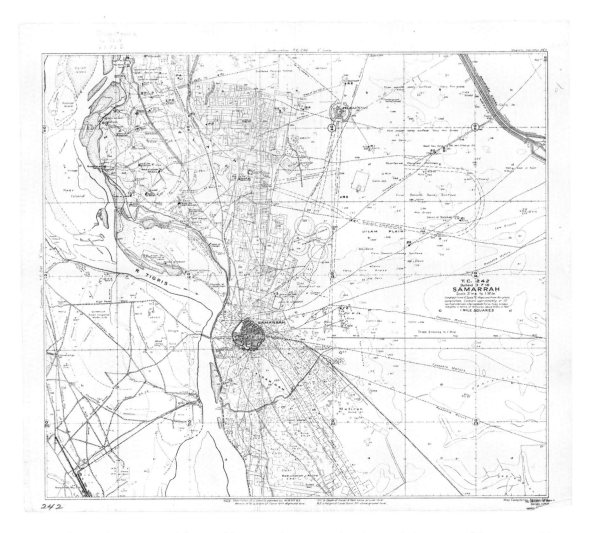

Figure 3. This British Survey map of the city of Samarra in Iraq was produced in 1918. It shows parts of this important Islamic capital and UNESCO World Heritage Site that have since been obscured or even destroyed. Thanks to a donation of the map for digitization by Dr. McGuire Gibson, this early map is now part of CAMEL's digital archive. This will facilitate access to this map by researchers, students, and everyone interested in what was visible at Samarra in the early twentieth century. Donations of paper maps and aerial photographs pertaining to the Near East are always welcome at CAMEL

CHICAGO ASSYRIAN DICTIONARY (CAD)

Martha T. Roth

2010–11 saw the publication of the final volume of the Chicago Assyrian Dictionary. The last detailed tasks occupied Manuscript Editor Linda McLarnan, Research Assistant Anna Hudson Steinhelper, and me for much of the year. Below is an edited version of the lecture I presented at the celebratory symposium for the completion of the project, held at the Oriental Institute on 6 June 2011. For more detailed histories, the reader is referred to I. J. Gelb's "Introduction" to CAD A/1 (1964) and Erica Reiner's *An Adventure of Great Dimension* (2002).

The CAD was ambitiously begun in 1921 under the guidance of James Henry Breasted, whose vision for collaborative projects launched the Oriental Institute, the University of Chicago's first research institute. Housed originally in the basement of Haskell Hall and under the direction of Daniel D. Luckenbill, the small staff of scholars and students began to produce the data set by typing editions onto 5 x 8 cards, duplicating with a hectograph, parsing, and filing. Luckenbill died unexpectedly in 1927 at the age of 46, and Edward Chiera was called to Chicago from the University of Pennsylvania to take over the project. The enlarged resident staff was augmented by some twenty international collaborators, and in 1930 the project moved into its current home in the new building, to a spacious room on the third floor that was specially reinforced to hold the weight of tons of file cabinets and books. Technological advances allowed the old hectograph to be replaced with a modern mimeograph machine for duplicating the cards. Alas, Chiera too died young, at the age of 48, in 1933, and the directorship of the project passed to Arno Poebel, who came to Chicago in 1930 also from the University of Pennsylvania. Collecting of data continued under each successive editor — Luckenbill, Chiera, Poebel — and by 1936 more than one million file cards were in the banks of cabinets, alphabetized and arranged by key word. With the onset of World War II, work on the Dictionary came to a halt, but after the war and the retirement of Arno Poebel in 1946, I. J. Gelb, who had come to Chicago in 1928 from the University of Rome, assumed the helm.

The post-war years were the boom years for the project: the University brought into our midsts a number of scholars displaced by the European disaster, and the Oriental Institute benefited enormously: in 1947 Benno Landsberger (who had been a Dictionary collaborator since 1932, working from Leipzig and then Ankara) and A. Leo Oppenheim from Vienna, and in 1952 Erica Reiner from Budapest and Paris. By this time, too, the editors had given up on the ambition to collect every single known cuneiform text and to fully parse every occurrence of every word in favor of excerpting; the project no longer aimed to be comprehensive and eternal.

In 1950, Gelb went to Europe to see if he could acquire the data sets that had been assembled before the war by Bruno Meissner under the auspices of the Prussian Academy of Sciences since the mid-1920s. Meissner had died in 1947, at the age of 78, and the project had been inherited by Adam Falkenstein, then at the University of Heidelberg, and Wolfram von Soden. The two projects, in Chicago and Heidelberg, attempted a formal collaboration, the details of which were recorded in a document called "The Marburg Agreement" and formally ratified by the Union Académique Internationale in 1951. Alas, the projects and personalities could not be united and any formal collaboration quickly broke down, although informal contact and exchange of information continued until the completion of the German project, under the direction and almost the sole authorship of Wolfram von Soden, as a three-volume compendium, published in fascicles from 1965 to 1981.

Back in Chicago, the senior members of the faculty, Gelb, Jacobsen, Landsberger, and Oppenheim, jostled for dominance. The differences were, at this time, mainly theoretical and methodological: Gelb advocated for a highly rigid linguistic analysis and descriptive presentation, with each entry organized by grammatical categories; Landsberger insisted on a highly "semantic" approach. Oppenheim wrote in his comments to the differing proposals, "It is rather obvious that both these 'systems' reflect the individual psychological make-up of their originators; Landsberger prefers the dogmatic approach that is an adequate expression of his scholarly standing and temper, while Gelb wishes to follow the 'objectivity' of the American linguistic school" (quoted in Reiner 2002: 24). As Reiner wrote later in her history of the project, "It is quite clear that for Landsberger and Oppenheim the elucidation of the word's *meaning* was of primary importance, whereas for Gelb the orderly presentation of the evidence was crucial" (ibid., 25).

The internal strife and personality conflicts occupied the energies of the Director of the Oriental Institute, Carl Kraeling, as well as the offices of the Dean, Provost, and President. Finally, Gelb resigned at the end of 1954 and never again participated in the production of the Dictionary. As he wrote of himself in the third person a decade later in 1964: "Gelb went on leave of absence for one year, which was prolonged indefinitely due to his inability or unwillingness to adjust to the new spirit prevailing in the Dictionary" (CAD A/1, p. xix).

Oppenheim now took the helm in 1955 and proceeded to do what no one else had been willing to do for the preceding thirty-five years: produce a volume of the Dictionary. The first volume, devoted to the words beginning with the letter H, was sent to press in October 1955 and the second, G, to press in July 1956, appearing in print within a few months of each other in 1956 and 1957. The two volumes were largely the work of Oppenheim and the junior members of the team Reiner, Hallock, and Rowton, and came in for much — and much deserved — harsh criticism from scholars throughout the world and especially in Chicago. As one might imagine from the speed with which the volumes were actually written, edited, and published — what Benno Landsberger famously called "insane haste" — the process of citation checking suffered. The subsequent finger-pointing devolved into a raging and vicious feud between Thorkild Jacobsen and Leo Oppenheim, and centered on the publication of the third volume, E. The details of the feud that irreparably severed personal and professional ties has been recounted in Reiner's history of the project, *An Adventure of Great Dimension*. Volume E included several words key to Jacobsen's evolving positions on Mesopotamian religion (such as the words ēnu and ēntu, "priest" and "priestess," and erṣetu, "earth" and "nether world"), and the volume was sent to press in August 1957 without Jacobsen's input. Jacobsen prepared a long and detailed list of what he called "errors" in the volume and presented them to the voting members of the Oriental Institute along with an accusation directed at the Director of the Institute, Carl Kraeling, a biblical scholar, for dereliction of duty and an "inability to maintain the scholarly standards of the Institute." In an eleven-page defense of his directorship, Kraeling perforce defended the Dictionary and Oppenheim, without fully smoothing over the antagonisms, however. By 1959, when Oppenheim was offered a position at Johns

Hopkins and Reiner a position at Harvard, the two were tempted to leave and abandon the Dictionary. The University succeeded in retaining them, but, alas, with the consequence of further alienating Jacobsen, who resigned from the editorial board of the Dictionary. Once again, in 1960, Jacobsen prepared a detailed list of errors in the fifth volume, I/J. The director of the Institute then was the Egyptologist John Wilson, and he turned to Benno Landsberger to try to intercede, but to no avail. In 1962, Reiner again received an offer from Harvard. Edward Levi, then president of the University, in trying to retain her, downplayed the offer by telling Erica that "Everybody gets an invitation to Harvard." When she added that it was her second offer, he replied "Everybody who is somebody gets two invitations to Harvard."

With the strong support of the University administration and the appointment of Robert McCormack Adams to the directorship of the Oriental Institute, Reiner turned down the Harvard offer. Jacobsen promptly had the offer extended to himself and left Chicago in 1962.

The project was at that point forty years old, which calls to mind a first-millennium learned compendium from Sultantepe (STT 400) that outlines the following "ages of man":

40, the prime of life

50, a short life

60, maturity

70, a long life

80, old age

90, extreme old age

The Dictionary was thus in the "prime of life" at 40: robust, vigorous, active. Indeed it is at this time that three of the current members of the team first came to Chicago: Bob Biggs, Tony Brinkman, and Miguel Civil all began their affiliations with the Dictionary in 1963. Thus began what Erica Reiner later called "a dozen years of peace and progress," when the team worked and completed the volumes Z, Ṣ, A, B, K, and L. In 1970 Herman Hunger arrived in Chicago. By 1972, when Leo Oppenheim retired and left the Dictionary in the hands of Biggs, Brinkman, Civil, Hunger, and Reiner, eleven volumes had seen publication.

Oppenheim's unexpected death in 1974 was traumatic for Reiner and for the project. She wrote later: "Oppenheim's death occasioned a profound change in the life of the project as well as in my own relation to it. Gone was the reassurance.... No other senior Assyriologist was on hand to turn to when I needed advice. The attitudes of the members of the CAD staff were varied: Some, possibly resenting that a woman was in charge, offered [help] but their initiative soon petered out. At this juncture the importance of the contributions of Miguel Civil, not only in the field of Sumerian ... became evident. ... His expertise assured the quality of the Dictionary ... after Oppenheim's death" (2002: 69).

After a somewhat shaky start as editor-in-charge, Erica Reiner became a fierce and formidable advocate and defender of the project. Under her leadership, the National Endowment for the Humanities (NEH) began its invaluable support of the project. The NEH funded the Dictionary from 1975 through 2003. During this time of ample funding support, the project brought in dozens of junior and senior colleagues from institutions throughout the world. Among them were several who became more than transient visitors. I myself came to Chicago in 1979 on the NEH grant, a brand-new PhD from the University of Pennsylvania with experience on the Sumerian Dictionary project there. By now the Dictionary was sixty years old — maturity — and Erica Reiner and Miguel Civil warned me that there was no long-term future here, that the project would be completed shortly.

The Assyrian Dictionary was by then, in its maturity, a well-established, highly respected, and indeed indispensible project. Today's students simply cannot imagine learning Akkadian without the tools. I vividly remember as a graduate student eagerly awaiting the publication of the M volume. We anticipated the appearance of each new volume with a true hunger for the insights and wisdom of the Chicago Assyrian Dictionary team.

Although the people and operations of the Dictionary were not always smooth, the project never again experienced the turmoil and uncertainty of those years in the 1950s. Under Oppenheim's editorship, eleven volumes had been published, and under Erica Reiner's editorial eye and hand — trained by Oppenheim — five more volumes were published (M, N, Q, S, and Š) and one was in press (T). When Reiner retired in 1996 and I assumed the reins — similarly excruciatingly trained by Reiner — she continued to come to the office every day to work on the Dictionary and to look over my shoulder. It wasn't always easy or comfortable for me or any of us. We all, the in-house collaborators and editorial board — Bob Biggs, Tony Brinkman, Miguel Civil, Walter Farber, and Matt Stolper — had begun to move on to other projects, other intellectual pursuits. The Dictionary in 1996 when I assumed responsibility for the project, was, at seventy-five, in the terms of that Babylonian compendium, in the time of "long life" and "old age." It was, in other words, getting tired. It was time to move from a stance of keeping the project alive to one in which it would actually be finished.

One of my first tasks as editor-in-charge in 1996 was to retrieve the manuscript of the T volume from the publisher J. J. Augustin, based in Glückstadt, Germany, with its American office in Locust Valley, New York. Augustin was a distinguished publisher of some of the finest-quality technical humanistic books in the world, and had been the skilled compositor of every volume to date, first in "hot type" (molten lead cast into letters and lines of type) and then in "cold type" (typeset by computers and pasted up into pages). But the firm had run into financial difficulties and was holding up publication of the T manuscript, which we had sent to them in 1991. With the help of the University's legal office we succeeded in having the only marked-up copy returned to Chicago and sent then to Eisenbraun's for composition in 2000. Eisenbraun's became the compositor for every subsequent volume, and has been an outstanding partner.

The story is now drawing to an undramatic close. When I took over as editor-in-charge, the remaining volumes had all at least been started, to varying degrees. One by one, they have seen publication: R in 1999, P in 2005, T (belatedly) and Ṭ both in 2006. As each cleared the "pipeline," the project came closer to completion. Over the last years, our attention was focused exclusively on completing the very last volume, U/W, which went to press in 2007 and finally appeared this winter, in 2010/11.

The ninety-year chain of editorial direction — Daniel Luckenbill, Edward Chiera, Arno Poebel, I. J. Gelb, A. Leo Oppenheim, Erica Reiner, Martha T. Roth — was unbroken. The project has engaged eighty-nine scholars over its ninety-year history, some coming to Chicago for short sojourns before going off to teach and research in universities and museums all over the globe. The final U/W volume alone involved some twenty colleagues at all stages, scholars who are now teaching in Madrid, Vienna, New York, Helsinki, Leiden, Brigham Young, Loyola, Johns Hopkins, and Cornell — taking their Chicago experiences and lessons and passing them on to yet future generations of scholars.

Now, in 2011, the entire set of the Dictionary is available to the scholarly world, in print and online. After an initial thirty-five years of data-gathering, the teams of scholars here at the Oriental Institute produced twenty-six tomes over the next fifty-five years, a pace of publication of which we must all be extremely proud. I have had a hand in seven volumes: P, R, S, Š, T, Ṭ, and U/W — at the beginning as a first-draft writer, as a reader of galleys and proofs, as a critical-citation checker, as a first-run editor, as final editor with ultimate responsibility for the quality and accuracy of the published volume. Always, the University of Chicago seeks (in President Robert Zimmer's words "to make discoveries of lasting impact and to define the modes of inquiry for the future." We have engaged successfully in that task here at the Oriental Institute. Scholarship — enduring scholarship — progresses by the gradual accrual of knowledge over generations.

References

Reiner, Erica

2002   *An Adventure of Great Dimension: The Launching of the Chicago Assyrian Dictionary*. Philadelphia: American Philosophical Society.

STT = Gurney, Oliver Robert, and P. Hulin

1964   *The Sultantepe Tablets II*. Occasional Publications of the British Institute of Archaeology at Ankara 7. London: British Institute of Archaeology at Ankara.

Aage Westenholz and Johannes Renger (with backs to camera), Richard T. Hallock, A. Leo Oppenheim (by bookshelves), Jean Nougayrol, I. J. Gelb (with pipe), and Erica Reiner

Chicago Demotic Dictionary (CDD)

François Gaudard and Janet H. Johnson

The staff of the Chicago Demotic Dictionary, namely, Janet Johnson, François Gaudard, Brittany Hayden, and Mary Szabady, spent the year checking drafts of entries for the last letter files in progress. We have been assisted by Oriental Institute docent Larry Lissak, who scanned photographs of various Demotic texts and also part of Wilhelm Spiegelberg's *Nachlasse*. Letter files P (183 pages), M (312 pages), and, more recently, ꜣI (250 pages) have been posted online. As for the last two letters, T (297 pages) has been entirely checked and will be posted after a final style check, and S (400 pages), by far the largest of all the files, is currently being worked on. The numbers file (154 pages) is in the process of being double-checked. We would like to thank all our colleagues for their useful comments and suggestions, in particular, Joachim Friedrich Quack, Friedhelm Hoffmann, and Eugene Cruz-Uribe. Special thanks go to Veena Elisabeth Frank Jørgensen for providing us with various references from the files in Copenhagen.

In addition to everyday words, the CDD also includes specialized vocabulary (e.g., religious, legal, and mathematical terminology). Although we don't incorporate personal names unless there is a word of special interest in the name (the recently completed *Demotisches Namenbuch*[1] is an excellent resource), we do include many royal names and epithets, especially those of the Ptolemies and of the Roman emperors. For the latter, the various forms of an epithet or royal name are given for each emperor who bore them. Since most of the epithets and names of the Roman emperors were used by several different emperors, each of these entries is organized by emperor, indicating distinctive combinations of epithets used by the different rulers. It is hoped the user of the Dictionary will be able, this way, to avoid the confusion inherent in dealing with a name or epithet borne by several rulers by comparing the disparate writings of the name or epithet or by identifying the full list of titles of various emperors. However, for very common epithets used by almost all emperors, such as *Autocrator* (Greek "absolute ruler," corresponding to Latin *Imperator* "emperor"), *Caesar* (Greek but used as royal name by Augustus and as imperial title by subsequent emperors), and *Sebastos* (Greek equivalent of Latin *Augustus*), the reader will have to consult each emperor's individual entry for further information.

On September 2, 31 BC, the defeat of the joint forces of Mark Antony and Cleopatra VII by the fleet of Octavian at Actium, a promontory on the western coast of Greece, settled the fate of Ptolemaic Egypt. Octavian entered Alexandria on August 1, 30 BC, and Mark Antony and Cleopatra committed suicide. Later, Octavian changed his name to Augustus and became the first Roman emperor. Now a Roman province, Egypt was given a special status by being placed under the direct control of the emperor and being administered by a prefect accountable exclusively to the latter. No senator or member of the imperial family could even enter the country without the emperor's permission. This new status meant a loss of all political power for Egypt, which was no longer independent. Although the new rulers were not favorably disposed toward Pharaonic culture and society, the Egyptian priesthood depicted them as Pharaohs on the monuments, following the Pharaonic and Ptolemaic tradition. It is also interesting to note that in places as remote as the temple of Philae, located at the First Cataract just south of modern Aswan and Elephantine, the names even of obscure emperors are attested. Such is, for example, the case with Gordian III (Γορδιανός) (AD 238–244) ϛϡ𐤓𐤓𐤓 *Gwltn3*(?),[2] or with Valerian and Gallienus, interestingly referred to as 𐤓𐤓𐤓 [3] (var. 𐤓𐤓𐤓 [4]) *Wlry3nn3* (var. *W3lry3nn3*) *n3 Pr-3.w*, namely, "(the two) Valerians, the kings," during their co-rule (AD 253–260).

However, the non-conciliating attitude of the Roman emperors seems to have been reflected in the way their epithets and titles were rendered in Demotic. While the epithets and titles of the Ptolemies were almost always translated into Egyptian, those of the Roman rulers were usually given as a simple transcription of their Greek equivalent. For example, let us examine some traditional Greek epithets of the Ptolemies and their rendering into Demotic:

Ptolemy I:	σωτήρ "savior": most frequently 𐤓𐤓𐤓 *P3-Swtr*, or simply 𐤓𐤓𐤓 *Swtr* "(the) savior," but also *p3 ntr nt nhm* "the god who saves" or *nt rk hb* "who removes evil"
Ptolemy II:	φιλάδελφος "loving his sister": *p3 mr sn(.t)* "he who loves (his) sister"
Ptolemy III:	εὐεργέτης "beneficent": *p3 (ntr) mnh* "the beneficent (god)"
Ptolemy IV:	φιλοπάτωρ "loving his father": *p3 (ntr) mr it∙f* "the (god) who loves his father"
Ptolemy V:	ἐπιφανής "coming to light, appearing": *p3 ntr nt pr* "the god who comes forth"

Note that except in the case of σωτήρ rendered as *(P3-)Swtr*, which is a transcription, all the other Demotic epithets are translations of their Greek equivalents. For comparison, here are some traditional epithets used by various Roman emperors:

Caesar:	𐤓𐤓𐤓 [5] *Gysrs* (Καίσαρος [genitive singular of Καῖσαρ]) "Caesar"
Augustus:	most frequently 𐤓𐤓𐤓 [6] *Sbsts* (Σεβαστός) "August," but also attested in translation as *(p3 ntr) nt hwy* "(the god) who is august" or *p3 hw* "the August One"
Imperator:	most frequently 𐤓𐤓𐤓 [7] *3wtwgr3twr* (Αὐτοκράτωρ) "absolute ruler," but also attested as *(p3 ntr) nt mh(t)* "(the god) who seizes (control)" or *(p3 ntr) iir mh(t)* "(the god) who has seized (control)"
Maximus:	𐤓𐤓𐤓 [8] *Mgyste* (μέγιστος) "the Greatest One"
Felix:	𐤓𐤓𐤓 [9] *Flgys* "the Lucky One"

Some epithets of the Roman emperors reflected military conquests made by the emperors who bore them,[10] and for the first time far-off places like Germania were referred to in Demotic. Such epithets include:

Armeniacus:	𐤓𐤓𐤓 [11] *Hrmynqywe* (Ἀρμενιακός) "conqueror of Armenia"

Dacicus:	¹² *Tkqᶜ(?)* (Δακικός) "conqueror of Dacia"
Germanicus:	¹³ *Grmnyqs* (Γερμανικός) "conqueror of Germania"
Parthicus:	¹⁴ *Prṭsyṯqwe* (Παρθικός) "conqueror of Parthia"
Sarmaticus:	¹⁵ *Srmtsygw* (Σαρματικός) "conqueror of Sarmatia"

All of these Roman epithets are rendered as transcriptions of their Greek equivalent, and among them, only *Augustus* and *Imperator* are also attested as translations. It is also worth noting that, as was true with other foreign words and titles, the epithets of Roman emperors were followed in most cases by the "foreign" determinative (written, for example, ⟨ ⟩, ⟨ ⟩, ⟨ ⟩, ⟨ ⟩, ⟨ ⟩, or ⟨ ⟩), indicating that the Egyptian scribes were thinking of these rulers as foreigners. The same is true of the writing of their names, as one can see from the following selection (the determinative comes at the end of the word; since Demotic is written from right to left, this means that this determinative comes at the left end of the word/name):

Claudius:	¹⁶ *Qrwts* (Κλαύδιος)
Nero:	¹⁷ *Nerwne* (Νέρων)
Domitian:	¹⁸ *Twmtyꜣns* (Δομιτιανός)
Nerva:	¹⁹ *Nlwᶜ* (Νέρουας)
Trajan:	²⁰ *Trꜣyns* (Τραιανός)
Hadrian:	²¹ *ꜣtryns* (Αδριανός)
Marcus:	²² *Mrqse* (Μᾶρκος)
Commodus:	²³ *Kᶜmyts* (Κόμμοδος)
Severus:	²⁴ *Swry* (Σεουῆρος)
Gallienus:	²⁵ *Gllyꜣny* (Γαλλιηνός)

However, the above-mentioned Ptolemaic epithets and the royal name "Ptolemy" itself, ²⁶ *Ptlwmys* (Πτολεμαῖος), were not followed by the "foreign" determinative. This can be taken as an indication of the better integration of the Ptolemies into Egyptian society. Although they formed a dynasty whose founder was a foreigner, they themselves lived in Egypt.

Although the Roman emperors were referred to in Egyptian inscriptions and temple scenes as Pharaohs, and their names were cited in dating formulae of legal and administrative documents (including tax receipts), most of them never set foot in Egypt. A notable exception is Hadrian, whose visit to Egypt in AD 130 has remained famous. After leaving Jerusalem, the emperor entered the country at Pelusium and stopped in Alexandria in the early fall. From there, he sailed up the Nile as far as Thebes, modern Luxor, where he arrived by the end of November. On the west bank, he visited the Valley of the Kings and the so-called "Collossus of Memnon," one of the twin monumental statues of Pharaoh Amenhotep III (1390–1352 BC), standing at the entrance of his now destroyed funerary temple. In 27 BC, an important earthquake seriously damaged the northern collossus. The upper part of the statue collapsed and its lower part became cracked. When struck by the sun's rays at dawn, it produced a sound described by the ancients as the breaking of the string of a lyre or a kind of whistling, perhaps caused by the wind or the evaporation of dew inside the stone.[27] This intriguing phenomenon, reported by, among others, Strabo, Pausanias, Pliny, and Juvenal, had become a real tourist attraction in antiquity and was at the origin of the appelation "Collossus of Memnon." Indeed, since in Greek mythology Memnon, king of Ethiopia, was the son of Tithonus and Eos, killed by Achilles in the Trojan war, the sound of the statue was interpreted as Memnon's greeting to his mother, the goddess of the dawn. Julia Balbilla, a noble Roman woman and poetess who escorted Hadrian and his wife Vibia Sabina during their travels throughout the Roman empire, composed metrical inscriptions that were inscribed as graffiti in the lower parts of the collossus. They consist of four epigrams in Aeolic Greek commemorating the occasion, of which here is the first, dating to November 20, AD 130:

[The Inscription] of Julia Balbilla when the August Hadrian heard Memnon:

"I had been told that when the sun's rays lit Egyptian Memnon he spoke from the Theban stone, and now, when he beheld the all-ruler Hadrian before the sun rose, he bade him what welcome he could; but when Titan, driving through the sky with his white horses, kept in the shadow the second division of the hours, then again did Memnon speak, joyfully now with a clear voice as of smitten bronze, and spoke a third time; then the Emperor Hadrian greeted Memnon in return, and left engraven for posterity verses showing what he saw and heard, thus making it manifest to all that he is beloved of the Gods."[28]

Earlier in the same journey, on October 30, AD 130, Hadrian had founded the city of Antinopolis in memory of his favorite courtier, Antinous, whose mysterious death by drowning in the Nile was officially attributed to an accident but was said by some to be a suicide, a murder, or a (voluntary?) sacrifice for the sake of the emperor.

The CDD is a lexicographic project, intended to help Demotists, Egyptologists, Greek papyrologists and others read and translate texts, but, as one can see from the example of the names and epithets of the Roman emperors, it can be at the same time a mine for political history (or socio-economic history, the history of culture, religious studies, legal studies, and many other fields). As is often the case, the preparation and publication of a basic resource, in this case a dictionary (or, more rightly, a glossary), has implications and importance for research far beyond the restricted field which its title defines.

Notes

[1] Erich Lüddeckens et al., *Demotisches Namenbuch* (Wiesbaden: 1980–).
[2] G. Philae 384, 3.
[3] G. Philae 273, 3.
[4] G. Philae 301, 5.
[5] O. Berlin 6271, 1.
[6] O. Berlin 1660, 4.
[7] S. Cairo 31146, 5.
[8] G. Philae 433, 5.
[9] O. BM 20300, 8.
[10] At least the first time such epithets were used.
[11] G. Philae 433, 5.
[12] P. Berlin 7056, 10.
[13] O. Berlin 1660, 5.
[14] G. Philae 433, 6.
[15] S. Cairo 50057a, 16.

[16] P. Berlin 6857+30039, 1/1.

[17] O. Bodl. 802, 5.

[18] O. BM 15796, 5.

[19] P. Berlin 7056, 9.

[20] P. Berlin 23503B, 3.

[21] G. Philae 272, 1.

[22] G. Philae 433, 4.

[23] O. TTO 31, 8.

[24] G. Philae 326, 14.

[25] G. Philae 326, 13.

[26] P. Turin 6081, 1.

[27] In the third century, it seems that the colossus became dumb, after the Roman emperor Septimius Severus (AD 193–211) decided to repair it.

[28] Translation based on J. M. Edmonds, "The Epigrams of Balbilla," *The Classical Review* 39, no. 5/6 (1925): 108, and on André and Étienne Bernand, *Les Inscriptions grecques et latines du Colosse de Memnon,* Bibliothèque d'Étude 31 (Cairo, 1960) no. 28, pp. 80–85, with some modifications.

CHICAGO HITTITE AND ELECTRONIC HITTITE DICTIONARY (CHD AND eCHD)

Theo van den Hout

Last year's Annual Report on the Chicago Hittite Dictionary told of the final batch of words starting in *ši-* that had been sent of to our outside consultants Gary Beckman (Ann Arbor), Craig Melchert (UCLA), and Gernot Wilhelm (Würzburg, Germany). Their remarks have now all been incorporated. Originally, senior editors Harry Hoffner and Theo van den Hout planned on adding the *šu-*words to that material and publishing one big fascicle to finish the letter Š. However, the material for the *ši-*entries now looks so large that it may be advisable to devote a single fascicle to them. Important words such as "to libate, offer," "god," and "day" are partly responsible for this but, as so often, it's the shortest words that take up most space: page-wise the biggest entry will be *šer* "up, above, over" written by junior editor Petra Goedegebuure.

Our two other junior editors, Richard Beal and Oğuz Soysal, have done important work on the *šu-*words that will make up the fourth and last installment of the letter Š. The second half of this is ready to go to our outside consultants and work on the first half will start this summer. Apart from this, Beal and especially Soysal have continued writing words starting in T, ensuring a smooth transition once the Š is completely done.

The electronic version of the Chicago Hittite Dictionary (*eCHD*) has recently benefited from a major upgrade by our digital specialists Sandra Schloen, Dennis Campbell, and Seunghee Yie. The upgrade concerns both the underlying server hardware, which powers the *eCHD*, as well as the software that provides its functionality. Faster processing, better internal indexing, and a simplified interface combine to allow for a more productive online experience for the users of the electronic version.

The new query facility presents a standard list of ready-made queries for the casual user. An advanced option allows for the creation of more complex queries by allowing the user to combine query results (using Boolean AND, OR, and NOT logic) as well as to nest queries (using the result of one query to define the scope of the next query). New output formats, including a tabular view of relevant results and an outline view (for example, of subordinate forms or meanings), provide useful means of viewing query results. Additionally, the search engine can now ignore many kinds of punctuation so that a search for *memai* "he/she speaks" will result in matches on *mema*[i], [*memai*], [*me*]*mai*, etc., thereby greatly reducing the number of near misses. The square brackets here indicate what is actually preserved on the tablet and what is not. Given the almost always broken and fragmentary state of clay tablets you can imagine how often we use these in print! A new user's guide to the intricacies of the query facility is forthcoming.

An important personnel change took place among the students working for us. Kathleen Mineck, who has been working for the Dictionary for many years and who took over from Hripsime Haroutunian in 2002 the important job of keeping up our files and coordinating student work, gave up her position this past May in order to concentrate on her job as managing editor of the *Journal of Near Eastern Studies* as well as on her dissertation. In this place we all thank her for years of dedicated service to the CHD! Oya Topçuoğlu, a PhD student working on Old Assyrian seals found in Anatolia, is Kathy's successor and she is now responsible for adding new texts to our files and thus ever-expanding the basis of the CHD. Oya is assisted since the beginning of the past academic year by Joanna Derman, a third-year student in the College. The two make a formidable team and we welcome Joanna to the Dictionary staff!

Finally, we had two visitors. Gordon Johnston, associate professor in Old Testament studies at the Dallas Theological Seminary, spent his sabbatical year in Chicago to deepen his knowledge of the Hittite language and familiarize himself with the files and other collections of the CHD in Room 323. In June we had Professor Piotr Taracha of Warsaw University, Poland, here working on his new book and using our files and photo collection to put in the final touches.

———————————

DIYALA PROJECT

Clemens Reichel

Another message came in as I was replying to the previous one. "I changed the layout, rearranged the find number display. Comments, please." Switching over to the web browser again, reloading the page that had already been discussed in various e-mails. "Looking a lot better that way — now could you ...?"

I am in my office at the Royal Ontario Museum in Toronto. It's a Friday afternoon. Friday means the end of the week, no teaching — and catching up with the "real" work. Friday also means that George Sundell is sitting in room 226b at the Oriental Institute, bombarding me with questions. A good dozen today, certainly more to come ....

Two and a half years have passed since I left the Oriental Institute for Toronto. I had been told that one never really leaves the OI — something that I have come to realize over time. My own research has not changed much in focus. I continue to co-direct Hamoukar (see separate report) as a joint Syrian Department of Antiquities-Oriental Institute project. From my daily e-mail, which contains numerous exchanges with colleagues in Chicago, it would be hard to tell that I am even outside of the building. And yet a lot has changed. Phone and Internet are useful means of exchanging information, but they cannot replace the personal interaction with colleagues. Great ideas and big solutions develop over long discussions, not during five-minute phone calls. The dynamics that develop when looking at objects together or even just pointing at an item on a computer screen will only be appreciated fully when they are missed.

Nowhere did I feel this change more than in the Diyala Project. Having written my dissertation on the material and taken over this project in 2001 after my graduation, it had become my raison d'être at the Oriental Institute. Even more than Hamoukar, the Diyala excavations are intrinsically connected to the Oriental Institute. The significance of these excavations for Mesopotamian archaeology can hardly be overstated. Throughout the nineteenth century much of Near Eastern archaeology was little more than a treasure hunt, largely organized by Europe's and North America's great museums in their quest to acquire more artifacts for display. A focus on "museum-quality" artifacts had little use for the many items of daily use, such as tools, weapons, implements, or toys made of stone, clay, metal, or bone found during excavation, which generally were not collected at all. Archaeological and architectural contexts, if recorded at all, were of secondary importance. Despite notable exceptions — such as the French expedition at Khorsabad during the 1840s and 1850s and the German projects at Babylon and Assur between 1897 and 1917 — this situation had not improved much by the early twentieth century. New standards of excavation and recording were reached during Leonard Woolley's groundbreaking work at Ur, sponsored by the British Museum and the University of Pennsylvania Museum. By the end of the 1920s, however, Mesopotamia's early history still was patched together from historical and pseudo-historical sources of Mesopotamian and biblical origin. Artifacts largely were dated through inscribed items. Scholars knew more about Akkadian sculpture and seals than about Akkadian palaces, temples, or houses, let alone about the way that an Akkadian family would have lived. Most of what was known about prehistory was patched together from mythological sources, with prehistoric artifacts almost randomly assigned to "flood" or "pre-flood" strata.

Excavation and recording strategies of the Diyala Expedition differed radically from those approaches. Directed by Henri Frankfort, four large sites (Tell Agrab, Tell Asmar, Ishchali, Khafaje) in the Diyala region to the northeast of Baghdad were excavated between 1930 and 1938 on a large and comprehensive scale. In addition to administrative and cultic complexes, some of the largest exposures of domestic architecture ever were made at Khafaje and Tell Asmar. Wherever possible, buildings were excavated layer by layer, revealing their architectural history and allowing a stratigraphic recording of finds. In several areas, excavations were taken to virgin soil, in one case extending over a total depth of 16 meters. All archaeological finds, including pottery, were collected and cataloged carefully. The data recovered by the Diyala excavation for the first time allowed the reconstruction of Mesopotamia's early archaeological history from the late fourth (Jemdet Nasr period) to the early second millennium BC (Old Babylonian period). Dates like "Akkadian" or "Ur," periods that previously had been defined by inscriptional evidence and datable artwork, now received archaeological components by adding architectural complexes, pottery types, and tools and utensils associated with daily use to their known inventories. The proto-historic periods of the earlier third millennium, whose dating so heavily had been interwoven with the biblical and Mesopotamian flood stories (for example, during the Field Museum's excavations at Kish Y Cemetery), now were phased into Early Dynastic periods that were based on archaeologically manifested levels and artifact assemblages. To the present day, the Diyala sequence (together with the subsequently excavated Nippur Inanna Temple sequence; see separate report on Nippur) remains the backbone of Mesopotamia's early historical chronology. With most excavations in Iraq still on hold, much more restrictive funding, and the large-scale destruction of many sites in Iraq due to post-war looting, this situation is unlikely to change soon.

As pointed out in earlier reports, the Diyala excavations were followed by a large-scale publication project between 1938 and 1988, during which five architectural and four artifact-based volumes appeared. Ironically, the vast corpus of 15,000 "miscellaneous" items such as tools, weapons, jewelry, beads, implements, over 1,000 tablets, and several hundred sealings, had remained unpublished. More than half a century had passed since the end of the excavations when in 1992 McGuire Gibson launched the Diyala Project with the intent of finally getting these items published. In previous *Annual Reports* I have written extensively about the way that our changing approaches to this data set also changed the planned end product. What originally had been planned as a multi-volume book publication and a CD set later on eventually turned into a web-based database.

Technological advances during these times turned into both a blessing and a curse. Database applications for desktop computers were a relative novelty in 1992, but they turned into a perfect vehicle to manage data from field registers and object cards. Relational components allowed us to add links to individual images or type drawings without the need of duplication. In some respects, however, rapid technological advances also impeded our progress. We were forced to change database applications twice, and finally decided to use Oracle as the underlying back-end application. Since 2003 George Sundell, who joined the project in 2000 as data architect, systematically transferred the data into an Oracle-based layout.

There is no denying that there have been, and still are, numerous hitches and snags. The data layout had to be modified and expanded, all of which took a lot of rethinking. The most significant impediment, however, was not connected to computers or technology at all but to the idiosyncrasies of analog paper trails. Calling some of the Diyala records idiosyncratic does not mean that they are "bad." On the contrary — many of them are very detailed, but they do not lend themselves to systematic computer entries (fig. 1). Moreover, years of excavation and post-excavation work left visible marks of ongoing thought processes — some entries had been crossed out, written over, or augmented. Some of these changes represent improvements, but quite often details were sacrificed toward more simplified entries. Perhaps the most important recognition of all was the realization of how much archaeological data was recorded in the field and how comparatively little in the end was published. Substantial buildings such as the Northern Palace at Tell Asmar, for which hundreds of pages of field notes and locus and object cards exist, were summarized in a few pages.

Why did this matter so much to us in the context of object publications? The physical description of an object, if

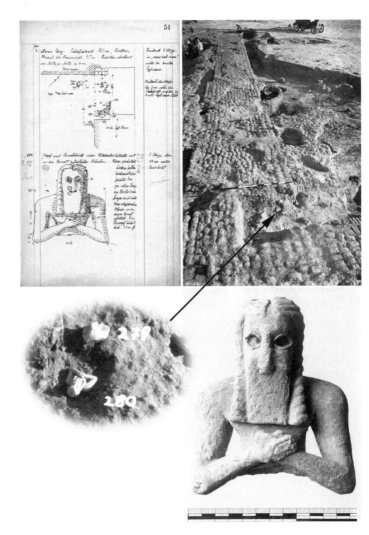

Figure 1. Top left: Entry by Conrad Preusser into 1930/31 field register for statue fragment Kh. I 280 (OIM A9049) from Khafaje, indicating details of provenience in narrative and sketch. Top right: photo of Temple Oval at Khafaje, showing findspot of Kh. I 280; bottom left: close-up of Kh. I 280, showing find relationship with alabaster head Kh. I 279 (OIM A9055A); bottom right: photo of statue fragment Kh. I 280

available for study, can be verified and improved upon if necessary. As far as the archaeological context of an object is concerned, however, we have to rely on the words of the excavators. Since the 1930s the way in which archaeological data is being used clearly had changed. The primary purpose of recording artifact contexts during the Diyala excavation was the establishment of a chronological framework. Datable artifacts could date a building level, while building levels, in turn, could organize otherwise undatable artifacts into a relative sequence, often providing an absolute date by association with a datable artifact. The idea of a functional analysis of buildings by studying artifact patterns and distributions on a horizontal scale, as often is done today, had not really been developed in the 1930s and is certainly not reflected in the published Diyala volumes. The notes of some of the excavators, however, clearly indicate that they were thinking along such lines. Some of them were far ahead of their times, as shown in the field register entries by Conrad Preusser for 1930/31. Preusser, a former member of Walter Andrae's Assur expedition, carefully recorded proveniences of artifacts either by sketching their findspots or by triangulation (fig. 1). The recordings of tablet findspots and sealings by Thorkild Jacobsen, the expedition's field epigrapher, at the Palace of the Rulers were detailed enough to allow me to undertake a pattern analysis for a detailed functional study of the building over its 250 year lifetime (fig. 2).

In short, while Iraq itself was inaccessible for archaeological work the potential of "re-excavating" an old excavation through their documentation existed, having been undertaken successfully by other scholars at the sites of Nippur, Assur, and Ur. In order to provide scholars worldwide with access to the unpublished archaeological data we had to make it accessible. This proved to be a monumental task. Supported by two National Endowment for the Humanities grants between 2004 and 2010, we scanned and photographed over 30,000 notebook pages, object cards, maps, and field negatives. Karen Terras, project volunteer since 2004 and staff member between 2007 and 2009, scanned field notebooks and diaries and indexed the correspondence exchanged between the Diyala Expedition and the Oriental Institute administration. Robert Wagner took on the formidable task of scanning all the Diyala negatives. Field registers that were too large or documents that were too brittle to be scanned were photographed by Larry Lissak with a high-resolution Digital SLR camera. While the digitization of these materials is now complete, the process of indexing them continues, undertaken jointly by myself and Mike Fisher, student assistant and project coordinator.

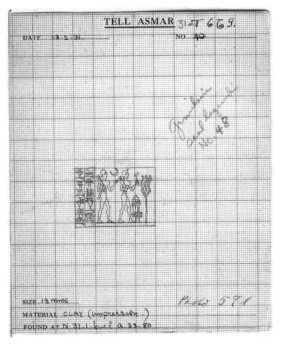

The Diyala database continues to be developed by George Sundell. In the past year much of the archaeological data — field registers, diaries, object and locus cards, and photographs — were added to the database. Keyword schema for objects, buildings, and loci are either in full development or in revision. George has been busy with the development of new screens and layouts. Over the past two years, four releases of the database have been sent to the University of Chicago's IT services. After completing archival photography, Larry has focused on photographing those artifacts that either were not documented at all or only insufficiently. We are getting close to a public release of the database, though data revisions need to be

Figure 2. Top: Object card for As. 30:T.216 with seal of Ašubliel (a servant of Ešnunna's ruler Ibalpiel) recording find date and provenience of sealing; bottom: photograph of As. 30:T.216

completed beforehand. While our own work continues, our digital acquisition of the Diyala documentation has already benefitted others. Using our scans, the Publications Office was able to significantly improve the quality of the images in their PDF reproduction of Henri Frankfort's 1955 *Stratified Cylinder Seals from the Diyala Region* (OIP 72).

The often administrative and downright "clerical" nature of much of this work occasionally might overshadow our fundamentally academic interest in this material, though this picture truly is misleading. Over the past two years I was able to re-study and re-photograph all the clay sealings and sealed tablets from the Palace of the Rulers at Tell Asmar. Angela Altenhofen, who

Figure 3. Top: photographs of As. 35:T. 99, a clay tag with two impressions of a seal held by Ilanum, a servant of Ešnunna's ruler Uṣrawassu (ca. 1980 BC); bottom: composite drawing of the seal by Angela Altenhofen

already worked as an illustrator for Karen Wilson's Bismaya project, undertook the arduous task of drawing the Diyala seal impressions, often from as many as twenty or more partially overlapping (but always incomplete) impressions (fig. 3). The fact that many of them were inscribed provided an extra challenge — one, however, that Angela mastered most admirably by teaching herself the basics of cuneiform writing. By the end of the year I hope to be done with the description and editing of more than 2,000 photographs and more than 100 composite seal drawings, allowing me to finally publish a revised version of my dissertation on the Palace of the Rulers.

A colleague once remarked to me that "once you publish your stuff, work on it only begins." I have no illusions about the fact that the Diyala material will not disappear from my life even after the launch of the Diyala website and the publication of my volume. It is a great testimony to the diligence of the Diyala excavators that, eighty years after the end of the excavation, their work holds up and still continues to inspire us.

EPIGRAPHIC SURVEY

W. Raymond Johnson

On April 15, 2011, the Epigraphic Survey, in cooperation with the Egyptian Supreme Council of Antiquities (SCA)/Ministry of State for Antiquities Affairs (MSA), completed its eighty-seventh, six-month field season in Luxor. Because Luxor remained secure during the enormous changes that took place during Egypt's revolution this winter, Chicago House's activities ran uninterrupted from October 15, 2010, through April 15, 2011. Projects included epigraphic documentation, conservation, and restoration work at Medinet Habu (funded by a grant from USAID Egypt); the inauguration of a new documentation program at the Theban Tomb 107 of Nefersekheru; salvage documentation at Khonsu Temple at Karnak (in cooperation with the American Research Center in Egypt [ARCE]); and conservation, restoration, and maintenance of the blockyard open-air museum at Luxor Temple (funded by the World Monuments Fund [WMF]), as well as documentation of blocks from the Basilica of St Thecla in front of the Ramesses II eastern pylon (kindly funded by a grant from Nassef Sawiris).

Medinet Habu

Work at Medinet Habu this year was supervised by SCA inspectors Mr. Gamal Amin Ebaid, Mr. Mostafa Mohammed Salah Taha, Mr. Hassan Youssef Mohammed, Mr. Eweis Abd el-Radi Ataya, and Mr. Ali Saad Mohammed. Epigraphic documentation, supervised by senior epigrapher Brett McClain, senior artists Susan Osgood and Margaret De Jong, and Egyptologist/artist Krisztián Vértes and artist Keli Alberts, continued in the small Amun temple of Hatshepsut and Thutmose III. Work continued primarily in the Thutmoside bark sanctuary ambulatory and its facade. Epigrapher Virginia Emery assisted in the collation process during the month of January.

Our documentation priorities continue to be completing drawing enlargements for our next volume, *Medinet Habu* Volume X, which will contain the documentation of the following portions of the temple:

- the facade (including the Eighteenth Dynasty decoration as well as all later revisions of the decorative scheme)
- the pillars of the Thutmoside peripteros (including the interior and lateral pillar faces, but excluding the exterior Ramesses III decoration)
- the interior architraves of the Thutmoside peripteros

Work on facsimile drawings for the following volume, *Medinet Habu* Volume XI, has continued when time permitted. This volume is planned to consist of the following elements:

- the exterior scenes and texts added to the temple under Ramesses III
- the marginal inscriptions of Pinedjem
- the columns, gateway, and blocking stones of Achoris

The next volume, *Medinet Habu* Volume XII, will contain the publication of the bark shrine, while the Kushite pylon and portico will appear in *Medinet Habu* Volume XIII. Finally, *Medinet Habu* Volume XIV will document the great Ptolemaic pylons and Roman court of the complex.

Sue's work this season was concentrated primarily in the ambulatory and on the facade of the Small Temple, in particular on the Thutmoside architrave inscriptions and adjoining architectural elements of the facade, and on the pillars of the ambulatory. Sue and Margaret were responsible for the overall organization and coordination of the Medinet Habu staff on-site, including the ordering of additional photography and drawing enlargements, in consultation with Brett. Krisztián finished recording a Thutmoside pillar on the eastern facade, north end, partially hidden by the addition of the Ptolemaic "court" walls. Tina Di Cerbo and Richard Jasnow continued to document graffiti throughout the Medinet Habu complex, particularly on the roof of the Ramesses III mortuary temple.

Medinet Habu Blockyard

This season the Medinet Habu conservation team, supervised by senior conservator Lotfi Hassan (fig. 1), finished the moving of fragmentary material from the old Medinet Habu blockyard to the new, protected blockyard built by Chicago House against the southern Ramesses III enclosure wall. In all, 3,500 blocks and block fragments from all parts of the complex were moved during the last three seasons, and 2,450 have been documented and entered on the Medinet Habu fragment database by Egyptologist Julia Schmied assisted by Egyptologist Christian Greco. Also included in the move to the new storage facility was the area behind the Gods Wives Chapels, where fragments and blocks were stored on cement platforms. That area is now clean, the objects and blocks moved to the new blockyard, and the platforms dismantled by Chicago House. New security lighting was also installed by Chicago House at the request of the SCA for the facade of the blockyard. Once the moving of blocks and fragments was finished, the old mudbrick-walled blockyard east of the king's palace was dismantled (in March)

Figure 1. *Lotfi conserving a palace door in front of the new blockyard. Photo by Ray Johnson*

and the area leveled as part of the site-management program of the Medinet Habu precinct. This project was proposed to Chicago House by former SCA Gurna Director Ali Asfar five years ago, and it is a great pleasure to get to this point.

At the beginning of February, at the request of the SCA, Chicago House undertook the inventory of fragments stored within the last remaining storage room in the great mortuary temple of Ramesses III (Nelson's Room 16). By the end of March, all the approximately 500 fragments stored in that room were numbered and photographed and included in the Medinet Habu fragment database. Most of the material — from the Ramesses III complex and later monuments within the Medinet Habu precinct — was moved to the new secure blockyard. Copies of the Chicago House Medinet Habu database lists were given to the Gurna Inspectorate.

A special covered area against the back wall of the blockyard was built and designated as a conservation treatment area, where conservation supervisor Lotfi, assisted by Nahed Samir Andraus and Mohamed Abou El Makarem and the conservation workers, now consolidate and re-assemble some of the fragmentary material stored in the facility. SCA conservators who worked with Lotfi this season included Ramadan Mohamed Salim, El Azab El Tami Mohamed Ahmed, and Aly El Tayib Mohamed Hassan. Next season will mark the completion of a small open-air museum component in front of the new blockyard that has been specially constructed by Lotfi and the team for appropriate joined fragment and display groups. These include some beautiful decorated doorways from Ramesses III's mortuary temple palace, and a red-granite false door, broken in three pieces in the medieval period (and used as an olive press), quarried and re-used in the Ptolemaic period from Amenhotep II's mortuary temple north of the Ramesseum.

The Domitian Gate

This season marks the beginning of a new chapter of our Medinet Habu restoration work. Last season we noted that the first-century AD sandstone gate of the Roman emperor Domitian behind the small Amun temple, reassembled by George Daressy from scattered blocks in the late nineteenth century, was in danger of collapse due to groundwater salt decay of its foundations. The northeastern corner was actually turning to sand. After consultation with the SCA and our structural engineer, Conor Power, it was decided that the gate had to be dismantled in order to properly replace the foundations with new sandstone, specially damp-coursed against any future groundwater problems. Permission was granted by the SCA to begin that work this season.

In January 2011 the monument — although Roman period it is Egyptian in style — was thoroughly photographed by Chicago House photographer Yarko Kobylecky assisted by Ellie Smith. Afterward the gate was carefully surveyed and architectural drawings were generated by stonemason Frank Helmholz. Because the USAID-funded, west bank dewatering program was inaugurated earlier (in September of 2010), the ground was already showing signs of drying out by the new year. I should mention that by the time we finished work in mid-April, the water level in the Medinet Habu sacred lake was down three meters and back to levels

Figure 2. Domitian gate dismantling, March 3, 2011. Photo by Ray Johnson

recorded during the Oriental Institute's first work at Medinet Habu in the 1920s and 1930s — a great success. In February dismantling of the gate commenced by Frank and the Chicago House workmen, and continued during March (fig. 2). Forty-three blocks (out of 68 total) are now stored on protected platforms immediately to the north of the gate, and will undergo any conservation and consolidation necessary next season. Three courses of stone blocks remain, and now that there is much less weight pushing down on the stones, there is no longer any threat of collapse. The dismantling will be finished next season, and during that time Frank and his team will also cut and shape new foundation blocks for the re-erection of the gate, scheduled to begin in 2012.

The Tomb of Nefersekheru (Theban Tomb 107)

In 2009–2010 the Epigraphic Survey initiated a condition study and preliminary, photographic documentation at the tomb of Nefersekheru (TT 107), in western Thebes. Nefersekheru was steward of Amenhotep III's great jubilee palace south of Medinet Habu at Malkata (Luxor's own "Amarna") and his tomb is one of the largest late-Amenhotep III-period private tombs in Thebes. No complete plan has ever been made for the tomb, nor has it ever been cleared. The only decoration known so far is along the outside of the broad hall, in sunk relief that is every bit as beautiful as the raised relief of the contemporary tomb of Kheruef nearby that the Epigraphic Survey documented in the 1960s.

In February of 2010 staff photographer Yarko assisted by Ellie photographed the portico reliefs in preparation for drawing. Because of the fragile condition of the stone, non-invasive drawing on photographic enlargements was chosen as the medium of documentation. This season, 2010–2011, saw stabilization, documentation, and study of the tomb. Before drawing began this season, and at the recommendation of structural engineer Conor Power, Chicago House erected a series of reinforcing screw jacks and wooden beams along the inside of the potentially unstable portico. The equipment was kindly lent to us by colleague and former Chicago House director Kent Weeks, who had faced similar conditions during his work in KV 5 in the Valley of the Kings on the other side of the cliffs.

Once the portico was stabilized, artists Sue and Margaret began penciling the exquisite reliefs and inscriptions, starting in January 2011. SCA inspectors who worked with us this season included El Sayed Mamdouh El Sayed and Zeinab Ali Mohamed (fig. 3). Documentation will continue next season, and collation is expected to be finished late in 2012. Cleaning and more permanent stabilization measures for the portico will follow, including restoration of the missing limestone columns.

Figure 3. Margaret and SCA inspector Zeinab in TT 107, March 2011. Photo by Marie Bryan

Khonsu Temple, Karnak

This year marked the third season of an Epigraphic Survey and American Research Center in Egypt collaboration at

Khonsu Temple, Karnak, part of the USAID-funded ARCE Groundwater Lowering Response Initiative. Part of ARCE's program focuses on conservation and restoration work in Khonsu Temple, including restoration of floor blocks where they are missing. Because Ramesses III wanted his new temple built quickly, every single block in Khonsu Temple, including the floor and foundation stones, is reused from earlier monuments (among them the mortuary temples of Amenhotep III and Ay/Horemheb) and they often preserve earlier inscribed surfaces. The temple is a gold mine of information about those earlier structures.

Chicago House senior epigrapher Brett McClain supervised the epigraphic team (Egyptologist Jen Kimpton, Egyptologist/artist Krisztián Vértes, and artist Keli Alberts) in the recording of the inscribed stone blocks reused in the flooring, foundations, and western roof area of Ramesses III's Khonsu Temple. This documentation is necessary before ARCE's floor restoration work, involving repaving whole areas, makes the reused material inaccessible. SCA inspectors who worked with us this season included Fawzi Helmi Okail, El Tayib Gharib Mahmoud, and Ghada Ibrahim Fouad (fig. 4).

All Chicago House recording work was done in coordination with ARCE Luxor director John Shearman and Karnak director Ibrahim Suleiman, and is an essential documentation component of the ARCE/SCA restoration program. All cleaning was done by the SCA/ARCE workmen; Chicago House's work was strictly documentation. Before floor repair occurs, ARCE and the SCA's workmen carefully remove the modern dirt fill between the stones and areas where the stone is missing, exposing any earlier surfaces. A Chicago House artist then traces the inscribed surface of the block on tracing film, or, when space is restricted, produces an aluminum foil rubbing of the inscribed surface, which is later traced, scanned, and collated in increments before restoration of the flooring once more conceals the earlier inscriptions from view.

In two seasons of work there we have learned that the Khonsu court floor blocks are made up of material primarily from the time of Sety I, including a gigantic lintel several meters long inscribed with names and figures of this king worshipping the divine triad of Thebes. Thanks to the careful cleaning of the ARCE workmen and the expertise of artist Krisztián Vértes, we were able to record the entire lintel and many other blocks of Sety I in that part of the temple. Both Krisztián and Keli have proven to be tremendously adept at teasing out data from hard to reach places.

Once each block is traced, scanned, collated, and approved by the Chicago House director, 1:4 scale reductions of the collated drawings are then inked by Krisztián and Keli according to the standard conventions of the Epigraphic Survey. We have modified the damage convention, which is done minimally if at all, for clarity, and speed, since these draw-

Figure 4. Khonsu Temple, inspector Fawzi and Krisztián. Photo by Ray Johnson

ings must be produced — and collated — quickly, in order to keep to ARCE and the SCA's restoration schedule.

The material Chicago House has documented in the flooring of the rear sanctuary areas of Khonsu Temple suggests that Ramesses III dismantled a smaller, Eighteenth Dynasty, square-pillared sanctuary of Khonsu from the time of Thutmose III and utilized the stone from that structure in the foundations and flooring of his much larger structure. Most of the offering scenes preserved in the flooring depict or refer to the god Khonsu, and most of them show clear signs of restoration, which dates them to the pre-Amarna period. Blocks inscribed with the names of Thutmose III, Amenhotep II, Thutmose IV, Ay, Horemheb, Sety I, Ramesses II, and Sety II have all been documented in the flooring. Some limestone blocks appear to be much earlier, perhaps even from the Middle Kingdom. Many of the Thutmoside raised-relief offering scenes show signs of reworking in sunk relief and appropriation by Ramesses II. In one block the ancient artists recarved the raised-relief name and figure of Horemheb into a sunk-relief representation of Ramesses II in the same way he appropriated and converted raised relief scenes of his father Sety I in the Karnak Hypostyle Hall.

We are pleased and surprised at the amount of material that it has been possible to document. To date, the reused blocks and fragments recorded at Khonsu Temple during the 2008–2009, 2009–2010, and 2010–2011 seasons now total 652. In situ blocks from the flooring and foundations of Khonsu Temple total 309, while loose blocks and fragments total 343.

Luxor Temple

We are pleased to report that a gift from Nassef Sawiris has allowed the Epigraphic Survey to begin cataloging, documenting, and surveying the remains of the sixth-century AD basilica of St Thecla. Built just north of the Roman enclosure wall that abuts the eastern Luxor Temple pylon, it is the earliest known basilica/church in Luxor. This new project will allow us to integrate the church into the Roman fortification-wall study, and is expected to provide vital information about the transition period between the pagan and Christian religions, a hitherto little known chapter in the history of Luxor Temple. Already 102 blocks from the basilica sanctuary have been located and moved to a special processing area east of the Colonnade Hall for cleaning by conservator Hiroko Kariya, and recording by architect Jay Heidel. Jay (fig. 5) has drawn and entered 118 blocks (some too big to move) into a specially designed database and is preparing AutoCAD drawings for their reconstruction on paper this summer. Already numerous joins among the blocks have been noted, including blocks from a large, beautifully carved central arch, and the two granite columns and sandstone capitals that supported it. Future plans include a feasibility study for physically reconstructing some of the sanctuary blocks and architectural elements in situ as part of the comprehensive site management program for that area.

Educational signage for the main axis of the temple has also been designed, beginning with an orientation panel for the entire temple complex that will appear outside the main entrance (now on the east side of the temple) in English and Arabic. Panels that have already been designed and are being translated now include an "Ancient Thebes Orientation and Sphinx Avenue" in front of the temple, "The Ramesses II Pylon Entryway," "The Ramesside Court," "The Great Colonnade Hall," "The Amenhotep III Court," "The Roman Sanctuary," and "The Luxor Temple Sanctuary."

The Luxor Temple Blockyard Project

The Luxor Temple blockyard conservation program was coordinated by Hiroko Kariya and assisted by Tina Di Cerbo and Nan Ray. SCA inspectors who worked with us this season included El-Kazafi Abdul Rahman Azab, Omar Youssef Mahmoud, and Ahmed Abd El Nazeer Abd El Wares. The program this season focused on the Luxor Temple block-yard open-air museum, a project supported by the World Monuments Fund (a Robert W. Wilson Challenge to Conserve Our Heritage Grant).

The blockyard open-air museum was completed and opened to the public on March 29, 2010. It features a total of 169 pieces/groups (308 fragments including single and joined pieces) on twelve thematic mastaba platforms (a total of 142 m in length). Displayed on these mastabas are sixty-two fragment groups arranged in chronological order (from the Middle Kingdom to the present) accompanied by educational signage. There are also mastabas on which fragments are organized thematically; a rotating display currently featuring ancient Egyptian creatures, large blocks from the Amenhotep III sanctuary of Luxor Temple, statues, stelae, door

Figure 5. Luxor Temple, Thecla Church. First join by Jay. Photo by Ray Johnson

jambs, capitals, fragments showing ancient Egyptian masonry and conservation techniques, and finally, fragments uncovered during the Luxor Temple dewatering project. The display also includes the in situ presentation of the great eastern Roman *tetrastyle*. The 200 m long paths adjacent to the display platforms were paved and metal railings installed for the protection of the fragments. A total of fifteen large and forty-three small explanatory signs were installed. Thirty-four spotlights were installed for illuminating the display after dark.

This season a fragment that is part of the displayed fragment of Thutmose III was identified and was added to the displayed piece. The loss area was filled with brick and a mortar surface on which the missing decoration was painted by Ray.

A massive brick/mortar support for a large granite stela on display was partially dismantled and replaced with a new metal support. The metal support was locally prefabricated and assembled in the temple. It was then painted for visual integration with the stela.

The condition of each fragment on display was examined and compared to that of the last season, and the information was entered into the Luxor Temple blockyard database by Nan. The condition of the majority of the fragments did not change. A digital image of each displayed fragment was taken by photographer Yarko that will serve as a reference for condition surveys in the future.

Initial cleaning of loose as well as accumulated compact dirt on each fragment in the blockyard museum display area was carried out. This was followed by cleaning tests and intensive cleaning (both mechanical and chemical) in order to reveal details of relief and paint decoration of some fragments. Two fragments disfigured by hard mineral encrustation and dark ferrous inclusions were extensively treated.

In order to reduce the amount of dirt/dust on the pavement, additional gravel was placed approximately 1 m wide along the western side of the paved path upon approval by the SCA. This has had a very positive effect of cutting down the dirt tracked onto the paving.

In the blockyard storage area an annual condition survey of selected fragments was carried out. Also, the fragments that were previously treated and/or protected in covered mastabas or covered shelves were examined and their condition checked.

Luxor Temple Structural Condition Study

This season structural engineer Conor Power continued his condition study of the Luxor Temple structure, and found that the temple is stable. He found no discernible movement or destabilization of the Ramesses II pylons or great Colonnade Hall columns. Based on a comparison with photographs taken in the year 2000, Conor found that there is a noticeable reduction of overall moisture levels in the temple, and that moisture wicking has subsided. His conclusion is that the groundwater lowering engineering project, activated in 2006, has had a positive effect on Luxor Temple with a reduction of salt efflorescence and moisture levels in the structure. Excellent news!

Chicago House

The Marjorie M. Fisher Library, Chicago House

The Marjorie M. Fisher Library, Chicago House, opened for the season on October 22, 2010, and closed on April 8, 2011, under the supervision of librarian Marie Bryan. During that time we had 778 visitors/users, and I am pleased to report that we remained open for our Egyptian and foreign colleagues during the months of revolution. Use of the library by our Egyptian colleagues increased dramatically this season, and we noted a huge increase in use particularly during the last two weeks we were open in March and April.

This season 205 titles (218 volumes) were added to the collection, of which 110 were monographs/books, seventy were journals, twenty-four were series volumes, and one was a pamphlet. One hundred eleven volumes were repaired during the season and thirty-two spine labels were repaired or replaced.

Physical conversion to the Library of Congress classification system continued on November 10, 2010, shortly after the arrival of Oriental Institute Visiting Committee members Andrea Dudek and Joan Fortune, who were Marie's library slaves until November 29. These two "relentless" workers managed to convert 334 titles (424 volumes) in the brief time they were here. Anait Helmholz started work on January 4 and finished conversion of 206 titles (382 volumes) by March 15, despite a fractured leg that impeded her mobility somewhat! A total of 640 titles (806 volumes) were completely converted this season.

As usual, our friends in the field continued to make kind donations of books to the library, a grand total of eighty-seven titles, over 40 percent of our entire acquisi-

Figure 6. Chicago House library in April

tion list this season. Marie herself has generously donated funds to purchase most of our French Institute/Institut Français d'Archéologie Orientale (IFAO) publications, all of which are now being purchased directly from the Institute in Cairo at a 25 percent discount. Kent Weeks very kindly donated $1,000 to set up a Susan Weeks Memorial Fund. He is designing a special bookplate for the books purchased through this fund. Our dear friend Ken Ostrand continues to bring books as gifts, many donated by Peppy Bath. Foy Scalf of the Oriental Institute Research Archives and Vanessa Desclaux of the IFAO library in Cairo helped us out with scans of several articles for our users and to repair damaged volumes. Sincerest thanks to you ALL.

The Tom and Linda Heagy Photographic Archives

Photo Archives registrar Ellie Smith registered 189 large-format negatives this season, and among a million miscellaneous tasks assisted staff photographer Yarko photographing the Domitian gate at Medinet Habu, numerous block fragments in the Medinet Habu blockyard, and a dozen Khonsu Temple blocks. Yarko valiantly kept up the site photography as well as photographic drawing enlargement production, collation blueprint production, and bleaching of finished inked drawings. He took a series of conservation reference shots of restored fragment groups in the Luxor Temple blockyard open-air museum, as well as reference photos of the museum displays lit for nighttime viewing. Yarko also continued the digital documentation of the changing face of Luxor during the Government of Egypt (GOE) urban renewal program, which had slowed down considerably by the time we left in April as the new GOE reevaluates the program, and spent much of his evening hours organizing and optimizing the hundreds of digital images he took during the day. Archivist Sue Lezon supervised the upgrading of the computers in the Photo Archives (and the replacement of the Chicago House main Internet hub that blew during a power surge) and helped a number of visiting scholars find what they needed in the archives. She and Brett continued planning the production of the next Medinet Habu publication, while she and Ellie began the re-organization of the Metropolitan Museum of Art tomb photographs in new archival housing generously donated by Ellie. Sue worked with Tina and Yarko on recent negative scans and produced CDs of those images, and optimized 100 scans of the Jacquet archive for the Chicago House Photo Archives database currently being worked on by Alain and Emmanuelle Arnaudiès. The Arnaudiès spent two weeks in March with us (fig. 7) and continued to develop the large-format image database as well as input new data. Alain added two new features to the Photographic Archives toolbox: an access list to the various Chicago House collections and information giving short historical backgrounds for each of them. The new data input included 2,090 refer-

Figure 7. Alain and Emmanuelle Arnaudiès at work in March. Photo by Ray Johnson

ences in the bibliographical file concerning the Theban area and the Chicago House and staff activities, and 583 PDF files in the virtual library. Emmanuelle Arnaudiès carried on the documentation of the Nelson numbers in Medinet Habu and added those of the small Amun temple (section B, Medinet Habu B). 236 new Nelson numbers were documented (description, bibliographical cross references, bibliography update, including the translations of the *Medinet Habu* Volume IX publication). Tina has spent a fair amount of time and expertise organizing and archiving the entire Photo Archives image holdings for uploading into the University of Chicago's offsite data storage as well as new multi-terabyte external hard drives for the Chicago House network, thanks to an ARCE Antiquities Endowment Fund grant.

Chicago House

Tina came early and stayed late to open and close up the Chicago House (CH) facility before and after our 2010–2011 season; bless you, Tina. Chicago House finance manager Safi Ouri (fig. 8) and administrator Samir Guindy continued to make sure that all our archaeological fieldwork was properly supported financially, and this season administrative assistant Samwell Maher joined the team to assist in that process. Sadly, I must report that Safi was obliged to return to Jordan in January to take care of family matters and has left the full-time employ of Chicago House. She continues to consult with us on our grants management from afar, but Chicago House is a very different place without her. Let me express my heartfelt thanks to Safi for her eleven years of brilliant financial management, total dedication, and very, very hard work on our behalf. She helped raise the Epigraphic Survey to a new level of excellence that we are committed to maintaining, and her expertise has allowed us to build a foundation solid enough to support that work. Thank you, Safi; we wish you great success back in Jordan. The good news is that Safi kindly helped us find her replacement, senior accountant Essam El-Sayid, who started work with us on March 1. Welcome, Essam! Mention must also be made of Carlotta Maher, who kindly assisted us for two weeks in November and brought great joy to visitors and staff alike! I would also be remiss if I didn't mention the visit on New Year's day of Prince Albert of Monaco, his fiancée (now wife), and a few friends. We don't get much royalty through Chicago House and this visit was a treat.

Figure 8. Finance manager Safinaz Ouri

* * * * * * * * * *

The Epigraphic Survey professional staff this season, besides the director, consisted of J. Brett McClain as senior epigrapher, Jen Kimpton, Christina Di Cerbo, Virginia (Ginger) Emery, and Christian Greco as epigraphers; Boyo Ockinga and Susanne Binder as archaeologist/epigraphers; Margaret De Jong, Susan Osgood, Krisztián Vértes, and Keli Alberts as artists; Julia Schmied as blockyard and archives assistant; Jay Heidel as architect/surveyor; Yarko Kobylecky as staff photographer; Susan

Lezon as photo archivist and photographer; Elinor Smith as photo archives registrar and photography assistant; Carlotta Maher as assistant to the director; Safinaz Ouri as finance manager; Essam El-Sayid as senior accountant; Samir El-Guindy as administrator; Samwell Maher as administrative assistant; Marie Bryan as librarian; Anait Helmholz as librarian assistant; Frank Helmholz as master mason; Lotfi K. Hassan as conservation supervisor; Nahed Samir Andraus and Mohamed Abou El Makarem as conservators at Medinet Habu; and Hiroko Kariya as conservation supervisor at Luxor Temple. Nan Ray worked as Hiroko's assistant in the Luxor Temple blockyard; Alain and Emmanuelle Arnaudiès worked on the Chicago House Digital Archives database; Louis Elia Louis Hanna worked as database architect; Conor Power worked as structural engineer; Helen Jacquet-Gordon and Jean Jacquet continued to consult with us from Geneva; and Girgis Samwell worked with us as chief engineer.

Chicago House staff, 2010–2011. Back row, left to right: Artist Keli Alberts; Egyptologist/epigrapher Christian Greco; Egyptologist/epigrapher Jen Kimpton; Egyptologist/senior epigrapher Brett McClain. Second to the top row, left to right: Egyptologist/epigrapher Tina Di Cerbo; Luxor Temple conservator Hiroko Kariya; senior artist Margaret De Jong; chief engineer Girgis Samwell; librarian Marie Bryan; stonemason Frank Helmholz; assistant administrator Samwell Maher. Second from bottom row, left to right: conservator Mohamed Abou El Makarem; Egyptologist/artist Krisztián Vértes; Egyptologist/epigrapher Julia Schmied; Egyptologist/director Ray Johnson; architect Jay Heidel; assistant librarian Anait Helmholz; administrator Samir Guindy. Bottom row, left to right: senior accountant Essam el-Sayyid; conservator Nahed Samir Andraus and daughter Joia; Medinet Habu senior conservator Lotfu Khaled Hassan and son Hany; conservator Dina Hassan and son Karim; photo archivist/ photographer Sue Lezon; Pia Kobylecky; and staff photographer Yarko Kobylecky. Photo by Yarko Kobylecky and Sue Lezon

To the Egyptian Ministry of State for Antiquities and Supreme Council of Antiquities we owe sincerest thanks for another, fruitful collaboration this season: especially to Dr. Zahi Hawass, first Minister of State for Antiquities and former Chairman of the SCA; Dr. Mohamed Ismail, General Director of Foreign Missions; Dr. Sabry Abdel Aziz, Head of the Pharaonic Sector for the SCA; Dr. Mansour Boraik, General Director of Luxor and southern Upper Egypt; Mr. Mustafa Waziri, General Director for the West Bank of Luxor; Dr. Mohamed Assem, Deputy Director of Luxor; Mr. Ibrahim Suleiman, Director of Karnak Temple; Mr. Sultan Eid, Director of Luxor Temple; and Mme. Sanaa, Director of the Luxor Museum. Special thanks must go to our inspectors this season, noted above. It was a pleasure working with everyone, especially during this extraordinary time in Egypt's history.

It is a pleasure to acknowledge the many friends of the Oriental Institute whose support allows Chicago House to maintain its documentation, conservation, and restoration work in Luxor. Special thanks must go to the American Ambassador to Egypt, the Honorable Margaret Scobey; former American Ambassador to Egypt Frank Ricciardone and Dr. Marie Ricciardone; former Ambassador to Egypt David Welch and Gretchen Welch; Haynes Mahoney and Helen Lovejoy, Cultural Affairs Office of the U.S. Embassy; Jim Bever, director of the United States Agency for International Development in Egypt, and former director Hilda (Bambi) Arellano; Ken Ellis, former director of the USAID Egypt; Dr. Marjorie M. Fisher; David and Carlotta Maher; O. J. and Angie Sopranos; Misty and Lewis Gruber; Mark Rudkin; Dr. Barbara Mertz; Daniel Lindley and Lucia Woods Lindley; Eric and Andrea Colombel; Piers and Jenny Litherland; Dr. Fred Giles; Tom Van Eynde; Helen and Jean Jacquet; Marjorie B. Kiewit; Nancy N. Lassalle; Tom and Linda Heagy; Shafik Gabr, ARTOC Group, Cairo; Judge and Mrs. Warren Siegel; Barbara Breasted Whitesides and George Whitesides; Miriam Reitz Baer; Andrea Dudek; Khalil and Beth Noujaim; James Lichtenstein; Jack Josephson and Magda Saleh; The Secchia Family; Emily Fine; Nan Ray; Anna White; Janet and Karim Mostafa; Waheeb and Christine Kamil; Caroline Lynch; Polly Kelly; Howard and Diane Zumsteg; Louise Grunwald; Lowri Lee Sprung; Andrew Nourse and Patty Hardy, Kate Pitcairn; Drs. Francis and Lorna Straus; Donald Oster; Dr. William Kelly Simpson; Dr. Ben Harer; Dr. Roxie Walker; Tony and Lawrie Dean; Mr. Charles L. Michod, Jr; Dr. Gerry Scott, Kathleen Scott, Mary Sadek, Amira Khattab, and Jane Smythe of the American Research Center in Egypt; Dr. Jarek Dobrolowski, and Janie Azziz of the Egyptian Antiquities Project; Dr. Michael Jones of the Egyptian Antiquities Conservation Project; and all of our friends and colleagues at the Oriental Institute. I must also express our gratitude to British Petroleum, the Getty Grant Program of the J. Paul Getty Trust, LaSalle National Bank, Mobil Oil, Coca Cola Egypt (Atlantic Industries), Vodafone Egypt, and the World Monuments Fund (and especially Robert Wilson) for their support of our work. Many, many thanks to you all!

* * * * * * * * * *

ADDRESSES OF THE EPIGRAPHIC SURVEY

October through March:
Chicago House
Luxor
Arab Republic of Egypt
tel. (011) (20) (95) 237-2525
fax. (011) (20) (95) 238-1620

April through September:
The Oriental Institute
1155 East 58th Street
Chicago, IL 60637
tel. (773) 702-9524
fax. (773) 702-9853

HAMOUKAR

Clemens Reichel

"I know that you are walking to 'B,' but I need to show you something in 'E' ...... it's great but not what I am looking for ...." Since I couldn't get more out of Kate I changed course. Instead of the well-trodden path from our dig house to Area B, our main excavation area on the high mound — across the village's soccer field and Hamoukar's only paved road, up the slope and across several ridges, crossing the front yards of several houses while fighting off several wildly barking dogs — I turned right and walked to Area E to the south of the dig house, where two trenches were in process of excavation. All I had gotten out of Kate in the meantime was "I am not in a Ninevite V level, but I don't think that I can go deeper here ...." When I got to the edge of the eastern trench I understood what she meant. The trench literally was covered in baked brick — a paved courtyard in front of an elaborately constructed facade, the lower courses of which also had been built of baked bricks. Clearly a public building from the later Early Bronze Age. A great discovery but not what she had been looking for. The site had tricked us again.

Surprising as this reaction may be to an unprepared reader, it is all too familiar to our excavators. There really is no shortage of finds at Hamoukar, but sometimes these finds aren't at all what we are hoping for, forcing us to rethink our understanding of this site's history and our approach to it.

It was early June — our 2010 field season, which had started in late April, soon was to be wrapped up. A lot had changed for me since our previous field season, which had taken place in September/October 2008. In December 2008 I had left Chicago for a position as assistant professor at the University of Toronto and curator at the Royal Ontario Museum. My continued directorship of Hamoukar, a joint project between the Oriental Institute and the Department of Antiquities in Damascus, represents one of the few lasting factors of my life. My teaching schedule, however, no longer allows me to undertake fall seasons, hence in 2010 we opted for a spring season. It was to begin in late April 2010, after most of us took the opportunity of attending ICAANE (International Conference for the Archaeology of the Ancient Near East) in London. Unfortunately, the volcanic eruption in Iceland grounded some of us for over a week. Getting to Syria from London became an adventure, to no one more so than to Chicago students Kate Grossmann and Tate Paulette, who had planned on getting married in Italy after ICAANE and who ended up hitchhiking across Europe to make their wedding date.

The 2010 season saw a number of familiar faces: Salam al-Kuntar (Department of Antiquities, Damascus) continued as Syrian co-director; Mahmoud el-Kittab (Raqqa Museum), a member of the Hamoukar expedition since 1999 and more recently of the Tell Zeidan expedition, as driver and housekeeper; Tate Paulette, Kate Grossman, and Mike Fisher (NELC, University of Chicago) as excavators. In addition to Syrians and Americans, however, Hamoukar 2010 was a truly international team with members coming from Belgium, Canada, Germany, Lebanon, Spain, Turkey, and the UK. Archaeologists included Yvonne Helmholz (University of Münster); Tracy Spurrier, Khaled Abu Jayyab, Jad Kaado, Joanna Velgakis, Aaron Shapland (University of Toronto); Rasha Elendari (Damascus University); Ian Randall (University of Chicago), Amanda Schupak (New York); Tuna Kalaycı (University of Arkansas); Max Price

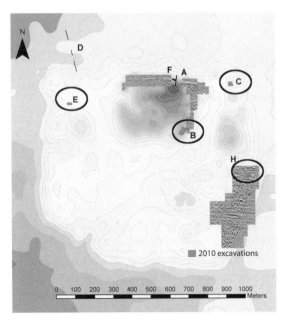

Figure 1. **Map of Hamoukar's Main Site:** *2010 excavation areas are circled; 2007–2008 magnetometric surveys on the high mound and in the outer town are superimposed*

(Yale); Jill Goulder (University of London); Steve Renette (Ghent University); and Alejandro Gallego-Lopez (Madrid University). Björn Oldsen (Alpirsbach, Germany) joined our team as site and object photographer.

In 2010 our main efforts were expended on two areas of the main mound: Area B at the southeast corner of the high mound with its Late Chalcolithic architecture, and Area C in the northeast corner of the outer town with a large Early Bronze Age building complex. In addition to that, Kate Grossman, our faunal analyst since 2006, pursued her dissertation research on urban developments throughout the Ninevite V period by opening several trenches in search of forerunners to Hamoukar's Early Bronze Age city, which covers most of the outer town (fig. 1).

As explained in earlier reports, the ridge on which Area B is located has seen considerable erosion over the millennia, giving us access to levels dating to Late Chalcolithic periods 3–4 (ca. 3500 BC) right below the surface. In 2001, 2005, and 2006 we exposed remains of two large administrative complexes (C-A and C-B) that had been destroyed by fire. Thousands of clay sling bullets found in the burnt debris indicated that these buildings had been destroyed by warfare. Numerous pits full of Uruk pottery, which had been dug from a higher, now eroded floor, indicated that this attack most likely had been launched around 3500 BC during the takeover of northern Syria by southern Mesopotamia's superpower. In 2008 we expanded our excavations to the north of these two complexes to contextualize them within the fabric of the Late Chalcolithic city. Nothing, however, seemed to match up. The architecture found here was more substantial than the burnt complexes and did not align with them (fig. 2). More seriously, no traces of destruction were noted — it appeared as if the conflagration had stopped right at the northern wall of C-A. On the last days of the 2008 season, during cleaning along the northern edge of the trench, we finally came across a stretch in which ash and burnt debris was pouring out of the baulk. Relieved to discover that my warfare theory had not been altogether wrong, I still felt as if I had exaggerated the extent of the destruction, which now looked more localized and patchy. I hypothesized that only areas of political and economic significance were defended and accordingly attacked and destroyed, with domestic areas surviving relatively unscathed. Even a casual look at the plan of the 2008 excavations, however, showed that the architectural remains excavated in 2008 were more substantial than Complexes A and B and clearly did not look "domestic."

Yvonne Helmholz, who currently is collecting data for a dissertation on socioeconomic complexity in Late Chalcolithic Hamoukar, managed to solve this mystery while removing unexcavated "lumps" and badly eroded baulks between trenches left by others after different seasons. When articulating the northern wall of Complex B she noted a strip of densely packed soil of irregular width extending along it. As she went deeper it became nar-

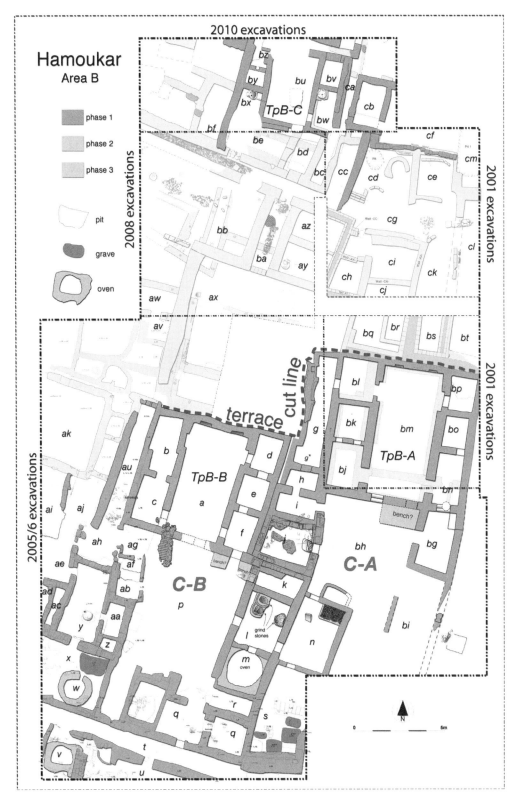

Figure 2. **Early Urban Structures:** *Plan of Late Chalcolithic architecture in Area B, showing major phases of occupation (Level 1 = burnt phase)*

Figure 3. **Terracing:** *Ancient cut line through Area B, separating terrace with burnt buildings to the south from earlier levels to the north (Yvonne Helmholz and Clemens Reichel excavating)*

rower but followed the line of the Complex B wall all the way down (fig. 3). It was a cut, but not just for a wall — the whole terrain that contained Complexes A and B had been leveled to counter the slope along the edge of the mound. Though the burnt level was lower in elevation than the architectural remains exposed in 2008, it actually was later than those. Walls to the north of and contemporary with Complex B would have been on a higher terrace, now lost to erosion. Fire-hardened sling bullets, found in 2008 just below the surface, must have been imprints of this destruction level, having survived wind and water erosion much better than mudbrick architecture. The gap in the destruction level, accordingly, was an environmental phenomenon, not an ancient lack of thoroughness in wiping out a city.

Another tripartite building (TpB-C) was found in a 5 x 15 m trench supervised by Tracy Spurrier and Rasha Elendari, to the north of the spot where burnt levels had appeared in the baulk in 2008 (fig. 2). Badly damaged by Uruk pits, its function remains uncertain, though some functional indication might be given by two almost identical installations found in rooms -bw- and -bx-, consisting of large, shallow bowls on benches made of mud and broken bricks (fig. 4). Their surfaces showed significant abrasions, suggesting that they were used as stationary grinders, but it remains unclear what would have been processed in them. Central holes in both bowls allowed for ground substances to be collected from below in bowls or jars. Channels below these features, leading into room/courtyard -bu-, might have

Figure 4. **Mystery Grinding Bowl:** *One of two large, shallow bowls from TpB-C (room -bw-; see fig. 2) apparently used for grinding; dashed line indicates the course of a water channel (partially removed) leading into central room/courtyard -bu-*

carried away wastewater after cleaning these installations. Neither channel was coated in bitumen or plaster, suggesting that they were secondary and somewhat ramshackle installations, possibly constructed during the crisis that preceded the destruction of these buildings.

The more substantial size of the earlier walls excavated in 2008 contrasts sharply with the flimsy nature of some of the walls from the destruction level (fig. 2). Did the latest level of Area B architecture already represent an impoverished phase? In order to address this question we decided to remove parts of Tripartite Building (TpB) -A- (fig. 2). Supervised by Aaron Shapland, we encountered the remains of an earlier, much more substantial building below TpB-A that largely, though not entirely, corresponded with the outline of its successor. A deliberate infill of this building with sterile soil at first made it look like a foundation to TpB-A. The discovery of doorways, secondary alterations in the architecture, and of wall plaster made it clear, however, that these were rising walls (fig. 5). Future seasons hopefully will help us to understand why this building was filled in, only to be replaced with a much more modest construction.

Along the bottom of the mound in Area B Khaled Abu Jayyab, helped by Joanna Velgakis, resumed work that initially was undertaken in 1999 by Judith Franke. One of Judith's first trenches, along the perimeter of the mound, had encountered a zone of dense, clay-rich but virtually sterile soil, leading McGuire Gibson to suggest that this "strip" was part of a 3 m wide wall that had been discovered earlier during that season in a step trench along the slope of the high mound several hundred meters to the north. His hypothesis was confirmed in 2008, when a geophysical survey along the slope of the mound managed to follow its line from the step trench to the bottom of Area B (fig. 1), suggesting that it indeed was a Late Chalcolithic city wall (see *2008–2009 Annual Report*). A sounding along the inside of the wall, undertaken by Khaled in 2005, showed that it had been set against earlier levels with no floors associated with the wall that would have dated it securely. In the hope of finding a better context in Area B we opened a 3 m wide trench across the line of the wall. The inner face of the wall was reasonably well defined with several abutting floors and features. The pottery samples retrieved from them were limited but they confirmed a date to Late Chalcolithic 3 (4000–3700 BC), hence several centuries earlier than the burnt level on top of Area B. Several big ovens against the wall indicate that large-scale food production in Area B, as attested through in the ovens of Complexes A and B on top of the mound, already was pres-

Figure 5. **Forerunners:** a) Area B from east with TpB-A partially removed, exposing substantial earlier building below (phases separated by dashed lines); b) A. Shapland articulating infant burial

Figure 6a–f. *Early Bronze Age Public Architecture:* a) Aerial view of Area C, arrows indicating viewpoints shown in pictures b–d; b) niched facade excavated in 1999; c) room with niched doorways and partially excavated "podium" (circled) in 2008; d) room with excavated "podium" and fire installations after 2010 season; e–f) close-ups of fire installations

ent centuries earlier. Defining the outer wall remained tricky, and more work will be needed to firmly determine its full width.

Much of the excitement during the 2010 season focused on those areas in which Hamoukar's second, and greatest, urban expansion was addressed. Jason Ur's site survey (recently published as Oriental Institute Publications 137) indicates that by the late Early Bronze Age the city had expanded to a size of almost 100 hectares, extending into an outer town that nowadays makes up most of the main site. Excavations in Area C in 1999, 2001, 2006, and 2008 had uncovered remains of two large building complexes that are separated by an alley (fig. 6a). A relative wealth is indicated by the presence of baked-brick pavements in almost every room, a major expense in an area devoid of abundant fuel sources. The recovery of numerous clays sealings suggested the presence of some level of administrative complexity. The exact function of these buildings, however, continued to elude us. A niched facade above a podium, discovered in our initial 1999 sounding, first suggested it to be a temple, but the facade turned out to be located inside a small square room (fig. 6b). Similar but larger podiums with niched facades have been found in courtyards of the palace at nearby Tell Beydar. No further evidence for cultic activities was found in this area until 2008, when we found a plastered, multiply recessed doorway that led into a large, elongated room in the southeastern edge of the excavation area (fig. 6c). Its opposite end was beyond the reach of the excavation that year, a fact made worse by the last-minute discovery of a brick podium whose front was level with the line of the baulk, right where a cult podium would be expected in a cella. There was no time to expand the excavation, so we had to contain our curiosity until 2010. This time we widened all of Area C to a 30 x 30 m excavation, but unfortunately the full extent of this room still remains beyond the excavation's limit. We do, however, have a better understanding of its placement within Area C. Accessed from the alleyway mentioned above it is preceded by an anteroom paved with baked bricks that opens to the main room. Both rooms contained fire installations of seemingly secondary nature, possibly of metallurgical nature, built against their walls (fig. 6e, f). Those in the main rooms were made of large broken cooking pots that were set against the walls and encased by upright baked bricks. While the "podium" from 2008 unfortunately turned out to be a ramshackle, secondary feature (fig. 6d), a cultic function nonetheless is suggested by a curious square pottery basin with incised decoration (fig. 7), of which fragments were found on top of and scattered around the podium. Several spouts along its base suggest that it was used for libations. Just how much farther this room still extends remains unclear. The function of a large square mudbrick feature, located off-center close to the right (western) side of the room behind the "podium," will have to be investigated next season. A cache consisting of numerous beads and fragments of a cylinder seal, found on the floor right behind the "podium," possibly was dropped during the ransacking and looting of this building.

Just as other Upper Khabur sites, Hamoukar reached its largest extent during the later Early Bronze Age (2500–2200 BC). Expanding into a large outer town it extended over almost 100 hectares. The origins of this expansion, however, appear to be much earlier. Ur's site survey already indicated that pottery from the preceding Ninevite V period (ca. 2900–2600 BC) in the outer town covered almost the same area as the later city. In 2008 Kate Grossman had dropped several soundings in search of architectural remains from this time period. Supported by a Wenner-Gren dissertation grant in 2010, she reopened two areas (E and H) that previously had been excavated, hence provided "windows" below the omnipresent late third-millennium architecture. Excavations in 2001 in Area H, located at the eastern edge of the village in agricultural land outside the officially

Figure 7. Libation bowl from Area C, found in association with the "podium"

Figure 8. **Bricked Complexity:** *Baked bricked facade and paved courtyard, Area E; date: ca. 2400 BC*

designated boundary of the site, uncovered the remains of well-built houses (see the *2001–2002 Annual Report*) with paved courtyards very close to the surface. Below them Kate was able to uncover remains of three sizable building units that were associated with Ninevite V pottery. Several ovens and large storage jars indicate that food storage and processing played a major part in some of the rooms or open spaces. In Area E on the western edge of the site, where work had been called off in 2001 due to lack of results, she reopened two 10 x 10 m trenches. The results were unexpectedly rich, even if not for the time period that Kate was looking for. The eastern trench, supervised by Tuna Kalaycı, contained the late third-millennium baked brick building and court described at the outset (fig. 8). The obvious display of wealth, evident from the building materials chosen, leaves no doubt that this is a non-domestic, representative building, but a larger excavation will be necessary to understand its function. The western trench (supervised by Max Price) contained numerous burials from the mid- to late

Figure 9. **Glyptic Firsts:** *Cylinder seal of green stone from Area E, with rolled-out modern impression showing erotic scene; date: ca. 2400 BC*

THE ORIENTAL INSTITUTE

Early Bronze Age — some of them quite rich in grave goods, especially in miniature vessels. The status of the buried not only could be appreciated from the grave inventories but also by the jewelry found in association with the deceased — rings, bracelets, and pendants made of copper and bone. Perhaps the most spectacular find of this area — if not of the whole season — was a cylinder seal that had been worn as a necklace. Once the seal had been cleaned we were stunned to see that the theme of our first cylinder seal was quite naughty... (fig. 9). In addition to that seal, numerous seal impressions were found in both Areas H and E (fig. 10).

More than a year has passed since the end of the 2010 season, yet we are far from being done with our analysis and data processing toward publication. In light of the current events in Syria the timing of our next field season — scheduled for spring 2012 — remains speculative. During a recent trip to Hamoukar, Salam undertook some repairs on our house, which had suffered some damage due to winter rains. The site is guarded and, apart for the ongoing problem of illegal house constructions on site, protected. Our main concern presently has to be for the safety and well-being of our Syrian colleagues and friends.

Figure 10. **Mesopotamian Parallels:** Seal designs showing parallels with Mesopotamia glyptics: (top) row of four human figures with bird-shaped heads and large circular eyes, facing left; left arms are raised, right arms are lowered; oblique lines crossing bodies at waist height, probably indicating weapons; date: ca. 2400 BC; (bottom) eagle holding two lions, approached (or attacked?) by a male figure from right side

In closing, I would like to thank those individuals and institutions who have made the 2010 season a resounding success. The Syrian Department of Antiquities, notably Dr. Bassam Jamous (Director General of Antiquities and Museums) and Dr. Michel al-Maqdissi (Director of Excavations), issued our excavations permit quickly and provided us with logistical support throughout the season. The Oriental Institute not only supported our work logistically but also financially. In 2010–11 the University of Toronto provided two Research Opportunity Program (ROP) positions to allow me to train undergraduate students in data analysis. Last but by no means least, several sponsors have contributed generously over the past few years: Howard Hallengren (New York); the late Alan Brody, Carlotta Maher, Cathy Brehm, Rita and Kitty Picken, Toni Smith, Anton and Sonia Koht, Virginia O'Neal (Chicago), and the Royal Ontario Museum (Toronto). Without their unwavering support this season would not have been possible.

ICONOCLASM AND TEXT DESTRUCTION IN THE ANCIENT NEAR EAST AND BEYOND

Natalie Naomi May

On April 8–9, the Oriental Institute held its annual seminar, which traditionally takes place in the Breasted Hall. The title of this year's seminar was Iconoclasm and Text Destruction in the Ancient Near East and Beyond, and was organized by Natalie N. May, the Oriental Institute post-doctoral scholar.

The purpose of this conference was to analyze the cases of and reasons for mutilation of texts and images in Near Eastern antiquity. Destruction of images and texts has a universal character; it is inherent in various societies and periods of human history. Together with the mutilation of human beings, it was a widespread and highly significant phenomenon in the ancient Near East. However, the goals meant to be realized by this process differed from those aimed at in other cultures. For example, iconoclasm of the French and Russian Revolutions, as well as post-Soviet iconoclasm, did not have any religious purposes. Moreover, modern comprehension of iconoclasm is strongly influenced by its conception during the Reformation.

The primary goal of this seminar was to explore iconoclasm and text destruction in ancient Near Eastern antiquity through examination of the anthropological, cultural, historical, and political aspects of these practices. Broad interdisciplinary comparison with similar phenomena in other cultures and periods contributes to a better understanding of them.

Pictured, left to right: (front row) Marian Feldman, Hanspeter Schaudig, Joan Goodnick Westenholz, Claudia Suter, Irene Winter, Angelika Berlejung; (middle row) Seth Richardson, JoAnn Scurlock, Robin Cormack, Natalie N. May, Betsy M. Bryan; (back row) Silke Knippschild, Nathaniel Levtow, Petra Goedegebuure, Walter Kaegi, Christopher Woods. Not pictured: Janet Johnson, Richard Neer, Miguel Civil, Robert Biggs, W. J. T. Mitchell, Lee Palmer Wandel

Despite its importance, iconoclasm in the ancient Near East has not received proper scholarly attention. In 1995 Bahrani defined the totality of relevant research as "three brief articles," those of Nylander (1980), Beran (1988) and Harper (1992). We can now add to the list two articles by Bahrani herself (1995, 2004) , another contribution by Nylander (1999), an earlier one by Brandes (1980) and recent articles by Porter (2009) and May (2010). All these studies either treat particular cases of mutilation or certain aspects of its significance.

Mutilation of image and text in the ancient Near East as a phenomenon remains a field awaiting systematic research. The specific framework for the previous scholarship has been assault on royal and divine effigies, although the phenomenon was in fact much more universal. The seminar and the resulting publication of the proceedings are an important step in advancing the entire field.

The problems examined can be summarized as follows:

- The purposes of the mutilation, in the framework of the choice of images and texts meant to be damaged
- The types of damage inflicted as a key to its meaning
- Iconoclasm and aniconism
- The thoroughness of the injury inflicted on complexes of images and monuments
- The significance of the destruction and spoliation of pictorial and textual monuments in respect to territorial domination
- The significance of the mutilation and superimposition of texts
- Iconoclasm and text destruction in European and Oriental Middle Ages and beyond — legacy or universality of phenomenon?

The Oriental Institute Seminars are conceived as interdisciplinary discourse. Thus this seminar embraced all historical periods starting with Sumer and concluding with modernity. Among the participants were such internationally celebrated scholars as Angelika Berlejung (University of Leipzig and University of Stellenbosch; ancient Near East), Robin Cormack (University of Cambridge, UK; Byzantium), W. J. T. Mitchell (University of Chicago; English literature and modern art), and Irene Winter (Harvard University; ancient Near East), together with young and promising scholars such as Silke Knippschild (University of Bristol; classics), Nathaniel Levtow (University of Montana; Hebrew Bible), and Hanspeter Schaudig (University of Heidelberg; Assyriology). The renowned specialists contributed papers in their field of expertise: Betsy Bryan (Johns Hopkins University; Egyptology), Joan Goodnick Westenholz (New York University; Assyriology), Lee Palmer Wandel (University of Wisconsin-Madison; Reformation), and Claudia Suter (University of Basel, Switzerland; ancient Near Eastern art). On behalf of the Oriental Institute, lectures were delivered by Petra Goedegebuure (Hittitology), Natalie N. May (Assyriology and ancient Near Eastern art), Seth Richardson (history of the ancient Near East), and Christopher Woods (Sumerology). The conference was attended by about 120 people and attracted international scholarly attention. The scholarly community all over the world expressed to Natalie N. May great interest in the seminar itself and anticipation of the subsequent publication of the seminar papers.

The proceedings of the seminar will be published in the eighth volume in the Oriental Institute Seminars (OIS) series. The book, to be published in early 2012, is expected to be substantial, with color images.

References

Bahrani, Zainab

  1995   "Assault and Abduction: The Fate of the Royal Image in the Ancient Near East." *Art History* 18/3: 363–82.

  2004   "The King's Head." *Iraq* 64: 115–20.

Beran, Thomas

  1988   "Leben und Tod der Bilder." In *Ad bene et fideliter seminandum: Festgabe für Karlheinz Deller zum 21. Februar 1987*, edited by G. Mauer and U. Magen, pp. 55–60. Alter Orient und Altes Testament 220. Neukirchen-Vluyn: Neukirchener Verlag.

Brandes, M. A.

  1980   "Destruction et mutilation de statues en Mesopotamie." *Akkadica* 16: 28–41.

Harper, Prudence O.

  1992   "Mesopotamian Monuments Found at Susa." In *The Royal City of Susa*, edited by P. O. Harper et al. New York: Abrams.

May, Natalie Naomi

  2010   "Decapitation of Statues and Mutilation of the Image's Facial Features." In *A Woman of Valor: Jerusalem Studies in the Ancient Near East in Honor of Joan Goodnick Westenholz*, edited by W. Horowitz, U. Gabbay, and F. Vukosavović, pp. 105–118. Biblioteca del Próximo Oriente Antiguo 8. Madrid: Consejo Superor de Investigaciones Científicas.

Nylander, Carl

  1980   "Earless in Nineveh: Who Mutilated 'Sargon's' Head?" *American Journal of Archaeology* 84: 329–33.

  1999   "Breaking the Cup of Kingship, an Elamite Coup in Nineveh?" *Iranica Antiqua* 34: 71–83.

Porter, Barbara N.

  2009   "Noseless in Nimrud: More Figurative Responses to Assyrian Domination." In *Of God(s), Trees, Kings, and Scholars: Neo-Assyrian and Related Studies in Honour of Simo Parpola*, edited by M. Luuko, S. Svärd, and R. Mattila, pp. 201–20. Helsinki: Finnish Oriental Society.

JERICHO MAFJAR PROJECT AND ISLAMIC ARCHAEOLOGY

Donald Whitcomb

In the last *Annual Report* for the Oriental Institute, I reported on publications and meetings in this field of research. This delineated the exciting new features of Islamic archaeology which came to my attention. Sadly, this year rather less news has come into my ken, perhaps because I have had my nose pressed to the ground, almost literally, with new digging.

This new archaeological research is located in the Jordan valley near Jericho. To reach Jericho one must descend east from Jerusalem, from highlands at Ramallah (2,500 ft) into the *ghor* (literally, the depths) some 850 ft below sea level. Jericho is reputed to be the lowest city in the world, a sub-tropical environment of palms, citrus fruits, bananas in lush vegetation, where there is access to water. Jericho is a virtual oasis, with the city located on the wadi al-Qilt, and springs of ʿAin Duyuk, Naʾaran, and Nuwaiyma providing copious waters. Perhaps the most important was (and remains) the ʿAin al-Sultan at the foot of the massive mounds of biblical Jericho, known as Tell al-Sultan (fig. 1).

When one mentions the archaeology of Jericho, it evokes the famous excavations of Kathleen Kenyon (1952–59) and the search for the fallen walls of Joshua. Her methodology remains the standard for modern archaeological fieldwork, but also recalls Robert Braidwood of the Oriental Institute and his debate with the formidable Dame Kathleen on the nature of urbanism and the Neolithic period in the Near East. The questions are past and the city of Jericho is celebrating 10,000 years of urbanism, making it also the oldest city in the world. Muqaddasi

Figure 1. Mounds of the site of Tell al-Sultan, biblical Jericho. Photo by Donald Whitcomb

sang of its reputation in the tenth century, "Ariha is the city of giants and herein is the gate indicated by God to the children of Israel. This a land of indigo and palms. Its rural district is the Ghor, where the fields are watered by springs. ... one drinks there the lightest water in Islam; bananas, fresh dates, and fragrant flowers are abundant" (al-Muqaddasi 1906: 174–75).

Ariha

This is a rendition of the name Jericho in earlier times and should be reflected in specific archaeological remains. Invariably, discussion of Hashmonean, Herodian, Roman, Byzantine, and Islamic occupation has placed the main settlement under the modern town of Jericho (or occasionally at Tell al-Sultan). The only published archaeological site in the town is the church at Tell Hassan, where Baramki found remains of the Byzantine and Islamic periods. There are two important sites along the Wadi al-Qilt: to the east is Khirbet al-Nitla, and Tulul Abu al-ʿAlayiq is on the west (fig. 2).

The site of ʿAlayiq has been labeled New Testament Jericho and a long series of excavations, both before the 1950s and more recently, have revealed palatial complexes of Hashmonean and Herodian times. Islamic occupation is reflected on the summit of Tell 1, south of the Wadi Qilt, where ceramic diagnostics reliably place it within the Abbasid period, despite an absence of glazed wares. George Miles was entrusted the publication of 266 Islamic coins from this site (while curiously both Nitla and even Mafjar have no numismatic information).

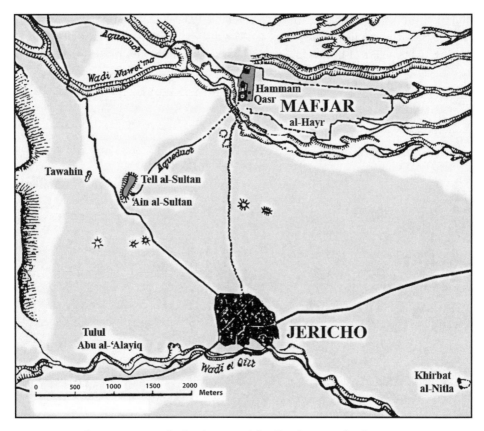

Figure 2. Map of some remains in the Jericho region (after Hamilton 1959: fig. 1)

An important corpus of Umayyad and earliest Abbasid issues gives a very clear picture of the regional economic and political context of Ariha. Coins from Damascus, capital of Bilad al-Sham (Syria), are predominant, then those of al-Ramla, the capital of Filistin, and then a large number of coins from Egypt, indicating commercial connections.

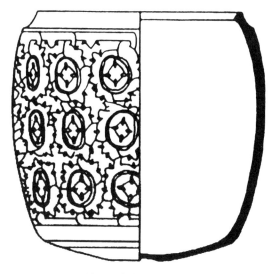

The site of Khirbet al-Nitla is 2.5 km east of Jericho and produced, in the words of its excavator, buildings that were "architecturally of no consequence." One structure was a church with at least four architectural phases, from the late fourth through the ninth centuries. Baramki treated the ceramics from Nitla in careful detail, since he recognized in this assemblage Byzantine and early Islamic periods (eighth–ninth centuries) directly compa-

Figure 3. Painted bowl of Abbasid "palace ware" (after Kelso and Baramki 1955: pl. 30, A121)

rable in fact to the ceramics of Mafjar (fig. 3; see below). In his enthusiasm for the ceramic assemblage from Nitla and Abu al-ʿAlayiq, he clearly notes that "... the two sites give a cross-section of Palestine pottery from the close of the Hellenistic period through the Roman and Byzantine and into the Early Arabic" (Kelso and Baramki 1955: 52).

Khirbet al-Mafjar

During the survey of western Palestine in 1894, F. J. Bliss described a series of three large mounds north of the town of Jericho. Even at this relatively early date, these ruins were utilized as a source of building stones for the modern town, and the site was much disturbed. Dimitri Baramki was antiquities inspector for the Palestine Department of Antiquities and responsible for securing this site among so many others; he recognized its extraordinary potential and directed some twelve seasons of excavations, from 1934 until 1948. He was joined by Robert W. Hamilton, Director of Antiquities under the Mandate, during the

later seasons of the 1940s when the bath hall was uncovered. Hamilton went on to publish a monograph on the site in 1959 (with the assistance of Carl Kraeling, then director of the Oriental Institute).

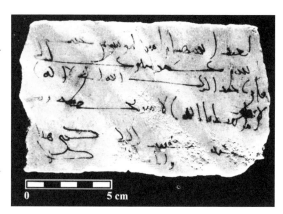

The identity and character of Khirbet al-Mafjar have always been problematic — there is no ancient or medieval reference in literary or historical texts. The site is anepigraphic, without inscriptions except for a number of ostraca in Arabic. Two of these scraps of marble provide a clue: the name of the caliph Hisham, who ruled from 727 to 743 (fig. 4). Thus, the site became Qasr Hisham ("Hisham's

Figure 4. Ostracon with name of Hisham (after Hamilton 1959: pl. 57:1)

Figure 5. Palace facade with stucco work (after Hamilton 1959, fig. 52)

palace") for Baramki and indeed this remains the popular name in Palestine (and is reflected in the Wikipedia entry on the Internet). Hamilton went on to weave an alternative interpretation, assigning foundation stories to Walid II, before his brief caliphate in 743–47. At present, the more neutral site name of Khirbet al-Mafjar ("flowing-water ruins") seems preferable.

The Khirbet al-Mafjar excavation produced some of the most stunning art work of the early Islamic period, setting a standard for evaluating this period throughout the region. Khirbet al-Mafjar is one example of an amazing phenomenon, the settlement of marginal lands by the early Muslims employing the bounty resulting from the conquests. An aqueduct brought water from springs to irrigate about 150 acres of garden or parks enclosed in a long boundary wall. The principal building was the Great Hall and bath, a reception hall not unlike the Sasanian palace at Firuzabad in Iran. It is not difficult to imagine the mosaics as so many Persian carpets spread throughout the hall floors. Perhaps the most extraordinary element is the ceremonial entryway, the porch, with a high central niche carrying a figure with sword standing on two lions, very likely the caliphal patron himself, Hisham (fig. 5). The Palace is more typical of Umayyad residences but no less wonderfully decorated with stuccoes and frescoes. Together with the pavilion and mosque, this architectural complex stands analogous to Fustat (Cairo) and Samarra in Iraq as a testament to the beginning of Islamic archaeology, in this case for Palestine.

To Return to Mafjar

This archaeological site witnessed fine excavations that produced monuments of magnificent art and archaeology. The documentation is exemplary in Baramki's preliminary reports and Hamilton's monograph, a record many excavations might emulate. Interpretation of the history and functions of the site remains debatable, and the archaeological evidence is obviously incomplete. In contemplation of a return to these remains, two aspects appear foremost as research agendas.

The original chronological assumptions on the buildings and their occupation seems erroneous. The original ceramic analysis by Baramki (1944) was admirable but never consistently utilized, as suggested in my study in 1988. A new stratification indicates four phases of occupation, which have been confirmed by sondages by Hamdan Taha in 2006. The suggested periods are proposed with the following features:

1. Construction and destruction debris mixed with painted wares. 700–750

2. Further occupation and destruction, suggesting more extensive damage from an earthquake in the ninth century; ceramics seem transitional types, similar to the Mahesh phase at Aqaba. 750–800

3. Major reoccupation of the site in the Abbasid period; continuities and introduction of cream wares (popularly known as Mafjar ware), incised, molded and glazed ceramics. 800–950

4. Medieval reoccupation in the Ayyubid-Mamluk period; final destruction of roofed structure. 1100–1300

Creswell pointed out long ago (1932) that the palace is based on a different cubit from the bath and pavilion. His concern was to understand the sequence of these structures, pointing out the secondary history of occupation after the foundation. These aspects have been consistently ignored and the evidence presumed to have been destroyed.

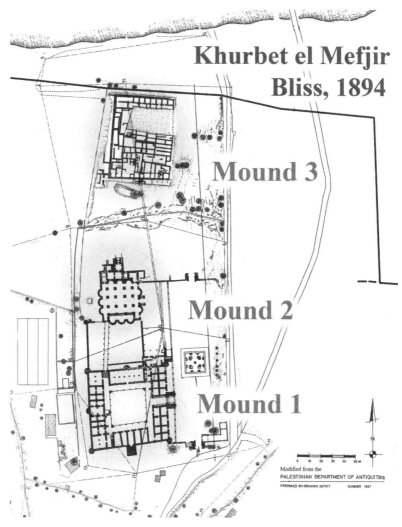

Figure 6. Plan of the mounds described by Bliss in 1894 and structures excavated

There is an important lesson in archaeological research that one should return to the first excavations of a site, in this case that of Bliss and Hunter in 1894. They noted three separate mounds: one with a hollow center in the south (the palace with its large courtyard), a massive mound in the center (the bath with its massive fallen superstructure), and a badly robbed complex on the north. They planned this latter structure and suggested an identification as a khan or caravanserai (fig. 6). A visit to this area reveals extensive archaeological excavations, squares with baulks still standing. This was the work of the Jordanian Department of Antiquities between 1957 and 1967 by Awni Dajani. It is a profoundly sad instance where only a few minimal lines have been written and all records and objects apparently lost, perhaps in a flood in central Amman in 1970.

This has been characterized as a laborers' settlement or "domestic quarters for servants and slaves" by Lancaster Harding (1967: 177), but fine architectural elements suggest a more important role for this settlement. Two other hypotheses might be considered: first, that these northern structures represent the original settlement around another "palace," along the lines of Qasr al-Hayr al-Sharqi; or alternatively, the palace and other structures represent a major Abbasid settlement. There seem to be sufficient unexcavated areas to test these and other hypotheses.

Islamic Archaeology in Palestine

The late professor Albert Glock was a strong advocate of Palestinian archaeology and yet wondered whether such a focus, having explicit political intent, might not perpetuate the problems of Western-oriented biblical archaeology. Searching for a remedy, he noted the potential of the field of Islamic archaeology but lamented the domination by art historians and preoccupation with Jerusalem to the exclusion of the remainder of Palestine (1994). The field is not quite as bleak as he imagined and an impressive amount of high-quality fieldwork has been undertaken. That there has been no synthesis is perhaps more typical of present archaeology than the relative importance of Islamic archaeology. One may suggest that archaeological research at Jericho has a potential for defining an aspect of Palestinian archaeology and the general discipline of Islamic archaeology at the same time (fig. 7).

For Hamilton, who pondered the social context of Khirbet al-Mafjar for over fifty years, this was "... the mansion of a Muslim personage of princely status.... Yet here there was no capital. There was not even a centre of population. No trace of any settlement, village or town, can be seen nearer than Old Jericho, now Tell es-Sultan" (Hamilton 1959: 3). His assumption of an

Figure 7. Recent view of entry through the south gate into Khirbet al-Mafjar. Photo by Donald Whitcomb

absence of archaeological evidence for the city of Ariha seems mistaken, perhaps clouded by a superficial view of the role of the "desert castles." Impressive new research, especially by Denis Genequand, has refined the understanding of these elite residences, villas, or estates of the Umayyad period. One nuance is the idea that these settlements were proto-urban, or rather intended to become urban entities in an Islamic landscape. Thus one may posit that the northern area was intended to develop into the town adjacent to the palatial complex. What is more important and interesting is the continuing existence, and even prosperity, of a Christian occupation in Ariha, now obscured by the modern city of Jericho. Clearly an eventual investigation of these dual settlements in the early Islamic period has historical importance for Palestine and the Middle East.

References

Al-Muqaddasī, Muhammad ibn Ahmad

1906   *Kitāb Ahsan al-Taqāsīm fī Ma'rifat al-āqālīm.* Bibliotheca Geographorum Arabicorum 3. 2nd edition. Leiden: Brill.

Baramki, Dimitri C.

1944   "The Pottery from Khirbat el Mefjar." *The Quarterly of the Department of Antiquities in Palestine* 10: 65–103.

Bliss, F. J.

1894   "Notes on the Plain of Jericho." *Palestine Exploration Fund Quarterly Statement,* pp. 175–83.

Creswell, K. A. C.

1932   "Khirbat al-Mafjar." In *Early Muslim Architecture,* edited by K. A. C. Creswell, vol. 1, pt. 2, pp. 545–77. Oxford: Oxford University Press.

Glock, Albert

1994   "Archaeology as Cultural Survival: The Future of the Palestinian Past." *Journal of Palestine Studies* 23: 70–84.

Hamilton, Robert W.

1959   *Khirbat al Mafjar: An Arabian Mansion in the Jordan Valley.* Oxford: Clarendon Press.

Harding, G. Lancaster

1967   *The Antiquities of Jordan.* Revised edition. London: Lutterworth.

Kelso, James L., and Dimitri C. Baramki

1955   *Excavations at New Testament Jericho and Khirbet en-Nitla.* The Annual of the American Schools of Oriental Research 29–30. New Haven: American Schools of Oriental Research.

Taha, Hamdan

2006   "New Excavations in the Bath Area at Khirbet el-Mafjar" (unpublished manuscript).

Whitcomb, Donald

1988   "Khirbet al-Mafjar Reconsidered: The Ceramic Evidence." *Bulletin of the American Schools of Oriental Research* 271: 51–67.

KERKENES DAĞ PROJECT

Scott Branting

http://www.kerkenes.metu.edu.tr/

The 2010 season at Kerkenes Dağ saw the continuation of the multi-year program of excavation and restoration within the Cappadocia Gate as well as the undertaking of larger-scale excavations within the west-central portion of the city (fig. 1). Dr. Sevil Baltalı Tırpan was added to the project staff this year as Assistant Director. Sevil and I were once graduate students together here at the University of Chicago and I am extremely pleased to welcome her as a collaborator on the project. In addition to the excavations, geophysical surveys were conducted in the southern and west-central portion of the city and restoration work was undertaken both at the Cappadocia Gate and in the Kerkenes gallery of the Yozgat Museum. Complimenting this extensive program were new paleoenvironmental and ethnographic research projects and continuing projects involving Anatolian metallurgy and the Kerkenes Eco-Center.

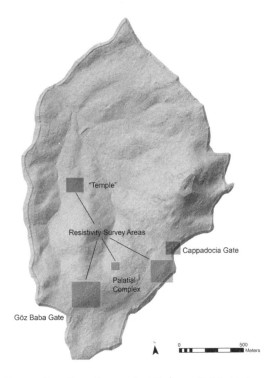

Figure 1. Locations of research at Kerkenes Dağ in 2010

Geophysical Investigations

Four areas of resistivity survey covering a total of 69,200 sq m (6.9 ha) were completed in May of 2010. Three of these areas are in the southern portion of the city (fig. 2). The first area, to the east of the Palatial Complex and just south of the Cappadocia Gate, extends to the south the area surveyed in 2009 (see *2009–2010 Annual Report*, p. 66). The second area, to the north of the Palatial Complex, extends the western extent of the 2009 survey. The third area, between the Palatial Complex and the Göz Baba Gate, extends the western extent of the 2007 and 2008 surveys (see *2007–2008 Annual Report*, pp. 86–87, and *2008–2009 Annual Report*, pp. 88–89). In addition, a fourth small area was surveyed around the "Temple" in the lower west-central part of the city in preparation for the excavation undertaken there in June and July.

All told, the past four seasons have surveyed 18 ha of the high southern ridge between the Kale, the Cappadocia Gate, and the Göz Baba Gate. This includes the entire Palatial Complex and many of the urban blocks in its vicinity. A good portion of the urban blocks facing the street running between the Cappadocia Gate and the Göz Baba Gate have also now been

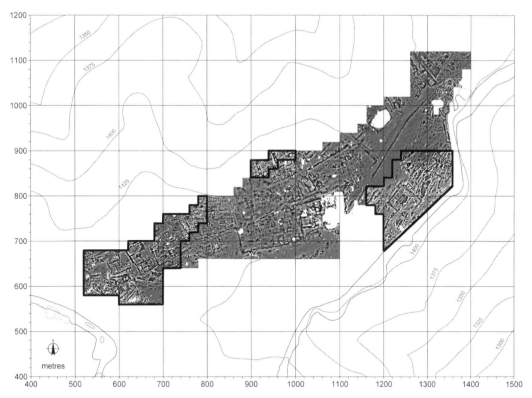

Figure 2. The resistivity survey data collected between 2007 and 2011 on the southern ridge of the city. The areas covered in 2010 are outlined in black

surveyed, as well as the open areas in front of the Palatial Complex and the Cappadocia Gate. This includes the urban block and associated structures on a small rise just inside the city wall to the south of the Cappadocia Gate, which may have had some special relationship to the Palatial Complex, given their isolated position opposite it in a wide open area. It also includes the narrow structures and water storage ponds surveyed last year opposite the Cappadocia Gate. The characteristics noted in the urban blocks across this area are varied. In the Palatial Complex and adjacent urban blocks there do seem to be more large structures, perhaps with a public or elite function. In more distant urban blocks, back toward the Göz Baba Gate, the buildings within the urban blocks are more in keeping with the character of urban blocks seen elsewhere in the city. Of course the uses to which these more typical buildings were put remains unknown. This area may have been filled with workshops and storerooms in the long narrow rows of rooms seen throughout the area, and interspersed with residences for craft specialists and others linked to the palace. While the resistivity survey provides us with knowledge of the forms of the structures, their functions remain a mystery. Just beyond the westernmost extent of this survey area is a large and likely important urban block just inside the Göz Baba Gate. Survey here in future years may well change interpretations of the urban blocks in its vicinity.

On the slopes to the west of the central part of the city, a small area of resistivity survey revealed a range of buildings around a large burnt hall (fig. 3). This impressive structure was clearly visible in the magnetometry data, yet the buildings in the urban blocks around it were very difficult to discern. Surveying this area in May allowed better decisions to be made as to

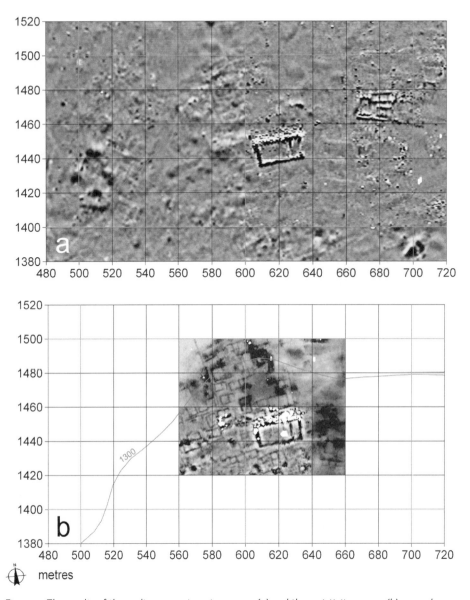

Figure 3. The results of the earlier magnetometry survey (a) and the resistivity survey (b) around the "Temple"

where to place the trenches excavated in June and July, including identifying a small square building behind the large hall that was a focus of the excavations.

Excavations in the "Temple"

Using the results of the geophysical surveys, trenches TR27 and TR28 were situated so as to uncover precisely half of a large two-roomed hall (Structure A) and a quarter of a square building behind it (Structure B) (figs. 4 and 5). Structure A, measuring 26.5 x 12.5 m, is one of the largest buildings so far seen at Kerkenes Dağ. Parallels for similar free-standing halls on this scale at Kerkenes Dağ are found within the Palatial Complex, in an adjacent urban block

Figure 4. Photograph of Trenches TR27 and TR28 after excavation

to the Palatial Complex, and in two urban blocks in the north of the city including the one in which the unique carved ivory plaque was found in 1996. While these contexts for similar large halls suggest their use by elites, Structure A is unique among the large halls in being situated outside of any of the walled urban blocks that fill an overwhelming majority of space within the city. Evidence from the magnetometry survey also revealed that Structure A was intentionally set on fire in the final destruction of the city. Given this evidence it has been suggested that Structure A might be an important public structure such as a temple.

Trench TR27 exposed not only Structure A but also an area in front of the building, a narrow alleyway running along its northern side, and the wall of the adjacent urban block to the north. This expanded area allowed a majority of the stone collapse from the structure to be examined for any evidence of decoration or inscription that may have once been on or in the building. The excavations, however, revealed no such finds. The meter-wide foundation wall terracing the northern side of Structure A was preserved up to 1.4 m, but erosion over the past two millennia had washed away nearly all evidence of the floors, installations, and superstructure. Scattered nails and some charcoal were all that remained in the area, evidence of the large wooden superstructure and presumed thatch roof. Given the level of erosion in this area, excavations in TR27 were stopped after exposing half of the anteroom

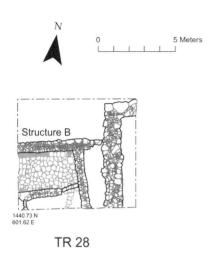

TR 28

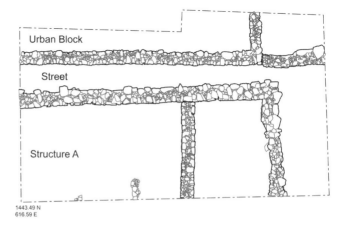

TR 27

Figure 5. Plans of trenches TR27 and TR28

and over a quarter of the large internal room. One benefit of this destruction is that the collapse of the building had very effectively sealed the surface of the alleyway alongside it and prevented any erosion. The alley was unpaved and had clear evidence of layering and soil formation similar to streets excavated elsewhere in the city (fig. 6). Soil and micromorphological samples were collected from this alleyway for analysis at Cambridge University as part of an ongoing study of transportation in the city.

Figure 6. Section in trench TR27 bisecting the alleyway running to the north of Structure A

Trench TR28 was originally situated so as to expose one quarter of Structure B. It was subsequently expanded to include a portion of Structure A in order to examine the state of preservation in the back of the large room and to examine stratigraphic sequencing. The back end of Structure A exhibited the same extensive erosion as was found in TR27. No traces of flooring or installations were preserved. However, at the base of the northwest foundation wall evidence was found for older layers of the same distinctive street surface, noted in the adjacent alleyway, running beneath the lowest course of stone before natural soil was reached. This evidence, combined with the position of the structure outside of an urban block and the lack of the characteristic external stone paving in front of the structure suggests that this building was constructed well after the foundation of the city.

Structure B, unlike the terraced Structure A, was well preserved. A portion of two adjoining rooms with a doorway connecting them were uncovered. The wooden door that originally stood in the doorway was found burned on the floor in the northern room together with a short iron strip and nails that may have held it together. Inside the northern room a raised stone floor with recessed slots and stones for the bases of the wooden posts that supported the wooden superstructure were discovered. Several medium and larger-sized broken pottery vessels, a tripod-footed stone bowl, a copper alloy arrowhead, a small tin-antimony alloy bead, and two star-shaped silver objects were found on the paved floor along with carbonized wheat and grape pips recovered by flotation (figs. 7 and 8). In the southern room, a raised paving stone walkway laid back across the room from the doorway was the only feature of note in an otherwise empty portion of the room.

Following excavation and recording the walls and surfaces were covered with geotextile and backfilled. The tops of the walls were rebuilt to extend three courses above the modern ground surface so as to allow visitors to the site to see the locations and orientations of the ancient structures while preserving the Iron Age walls.

Figure 7. One of the star-shaped silver objects from the paving in TR28

Figure 8. The stone tripod-footed bowl found in TR28

Paleoenvironmental Research

A new program of paleoenvironmental research was begun at Kerkenes Dağ by Mac Marston of Brown University during the excavations in TR27 and TR28. This program encompasses not only flotation of excavated contexts for fauna and flora using a SMAP-style flotation machine, but also an ecological survey of the modern landscape within the boundaries of the ancient city and in the surrounding region. Mac, along with Naomi Miller, was able to conduct basic field identification and collection of plant species at Kerkenes Dağ and to identify tentative locations for systematic botanical survey transects in future seasons. The beginnings of a comparative collection of local seeds were also collected as a reference for identifying seeds recovered in the excavations. A similar type of ecological research program, involving both the ancient and modern environment, has been successfully undertaken for years by Naomi and Mac at the site of Gordion. It is hoped that the results of the intrasite research at Kerkenes Dağ, as well as intersite comparisons between the ecology of these two different Phyrgian cities will yield fruitful results.

Metallurgical Analysis

Joseph Lehner continued his program of analyzing metal objects and fragments excavated at Kerkenes Dağ. This season he was able to make use of a portable x-ray fluorescence device to give characterizations of objects in the field in order to guide additional discrete sampling for more detailed analysis at the Costen Institute of Archaeology and the Laboratory for Molecular and Nanoarchaeology at the University of California, Los Angeles (UCLA). This program is a part of a larger project involving material from both Kerkenes Dağ and Boğazkale that is looking at changing patterns of metal sources and production across the Late Bronze and Iron Ages in Central Anatolia.

Ethnographic Studies

A new program of ethnographic research was also started in 2010 under the direction of Assistant Director Sevil Baltali Tirpan of Istanbul Technical University. The primary focus of this research is to better understand how the site and the archaeological project have been and are perceived and integrated into the village of Şahmuratlı. Additional work this year involved explorations of past agricultural practices, knowledge that will play a critical role in the new paleoenvironmental research program.

Restoration and Installation of Objects in the Yozgat Museum

In 2008, a Kerkenes Dağ gallery was established in the local Yozgat Museum (see *2008–2009 Annual Report*, pp. 92–94). Thirty-six of the most important excavated pieces were installed within this gallery under the direction of Oriental Institute Museum Preparator Erik Lindahl. Two notable pieces not ready for installation in 2008 were the semi-iconic stela discovered in situ in the Cappadocia Gate and one of the various large semi-iconic idols found in the Monumental Entranceway to the Palatial Complex. This year, we were able to make use of Erik's services once again and complete their installation within the Yozgat Museum (fig. 9). Conservation of both large pieces was completed by Noël Siver, assisted by Oriental Institute Conservator Alison Whyte (fig. 10). Steel frames were constructed by Erik for support, and missing portions of both pieces were restored by Noël, Erik, and Alison. Both pieces are now proudly on display in Yozgat (figs. 11 and 12).

Clockwise from upper left: (Figure 9) Erik Lindahl installing the idol block from the Palatial Complex Entranceway in the Yozgat Museum; (Figure 10) Noël Siver and Alison Whyte completing the restoration of the idol block; (Figure 11) Noël Siver standing next to the restored idol block installed in the Yozgat Museum; (Figure 12) The restored Cappadocia Gate stela installed in the Yozgat Museum

Excavations in the Cappadocia Gate

The central focus of excavations during the 2009 season was to start the multi-year clearance of collapse from the Cappadocia Gate in preparation for a major restoration initiative (see *2009–2010 Annual Report*, pp. 67–69). Masses of burnt and fallen stone were removed from the gate passage in 2009, evidence of the final fiery destruction of the city. Care had to be taken, both because of the instability of the high, freestanding walls left behind by the clearance and to protect the stone paved floor of the gate. In addition, work was undertaken along the glacis on the outside of the gate.

Excavation resumed within the Cappadocia Gate in the later part of the 2010 summer season (figs. 13 and 14). The remainder of the gate passage was cleared to a point in line with the platform upon which the semi-iconic stela had been found. Here a line of large threshold stones were uncovered at the edge of the paving, spanning much of the width of the gate passage. An iron band, similar to those found in the entranceway to the Palatial Complex, was also found here as clear evidence of the doorway to which the threshold belonged. Clearance inside this doorway and in the area between the North and West Towers was left for 2011.

While this work was ongoing the remainder of the gate chamber was also cleared of collapse. This left the original walls of the chamber standing in places over 4 m high. The structural integrity of these walls had been compromised when the horizontal timbers, originally set into the faces of the walls at roughly 1 m vertical intervals and covered with plaster, were destroyed during the intense burning of the gate. Smaller stones from the core of the wall slid over time into the ca. 25 cm gaps left by the burnt beams, and this makeshift fill has supported the walls after clearance. However, the overall structural integrity of the walls is suspect. This was demonstrated all too clearly when a portion of the wall of the Middle Tower collapsed during the heavy rains that brought the season to a close. Restoration work within the Cappadocia Gate will make these walls more stable.

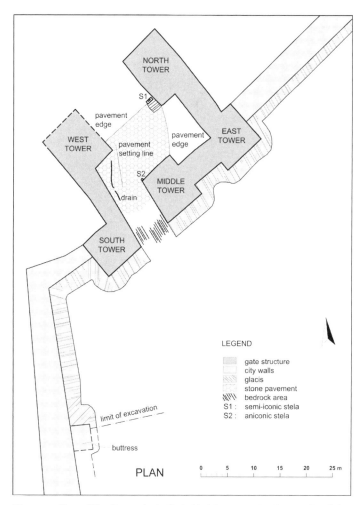

Figure 13. Plan of the Cappadocia Gate that incorporates the results of this year's excavations

The stone paving that was uncovered within the gate passage extended well into the gate chamber. It had been laid up to a line running from the southern corner of the North Tower down to the northern corner of the Middle Tower. The pavement clearly was meant to end here, with the dirt floor in the rest of the gate chamber pocked by the heavy stones that fell from the gate during its destruction and collapse. On this dirt surface a second victim of the destruction of the city was found (fig. 15). This skeleton, like the first one uncovered in the gate passage last year, was apparently killed by the collapsing stones and beams of the gate. No objects were discovered with either body. While both individuals were found in the gate, there is some distance between the locations of their bodies. There is no evidence that they were together. However, how they came to be in the gate during its destruction still remains a mystery. This individual's body was so badly crushed beneath the falling stones that the position is difficult to discern. The heavy rains that brought down the wall of the Middle Tower in the last days of the season made lifting the skeleton this year impossible. It was covered and reburied awaiting full excavation and analysis in 2011.

Figure 14. The extents of the Cappadocia Gate passage so far exposed and the full gate chamber

Figure 15. The skeleton, knees bent, was crushed by the large stones falling from the top of the walls

Restoration of the Cappadocia Gate

While excavations continued inside the Cappadocia Gate, the start of an extensive program of conservation and restoration on the outside of the gate commenced (fig. 16). The work has been the subject of architectural and engineering studies for the past several years. It was supervised by Nilüfer Baturayoğlu Yöney of Istanbul Technical University and undertaken by Erkan Kambeck and five master stone masons from Manisa. Heavy machinery generously provided by the Sorgun District governor and the Sorgun mayor allowed the masons to remove and replace several of the large granite glacis stones along a sizable stretch of wall as

Figure 16. The Cappadocia Gate glacis before the start of restoration work

Figure 17. Reconstruction of the Cappadocia Gate glacis in progress

Figure 18. Restored section of the Cappadocia Gate glacis and wall

well as shore up the loose rubble core behind the glacis (fig. 17). Once the base was stabilized, the glacis was reconstructed back to its original height, all the way up to the face of the outer wall of the gate. The wall itself was rebuilt several courses above this point (fig. 18). It is expected that this reworked section will help to stabilize not only the glacis but also the structural walls of the gate. At the same time, it provides an extremely impressive vision of what the city wall and gates would have looked like during the life of the city.

Kerkenes Eco-Center

This sister project to the archaeological excavations continues to promote and explore new avenues for rural sustainability. With funding from the United Nations Development Programme's (UNDP) Global Environment Fund (GEF) several new designs for solar cookers and driers were produced by Güner Mutaf of Middle East Technical University and his team. One of these designs minimizes a key issue with the earlier designs, needing to continuously turn the parabolic device to keep it optimally focusing the sun's rays. The new cooker has a solar-powered motor and automatically turns to follow the sun during the day. This work was in addition to ongoing educational activities and public outreach efforts.

Acknowledgments

The Kerkenes Dağ Project is a joint project between the Oriental Institute and the British Institute of Archaeology in Ankara. It is co-directed by Dr. Geoffrey Summers of Middle East Technical University (METU) and myself. Dr. Sevil Baltalı Tırpan of Istanbul Technical University (ITU) is Assistant Director. The Kerkenes Eco-Center Project is directed by Françoise Summers of METU, who is also jointly directing the restoration work within the Cappadocia Gate with Geoffrey Summers and Dr. Nilüfer Baturayoğlu Yöney of ITU.

Our thanks go to General Director Murat Süslü and staff of the General Directorate of Cultural Assets and Museums and to their representatives, Özge Yurdakul, Kenan Sürül, and Resul İbiş. Thanks are also due to former Yozgat Director of Culture and Tourism, Bahri Akbulut, his successor Lütfi İbiş, and to the staff of the Yozgat Museum, especially Director Hasan Şenyurt. We are grateful to the Governor of Yozgat, Necati Şentürk, the Yozgat Mayor, Yusuf Başer, the Directors of the Provincial Authority, TEDAŞ, and Türk Telekom, who with their staff continue to support the project in many ways. We thank the Sorgun district governor, Levent Kılıç, and Sorgun mayor, Ahmet Şimşek, and their staff for their continuing assistance.

Principal sponsors in 2010 were the Women's Board of the University of Chicago, the Oriental Institute, the Loeb Classical Library Foundation, the U.S. Ambassador's Fund for Cultural Preservation, the Archaeocommunity Foundation, Andrea Dudek, an anonymous American donor, the AICC, the Bernard and Innes Burrows Memorial Award of the Anglo-Turkish Society, the Binks Trust, the Charlotte Bonham-Carter Trust, Çimpor Yibitaş Yozgat Çimento, the Erdoğan M. Akdağ Foundation, MESA, METU-BAP grant, Peter Sommer Travels, the UCLA Cotsen Institute of Archaeology, and Yenigün. A full list of all participants and sponsors can be found on our website.

KHORSABAD RELIEF FRAGMENT PROJECT

Eleanor Guralnick

For more than three summers progress has been made on uncrating, cleaning, conserving, photographing, registering, and cataloging the hundreds of fragment of Khorsabad sculptures and inscriptions that have been stored in the Oriental Institute since 1930. This major project has resulted in the registration of some ninety-one large fragments of sculpture and several groups of adjacent sculptures. These groups are collected under a single registration number. One has thirty-six separate fragments that fit perfectly together. Other groups have as many as five to fourteen fragments. Several interesting individual pieces have been identified, while the majority of the pieces fill in most of the sculptured decoration of room 10 of the palace at Khorsabad, in northern Iraq.

A number of people from the Oriental Institute staff have dedicated their time to the several aspects of this project. Erik Lindahl, Laura D'Alessandro, Alison Whyte, Anna Ressman, Helen McDonald, and Susan Allison. John Brinkman is compiling the inscriptional material for future study. Without the help of this team of specialists this project could not be undertaken. The project is partially supported by grants from the Shelby White-Leon Levy Program for Archaeological Publication. Gil Stein has assigned the essential Oriental Institute staff to this project. His support has been essential to advancing this project.

In the very first stage 355 small sculpture fragments were registered and cataloged. These included some interesting pieces including two fragments from the palace throne room. One is a fragment with a man fleeing on a camel. The other is a fragment with a date palm with the limb of a falling man (fig. 1). Both confirm that the throne room was decorated with battle scenes from southern Mesopotamia. Several fragments reconstruct the head of a monumental foreigner in a turban, probably from room 8. These may be the only fragments surviving from this room in the West. At least three other fragments must be from the upper registers of room 13 or 14 (fig. 2). They were

Figure 1. Date palm and limb of falling man. Throne Room. OIM A150532

Figure 2. Falling warrior. Room 13 or 14. OIM A70605

Figure 3. Evergreen tree. Room 7. OIM A150565

Figure 4. Lower half of winged genie with branch of poppy pods or pomegranates. Entrance to room 7. OIM A58121

found in the fill above room 10. Two of these fragments show parts of falling warriors from battle scenes. The third fragment shows a feathered horse crest, smaller and carved to a different style from those in room 10. The feathers of the crest alternate with red and blue pigments and are well preserved. This confirms Botta's observation that the sculptures of rooms 13 and 14 are brightly painted. More than twenty-six fragments of evergreen trees from room 7 have been discovered, nearly all with substantial remains of blue pigment on the spines. One example, shown in figure 3, retains a small amount of green coloration as well. Research on the blue pigments is planned to determine whether the original color of the trees was blue or green, and the nature of the blue pigment. Two interesting large fragments each present the lower half of a winged genie. The larger of the two, probably from the entrance doorway to room 7, is presented in figure 4. It has remains of red pigment on the stemmed poppy pods or pomegranates it carries. This one was registered but undescribed in 1930. The other is among the newly registered.

Figure 5. Assyrian courtier followed by a foreigner. Room 10, southwest wall, lower register, slab 8. OIM A150587A–B

Most of the newly registered and cataloged large fragments are from the corridor named room 10. Among the groups of fragments of special interest are the fairly well-preserved, well-fitting pieces registered as A150587A–B, from the southwest wall, lower register (LR), slab 8, with an Assyrian courtier followed by a foreigner, leading the procession of foreigners with horses toward the inner courtyard of the palace (fig. 5). These two large fragments are enhanced by the small fragment A62133 with the excellently preserved right boot of the foreigner on A150587B and part of the slab base. Substantial remains have been cataloged for the other three courtiers who lead the other three processions of room 10, southwest wall, upper register (UR), slab 8 and the northeast wall, UR and LR of slab 9. Several large groups of fragments comprise nearly all of several LR compositions of foreigners and horses. A detail photo from fragment group, A150591 of the southwest wall, LR, slab 1, shows the elaborate horse trappings with significant amounts of red pigment surviving on the reins and chest strap (fig. 6). The large tassels alternate red and blue pigments. Another fragment from the southwest wall, LR, slab 7, illustrates the fine carving of a horse head held by a lead by a partially preserved man on the right wearing a furry cloak (fig. 7). A composition from the northeast wall, LR, slab 11, is composed of several closely fitting fragments (fig. 8). It offers a sense of what can be reconstructed for exhibit with a minimum of infilling, providing an example of excellently preserved, high-quality carving. On the whole, the fragments from the lower register are better preserved than those of the upper register. The latter are often damaged by fire and water. The lower register fragments are mainly broken with some weathering and water damage. The upper registers fell to the ground partially protecting the in situ sculptures.

Informal agreements have been reached with the Louvre, the British Museum, and the Iraq Museum in Baghdad for the exchange of photographs of all Khorsabad sculptures so that the publication will, in principle, address all the surviving sculptures in museums from that site. The situation in Iraq may limit the ability of the Baghdad Museum to cooperate. A list of all sculptures in the British Museum indicates that nearly all the inscribed display inscription from room 10 is in that museum. Many of the inscribed fragments have attached heads, horses' heads from the lower register, and feet, legs, and horse hoofs and legs from the upper register. This suggests that at least some of the missing pieces in the Oriental Institute compositions will be filled in by the fragments from the

Figure 6. Detail with horse trappings with red and blue pigments. From room 10, southwest wall, lower register, slab 1. From OIM A150591

Figure 7. Horse head and groom. Room 10, southwest wall, lower register, slab 7. OIM A150506

Figure 8. Horses and accompanying foreigners. Room 10, northeast wall, lower register, slab 12. OIM A150501A-F

British Museum. The Louvre has about one and a third slabs from the lower register of the southwest wall, room 10, on display. This will help complete that wall. Both these museums also have a number of individual heads, several of which should find places in the room 10 compositions.

At this point it appears that by the end of the current season we will have uncrated, cleaned, conserved, photographed, registered, and cataloged the remaining Khorsabad sculptures. The process of analyzing pigments and initiating the publication phase of the project will begin.

Further Reading

Albenda, Pauline

1986   *The Palace of Sargon, King of Assyria: Monumental Wall Reliefs at Dur-Sharrukin, from Original Drawings Made at the Time of Their Discovery in 1843-1844 by Botta and Flandin.* Synthèse 22. Paris: Éditions Recherche sur les civilisations.

Albenda, Pauline, and Eleanor Guralnick

1986   "Some Fragments of Stone Reliefs from Khorsabad." *Journal of Near Eastern Studies* 45/3: 231–42.

Botta, Paul Emile

1846–1850   *Monument de Ninive.* 5 volumes. Paris: Imprimerie nationale.

Guralnick, Eleanor

2002   "New Drawings of Khorsabad Sculptures by Paul Émile Botta." *Review Assyriologique* 96: 23–56.

2008   "Bronze Reliefs from Khorsabad." In *Proceedings of the 51st Rencontre Assyriologique Internationale (July 18–22, 2005),* edited by Robert D. Biggs, Jennie Myers, and Martha T. Roth, pp. 389–404. Studies in Ancient Oriental Civilization 62. Chicago: The Oriental Institute.

2008   "Assyrian Clay Hands from Khorsabad." *Journal of Near Eastern Studies* 67/4: 241–46.

2009   "Khorsabad Sculptured Fragments." In *Proceedings of the 5th International Congress of the Archaeology on the Ancient Near East (5-8 April 2006),* edited by Joaquín M. Córdoba, Miquel Molist, M. Carmen Pérez, Isabel Rubio, and Sergio Martínez, pp. 127–41. Madrid: Universidad Autónoma Madrid.

2010   "Color at Khorsabad: Palace of Sargon II." In *Proceedings of the 6th International Congress of the Archaeology of the Ancient Near East*, edited by Paolo Matthiae, Frances Pinnock, Lorenzo Nigro, and Nicolò Marchetti, vol. 1, pp. 781–91. Wiesbaden: Harrassowitz.

Loud, Gordon

1936   *Khorsabad 1. Excavations in the Palace and at a City Gate.* Oriental Institute Publications 38. Chicago: University of Chicago Press.

Loud, Gordon, and Charles B. Altman

1938   *Khorsabad 2. The Citadel and the Town.* Oriental Institute Publications 40. Chicago: University of Chicago Press.

Musée du Louvre

1936   *Encyclopédie photographique de l'art,* vol. 1. Paris: Editions "TEL."

Place, Victor

1859–1865   *Ninive et l'Assyrie.* 3 volumes. Paris: Imprimerie impériale.

MARJ RABBA

Yorke M. Rowan

The Chalcolithic period (ca. 4500–3600 BC), a key transitional time between the Neolithic and Bronze Ages, witnessed the first metallurgy, the first pottery formed on a wheel, and dramatically new burial practices for the dead. Yet in contrast to regions such as the Negev or Jordan Valley, our knowledge of life in the Galilee during the Chalcolithic period is very limited. For example, we have no radiocarbon dates for a Chalcolithic settlement in the Galilee, nor do we have an architectural plan. The second year of excavations at Marj Rabba (also know as Har ha-Shaʾavi, west — southwest, lat/long: 749780–226350; northeast, lat/long: 749950–226800) — the initial undertaking of the multi-site Galilee Prehistory Project — demonstrated that this site may be pivotal to a greater comprehension of this under-investigated area and time period. This research initiative is designed to examine the dramatic changes in the relationship of villages, ritual sites, and mortuary practices during this poorly understood period.

In 2009 we discovered intact sub-surface architecture, collected material culture and faunal samples, and sought to determine the depth of anthropogenic strata. Based on the good preservation of architectural features and faunal remains, Marj Rabba shows great promise for expanded, intensive investigation to offer insights into this key transitional era. During the 2010 season the excavation area was expanded and concentrated on the eastern area of the site, with particular effort put into excavation of squares B1, E1, F1, M1, and the northern half of squares E2 and F2.

Squares E1, E2, F1, F2

At the end of the 2009 season, a double-row, large fieldstone wall foundation (wall w7) was excavated which continued into the eastern section of square D1. Squares E1 and F1, and later E2 and F2, were opened in an effort to follow some of the features previously excavated in 2009 in square D1. Additionally, a large circular feature (locus L.23) almost 5 m in diameter and made of small cobbles was only half excavated and was expected to continue into square E1. The 2010 season revealed more architecture, more round features, and evidence for several phases of construction and habitation.

Excavation in both squares E1 and F1 began with the speedy removal of the topsoil by several volunteers and the workmen. There was significant modern material (plastic, bottle glass) mixed in with Chalcolithic pottery and lithics. Early in the season some larger stones emerged in E1 (w203) that appeared to be a continuation of wall w7, the east–west wall from the 2009 excavations in square D1. Additionally, there appeared to be a north–south wall on the western edge of E1 (w204) that adjoins w203 and would be a closing wall for the areas excavated in 2009. In F1 there also appeared an east–west wall (w201) that was assumed to be a continuation of w7 and w203.

During the initial days of topsoil removal, active mole-rat disturbance was noted in E1. This bioturbation continued throughout the excavation in E1 and F1. Daily, it was possible to see dirt and ancient material from different layers being actively pushed up by mole-rat activity (fig. 1). With the amount of ongoing soil disturbance visible in the short time we

Figure 1. Active mole-rat disturbance in square E1 (photo by A. Hill)

were on site and the quantity of burrows visible in subsoil layers, it must be assumed that significant amounts of bioturbation have disturbed much of the original context of finds at all levels.

Within the first week, the simple interpretation of the architectural pattern (continuation of the long wall (w7/w201/w203) with a north–south closing wall (w204) was called into question. At lower elevation but still in the topsoil, W.203 did not seem to continue past the middle of E1, w204 did not seem to actually connect to w203, and w201 seemed to jog north and not line up with w203. There were three well-defined wall fragments that appeared unrelated to each other. Nonetheless, significant Chalcolithic finds, including basalt groundstone fragments, flint axes, preserved bone, pottery, fenestrated basalt stand fragments, and ceramic spindle whorls, were recovered. The density of finds remained high in all areas throughout the rest of the season.

In the initial excavation of square F1 (figs. 2–3) we noticed a dense accumulation of very small pebbles in the western edge of the square. This concentration seemed to have an indistinct round edge. Initially we suspected that this was the fill of a pit, so we gave it a new locus number and excavated it separately. The dense, small pebbles gave way, however, after only a couple of centimeters, to densely packed medium cobbles at the same level with a very regular pattern and distinct edge. Rather than a pit this appears to be a round installation similar to others found throughout D1, E1, E2, F1, and F2. This feature was left in situ and will be removed during the 2011 season to more completely expose the floor level below. These installations were probably silo foundations. In the upper subsoil levels of F1 one of two obsidian blades found this season was pulled from the screen. Preliminary X-ray fluorescence (XRF) analysis suggests that the obsidian is from the Lake Van region of modern-day Turkey, reaffirming the existence of long-distance trade connections between Anatolia and the Levant during the Chalcolithic period.

In the eastern half of F1 we found a huge concentration of medium to large cobbles covering most of the square. This was a denser and larger concentration of stone than had

Figure 2. Squares F1 and F2, looking north

been found previously in Area E. After careful cleaning in and around this concentration, we eventually found two walls (w208
and w217) creating a room with w201. Wall
208 and w217 are both well-constructed
walls with two rows of regularly sized small
boulders. Unlike the walls in squares C, D,
and E, these walls do not use occasional
large standing boulders that are typically in
situ and often more than one course high.
There are at least two courses preserved
in w208 and w217. The north–south wall,
w208, seems to abut the first wall we discovered in F1, w201, even though it is significantly lower. Wall 201 has only one row
and one course preserved, is not particularly
straight, and appears to be a very late construction. However, there are large boulders
that may relate w201 to w208 and w217. Wall
231, below w201, is a better-constructed and
better-preserved wall that also appears to
adjoin w208. It has an opening that may be
a door, and then disappears into the western balk. W.231 appears to line up with the
walls from squares C, D, and E much better
than w201.

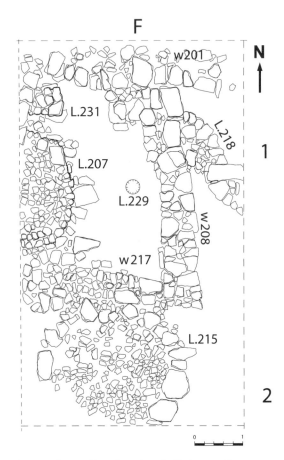

Figure 3. Square F1 and northern half of square F2

On the eastern side of w208, in square F1, we found another wall (w218) that runs diagonally southeast from the corner of w231 and w208 into the eastern section of F1. The purpose of this wall is unclear. It is not as well constructed as w231 or w208. Instead of two clear rows of uniformly sized field stones, this wall has very large stones (which may not be in situ) and some small cobbles in a more haphazard orientation. The wall seems to abut the corner of w231 and w208, but it also might articulate with w201, depending on which stones form part of the construction and which are from later destruction. It will not be possible to understand how this wall relates to the rest of the architecture in F1 without opening square G1 to the east, which we hope to undertake in the 2011 season.

Inside the room formed by w231, w208, and w217 there was a very dense and even distribution of cobbles and boulders at the bottom of L.210, a fill level. After photography and documentation, we removed the dense cobble layer. During removal of L.223, we recovered a nice mace-head fragment in the northwest corner. After about 10 cm and more cobble removal, a harder surface appears to be a floor (L.228), a light gray and very soft mix of silty soil, ash, and charcoal. Where preserved it is often sitting on top of flat sherds and appears to have been applied to them much like plaster. Unfortunately, we could only find portions of this layer in the southwest and northwest corners. In situ portions of the floor were carefully cleaned and photographed. Most of the floor is broken up by rodent burrows (see fig. 1 for evidence of mole-rat disturbance). In the middle of the room we found a small (ca. 26 cm diameter) round pit-like feature (L.229). This was a slightly irregular circle, clearly defined by a very hard irregular dark border (fig. 4). When broken, the boundary that defined L.229 seemed to be made of hard, burned, ash/charcoal/mud floor material. The feature continued approximately 26 cm down and was lined with small flat rocks and contained some fire-cracked small cobbles but very little in the way of finds. Although initially it seemed similar to "cupmarks" found at many Chalcolithic sites (e.g., Shiqmim, Gilat), this feature seems highly fired and unlike the cupmarks.

Recognizing that the architecture in square F1 continued to the south, we opened the northern half of square F2. Very quickly we noticed an apparent ragged circle of very large cobbles. This turned out to be a large round feature (L.215; see figs. 2–3) consisting of a large cobble border filled with uniformly sized medium cobbles. Although the circle is not particularly well preserved (some boulders have moved from the line of the circle, and some gaps exist), the feature is well defined. The border of L.215 is very close to w217, but because they do not abut the relationship between L.215 and the architecture in F1 remains unclear and will be clarified in the 2011 season.

Another round feature, very similar to L.215, was found in square E2. Eventually we came down on part of another round feature that has a diameter of approximately 2 m (L.226). This is similarly constructed with a border of larger fieldstones and a densely packed inner fill of medium cobbles. Less than half of this feature is in square E2; the rest disappears into the south section and the balk between E2 and F2.

Although some aspects of the dense cluster of features in square E1 remain unclear, there are at least four phases of construction (figs. 5–6). L.23, the large round feature, is the earliest and also largest feature. Unfortunately, it does not appear to be complete because the northeastern corner disappears just inside square E1. Next, L.230 is built on top of L.37, possibly reusing one edge of the earlier feature. Locus 225 may be contemporary with L.230 or might have been built during a similar phase. Then, the pit feature, L.214 (fig. 5b), cuts all three of these earlier features, Loci 23, 225, and 230. Finally, significantly later there is

Figure 4. Locus 228: room inside square F1 looking south. Arrows indicate preserved floor surface

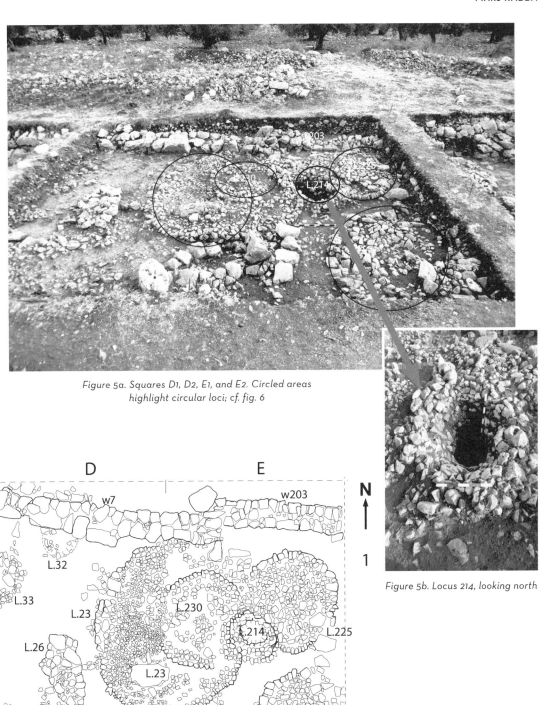

Figure 5a. Squares D1, D2, E1, and E2. Circled areas
highlight circular loci; cf. fig. 6

Figure 5b. Locus 214, looking north

Figure 6. Squares D1, E1, northern halves of D2, E2

the ephemeral wall construction w204. It is our hope that in season 2011 we will come to a better understanding of the function of these enigmatic features.

At the end of the season, as we dug into the subsoil level that contains all the large round features, we found that w203 continues. Wall 203 runs east–west across the entirety of square E1. North of w203 there continues to be a layer of dense cobbles, similar to the fill found north of w7, in D1 and C1. About 2 m from the western edge of square E1, w203 jogs to the north; it also only exists at a lower level after the jog (ca. 30–40 cm lower) and the construction method shifts. West of the jog, the wall continues, constructed in the same manner as in squares C1 and D1 with very large boulders in two rows, but often irregularly placed and with little uniformity of stone size. After the jog there are few large boulders and the rows are much more neatly and uniformly placed (similar to the walls in squares L1 and M1). Wall 203 disappears into the eastern balk and in both elevation and orientation seems to line up with w231. It remains unclear what the construction phases were for the wall. There is clearly a difference in construction at the jog, but whether w231 or w7 is constructed earlier may only be answered through further excavation. At the very end of the season we were just beginning to get some larger stones that might be a north–south wall adjoining w203 right at the jog. If this exists, then it would likely be a closing wall to w231, w208, and w217, making a complete room, running under all of the round features in E1. This would make the room in F1 an earlier phase than those in E1. This will be investigated in the 2011 season.

Square B1

Square B1 (fig. 7) was opened to explore the area immediately west of wall w6 in square C1, which was discovered in the 2009 field season. The intent was to uncover information pertaining to the construction of the wall and, perhaps, on the unique features found in C1 last

Figure 7. Square B1, looking north. Bedrock with sediment

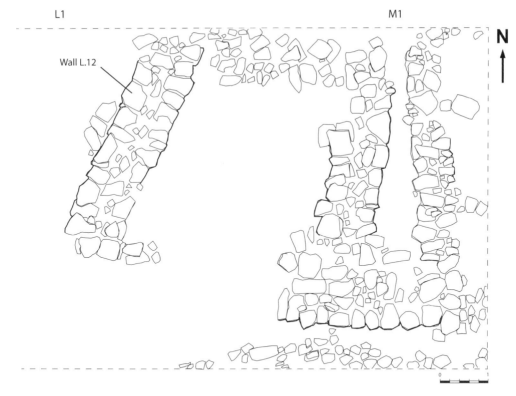

L1　　　　　　　　　　　M1

Wall L.12

N

Figure 8. Squares L1 (2009) and M1

Figure 9. Removal of topsoil in square M1. Exposure of possible walls. View toward north

year. Square B1 did not yield any architecture, yet there were quite rich cultural deposits, much of which was defined by mudbrick debris. Despite our best efforts, no convincing bricks were found in the square. Thus, B1 appears to have functioned as an extra-mural space during the Chalcolithic period. A great deal of bioturbation from both small animals (mostly rodents) and roots was present. Material from modern, Roman, Chalcolithic, and the Neolithic periods (one flint arrowhead) were found. Still, over 99 percent of the recovered artifacts dated to the Chalcolithic period.

Square M1

During the 2009 excavations in the East Area, one 5 x 5 m square was opened approximately 35 m to the east of the main excavation exposure. That square, L1, exposed a well-built wall (w12) with a double row of large cobbles, a small bench or pavement fragment (three stones to right of wall, farthest to right of in fig. 9). Wall 12 (see figs. 8–9) runs from the northeast corner of the square toward the southeast, terminating about one meter before the southern baulk.

In addition to this wall, the southern face of a wall (L.22; not shown on plan) was visible in the northern profile of the square, running east–west for almost 3 meters. The relationship between these two walls was unclear at the end of the season. With the goal of exposing any structures connected with w12, square M1 was opened. Removal of the dark topsoil exposed many stones, with the probably traces of walls, collapse, and random stones. The focus was primarily in the southern half of the square, where an east–west wall foundation appears, and where the dark, blocky, dry topsoil appears to dip lower than in the northern aspect of the square. During excavation of this locus, a small greenstone bead was found near the eastern face of w22. In this same area, some mudbricks were recognized in situ, probably part of the collapsed superstructure of w22. Also of interest, large pottery sherds at a relatively similar level in the northeastern corner of the square excavated together may fit together. We don't believe that this represents a surface, but probably only the fortuitous interface between the bottom of the plow zone and the archaeological layers.

By season's end, we believe that three different wall foundations were visible. One is an east–west wall line in the southern part of the square, and running parallel to the southern section of square M1. This wall seems substantial, but may not continue to the west as far as square L1. Instead, the wall may form a corner with a slightly curvilinear wall in the center of the square, running roughly north–south. More perplexing, another north–south wall is very close to the curvilinear wall, and thus may represent two different phases of building. Additional excavation is necessary to understand these walls, which were intentionally not exposed in order to protect them for full excavation in 2011.

Future Directions

After two seasons at Marj Rabba, we have at least six and possibly seven enigmatic round installations in squares E1, F1, E2, and F2. There seem to be two construction methods (with and without large fieldstone borders) and the diameter of the features ranges from as little as 2 m to as much as 5 m. The function of these installations remains unclear. There is no in situ evidence that these installations had any kind of superstructure, but they are very near the surface and so it is likely that plowing destroyed the upper portions of these features.

One potential function could be as silos, similar to those found at Tel Tsaf, although some of the Marj Rabba features are larger. Unfortunately, botanical preservation at this elevation is poor and although soil was removed from these installations for flotation, no preserved botanical remains have yet been recovered. We hope future seasons may clarify this question by uncovering lower and better-preserved installations.

Acknowledgments

On behalf of my co-director, Morag Kersel (DePaul University) and myself, we wish to thank the Israel Antiquities Authority for their continued support of this project. The project was made possible through the support of Professor Gil Stein, the Oriental Institute, and the generosity of private donors, for which we are very grateful. We would like to thank the staff at ORT Braude College in Karmi'el, particularly Ora Dahan and Maxine Noam, for their support and assistance during our stay. In Chicago, Steven Camp, Carla Hosein, D'Ann Condes, and Mariana Perlinac provided invaluable administrative support that ensured our fieldwork went much more smoothly. Particular thanks go to our Marj Rabba field staff: Austin Hill, Brittany Jackson, Max Price, and Dina Shalem, as well as the students, volunteers, and local workers.

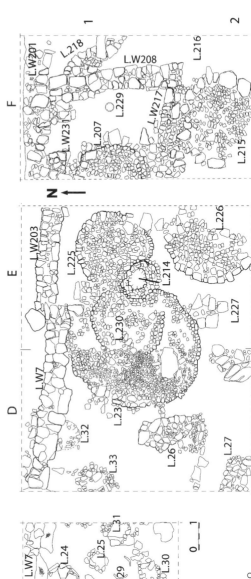

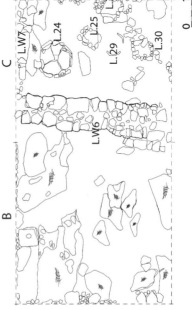

Figure 10. Composite of primary excavation areas, 2010

MUMMY LABEL DATABASE (MLD)

François Gaudard, Raquel Martín Hernández, and Sofía Torallas Tovar

The editors of the Mummy Label Database, namely, Sofía Torallas Tovar, the instigator of the project, Raquel Martín Hernández, and François Gaudard, have continued the laborious job of completing the database, including the task of revising existing editions, as well as publishing still-unpublished labels. For details on this joint project of the Instituto de Lenguas y Culturas del Mediterráneo y Oriente Próximo, Centro de Ciencias Humanas y Sociales – CSIC, Madrid, and of the Oriental Institute of the University of Chicago, readers can consult the *2008–2009 Annual Report*.

The MLD has now been integrated into a greater project named DVCTVS: La Memoria escrita: Recuperacion de los fondos papirologicos nacionales (FFI2009-11288), subsidized by the Spanish Ministry of Science and Innovation, which judged it excellent in its latest evaluation report. Thanks to this association the MLD will be able to hire a part-time new staff member, namely, Sergio Carro, whose role will be to arrange the photos and the fields of the database so that it can be launched online faster. The editors of the MLD would like to thank the Spanish Ministry of Science and Innovation for its generosity.

In March 2011, Sofía and François met at the Oriental Institute to discuss various aspects of the project. Sofía and Raquel visited the collection of the Abbey of Montserrat from September 18 to 22, 2010, and again from April 6 to 10, 2011, in order to identify new material for publication. Among others, they found an interesting mummy label that is currently being published by François in an article entitled "A Demotic-Hieratic Mummy Label in the Museu de Montserrat." Raquel wrote the two following articles: "Viajar por el Nilo en época greco-romana: El testimonio de los papiros," in *El viaje y sus riesgos: Los peligros de viajar en el mundo greco-romano*, edited by A. Alvar Nuño, pp. 115–29 (Madrid: Liceus, 2011), and "El transporte de momias a través del Nilo: El testimonio de las etiquetas de momia," which is in press and will be published in *Actas del V Congreso Español de Antiguo Oriente Próximo, Toledo 26–30 octubre de 2009*, edited by J. Oliva (Toledo: UCLM, 2011). She also delivered a paper entitled "El precio de la muerte en el Egipto Ptolemaico," at the III Jornadas de Papirología, held in Barcelona, from March 24 to 26, 2011. As for Sofía, she published "Linguistic Identity in Graeco-Roman Egypt," in *The Multilingual Experience in Egypt, from the Ptolemies to the ʿAbbāssids*, edited by A. Papaconstantinou, pp. 17–43 (Farnham and Burlington: Ashgate, 2010).

NIPPUR

McGuire Gibson

There is not much to say about Nippur itself. We get occasional reports from our guards that the site and the expedition house are safe. Besides our guards, there is a contingent of special guards from the government. Both the site and the house are slowing being weathered by rain and wind, but there is no looting. This next year will be a critical one in Iraq's history, with U.S. troops supposedly withdrawing (although I think that thousands will remain in several of the elaborate bases that have been built over the past decade). The withdrawal might lead to relative stability or its opposite. It may be possible to re-open investigations at Nippur in a year or two, but a team working at a very conspicuous site in a well-established house might present too tempting a target. Conditions seem to be fairly quiet in the south of Iraq, where Nippur is, and even farther south, they may be even better. Elizabeth Stone and Paul Zimansky are carrying out a short investigation of a site very close to Ur. This is a joint expedition with Abdul Amir Hamdani, an official of the Antiquities Service and also a doctoral student of theirs at Stony Brook. In addition, Abdul Amir is working with some Italians on another small site nearby, but that is also low-profile and essentially testing the waters. Carrie Hritz is planning an investigation of the area around ancient Girsu (modern Tello) and may start in the coming year.

Figure 1. View of the excavations at the Early Dynastic I Inanna Temple (ca. 2800 BC; level IXA). Note the curved platform for rituals

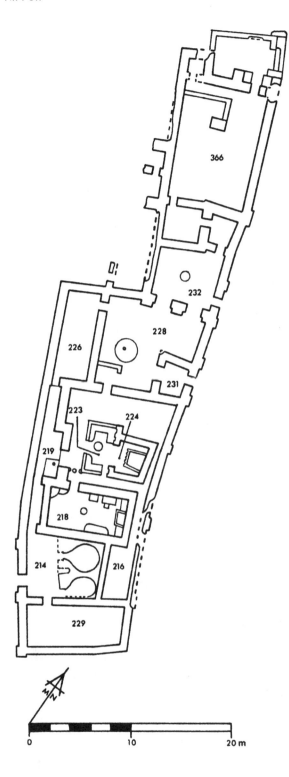

Figure 3. Two Early Dynastic statues of worshipers found in the Inanna Temple

Figure 2. Central section of the Early Dynastic Inanna Temple (ca. 2600 BC; level VIII). Note the two shrines (218 and 224), the second of which is probably the Uzu-mu-a, where Enlil struck his pick into the ground and the first human sprang out

Figure 4. Two of the bronze foundation statues of the Ur III king, Shulgi, buried under the temple when he built it. On his head is a basket of clay for the laying of bricks. Remnants of linen still cling to the statues

THE ORIENTAL INSTITUTE

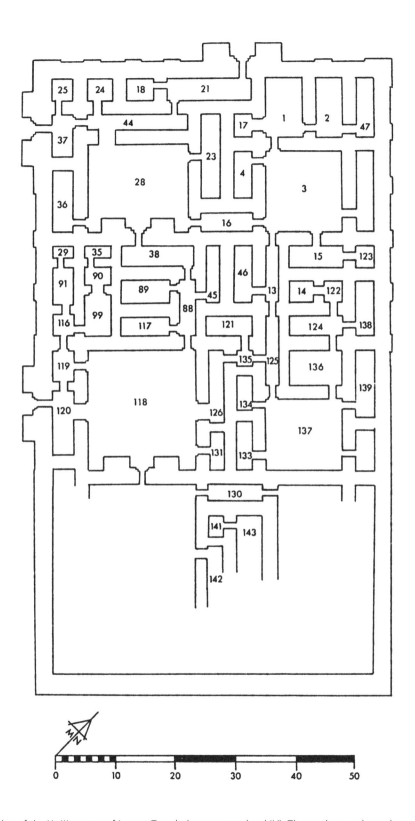

Figure 5. Plan of the Ur III version of Inanna Temple (ca. 2100 BC; level IV). The southern end was destroyed in antiquity, but we presume there were two shrines in the southern corner

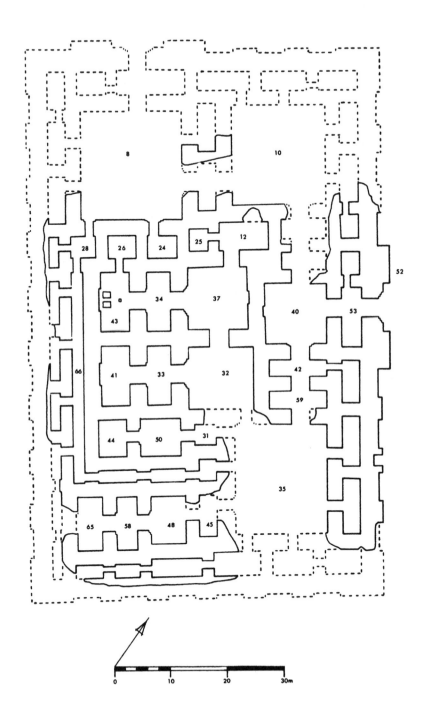

Figure 6. Plan of the Parthian version of the Inanna Temple (ca. AD 100; level II). Although more than six hundred years after the fall of Babylon, this temple, in classic Babylonian layout and detail, shows that the Mesopotamian religious tradition still held. Note the two shrines (rooms 41 and 43)

Meanwhile, we here at Chicago and elsewhere are hard at work on the preparation of reports on our years of work at Nippur. A National Endowment for the Humanities (NEH) grant, which supported the project for the past three years, is about to end. That funding has allowed us to bring the Inanna Temple report very close to completion. It is clear that this one is going to be a multi-volume publication. Richard Zettler, who took on the Inanna Temple for his dissertation research in the 1970s and then went on to teach at Pennsylvania, has completed a huge manuscript on the architecture alone. The careful excavation and recording done by Carl Haines, Donald Hansen, and James Knudsted have made it possible for him to lay out numerous alterations in the succeeding versions of the Early Dynastic temples (2900–2450 BC), in which hundreds of stone statues, reliefs, and other objects were found (figs. 1–3). Karen Wilson and Jean Evans have prepared manuscripts on the pottery, sculptures, and other objects. Ed Keall, in Toronto, has the responsibility for the Parthian version of the temple, which is one of the best examples of the persistence of ancient Mesopotamian religion and its architecture, which existed here for more than six hundred years after the last king of Babylon had died (fig. 6.). Robert D. Biggs is working on the inscriptions from the temple. The group is able to work together, despite being hundreds of miles apart, because we have used part of the NEH grant to scan into a computer database and make accessible hundreds of field notes, notebooks, drawings, photographs, and slides. We have been very fortunate to have Jeremy Walker carry out the laborious job of scanning. As a second step, Karen Terras has then gone through the database to choose crucial but badly preserved documents and images on which she has worked magic with Photoshop, giving us a greatly enhanced result. During the summer of 2011, Zettler will return to Chicago for a working session, in which the entire team will push the project toward its completion.

In addition to the Inanna team, James A. Armstrong is revising his manuscript on the Kassite through Neo-Babylonian periods, and he will also be in Chicago again this summer. When I find time, I am still preparing manuscripts on two seasons of my own work at Nippur since 1972. And lately, I have dug out the partially completed manuscript on Umm al-Hafriyat, an industrial site out in the desert about 30 kilometers southeast of Nippur, where we did one season of work in 1977. We had planned at least one more season at the site, but commitments elsewhere in the subsequent years delayed our return. I last saw the site in 2003, from a U.S. helicopter about a month after the war. The site was riddled with holes made by looters who helped to feed the international market for stolen antiquities during the 1990s. It may be so badly damaged that no archaeologist ever works there again, and our report will be the only record of a remarkable town.

———————

PERSEPOLIS FORTIFICATION ARCHIVE PROJECT

Matthew W. Stolper

The Persepolis Fortification Archive (PFA) Project continues to pursue the two urgent goals stated and repeated in earlier Annual Reports, namely, to make thorough records of the Archive that will sustain future research, and to distribute the records freely and continuously to enable current research. The records include digital images of thousands of tablets and fragments; readings and editions of thousands of complete and fragmentary texts in Achaemenid Elamite and Imperial Aramaic; identifications, catalog entries, collations, digital images and drawings of the impressions of thousands of cylinder seals and stamp seals. The team that compiles and processes these records includes students and faculty from Chicago and other colleges and universities. The means of distributing the results include two on-line applications, InscriptiFact (see http://www.inscriptifact.com/) and OCHRE (see http://ochre.lib.uchicago.edu/). As of mid-2011, the PFA Project has made usable records of more than 8,000 Persepolis Fortification tablets and fragments, and has made partial or complete records of almost 3,000 of them publicly available. The goal of a comprehensive record of the Archive is within reach. If it is accomplished it will sustain a generation of research on the languages, art, institutions, society, and history of the Achaemenid empire.

Image Capture

Thanks to continuing support from the Andrew W. Mellon Foundation (http://www.mellon.org/) and emergency help from the Farhang Foundation (http://www.farhang.org/) during a gap between grants, the collaboration between the PFA Project at the Oriental Institute and the West Semitic Research Project at the University of Southern California (http://www.usc.edu/dept/LAS/wsrp/) continues to capture and process very high-quality images of Persepolis Fortification tablets and fragments at increasing rates and with increasing quality. As the previous reports on the Project have described and illustrated — and as readers can see for themselves via InscriptiFact and OCHRE — many of these images are made with Polynomial Texture Mapping (PTM) technology, a kind of Reflectance Transformation Imaging (RTI) that gives the end user dynamic control over the apparent lighting in the image, allowing optimum viewing of features impressed on or in the tablet surface, like cuneiform signs and seal impressions; many others are made with a large-format, high-resolution BetterLight scanning camera, using polarized and filtered light to reveal details not easily seen in ordinary daylight, for example, faded ink traces, or ink obscured by surface discoloration. During 2010–11, Clinton Moyer (PhD 2009, Cornell), Miller Prosser (PhD 2011, NELC), and John Walton (PhD 2011, NELC) documented more than 700 tablets and fragments with one or both of these methods, making more than 6,000 new PTM sets of more than 640 pieces, and more than 3,500 new BetterLight scans of more than 130 pieces.

This phase of the Project gives highest priority to the categories of Fortification documents that have previously not been recorded and published, namely, the tablets with monolingual Aramaic texts accompanied by seal impressions, and the tablets with seal impressions unaccompanied by any texts. By mid-2011 more than 3,100 items were recorded with one or both of these kinds of imagery, including more than 690 Aramaic tablets, more than 1,800 uninscribed tablets, and more than 650 Elamite cuneiform tablets (about 220 of them also bearing short epigraphs in Aramaic).

InscriptiFact team members Marilyn Lundberg and Kenneth Zuckerman came to the Oriental Institute twice to train PFA Project imaging personnel in the use of a recently developed technique called Highlight-RTI. This is a method of capturing PTMs without the domed apparatus that the Project uses for Fortification tablets. Instead, one uses a stationary camera,

Figure 1. *Highlight-RTI imaging of Khorsabad relief in the Oriental Institute Museum: Clinton Moyer (left) and Miller Prosser move the light; Kenneth Zuckerman (back to camera) controls camera and light; reflective red ball at base of relief registers light position*

Figure 2. *PTM image of inscription from Khorsabad relief in the Oriental Institute Museum, obtained by Highlight-RTI method and displayed with InscriptiFact's stand-alone PTM Viewer (described in last year's Annual Report)*

a moving hand-held light, and a shiny black or red ball placed near the object. In a series of shots made with different lighting angles, the shiny ball registers a reflection, which software uses to establish the light positions, allowing PTM processing software to combine a series of shots into the final interactive PTM image. This technique is especially suitable for recording larger objects and immovable objects, like the Oriental Institute's Assyrian reliefs (figs. 1–2).

As mentioned in last year's *Annual Report*, grants from the Iran Heritage Foundation (http://www.iranheritage.org/) allowed the PFA Project to install two PTM post-processing stations at the Oriental Institute, where student workers Lori Calabria, Megaera Lorenz, Gregory Hebda (all NELC), Joshua Elek (Divinity), Amy Genova, and Daniel Whittington (both Classics) at Chicago complemented image processing done at USC by Bekir Gurdil, Claire Shriver, and Ashley Sands. By mid-2011, about 85 percent of the high-quality images had been processed, all but eliminating a backlog of several years' standing.

Calabria, Elek, Genova, Hebda, Lorenz, and Whittington, as well as Alexander Kornienko (History) and Tytus Mikołajczak (NELC), also made and edited about 10,000 new conventional digital images of about 1,650 more Elamite cuneiform tablets and fragments. Among them are some of those designated PF, published by the late Richard T. Hallock in his magisterial *Persepolis Fortification Tablets* (OIP 92 [1969]), many of those designated PF-NN, which the Project is preparing for publication, and many of those designated Fort., hitherto entirely unrecorded. By mid-2011, more than 5,500 Elamite documents had been recorded with ten to twenty conventional digital images each. After a complete review of earlier conventional images, these workers also continue the supplementary re-photography mentioned in last year's *Annual Report* to fill in gaps in the image record.

Conservation and Storage

A timely grant from the PARSA Community Foundation (http://www.parsacf.org/) allowed the PFA Project to address two urgent concerns, tablet conservation and data storage.

Since autumn 2009, when the Project lost the services of seasoned conservator Monica Hudak, we have been without a full-time tablet conservator. This was a grave problem, since many of the Persepolis tablets can be recorded only after skilled cleaning and stabilization. Robyn Haynie joined the Project in May 2011 to close this gap. She comes to the Project with a degree from the eminent conservation program of the Institute of Archaeology, University College London, academic background in Egyptology, and field experience in Greece and Turkey. A backlog of several hundred Persepolis items was waiting for her attention, and she began immediately to process the first batch and return the tablets and fragments to the editorial and imaging stream (fig. 3).

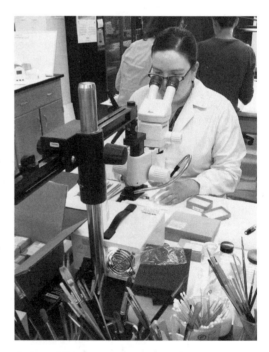

Figure 3. PFA Project conservator Robyn Haynie cleans a Persepolis Fortification tablet under binocular microscope (acquired with an earlier grant from the PARSA Community Foundation)

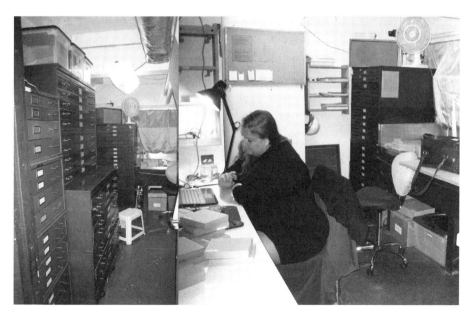

Figure 4. Left: extended basement storage of processed Fortification tablets. Right: PFA Project editor Annalisa Azzoni at work in subterranean seclusion

By the autumn of 2010, the accumulation of thirty-eight terabytes of editorial and image data had exceeded the capacity of the Project's dedicated server, maintained by systems administrator Elijah Buck at Humanities Computing. At the beginning of 2011, the addition of more than twenty terabytes of storage relieved the strain. As of mid-2011 the server holds about forty-five terabytes of Project data. This includes not only processed images and editions for online distribution, but also raw and intermediate images, scanned manuscripts and documents, and other tools used by Project editorial staff.

The growing number and volume of tablets and fragments recorded by imaging and editorial teams also began to strain the Project's physical storage capacity. Oriental Institute archivist John Larson and preparator Erik Lindahl made several banks of storage drawers available for PFA Project use, and in June 2011 Project editors Annalisa Azzoni, Mark Garrison, and Wouter Henkleman reorganized tablet storage in the Project's basement workspace (adding some decorative color to relieve the spartan gloom of the former photographic darkroom, fig. 4).

Digital storage capacity and physical storage capacity will both be recurrent problems, but they are welcome problems in the sense that they are the consequences of progress toward the Project's foremost goals.

Editorial

During two more spells of work at the Oriental Institute, PFA Project editor Wouter Henkelman (Free University of Amsterdam) continued to collate Elamite Fortification documents known from preliminary editions by Richard Hallock (PF-NN), preparing corrected, annotated editions and translations. The last such texts to be treated are the complex registers, documents that belong to formal types that Hallock designated as "journals" and "accounts." These registers compile, tabulate, and digest large amounts of information transferred from shorter memoranda in simpler formats on smaller tablets. Being larger, the registers are often more severely damaged than the memoranda; being denser and more complex, their damaged passages are often harder to reconstruct; being produced by the later phases of the information stream that the Fortification Archive records, they are of prime importance to understanding the Archive as a whole. For all these reasons, collating and editing these documents is slow going. By mid-2011, Henkelman had processed all but the last thirty-five of them in preparation for final publication. Editions and images of many are available on OCHRE.

I supplement these finished editions with preliminary editions of previously unexamined Elamite tablets and fragments, to be revised and collated with Henkelman. I give greatest attention to the journals and accounts, because they are numerically underrepresented in the published sample of the PFA. As of mid-2011, I had recorded about 750 new Elamite texts, among them about 400 registers. NELC student worker Tytus Mikołajczak reread about forty-five of these with me, making corrections, adding editorial and analytical notes, and supplying or verifying identifications of seals. Such new documents fill in more and more slots in the dense matrix of PFA data, and they also continue to yield surprises to delight the philologist, historian, and general tablet nerd — rare or entirely new Elamite and Old Iranian words, phrases, constructions and contents, and/or new seals.

I also continue to pore over the boxes of unrecorded tablets and fragments in a process of triage, to select Elamite tablets and fragments for conservation, photography, and/or reading.

The extraordinary harvest of Achaemenid art from the impressions of seals on Persepolis Fortification tablets continues to flourish under the overall supervision of PFA Project editor Mark Garrison (Trinity University). During six more visits to the Oriental Institute, Garrison systematically examined 275 more of the boxes of unprocessed tablets and fragments and selected 800 more uninscribed, sealed tablets that merit cataloging and recording. By mid-2011, he had examined more than two-thirds of the approximately 2,600 boxes and accumulated a collection of nearly 3,000 analytically useful tablets. Post-doctoral researcher Sabrina Maras (University of California, Berkeley) continues to catalog some of this material under Garrison's direction, processing about 170 tablets during 2010–11. Student workers visiting from other institutions are also doing preliminary cataloging under Garrison's direction: Jenn Finn (PhD candidate, Interdepartmental Program in Classical Art and Archaeology, University of Michigan) in July and August 2010, Jenny Kreiger (PhD candidate in the same program at Michigan), and Erin Daly (undergraduate, Cornell College) beginning in June 2011 (fig. 5).

During 2010–11 Garrison and his team identified almost 200 new seals from impressions on the uninscribed tablets, for a running total of almost 500 new seals in this subcorpus. Working with Mikołajczak, Garrison also examined about 300 more of the Elamite tablets texts being edited by Henkelman to verify seal identifications. They cataloged more than 140 more new seals, for a running total of nearly 600 new seals from review of about two-thirds of this subcorpus. Almost 2,800 distinct seals have been identified so far from impressions on Persepolis Fortification tablets. As last year's *Annual Report* emphasized, each of these seals represents the activity of a distinct individual or office, as distinct as a signature, and the whole corpus of seals is a collection of Achaemenid art without parallel for its size, range and precise context.

Working with research assistants at Trinity University, Garrison scanned final drawings of seals known from impressions on published tablets. All the scans of final drawings (and some of preliminary drawings) are available on the Project server to Project members work-

Figure 5. Jenny Kreiger (University of Michigan, foreground) and Erin Daly (Cornell College) classifying and cataloging uninscribed, sealed Fortification tablets

ing on all the subcorpora of the Archive. Garrison and his assistants have also begun to upload the drawings, accompanied with iconographic data, to OCHRE, where they can be linked to online display of the tablets. By mid-2011, they had entered about 320 of the seals, mostly those that appear in the two as-yet unpublished volumes of the ongoing publication of the seals on published Elamite Fortification tablets (the first volume, Oriental Institute Publication 117, by Garrison and Margaret Cool Root [University of Michigan], is available at http://oi.uchicago.edu/research/pubs/catalog/oip/).

During five more visits to the Oriental Institute, Project editor Annalisa Azzoni (Vanderbilt University) cataloged seventy more monolingual Aramaic tablets and fragments, for a running total of 738, all entered in OCHRE with preliminary readings and notes. Azzoni reviewed and formatted editions of fifty more of these for public distribution on OCHRE. Project editor Elspeth Dusinberre (University of Colorado), assisted in Chicago by student worker Emily Wilson (Classics), updated OCHRE records of 475 seals identified from impressions on the first 530 of the monolingual Aramaic Fortification texts (that is, all the Aramaic tablets recorded with autographed copies and draft editions by the late Raymond A. Bowman), completed final inked drawings of twenty of them and template drawings of more than forty more. Azzoni also examined all the known Aramaic epigraphs on Elamite Fortification tablets, the second major Aramaic subcorpus of the PFA. Of more than 220 epigraphs identified so far, she entered ninety for public distribution on OCHRE.

Distribution

During 2010–11, InscriptiFact Project members Marilyn Lundberg and Leta Hunt cataloged and uploaded more than 7,400 BetterLight scans and more than 2,700 PTM sets to display more than 530 additional Fortification tablets to the InscriptiFact database application. InscriptiFact is available for free download on application at http://www.inscriptifact.com/. As of mid-2011, users can view online or download for local use more than 17,000 high-resolution static images and more than 4,000 high-resolution PTM sets, documenting 1,060 Persepolis Fortification tablets. These include most of the Aramaic texts in the Archive (apart from Aramaic inscriptions in seal impressions): 688 of the 738 monolingual Aramaic tablets identified so far, and 185 of about 220 Aramaic epigraphs identified so far on cuneiform texts.

Oriental Institute post-doctoral worker Dennis Campbell continues to carry out the cluster of interlocking tasks involved in uploading, error-checking, and linking PFA texts, images and cataloging information for display in the On-Line Cultural Heritage Environment (OCHRE, available for free download at http://ochre.lib.uchicago.edu/index_files/Page494.htm), assisted by student workers Seunghee Yie (NELC), Wayne Munsch (Divinity), and Özgün Sak (History). More than 4,000 Elamite texts have been entered, more than 2,250 of them now publicly available. All of the known monolingual Aramaic tablets have been entered. More than 2,000 of the Elamite and Aramaic texts have associated images. More than 1,700 of the uninscribed tablets have been entered with basic cataloging and descriptive information, and more than 1,000 of them with linked screen-resolution PTM images.

Munsch has imported and edited images of about 400 Elamite tablets on OCHRE, and tagged about 2,000 of the images, linking the texts sign-by-sign to edited transliterations, and linking seal impressions to catalog entries and collated drawings of the seals. As new texts are entered, Yie continually revises and corrects Elamite glossary entries and the underlying text editions, and Campbell revises and corrects Aramaic glossary entries and the underlying text editions. This process underscores a notable property of the languages of the Fortification texts: of more than 3,000 lemmas in the Elamite and Aramaic glossaries so far, more than 70 percent are proper names. Considering that the texts are terse administrative records, this comes as no surprise, but it is startling to realize that this large corpus — the largest in Achaemenid Elamite and one of the largest in Imperial Aramaic — relies on scarcely a thousand items of common Elamite, Iranian-Elamite, Aramaic, and Iranian-Aramaic vocabulary, and it is sobering to recognize how much more of these languages we cannot know.

As the texts are cleaned up, those with explicit dates are linked to time periods (regnal years of Darius I, month when explicit, and modern expressions of ancient dates). This will allow users to include time as a variable in complex searches when examining patterns in choice of signs, choice of words, syntactic choices, volumes of commodities, and other matters.

The University of Chicago Library has upgraded the hardware that powers the PFA on OCHRE, and Internet data specialist Sandra Schloen, one of the creators of OCHRE, has upgraded the software. The results include faster processing, better internal indexing, and new

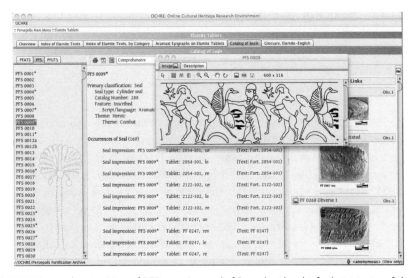

Figure 6. OCHRE Comprehensive View of PFS 0009*, a seal of Parnaka, the chief administrator of the Fortification administration, with his name in Aramaic engraved in the seal scene. The View shows a list of 160 impressions by tablet number and surface and by text number (left), with thumbnails of available images (right), and an opened link to show the collated seal drawing (center). Clicking on a text link opens an edition of the text associated with the particular impression

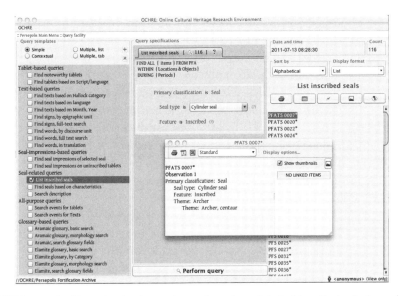

Figure 7. OCHRE query facility under development: search produces list of all inscribed cylinder seals; clicking on first-entry, PFATS 0007* (an inscribed seal first documented on Aramaic Fortification tablets), opens a terse catalog entry

functionality. New view formats include the "Comprehensive View," available for each seal in the Catalog of Seals, offering a concise presentation of each documented impression of the seal (including images) on tablets of all types, along with linked details of each tablet and its textual contents (if any) (fig. 6). A new query facility, still under development, allows a wide and flexible range of complex searches of properties of tablets, scripts, transliterations, translations, glossaries, seal impressions, seals, seal inscriptions, etc. (fig. 7).

Publications and Presentations

PFA Project staff members completed more than thirty-five articles, book chapters, and books based largely or entirely on PFA Project results. Publications that appeared in 2010–11 include Garrison's article on "The Seal of 'Kuraš the Anzanite, Son of Šešpeš (Teispes),' PFS 93*: Susa-Anšan-Persepolis," and Henkelman's article on "Parnaka's Feast: šip in Parsa and Elam," both in *Elam and Persia*, edited by J. Alvarez-Mon and Mark Garrison (Eisenbrauns, 2011), Henkelman's article on "'Consumed Before the King,' the Table of Darius, that of Irdabama and Irtaštuna, and that of his Satrap, Karkiš," in the conference volume *Der Achämenidenhof/ The Achaemenid Court*, edited by Bruno Jacobs and Robert Rollinger, Classica et Orientalia 2 (Harrassowitz, 2010), and "The First Achaemenid Administrative Document Discovered at Persepolis," by Charles E. Jones (Institute for the Study of the Ancient World, New York University) and Seunghee Yie, mentioned in last year's *Annual Report* and now available online at http://www.achemenet.com/document/2011.003-Jones&Yie.pdf.

The Project's weblog (http://persepolistablets.blogspot.com/, or on Facebook at http://www.facebook.com/pages/Persepolis-Fortification-Archive-Project/116290391782963), with sixteen new posts, was viewed more than 16,000 times during 2010–11 by more than 10,000 unique visitors.

Academic lectures and conference presentations by PFA Project members during 2010-11 included Azzoni's talk on "Aramaic at Persepolis" at the annual meetings of the American

Schools of Oriental Research and the Society for Biblical Literature in Atlanta, November 2010, and her lecture on "Digitizing the Past" at Loyola University of New Orleans in March 2011; a presentation by Garrison on "Observations on Persepolitan Glyptic and the Seal of Aršama," and six presentations by Henkelman on the PFA, its contents, its historical and sociolinguistic implications, all at series of workshops at Oxford in January, February, and May 2011; papers by Mikołajczak on "Visual Aspects of the Accounting Seals of the PFA" and by me on "'His Own Death' at Bisotun and Persepolis," both at the annual meeting of the American Oriental Society in Chicago in March 2011; and my keynote lecture on the PFA and the Project at a symposium on "Archaeologies of Text: Archaeology, Technology and Ethics," at the Joukowsky Institute for Archaeology and the Ancient World, Brown University, December 2010.

Among several local presentations, my keynote presentation on "Electronic Epigraphy to the Rescue of the Persepolis Fortification Archive," at the Umbrella Initiative Faculty Technology, tried to let members of the University of Chicago community who are not part of the Oriental Institute's ordinary constituency know that the work of the Oriental Institute belongs to the mainstream of the University's research mission in terms that are both technically adept and culturally responsible.

Conclusion

Another way in which the PFA Project carries out the University's mission is by supporting students who will populate the next generation of scholarship. Six graduate student workers have completed PhDs during the life of the Project, in fields that include Assyriology, Hittitology, Northwest Semitic philology (including Miller Prosser in 2011) and Hebrew Bible (including John Walton in 2011). In 2011, Tytus Mikołajczak completed an MA thesis on PFA material (including entirely original documentation), already the basis for two presentations at national meetings. Siwei Wang (Computer Science, PhD 2011) surmises that her investigation of PTM technology while volunteering for the PFA Project helped her earn a post-doctoral fellowship working on the Advanced Photon Source at Argonne National Laboratories. Undergraduate Project workers have gone on to graduate programs elsewhere, and in 2010–11 at least two of them (Elizabeth Davidson, Coptic and Early Christianity, Yale University; Ivan Cangemi, Anthropology and Interdisciplinary Program in Classical Art and Archaeology, University of Michigan) have reached PhD candidacy. As already mentioned, students from other colleges and universities have come to Chicago for summer work on the Project.

In this way, the aims, methods, accomplishments and temperament of the PFA Project contribute to the formation of scholars whose careers will take them far beyond the Project's topical focus. Unfortunately, some of them are moving forward in their careers before the Project is complete. This year, Clinton Moyer, the senior member of the high-resolution imaging team, who has been a key to developing and implementing its growing repertoire of methods, leaves to take up a post-doctoral fellowship at Wake Forest University, and John Walton, also part of the high-resolution imaging group, leaves for a teaching post at the University of Northern Iowa (fig. 8).

In spring 2011 came two pieces of good news that underscore the priorities of the PFA Project and that bode well for accomplishing the Project's goals. First, after long deliberation, a Federal appellate court panel handed down rulings on two motions in the lawsuit that still looms over the future of the tablets (see David Glenn, "U. of Chicago and Museums Win Key

Figure 8. PFA Project staff at farewell reception for departing workers. Left to right: Ben Thomas (NELC), Miller Prosser (PhD NELC, 2011), Annalisa Azzoni (Vanderbilt University), Stolper and Baxter, Clinton Moyer (PhD Cornell, 2009), Erin Daly (Cornell College), Wouter Henkelman (Free University of Amsterdam), and John Walton (PhD NELC, 2011). Walton's shirt shows the emblem of the Persepolis Football Club

Ruling in Legal Battle over Iranian Antiquities," *Chronicle of Higher Education* (http://chronicle. com/article/U-of-ChicagoMuseums-Win/126923/). Although these rulings are favorable to the Oriental Institute's position, it is important to realize that they concern procedural issues. The substantive legal issue remains to be determined by a trial on the merits and the date of that trial is not yet fixed. Thus, the urgency of the threat to the PFA is diminished but the substance of the threat remains. Whatever the outcome, the Oriental Institute will ultimately surrender custodial control of the Persepolis Fortification tablets, so a complete record of the PFA remains a compelling need.

Second, the Andrew W. Mellon Foundation, the PARSA Community Foundation, and the National Endowment for the Humanities (http://www.neh.gov/) renewed large grants to the PFA Project. These, along with supporting grants from the Iran Heritage Foundation and the Farhang Foundation and gifts from individual donors, will sustain our work at the present levels for the immediate future, bringing the goal of a complete record of the PFA within reach. As we proceed, the PFA Project continues to reveal the rich potential of the Archive's data for understanding the languages, art, and society of the Achaemenid Persian empire, and the intimate connections among them.

TELL EDFU

Nadine Moeller

The 2010 season of the Tell Edfu Project was marked by the longest field season in the project's history, which lasted for two and a half months, spanning the period from October to mid-December 2010. During this time it has been possible to considerably advance the excavation in the columned hall and silo area, which will be fully completed in 2011. The overall research focus of this project will then gradually shift to the exploration of the Old Kingdom settlement and the origins of the ancient town of Edfu. In this respect, major clearance work was carried out along the northeastern part of the tell, close to the Ptolemaic temple, where Old Kingdom settlement layers had been previously identified (see *Oriental Institute 2009–2010 Annual Report*). Furthermore, the Tell Edfu Project was expanded to incorporate a first reconnaissance survey at the Old Kingdom step pyramid situated about 5 km southwest of Edfu. This will be another new focus for future seasons.

Excavations in the Silo Court of the Second Intermediate Period

One of the main foci in the silo area has been the excavation of Silo 388, which is situated in the northern part of the granary court.[1] As noted already last season, its walls have been preserved to a considerable height, measuring more than 4 m from the silo floor to the last course of bricks, showing clearly the beginning of the vaulted top. We can estimate that it was about 80 percent intact at the time of its abandonment at the end of the Second Intermediate Period and any subsequent loss of the structure was minimal until the French expedition dug a deep trench in this area in the 1930s. This silo was built in the available space between Silo 316 and the northern enclosure wall (W 324) of the silo area (fig. 1). Therefore Silo 388 is slightly egg-shaped and not as round as some of the other silos in this area (fig. 2). Inside the silo numerous thick fill layers were excavated in which around seventy new Hieratic ostraca were discovered. They are inscribed with lists containing names, titles, and commodities, very similar to those found in the previous seasons.[2] The pottery from these layers consists mainly of sherds dating to the very end of the Seventeenth Dynasty to early Eighteenth Dynasty, which is the time

Figure 1. Northern part of excavation area with Silo 388 in the foreground and the Ptolemaic temple in the background

Figure 2. Silo 388, view from the top

when this area was being used for dumping large amounts of trash, an activity that continued at least until the mid-Eighteenth Dynasty.[3] Additionally, more hippopotamus bones were excavated in these layers and they will be part of a detailed zooarchaeogical study in the next season by Richard Redding (Museum of Anthropology, University of Michigan). It is interesting to note that relatively few broken mudbricks were found in these layers, which stands in sharp contrast to most of the other silos whose interior space was predominantly filled with the mudbrick demolition from the collapse of their upper parts. In the case of Silo 388, this might be related to the fact that it had been very well preserved with its walls standing up to a considerable height.

The full excavation of Silo 316, which is the largest (6.5 m in diameter) and probably oldest silo of the granary court, was also completed this season. In contrast to Silo 388, its interior was filled by a large quantity of broken mudbricks, which came from the collapsed roof and upper wall parts. A considerable number of hippopotamus bones have been found here, too (fig. 3). When the silo floor was reached, excavation continued underneath it in order to find the earlier remains belonging to the columned hall complex of the late Middle Kingdom (see below).

Figure 3. Hippopotamus bones inside the fill of Silo 316

Farther east, excavations also continued in the small space between the walls of Silo 316 and Silo 313. In order to create an additional storage space, a rounded wall was added between the two larger ones which then formed its own separate small silo (Silo 322). In the debris covering the mud floor of Silo 322 several pieces of decorated wood showing a *djed* pillar and a couple of *tjt* signs were found that had traces of colored plaster on their surfaces (fig. 4). Their original function remains speculative but it is likely

Figure 4. Wooden fragments of a small djed pillar

that they were part of some wooden furniture or boxes. Among those larger pieces were many smaller fragments of wood, some of them also showing remains of painted plaster on the surface. Hiroko Kariya (conservator for the Epigraphic Survey, University of Chicago) did some conservation on these pieces in the Elkab magazine where they are currently being stored.

The exterior space along the eastern sides of Silos 303, 393, and 405 was also investigated in depth (fig. 5). It is characterized by several succeeding floor levels showing multiple traces of settlement activity. The floors were covered with fireplaces and holes of various sizes for placing round-based pottery vessels as well as smaller holes for wooden posts. Two small col-

Figure 5. Exterior floor levels along the eastern sides of Silos 405 and 393

Figure 6. Street layers in southern part of excavation area

umn bases were also found in situ here (visible in fig. 5). These floor levels were cut by the very uneven foundation trenches for the construction of the later silos and thus must predate them. However, the analysis of the stratigraphic sequence linked to the late Middle Kingdom columned hall complex shows clearly that the floors are certainly later than the latter, too. Therefore, the analysis of the ceramic assemblage from this floor sequence will be very important because it contains pottery that belongs to the transitional phase between the end of the late Middle Kingdom tradition and the Second Intermediate Period. This will certainly shed light on the evolution of the ceramic tradition during this time period in Upper Egypt, which is still little understood due to the presence of few sites with a reliable stratigraphy.

At the beginning of the 2010 season we carried out some cleaning work and excavated a small trench along the southern limits of the silo area. We studied the thick east–west-running enclosure wall, which has its origins in the Old Kingdom when it functioned as the southern town wall. This enclosure continued to be in use for a long time thereafter and was re-used as the southern wall enclosing the silo area during the Second Intermediate Period. On the outside of this wall, we excavated two meters of densely stratified street layers, which are the remains of a major east–west street of the ancient town (fig. 6).

New Discoveries Related to the Columned Hall Complex

Excavations underneath Silos 316 and 308 reached the level of the earlier columned hall complex (fig. 7). During the previous seasons the columned hall itself had been excavated as much as possible but its continuation toward the north had not been explored yet because of the later silos lying on top of it. The excavations this season considerably changed this situation. Below Silo 316 we found a dismantled east–west-running mudbrick wall, which seems to have had an entrance to columned hall itself and a kind of bench along its northern face, delineating the columned hall to the north and separating it from another room, which had at least two columns, too (fig. 8). Two large empty holes were found in the mud floor where the column bases had been removed in ancient times. One of the holes had been filled with clean sand as foundation for the column base (fig. 9). The negatives left by the removal of the stone bases exhibit a larger diameter than those from the adjacent columned hall. Two seal impressions with the name of Sobekhotep IV have been found near the ripped-out columned bases in association with the mud floor of this room.

In order to better understand the floor levels and the traces of the east–west-running mudbrick wall, which was discovered underneath the floor of Silo 316, we excavated a 2 x 3 m trench immediately next to the exterior of Silo 316 and under Silo 308 (fig. 10). We recorded

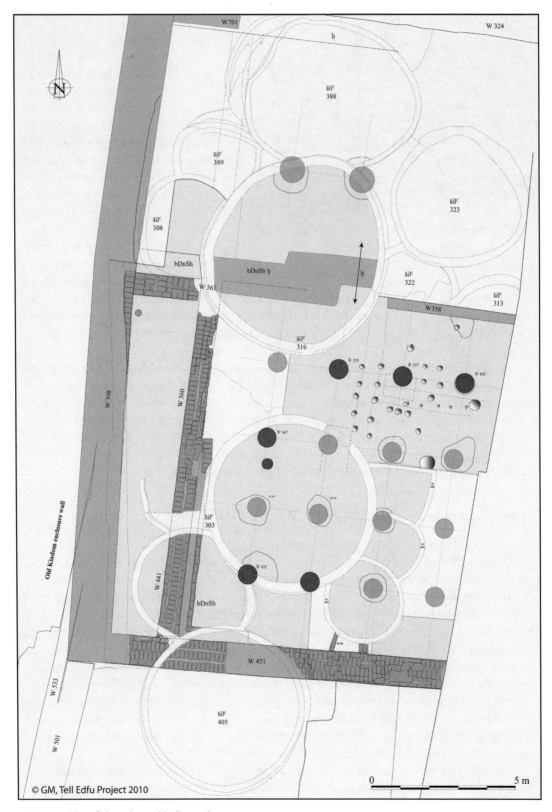

Figure 7. Plan of the columned hall complex

Figure 8. Northern extension of the columned hall complex visible underneath Silo 316

Figure 9. Emplacement of two column bases visible in the mud floor of the columned hall complex

the foundation trench of Silo 316 and discovered two floor levels that are contemporary with the columned hall complex. In the thick fill layer between these two floors, we found around 140 new seal impressions, many of them with private names of the late Middle Kingdom, together with sealings that are clearly of Second Intermediate Period date. Among them are a large number of sealings showing impressions made by scarabs that are of a northern origin (Tell el-Dabʾa and southern Palestine). The most unexpected discovery has been a group of eleven seal impressions showing the cartouche of the Hyksos ruler Khayan. Many of these broken sealings are peg sealings with the negatives of wooden fibers visible on their backs, which stem from the wooden boxes they were once attached to. Some jar sealings were found, too. This is the first time that Khayan is attested as far south as Edfu and this has important implications for the kind of contact between Upper Egypt and the Hyksos during the Second Intermediate Period which according to this discovery had been of economic nature at least for some of this period. We took several charcoal and wood samples from these contexts for radiocarbon dating.

Farther to the south, underneath Silo 303, several floor layers of the columned hall itself were excavated. In a layer of sandy silt covering the last layer of this floor which corresponds to the last phase of occupation of the columned hall before its final abandonment (US 2079), which is a very secure archaeological context. Three exceptional clay figurines were found in this layer: a broken figure of a striding male figure whose eyes were incised in the form of *wedjat*-eyes (fig. 11), a female figurine with a tripartite wig, and a mud "cocoon" with a headless

Figure 10. Lower floor level of the columned hall excavated on the western side of Silo 316 showing parts of a small bench, south view

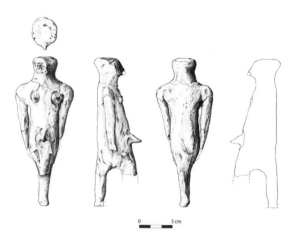

Figure 11. Mud figurine of striding male

female figurine inside it. All of them can be dated to the Thirteenth Dynasty according to the ceramic evidence. They were probably used for popular rituals related to fertility.

Another new discovery in the area was a large peg sealing stamped with an institutional seal in the form of a square stamp seal naming a mayor (ḥȝty-ꜥ) which was counter-sealed by another mayor's scarab seal. It was found among several hundred sealings mainly linked to the administrative activities taking place in the columned hall. Many of them belong to the category of private name sealings. They were found in a cluster along the western wall of the columned hall, providing evidence for the accumulation of sealings being discarded during administrative-activity.

Old Kingdom Settlement Remains

Major clearance work continues at Tell Edfu in the area where we have identified the oldest settlement remains (fig. 12). This area lies close to the Ptolemaic temple enclosure wall and was covered by several meters of debris and rubble left by the sebbakhin and also by A. Barsanti, who cleared an area 15 m to the north in order to place the decorated stone blocks

Figure 12. Area of Old Kingdom settlement remains at Tell Edfu

of the temple wall he dismantled in 1906.[4] A large group of local workers was employed for this purpose to advance the work as quickly as possible in order to reach the in situ layers underneath the rubble. This area will be a major focus of our excavations in the coming 2011 season. The aim is to find new information about the earliest settlement remains and the origins of the town of Edfu. The pottery samples we have found so far in this area date back to the Fourth to Sixth Dynasty but it is very likely that we will discover remains that date back even earlier than that. The presence of the Third Dynasty step pyramid in the vicinity (see below) and the reliefs in the Djoser complex mentioning the shrine of Edfu, provide some indication that the town of Edfu already existed back then.[5]

Edfu South Pyramid

A first survey has been carried out at the small step pyramid located 5 km southwest of Edfu, at the village of el-Ghonameya directed by Gregory Marouard (Oriental Institute, University of Chicago) with the collaboration of Hratch Papazian (University of Copenhagen) (fig. 13). This pyramid is a step pyramid and belongs to a series of almost identical small pyramids that have been discovered near several provincial centers in Egypt such as Elephantine, Hierakonpolis, Naqada, Abydos, Zawiet el-Meitin near Minya, and Seila in the Fayum. According to an inscription found at Elephantine that can be linked directly to this pyramid, it seems that the whole group dates to the reign of Huni, last ruler of the Third Dynasty. It is also clear from a study carried out by W. Kaiser and G. Dreyer in 1980 that these pyramids were not intended for funerary use. Their precise function has not yet been determined, but it has been suggested that they were markers of royal presence or a royal cult in the provinces.

Figure 13. Edfu South pyramid at el-Ghonameya in its current state

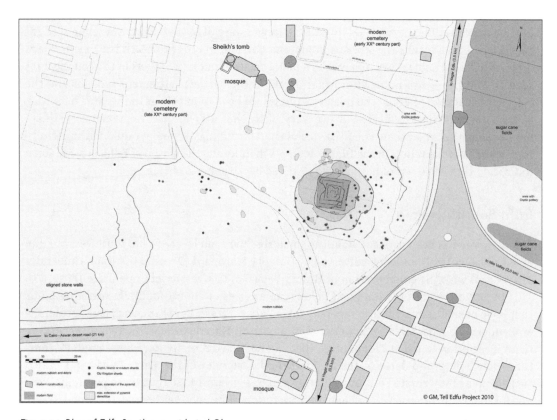

Figure 14. Plan of Edfu South pyramid at el-Ghonameya

The site is currently endangered by a fast developing modern cemetery and road works in the vicinity (fig. 14). This is the last pyramid of the group, which has so far been relatively untouched and has thus potential for the discovery of further data relating to its period of use and precise function. The monument in its current state of preservation has sides measuring 18 m in length; its height lies around 5.5 to 6.0 m consisting of four steps. The blocks are made of local sandstone.

Surface pottery was collected during this survey and the largest concentration of Old Kingdom sherds dating to the Third to early Fourth Dynasty was found along the eastern and northern sides. Within the frame of the Tell Edfu Project, we are hoping to continue next season with extensive cleaning and conservation work including some small-scale excavation along the eastern and northern sides of this monument, if granted permission and depending on the available funding. The Edfu South pyramid is still available for adoption!

Study of Unregistered Objects in the Magazine of Elkab

During much of the season, Kathryn Bandy, Lindsey Miller (Near Eastern Languages and Civilizations [NELC], University of Chicago), and Christiane Hochstrasser (freelance) spent time working on the unregistered objects, which are stored in the magazine of Elkab located 20 km north of modern Edfu. They were joined for a few days by Hiroko Kariya, who helped with the restoration of a pottery bowl with a hieratic inscription and several mud figurines. She also consolidated the color on two fragments of a limestone relief we found during this season in the silo area. Kathryn mainly focused her work on the study of the ostraca, and Lindsey worked on organizing and cataloging the seal impressions. Christiane did pencil drawings of the figurines and a selection of small finds, which will be prepared for publication. At the end of the season, Julia Schmied (Epigraphic Survey, University of Chicago) took photos of the objects, which included many seal impressions.

Acknowledgments

I would like to thank all the current team members of the project, and also the Edfu inspectorate for their ongoing support and collaboration, foremost Dr. Mohamed el Bialy (Aswan inspectorate), Mr. Mohamed Zenan, Ms. Nagwa Abdel Mageed, Mr. Mustafa Abdallah, and Dr. Sami Es-Zeidan Osman. A special thank-you also goes to Mr. Ramadan Hassan Ahmed, director of the Elkab magazine, for his collaboration and everlasting patience. Last but not least, I would like to thank Ms. Faten Abd el-Halim (Egypt Exploration Society) for her help with the translation of the final report into Arabic and other logistical matters occurring throughout the past year.

I am also very grateful for the ongoing support of many of our Oriental Institute members, foremost Misty and Lewis Gruber, Andrea Dudek, Arthur and Janet Ferguson, Daniel and Annette Youngberg, Stephen and Patricia Holst, Joan S. Fortune, Steve Camp, and Rosemary Ferrand. Additionally, I would like to thank the Oriental Institute and the National Endowment for the Humanities for their generous contribution to the Tell Edfu Project.

Notes

[1] For a general plan of the excavation area, see the *Oriental Institute 2009–2010 Annual Report*, p. 97, fig. 4.

[2] The ostraca are currently being studied by Kathryn Bandy (NELC, University of Chicago) as part of her PhD thesis.

[3] Natasha Ayers (NELC, University of Chicago) is analyzing the pottery from these layers as part of her PhD thesis.

[4] See Alexandre Barsanti, "Rapport sur les travaux exécutés à Edfou en 1902–1905 (réparations et consolitations)," *Annales du Service des antiquités de l'Égypte* 7 (1906): 97–109.

[5] See pages 27–28 and pl. 3 of Alan H. Gardiner, "Horus de Beḥdetite," *Journal of Egyptian Archeology* 30 (1944): 23–60.

TELL ZEIDAN

Gil J. Stein

2010 Field Work

The third field season of the joint Syrian-American excavations at Tell Zeidan, in the Euphrates River valley of north central Syria, was conducted from July 10 to August 8, 2010. The Tell Zeidan Project explores the roots of urbanism in Upper Mesopotamia (modern-day northern Iraq, north Syria, and southeast Turkey) by excavating a large regional center or town dating to the Halaf, Ubaid, and Late Chalcolithic 1–2 periods in the sixth and fifth millennia BC. Our excavations focus in particular on the Ubaid period, when we see the first evidence for the development of true towns, social stratification, irrigation-based economies, and centralized

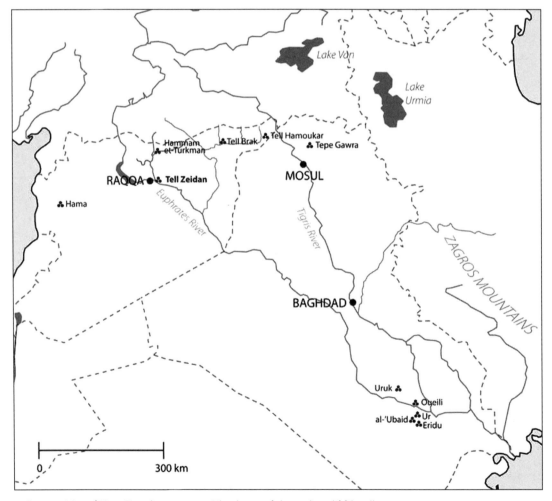

Figure 1. Map of Near East showing major Ubaid sites of the sixth and fifth millennia BC and the location of Tell Zeidan

political leadership in the Mesopotamian world. Together, these Ubaid-period developments of the fifth millennium BC laid the foundation for the later emergence of the world's first true cities and states in Mesopotamia during the fourth-millennium Uruk period.

Tell Zeidan is a 12.5 hectare prehistoric mound located approximately 5 km east of the modern city of Raqqa at the confluence of the Balikh River with the Euphrates (fig. 1). The site is a long triple mound oriented northwest to southeast located directly on the east bank of the Balikh. Tell Zeidan consists of a large southern mound 15 m in height, a lower town, and two smaller mounds — the northeast mound and the northwest mound. The first two seasons of excavation, in 2008 and 2009, identified four main occupation periods at the site: Halaf, Ubaid, Late Chalcolithic 1 (LC1), and Late Chalcolithic 2 (LC2) in a continuous radiocarbon-dated sequence ranging from about 5800 to 3800 BC. After an occupation gap lasting for almost a millennium, parts of Tell Zeidan were briefly re-inhabited in the early third millennium BC before the site was finally abandoned around 2800 BC.

Excavations at Zeidan are conducted jointly by the Syrian General Directorate of Antiquities and Museums through the Raqqa Museum, and by the Oriental Institute of the University of Chicago. We thank the General Director, Dr. Bassam Jamous, and the Director of Excavations, Dr. Michel al-Maqdissi, for their assistance and support in conducting these excavations.

The 2010 field season had four main goals:

1) Expand excavations to expose broader areas of the Ubaid and Late Chalcolithic 1 settlements
2) Geophysical/magnetometric mapping of subsurface features of the site
3) Field laboratory analyses of ceramics, chipped stone, animal bone, human remains, and carbonized plant remains
4) Test pits to assess damage to Zeidan by modern agricultural activities

Excavations

Excavations were conducted in nine 10 x 10 m trenches (called "operations") located in five areas across the site (areas A–E), along with three additional test trench sounding in areas F–H (fig. 2).

Area A: Operations 10 and 13 (northwest mound)

Area B: Operations 11, 14, and 18 (northeast mound)

Area C: Operation 9 (south mound)

Area D: Operation 17 (south mound)

Area E: Operations 15 and 16 (south mound)

Area F: Test trench — Operation 21

Area G: Test trench — Operation 20

Area H: Test trench — Operation 19

Area A: Northwest Mound — Operations 10 and 13

The 10 x 10 m Operation 10 continued to excavate fifth-millennium BC late Ubaid levels. In the southwest corner of the trench, excavations focused on an outdoor area enclosed by

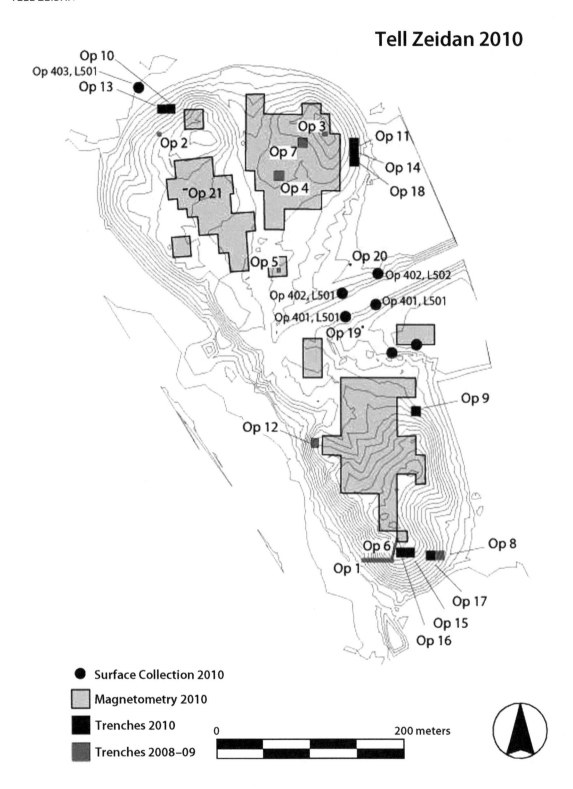

Figure 2. Topographic map of Tell Zeidan showing main excavation trenches, test pits, surface collection units, and areas where magnetometry/geophysical prospection was conducted. Note modern irrigation canal and triangular bulldozer cuts on the east side of the site

low walls, with a large above-ground oven or tannur (locus 81/89) made of packed clay and hardened by fire (fig. 3). The oven seems to have been constructed on top of a low platform made of packed mud. Accumulating up against the walls of the tannur structure, and also sealed off below it, were a series of thick wash layers with large amounts of ceramics, chipped stone, and some bone.

Excavations in Operation 13 (immediately to the west of Operation 10) exposed the corner of two mudbrick walls, loci 17 and 19, built on outdoor/ex-

Figure 3. Ubaid-period oven or tannur with surrounding mudbrick wall. Area A (northwest mound), Operation 10

terior surface 28. The northwestern half of Operation 13 was cut through by a very large modern borrow pit (locus 18) to take earth for road construction at some point in the last twenty years. The pit was removed down to the intact underlying Ubaid stratigraphy, which consisted of a series of thick wash layers with large amounts of ceramics, chipped stone, and some bone. The artifacts from these wash deposits match well with what one would expect in a domestic neighborhood of non-elite (commoner) households.

Overall, Area A seems to have been an exterior area, either a large courtyard or else an open space between houses. We can hypothesize that the actual houses were located in the (as yet) unexcavated area immediately to the south of Area A, based on the high volume of eroded trash, and on the presence of the tannur structure, wall fragments, pits, and compact surfaces found in Operation 10. Although occasional isolated Halaf sherds appeared in these wash layers, more than 99 percent of the ceramics were securely Ubaid, suggesting that Ubaid deposits in this open-air area continue downward in the two operations.

Area B: Northeast Mound — Operations 11, 14, and 18

Area B consists of three adjacent 10 x 10 m trenches (Operations 11, 14, 18) aligned north–south along the east slope of the northeast mound. All three operations have exposed domestic architecture dating to the Ubaid period. The walls and rooms can be linked between trenches, so that we can see Area B as a coherent complex of 300 sq. m of Ubaid houses in several overlapping phases (fig. 4).

Operation 11 had been opened as a 10 x 10 m trench in the 2009 field season and revealed several rooms of an Ubaid house (northernmost trench, on the right in fig. 4). In 2010, excavations uncovered a better-preserved earlier underlying level of Ubaid domestic architecture, consisting of at least seven rooms and a courtyard, constructed in two phases. This is the best and most completely preserved Ubaid domestic architecture recovered so far at Tell Zeidan. Three of the rooms in the house contained hearths that were in use contemporaneously, suggesting that an extended family might have lived here. One infant burial was found in the courtyard of the house. Calibrated accelerator mass spectrometry (AMS) radiocarbon dates

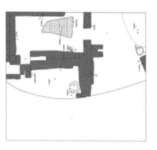

Figure 4. Photomosaic and composite top plan of Ubaid houses in (right to left) Operations 11, 14, and 18 in Area B (northeast mound)

from room floors and room fill date this house to a very early phase of the Ubaid occupation at Tell Zeidan — between 5100 and 5300 BC (table 1). The rooms and courtyard of this house continue into the west and south baulks of the trench. We hope to complete the exposure of the entire house in future seasons.

Figure 5. Ubaid ceramic boat model (ZD8215). These models are known from other Ubaid sites, such as Eridu and Mashnaqa. From Area B (northeast mound), Operation 14

Operation 14 was opened in 2010 as a 10 x 10 m trench immediately to the south of Operation 11 in order expand the exposure of Ubaid domestic architecture. The uppermost levels of Operation 14 reached Ubaid levels immediately and yielded an extremely rare find: a ceramic boat model (ZD8215; fig. 5). Very few Ubaid boat models are currently known, with the most notable examples deriving from Eridu, the Ubaid type site in southern Iraq, and from Mashnaqa in north Syria. In tandem with this distinctively Ubaid find, we also recovered a lightly baked clay figurine of a seated female, executed in a local north Syrian style (fig. 6). Excavations in Operation 14 reached Ubaid house levels from two superimposed

Table 1. Tell Zeidan 2009–2010 calibrated radiocarbon dates

ZD Number	Beta Number	Deposit Type	Op.	Loc.	Lot	Conventional Radiocarbon Age BP	2-Sigma BC Calibrated Maximum	2-Sigma BC Calibrated Minimum	2-Sigma BC Calibrated Mean	Cultural Period
3328	288105	Massif	12	4	—	4190 +/- 40 BP	2890	2630	2760	Early third millennium BC
5186	288110	Oven/kiln	16	4	9	4240 +/- 40 BP	2910	2710	2810	Early third millennium BC
1858	288097	Human burial	6	2	2	4340 +/-40 BP	3080	2890	2985	Early third millennium BC
9187	288115	Mudbrick collapse	21	15	31	5120 +/- 40 BP	3980	3800	3890	Late Chalcolithic 2
9145	288111	Room/floor deposit	16	79	113	5730 +/- 40 BP	4690	4470	4580	Late Chalcolithic 1
9339	288109	Mudbrick collapse	15	97	224	5780 +/- 40 BP	4720	4530	4625	Late Chalcolithic 1
3189	288102	Trash pit	10	57	95	5820 +/- 40 BP	4780	4560	4670	Late Chalcolithic 1?
7633	288112	Room/floor deposit	17	25	24	5880 +/- 40 BP	4840	4690	4765	Ubaid
5296	288101	Human burial	9	85	132	5960 +/- BP	4940	4730	4835	Ubaid
3221	288100	General room buildup	9	59	81	6010 +/- 40 BP	5000	4800	4900	Ubaid?
3150	288099	General room buildup	9	59	103	6040 +/1 40 BP	5040	4840	4940	Ubaid?
5626	288106	Wash	13	6	12	6060 +/- 40 BP	5050	4840	4945	Ubaid
3067	288098	Pyrotechnic feature	8	32	94	6120 +/- 40 BP	5210	4940	5075	Ubaid
6655	288107	Pit fill from two separate pits	14	6	61	6110 +/- 40 BP	5210	4940	5075	Ubaid
9451	288114	Mudbrick collapse	18	4	14	6120 +/- 40 BP	5210	4940	5075	Ubaid
8536	288113	Mudbrick collapse	18	4	9	6110 +/- 40 BP	5210	4940	5075	Ubaid
8193	288108	Floor/outdoor surface	14	33	142	6140 +/- 40 BP	5210	4970	5090	Ubaid
6468	288104	Room floor	11	75	96	6200 +/- 40 BP	5290	5040	5165	Ubaid
5698	288103	Room fill of room bound by walls 59-58-43 and west baulk	11	61	84	6270 +/- 40 BP	5320	5210	5265	Ubaid
2209	288095	Human burial	1	319	327	6550 +/- 40 BP	5600	5470	5535	Halaf
2782	288096	Indeterminate	1	340	365	6660 +/- 40 BP	5640	5520	5580	Halaf

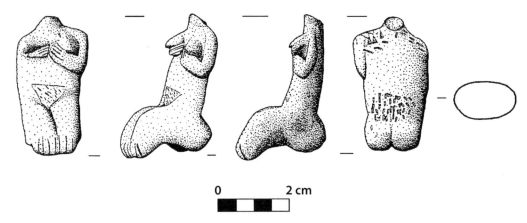

Figure 6. Lightly baked clay figurine of a seated female (ZD5545). Rendered in a north Syrian art style reflecting the localized character of the Ubaid-period culture at Tell Zeidan. From Area B (northeast mound), Operation 14. Drawing by Jack Scott

building phases. The upper phase consisted of three gray brick walls (loci 30, 35, 39), an associated floor surface (locus 36) and an infant jar burial that link to the latest building phase in adjacent Operation 11, but unfortunately were not as well preserved. These house walls immediately overlay an earlier building phase of yellowish brown mudbrick, forming four rooms and a possible courtyard. The uppermost floors in these rooms were reached. The architecture of this "yellowish-brown brick" phase is oriented northwest–southeast along the same lines as the architecture in adjacent Operation 11 to the north.

Finds from the yellowish-brown brick building level in Operation 14 included at least four spherical clay tokens and numerous over-fired kiln wasters of Ubaid bowls and other vessels. Possible prestige goods made from exotic raw materials were also found in this building level — notably a hematite mace-head fragment (ZD7790) and pieces of two chlorite/steatite carved stone bowls (ZD7762 and ZD7018).

Operation 18 was opened immediately to the south of Operation 14 as a 10 x 10 m trench, and was only excavated for a week at the end of the 2010 season. The uppermost well-preserved architecture in Operation 18 differs from the earlier houses in Operations 11 and 14 in that it is oriented directly north–south and east–west. Two adjacent rooms were defined. The western room had all four walls preserved (loci 3, 6, 8, 9), defining a space 4.3 m (north–south) x 2.5 m (east–west).

The most important discovery in Operation 18 was the remains of a chipped-stone tool production workshop. In room deposit 4, overlying the floor, we recovered a concentration of blade cores, flake cores, cortical flakes, production debris ("debitage"), and finished blades, blade tools, and flake tools (fig. 7). Most importantly, we also found, in association with the flint manufacturing debris, three pieces of carefully worked and polished deer antler (ZD9479), which were used as the punches to manufacture the blades either by indirect percussion with the "soft hammer" technique or by pressure flaking (fig. 8). Beneath the concentration of stone tools, manufacturing debris and antler punches, on floor 15 we found the preserved impression of a 2 x 1 m reed mat inside the room; this was clearly the actual workspace where the tools were made. This deposit and its related building phase can be radiocarbon dated to 5075 +/- 40 BC (table 1). It is extremely rare to find a securely dated workshop with the complete array of manufacturing tools, production debris, and finished chipped-stone

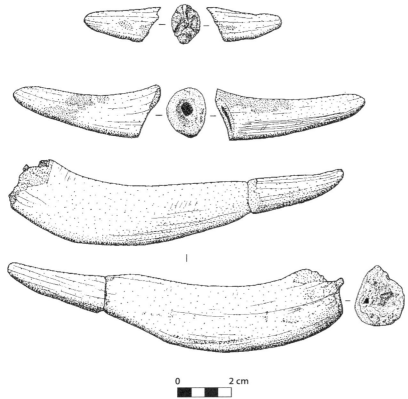

Figure 7. Chipped-stone tools, antler punches, and workshop debris recovered from a floor deposit on top of the remains of a reed mat inside an Ubaid house. From Area B (northeast mound), Operation 18, locus 4

Figure 8. Shaped and polished deer antler punches used for the manufacture of chipped-stone tools (ZD 9479). Area B (northeast mound), Operation 18, locus 4. Drawing by Jack Scott

0   2 cm

tools in the Ubaid period. This is good evidence for the existence of specialized craft production — an important line of evidence for emerging social and economic complexity at this time.

Area C: South Mound — Operation 9

Operation 9 excavations reached Ubaid levels and exposed a large 1.10 m thick mudbrick wall with 1 x 1 m buttresses on its north face (fig. 9). This wall may be the enclosure wall surrounding a large public building. Ceramics in deposits running up to both the north and south faces of the wall were securely dated to the Ubaid period. The wall is

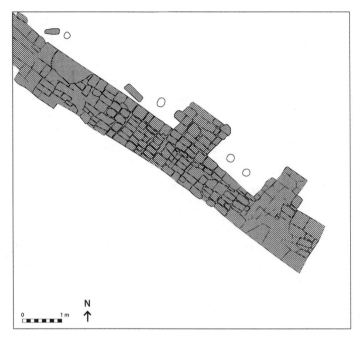

Figure 9. Buttressed wall 1.10 m thick from the Ubaid period. This may have been the enclosure wall for an area containing a large public building. Area C (South mound), Operation 9

quite large but is poorly preserved at its northwest and southeast ends. In future field seasons we hope to excavate farther inside the possible enclosure to determine whether a temple or other large public building was present here.

Area D: South Mound — Operation 17

Work in Operation 17 recovered a complex of mudbrick rooms oriented north–south and east–west. The walls were generally one brick-course wide and are preserved to a height of at least 1.0 m (fig. 10). The rooms were used for a long time, as can be seen in the number of superimposed floors and in the addition of later thin subdividing walls on the upper floor surfaces. The construction and use of these rooms date to the later Ubaid period. The uppermost in the sequence of associated room floors dates to the beginning of the Late Chalcolithic 1 period, while all floors below it can be securely dated to the Ubaid period. Operation 17 thus has the potential to give us valuable information about the Ubaid–Late Chalcolithic 1 transition. As an example, the baked clay "mullers" from Operation 17 pro-

Figure 10. Late Ubaid mudbrick architecture on southeast slope. Area D (south mound), Operation 17

Figure 11. Typical Ubaid-period ceramic "mullers" with plain, rounded heads (bottom) and Late Chalcolithic 1 mullers with crosshatch incised rounded heads (top)

vide good evidence for a stylistic change from mullers with smoothed, undecorated heads in the Ubaid period to mullers with crosshatch incised heads at the end of the Ubaid and in the Late Chalcolithic 1 (fig. 11).

Area E: South Mound — Operations 15 and 16

Operations 15 and 16 were opened as two adjacent 10 x 10 m trenches at the southern edge of the top of the south mound of Tell Zeidan. These trenches were opened to investigate the Late Chalcolithic 1 and 2 occupations of Zeidan from 4500 to 4000 BC. Imme-

diately beneath the surface, excavations revealed a cemetery area stretching across both trenches and containing approximately forty primary, secondary, and infant jar burials dating largely to the Late Chalcolithic 2 period, around 4200–4000 BC, although some burials are earlier (Late Chalcolithic 1) and some are almost certainly later in date (fig. 12). Only three of the forty burials contained any grave goods, and these were extremely simple — tiny white beads, a copper bead, and a bronze wire bracelet. The difficulty in dating these burials is compounded by the fact that they were cut down from Late Chalcolithic 2 and later floor

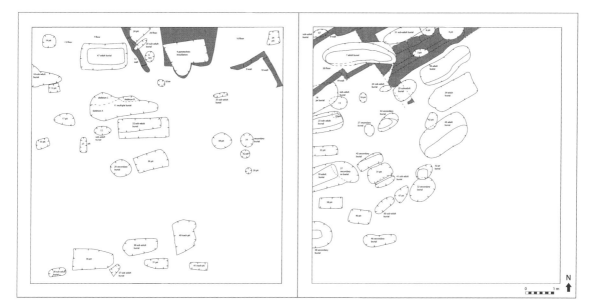

Figure 12. Operations 15 and 16 in Area E (south mound). Burials and other pit features were cut down from (now eroded away) Late Chalcolithic 2 and later levels cutting into Late Chalcolithic 1 architecture

levels that have been eroded away by the powerful winds that blow from the west across the site. The burials cut down into mudbrick architecture and associated deposits dating to the Late Chalcolithic 1 period, around 4500–4200 BC.

Once the forty burials in Operations 15 and 16 had been excavated, recorded, and removed, the underlying Late Chalcolithic 1 architectural levels were exposed. The uppermost two Late Chalcolithic 1 building levels in Operation 15 had been severely damaged by the intrusive burials and by erosion of the site slope. However, Late Chalcolithic 1 structures were much better preserved in the adjacent Operation 16. In the northern half of Operation 16, excavations exposed a row of three multiple-room structures whose mudbrick walls were a single course wide and oriented north–south and east–west (fig. 13). The easternmost of these three structures had two rooms, one with red-painted white plaster still surviving on its walls. The structures were built on compact, mud plastered floors from which microarchaeology samples were taken. The block of rooms appears to have been oriented east–west, and opened to the south onto what may have been a street or alley.

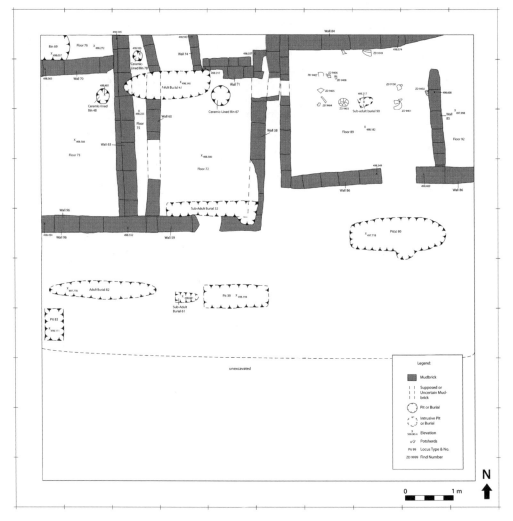

Figure 13. Operation 16 in Area E (south mound). Late Chalcolithic 1 period architecture – a series of rooms aligned east-west, facing onto a street or alley to the south

Area F: Northwest Mound — Operation 21

Operation 21 was a 1 x 5 m test trench on the south slope of the northwest mound excavated to investigate a possible ancient architectural feature detected by the magnetometry survey (see below). Immediately beneath the surface, excavations revealed a mudbrick structure with large amounts of coarse, wheel-made ceramics apparently dating to the early third millennium BC. Beneath this level was approximately 0.7 m of windblown (aeolian) silts, reflecting the post-Chalcolithic abandonment of Tell Zeidan after 4000 BC. Beneath the abandonment phase was a very large pyrotechnic feature consisting of a north–south-running wall of full-size bricks that had been heated to the point of vitrification. This wall seems to have marked the western edge of a kiln structure. Additional collapsed reddened brick and green-vitrified brick lay to the east of this wall. Although only a few ceramics were recovered from these deposits, diagnostics such as burnished gray ware carinated bowls and beaded lip hole-mouth jars allow us to securely date the use of the kiln to the latest phase of the Late Chalcolithic 2 occupation at Zeidan, contemporaneous with the latest Late Chalcolithic 2 phase in Operation 3, excavated in 2008.

Areas G and H: Lower Town — Operations 19 and 20

Parts of Tell Zeidan have been damaged over the past fifty years by agricultural development. Local farmers report that a portion of the northwest mound was bulldozed away to flatten the land to make it more suitable for irrigation. Much greater damage was done in 1958 by the construction of a raised irrigation canal that originates at almost the exact center of the mound, and then extends eastward to irrigate adjacent fields. Two large triangular areas in the lower town of Tell Zeidan were extensively dug out by bulldozers to borrow the large amounts of earth needed to create the berm or raised causeway for the canal. Based on the topographic mapping of the site, we estimate that the top three meters of archaeological sediments in these two parts of the lower town were removed in the excavation of the two bulldozer cuts to the north and south of the canal. A series of controlled surface collections and test pit excavations were conducted to assess the degree of site damage from these agricultural developments, while also determining whether any intact archaeological deposits still survived at the base of the north and south bulldozer cuts.

Operation 20 is a 2 x 2 m test pit excavated in the lower town, in the north bulldozer cut (fig. 2). The results of this test pit were extremely important and encouraging. Immediately beneath the surface, excavations recovered intact Late Chalcolithic 1 deposits characterized by high percentages of beaded lip flint-scraped bowls (37 out of 49 examined diagnostic ceramics in locus 2). Below 1.4 m, flint-scraped bowls no longer occurred, and this apparently marks the transition from Late Chalcolithic 1 to Ubaid deposits. By a depth of 1.9 m, ten out of eleven diagnostic ceramics were typologically Ubaid. These results are important in showing that: a) cultural deposits still survive intact in the bulldozed part of the site, b) the lower town was occupied in the Ubaid period, and c) Ubaid deposits are easily accessible in this area, just 1.4 m below the surface at the bottom of the north bulldozer cut. Apparently, the earth-moving activities associated with the construction of the irrigation canal removed all of the Late Chalcolithic 2 and possibly early third-millennium deposits, while leaving significant portions of the Late Chalcolithic 1 deposits intact, and all the underlying Ubaid deposits.

In parallel with Operation 20, a second 2 x 2 m test pit — Operation 19 — was excavated in the lower town, in the south bulldozer cut (fig. 2). Operation 19 sought to determine if any cultural deposits were still preserved. As with Operation 20, Operation 19 contained intact, stratified Late Chalcolithic 1 deposits immediately beneath the surface. Several intact mudbrick walls were located in the test pit, all securely dated by diagnostic ceramics such as beaded lip flint-scraped bowls to the Late Chalcolithic 1 period. By 1.4 m below the surface, secure trash deposits contained entirely Ubaid ceramics (with an occasional intrusive Halaf sherd, presumably re-deposited from earlier Halaf levels).

Together, Operations 19 and 20 confirm that the lower town was occupied in the Ubaid period, and that these deposits are accessible for excavation. We hope to open up 10 x 10 m trenches in one or both of these areas in future field seasons to explore the Ubaid of the Zeidan lower town in greater detail.

Magnetometry

Magnetometry or geophysical prospection is a remote-sensing technique used to search for architecture or other features beneath the surface of an archaeological site. Dr. Andrew Creekmore conducted these analyses (fig. 14). About 5 ha of Tell Zeidan's 12.5 ha area are flat enough to be amenable to magnetometric prospection. Of these 5 ha, 3 ha — 30,000 sq. m — were mapped and analyzed (see fig. 2 for locations). Subsurface mudbrick architecture can be difficult to detect with magnetometry, but other features such as kilns, ovens, stone walls, sherd-packed streets, or monumental architecture can be detected under the right conditions. A large number of magnetic anomalies were detected, but most of these seem to be modern — for example, the remains of modern houses, or modern metal trash (cans, pipes, wires, etc.).

Three magnetic anomolies were detected that seem to reflect ancient subsurface features. To investigate a strong magnetic anomaly on the northwest mound (fig. 15), Operation 21 was excavated and in fact did locate the remains

Figure 14. Andrew Creekmore conducting the geophysical (magnetometric) survey of Tell Zeidan, using a hand-held gradiometer

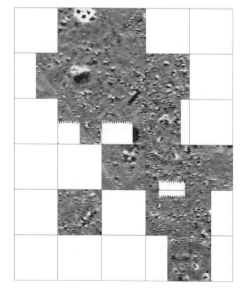

Figure 15. Magnetometry map of the northwest mound of Tell Zeidan. Each grid square is 20 x 20 m. The black areas indicate magnetic anomalies caused by stones, metal, or very high heat. The large oval-shaped anomaly at the upper left was explored in Operation 21, which determined that it represented a kiln dating to the Late Chalolthic 2 period

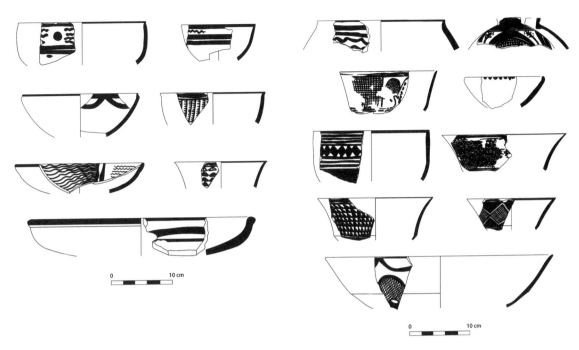

Figure 16. Earlier Ubaid painted pottery from Operation 11

Figure 17. Earlier Ubaid pottery from Operation 14

of a large kiln whose associated ceramics dated it to a late phase of the Late Chalcolithic 2 period (see above).

In-field Laboratory Analyses

Ceramics (Philip Karsgaard and Khaled Jayyab)

During the 2010 field season, 24,500 ceramic sherds (including 4,000 diagnostic rims, handles, bases, and painted ceramics) were analyzed. Ceramics were sorted by ware type, vessel function, and surface decoration. The ceramic analysis focused on recording the Ubaid pottery from both the earlier Ubaid levels in Operations 11 (fig. 16) and 14 (fig. 17) and the later Ubaid deposits in Operation 17 (fig. 18). The recording of Late Chalcolithic 1 and Late Chalcolithic 2 material focused on ceramics from Operations 3, 10, and 16. In addition, we worked on an intra-site comparison of Ubaid ceramics from the south and northwest mounds. Finally, work continued on the development of a ceramic typology for Tell Zeidan. One of the most interesting aspects of the Ubaid pottery at Tell Zeidan is the way it combines geometric stylistic motifs that are absolutely typical of southern Mesopotamia (figs. 16–17) with distinctively local north Syrian motifs, such as figural decorations of humans, birds, mammals, and even scorpions (figs. 19–21).

Chipped Stone (Dr. Elizabeth Healey)

More than 3,200 pieces of chipped stone were analyzed and recorded from Ubaid contexts in Operations 8, 11, and 14 from both the 2009 and 2010 field seasons. The chipped stone is overwhelmingly flint or chert of two varieties — rolled cobbles from the Balikh River and a very high-quality, fine-grained nodular flint, presumably from the limestone bluffs of the

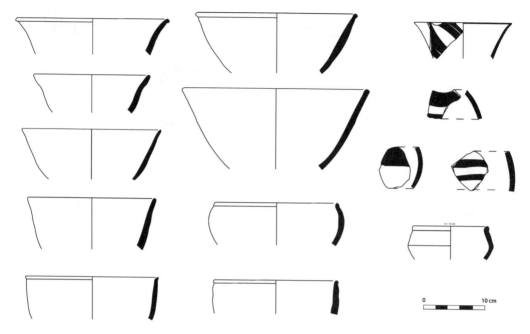

Figure 18. Later Ubaid pottery from Operation 17

Figure 19. Painted Ubaid sherd showing a group of dancers holding hands. Note the possibly elongated or deliberately shaped skull of the dancer

Figure 20. Painted Ubaid sherd showing a large bird, apparently an ostrich

Figure 21. Painted Ubaid sherd showing a segmented figure with appendages, probably a scorpion

Euphrates valley 3–4 km to the south of Zeidan. Obsidian (mostly from the Lake Van area in eastern Turkey) forms only about 4 percent of the analyzed chipped stone so far. The single most common type of flint tools are sickle blades made of fine chocolate-colored nodular flint, with silica gloss or polish on the cutting edge, proving that these blades were used to harvest cereals. This is good evidence for the importance of agriculture at Zeidan in the Ubaid period.

Human Remains (Dr. Kirsi Lorentz)

Seventy-four contexts with human skeletal material have been identified at Tell Zeidan from 2008 to the present. Thirty-eight partial and more complete skeletons were examined

Figure 22. Sub-adult skull from Operation 6, burial 2, whose elongated form shows clear signs of deliberate cranial shaping

from deposits spanning the Halaf, Ubaid, Late Chalcolithic 1, and Late Chalcolithic 2 periods. Males and females are both well represented, and there are far more sub-adults (juveniles, infants) than adults represented — suggesting high rates of infant and juvenile mortality. Whenever possible, we collected soil samples from the stomach area of the burials to see if we could recover the remains of intestinal parasites as a way to study ancient health conditions and pathologies. In addition, scrapings of subgingival calculus (dental plaque below the gum line) were taken from the teeth of as many burials as possible. The calculus scrapings can actually preserve food residues in the form of plant phytoliths, thereby giving us direct evidence for the different kinds of plant foods eaten in the ancient diet of the people at Tell Zeidan.

One of the most fascinating skeletal finds was the skull of a young child that had been deliberately shaped or molded into an elongated form (fig. 22). Cranial shaping can only be done while the bones of the skull are still pliable — up to the age of three. The shaping is usually done by swaddling a child in a cradleboard to flatten the back of the head, or by wrapping the head in cloth. The practice of cranial shaping does not seem to have any negative effects on brain size or intelligence. Cranial shaping serves as an unchangeable culturally created mark of a person's ethnic or tribal identity. Although cranial shaping seems alien and unusual to modern Westerners, in fact this practice is known from a number of seventh- to fifth-millennium BC sites across the Near East, and is known ethnographically among indigenous peoples in Africa, Asia, Andean South America, and even among relatively recent pastoral nomadic groups in the Near East. It is striking that Ubaid-period figurines from southern Mesopotamia are well known for depicting men and women with clearly elongated skulls. It is also notable that one of the painted Ubaid sherds we recovered at Zeidan shows a line of dancing human figures who also appear to have shaped, elongated skulls (see fig. 19).

Archaeobotany/Carbonized Plant Remains (Thomas Hart)

During the first two weeks of the 2010 season, soil samples were collected from the different excavation areas at Zeidan to recover ancient carbonized (burned) macro-botanical remains of seeds, plant parts, and charcoal. Most of the samples collected and processed so far were collected from Ubaid-period deposits.

Tom Hart and Mahmoud al-Kaitab worked together to construct a pump-powered flotation system (similar to those used at Abu Hureyra and Hamoukar). The flotation machine worked beautifully, enabling us to process a total of 108 flotation samples. In addition, a total of 128 samples were collected for phytolith and starch grain analysis. One of the most poignant archaeobotanical finds of the 2010 season was an Ubaid-period jar burial of an infant in Operation 9. Flotation samples taken from inside the burial urn showed the dried, unburnt remains of small flowers that apparently had been placed deliberately in the jar, perhaps by the child's parents (figs. 23–24).

Zooarchaeology/Animal Bone Remains (Kathryn Grossman, assisted by Miriam Hinman)

Kate Grossman analyzed and recorded approximately 9,000 fragments of animal bone from Ubaid and Late Chalcolithic 1 contexts in Operations 8, 9, 11, and 14 from the 2009 and 2010 field seasons. Miriam Hinman analyzed around 1,000 fragments of animal bone from Halaf deposits in Operation 1. These analyses show striking changes in the animal economy between the Halaf and Ubaid periods. In the Halaf period about half the bones at the site are those of wild animals such as wild cattle, wild donkey/onager, deer, and gazelle. But in the Ubaid period, 90 percent of the bones are those of domesticated herd animals such as sheep, goats, cattle, and pigs. In addition, there is a change in the proportion of sheep to goats. In the Halaf period, sheep and goats occur in roughly equal proportions, but in the Ubaid period, sheep outnumber goats by a ratio of almost three to one. Taken together, the animal bone evidence suggests that the economy of Tell Zeidan in the Ubaid period became much more focused on herding instead of hunting. The strong concentration on herding sheep suggests that the people of Zeidan may have begun to specialize in wool and textile production.

Figure 23. Ubaid-period infant jar burial ZD5902 from Operation 9. Archaeobotanical studies of soil samples from the jar showed that the child had been buried with fresh flowers

Figure 24. Unburnt dried flowers, the grave offerings recovered from infant burial ZD5902

Radiocarbon Dates and Chronology

Twenty-one samples of charcoal from Zeidan were processed by highly precise accelerator mass spectrometry (AMS) radiocarbon dating (table 1). Together with the dated samples we had processed earlier by the same method, we now have thirty-three radiocarbon samples as the basis for an absolute chronology of the site. The radiocarbon data show that the Ubaid occupation of Zeidan began around 5300 BC and lasted until about 4500 BC. These dates are consistent with the radiocarbon evidence from other Ubaid sites in north Syria, showing that the Ubaid expansion out of southern Mesopotamia began substantially earlier (in calendar years) than had traditionally been thought.

Summary: The Ubaid and Late Chalcolithic 1 Periods at Tell Zeidan

The 2010 field season at Tell Zeidan accomplished all its primary archaeological goals and made significant progress toward better understanding the structure of the settlement and its occupational history during the fifth millennium BC. We excavated nine 10 x 10 trenches and conducted magnetometry over an additional 30,000 sq. m of the site. We were able to make large horizontal exposures of 300 sq. m of houses dating to the Ubaid period in Operations 11, 14, and 18. We also documented the existence of Ubaid domestic areas on the northwest mound in Operations 10 and 13. In addition, we located the enclosure wall of a possible Ubaid public building in Operation 9. In Operations 15 and 16 we began to explore the Late Chalcolithic 1 occupation of the south mound, while Operation 17 began to yield important data on the Ubaid-to-Late Chalcolithic 1 transition. We conducted a magnetometry survey of the site and were able to detect a large Late Chalcolithic 2 period kiln structure based on that work. Our test pits in the lower town established the presence of an intact Ubaid occupation in the lower town area at the center of the site. Our in-field laboratory analyses of human bone, animal bone, archaeobotanical remains, chipped stone, and ceramics all made great progress as well.

Overall, the 2010 field season has given us significant new information about the Ubaid and Late Chalcolithic 1 periods at Tell Zeidan. We were able to recover large areas of Ubaid residential architecture and found the first traces of what may be large-scale public architecture at the site. We found good evidence for major economic changes in the Ubaid — notably the first strong evidence for craft specialization and specialized herding economies focused on raising sheep, perhaps for the purpose of wool and textile production. We also started to gain insights into the ideology of the Ubaid-period inhabitants of Tell Zeidan through their art on pottery, burial rites, and practice of cranial shaping as a marker of social identity. We hope to continue our explorations of the roots of social complexity in future seasons of fieldwork at Tell Zeidan.

Acknowledgments

We thank the Syrian General Directorate of Antiquities and Museums, most notably Dr. Michel al-Maqdissi, Director of Excavations, and Dr. Bassam Jamous, General Director, for their support and assistance in this project. The project was supported by the National Science Foundation, the Oriental Institute, and the generosity of private donors. I also gratefully acknowledge Mr. Muhammad Sarhan, director of the Raqqa Museum and Syrian co-director of the joint Syrian-American excavation project. The entire team owes its deepest appreciation to Mahmoud al-Kaitab of the Raqqa Museum for his hospitality, friendship, and invaluable assistance in the day-to-day logistics of operating the excavation and maintaining our dig house. We thank the Raqqa branch of the Syrian Ministry of Education for allowing us to use the Zeki al-Arsouzi Primary School as our excavation field house in 2010. In Chicago, Steven Camp, Carla Hosein, D'Ann Condes, and Mariana Perlinac provided invaluable administrative support and assistance. Finally and most importantly, I want to express my deep gratitude to the Zeidan Project field staff: Sarah Adcock, Andrew Creekmore, Rita Dayoub, Jean Evans, Michael Fisher, Kathryn Grossman, Katharyn Hanson, Thomas Hart, Elizabeth Healey, Miriam Hinman, Khaled Jayyab, Philip Karsgaard, Nabil Abu-l Kheyr, Kirsi Lorentz, Fahd Sbahi, Adam Schneider, Jack Scott, Stephanie Selover, Stefan Smith, Lise Truex, and Katherine Weber.

———————————

INDIVIDUAL RESEARCH

Richard H. Beal

Richard H. Beal spent his time updating, reference checking, and copy editing articles for the third fascicle of the Š volume and the beginning of the T volume of the Chicago Hittite Dictionary. Outside of office time his article "Hittite Anatolia: Political History" for the *Oxford Handbook of Ancient Anatolia* was pushed through the editing process and should appear in the coming year. An article in the *Reallexikon der Assyriologie* on "Seuche (epidemic)" among the Hittites is now in print. The article "Soldat (Hittite)" (Soldiers among the Hittites) is undergoing editing. He completed a review of a Festschrift for Silvin Košak, a predecessor of his as research associate on the Chicago Hititte Dictionary. He is working on reviews of a Festschrift for David Hawkins, the book *Rêves Hittites* by Alice Mouton, and the book *Hittite Votive Texts* by Jan de Roos.

Robert D. Biggs

Robert D. Biggs has continued his study of the mid-third-millennium BC cuneiform texts from the Temple of Inanna at Nippur, collaborating in particular with Karen Wilson and Richard Zettler on matters of dating of occupation levels. He has also resumed study of the second-millennium Babylonian texts dealing with extispicy (the Babylonian "science" of interpreting ominous signs in the internal organs of sheep) from the Hittite capital of Hattusha. With a fellowship from the American Research Institute in Turkey in the summer of 1972, he studied the originals in Ankara and Istanbul, and subsequently, in 1981, the originals now in Berlin. Although very fragmentary (with very few lines of text being complete), these texts nevertheless constitute a valuable source for the corpus of omens in the second millennium BC. He will be preparing an edition of the texts.

Scott Branting

Scott Branting continues as the director of the Center for Ancient Middle Eastern Landscapes (CAMEL) and co-director of the Kerkenes Dağ archaeological project in central Turkey. Reports for both of these endeavors appear in their separate sections of the *Annual Report*. He also is co-director of the SHULGI project with Argonne National Laboratory, continues to oversee the acquisition and installation of the Integrated Database for the Oriental Institute, and continues the partnership started last year with Wendy Ennes of the Public Education Department on the development of sixth-grade interdisciplinary curriculum. He serves as a committee member for the Archaeological Institute of America (AIA) and as a delegate to the American Research Institute in Turkey (ARIT).

During the year papers were presented at the American Schools of Oriental Research (ASOR) annual meeting and at the 33. Uluslar Arası Kazı, Araştırma ve Arkeometri Sempozyumu in Turkey. Public lectures were given to the Chicago Archaeological Society and at the Oriental Institute through the Member's Lecture Series. Grants were received from the Lloyd A. Fry Foundation and as part of the Institute of Museum and Library Services' Museums for America Collections Management Grant issued for the Oriental Institute's Integrated Database Project. Two new works appeared in publication: "Agents in Motion" in *Agency and Identity in the Ancient Near East: New Paths Forward*, edited by Sharon R. Steadman and Jennifer C. Ross (London: Equinox, 2010), and "The Kerkenes Project 2010" (with Geoffrey Summers, Françoise Summers, and Joseph W. Lehner) in *Anatolian Archaeology* 16. Several additional publications are in process.

Miguel Civil

Miguel Civil's book *The Lexical Texts in the Schøyen Collection* (CDL Press), his third book since retirement, was finally published in August 2010. It is an edition of 186 lexical tablets with the most varied contents, ranging from a Middle Babylonian tablet with the full text of the seventh tablet of HAR-ra, all the way back to a new group of Early Dynastic word lists. His edition of the Laws of Ur-Namma, king of Ur (2112–2095 BC), based on a new source almost contemporary with the promulgation of the laws, has just been published in a book edited by A. R. George, *Cuneiform Royal Inscriptions and Related Texts in the Schøyen Collection* (CDL Press). It is a philological edition, with special emphasis on lexical and grammatical aspects, to make the text of the laws accessible to legal historians. Miguel's minor publications of last year include "Sumerian Compound Verbs: Class II," a paper presented in the 53th Rencontre Assyriologique Internationale in Moscow, and printed in *Language in the Ancient Near East*, volume 1, part 2, edited by L. Kogan (Eisenbrauns). "Ur III as a Linguistic Watershed," a communication presented in the Meeting about Ur III studies (Madrid, July–August 2010), is in press. Miguel's paper in the April 2010 Oriental Institute Workshop on Linguistic Method and Theory, and several minor articles, are ready to go to press. He is working on several projects centered on Sumerian grammar and literary texts, such as an explanation (with the help of the Bible and Hellenistic Greek papyri) of Inanna's "watering with her foot" a sapling in Gilgameš and Enkidu, or an analysis of the verbal forms seen as a combination of a lexical verb with several auxiliaries/preverbs, rather than formed by a root and a string of affixes.

Fred M. Donner

Fred M. Donner spent much of the 2010–2011 academic year immersed in his duties as director of the University's Center for Middle Eastern Studies (CMES). After a tumultuous year in 2009–2010, this year was blissfully calm and CMES's many activities — including hosting numerous visiting lecturers, sponsoring workshops and conferences, mounting public education activities, and supervising CMES's burgeoning MA program — came off smoothly, thanks especially to the efforts of CMES's dedicated staff (Dr. Paul Walker, Dr. Thomas Maguire, Traci Lombre, and Alexander Barna). A number of CMES's events were co-sponsored by the Oriental Institute.

Of special interest to Donner was a two-day conference held in mid-June on Christians, Jews, and Zoroastrians in the Umayyad State that he and Professor Antoine Borrut (University of Maryland, College Park) organized. Ten invited participants and ten commentators, along with many visitors, convened for stimulating discussions focused on the role members of these non-Muslim communities played in the operation of the Umayyad state (660–750 CE). This event received major funding from the Franke Institute for Humanities and CMES, as well as greatly appreciated co-sponsorship and funding from the Oriental Institute, Department of Near Eastern Languages and Civilizations, Chicago Center for Jewish Studies, the Divinity School, and the University of Maryland Department of History. It is hoped that the papers will be published as a collected volume sometime in 2012.

Donner gave many lectures during the year. In July 2010 he participated in the third World Conference of Middle Eastern Studies, held in Barcelona, Spain, as part of a series of panels on ancient empires, presenting a paper on "An Empire in Crystallization: The Umayyads." At the Middle East Studies Association conference in November, he presented a paper entitled "Was Marwan ibn al-Hakam the First Real Muslim?" He also gave numerous presentations related to the theme of his recent book, *Muhammad and the Believers: At the Origins of Islam*, published in spring 2010 by Harvard University Press; this included talks at the Chicago Humanities Festival and at Chicago Alumni Day, and at York University in Toronto, the Noor Foundation in Toronto, Georgetown University, George Mason University, the University of Maryland, Ohio State University, and the University of Southern California. Less directly related to his own research, he was asked to deliver a plenary address at the annual conference of the American Oriental Society, on its theme of "Heritage." His talk was entitled "Heritage, Legacies, and Collectibles" and discussed how these concepts relate to the development of Islamic tradition.

Publications submitted during the year include the full version of his paper "Was Marwan ibn al-Hakam the First Real Muslim?," for a volume to be edited by Sarah Savant (Aga Khan University) on Genealogies and History, and "A Typology of Eschatological Concepts," submitted for a volume entitled *Roads to Paradise: Eschatology in the Islamic Tradition*, to be edited by Sebastian Günther (University of Göttingen) and Todd Lawson (University of Toronto). He is now at work on a very early Islamic papyrus found in the Oriental Institute collection.

François Gaudard

During the past year, **François Gaudard** continued working for the Chicago Demotic Dictionary (CDD; see separate report) and collaborating with Sofía Torallas Tovar and Raquel Martín Hernández as an editor of the Mummy Label Database (MLD; see separate report).

Two of François' articles, namely, "Ptolemaic Hieroglyphs" and "Fragment of a Funerary Shroud" (OIM E42046) both appeared in *Visible Language: Inventions of Writing in the Ancient Middle East and Beyond*, edited by Christopher Woods, with Emily Teeter and Geoff Emberling, pp. 173–75 and 176–77, cat. no. 86 (Oriental Institute Museum Publications 32). Despite their fragmentary condition, the texts of shroud OIM E42046, consisting mainly of offering formulae, are of particular interest, since they provide us with both unusual epithets of Osiris and some good examples of cryptography, the most interesting and innovative one being by far the sportive writing of the word *imntyw* "westerners" as 𓏏𓏏 instead of 𓈖𓏏 or 𓈖𓏏𓅱, occurring in the famous Osirian epithet *ḫnty imntyw* "foremost of the westerners." In this group, the sign 𓈖, which usually stands for the letter *n*, reads *imn*, while the signs 𓏏𓏏 represent number fifty, which was pronounced *tyw*.

François was also asked to contribute two articles, namely, "P. Berlin 8278 and Its Fragments: Testimony of the Khoiak Festival Celebration during the Ptolemaic Period," which is in press and will be published in a Festschrift for the Neues Museum in Berlin, and "A Demotic-Hieratic Mummy Label in the Museu de Montserrat," which will appear in a Festschrift honoring a colleague.

In addition, François is currently working on several articles, including the publication of the following texts: a major copy of *The Book of the Dead* from the Ptolemaic period, a Demotic priestly taxation list, a still unknown Late Ramesside letter (for details on this project, readers can consult the *2008-2009 Annual Report*), various Coptic texts and mummy labels, and, together with Sofía Torallas Tovar and Raquel Martín Hernández, a bilingual sale of a house in Soknopaiu Nesos from the Roman period.

In November, he was contacted by the *Salt Lake Tribune* to give his opinion on the discoveries made by Brigham Young University researchers on the edge of the Fayyum oasis.

François also attended the 62nd Annual Meeting of the American Research Center in Egypt, held in Chicago, from April 1 to 3, 2011.

McGuire Gibson

McGuire Gibson continues to work with Mark Altaweel and three Iraqi scholars to publish in English several reports on significant archaeological excavations carried out by the Iraqi State Board of Antiquities over the past thirty years. This project, funded by the State Department through The American Academic Research Institute in Iraq (TAARII), is nearing its end, but the final reports will be two book-length publications from the Oriental Institute. One will combine reports on two excavations conducted in the Diyala area, a region that was the focus of important Oriental Institute excavations from 1929 until 1936. In the 1950s, Robert McC. Adams did an innovative settlement pattern study in the same area. In addition to the Diyala publication, the project is finalizing a large manuscript on the Iraqis' work at the Assyrian capital Kalhu (modern Nimrud). This book will present the findings in the spectacular Queens' tombs, as well as other operations on the acropolis of the city.

This year saw the following additional publications by Gibson reach print:

- "The Dead Hand of Deimel" in *Beyond the Ubaid: Transformation and Integration in the Late Prehistoric Societies of the Middle East,* edited by Robert A. Carter and Graham Philip (Studies in Ancient Oriental Society 63; Chicago: The Oriental Institue, 2010).

- "Series Editor's Preface" in Hamoukar I. *Urbanism and Cultural Landscapes in Northeastern Syria: The Tell Hamoukar Survey, 1999–2001*, by Jason A. Ur (Oriental Institute Publications 137; Chicago: The Oriental Institute, 2010)

- Editing and additional comments to "Tell Abu Sheeja/Ancient Pasime: Report on the First Season of Excavations, 2007," by A. M. Hussein, H. A. Hamza, A. K. Thaher,

S. J. Kadhum, M. Hashem, H. M. Taha, M. R. Altaweel, and B. Studevent-Hickman, *Akkadica* 131 (2010).

He has in press an article assessing the Diyala sequence, which should appear this year in a book from Heidelberg University Press, and he has finished his report of the re-investigation of the Y Trench at Kish, which will appear as part of Karen Wilson's publication on Kish.

During the year, he convened a fact-finding and planning meeting in Philadelphia of archaeologists who have worked or wish to work in Iraq. This was the last time that many of the attendees had the opportunity to interact with Donny George Youkhanna, who died about two weeks later. The Oriental Institute had scheduled a lecture by Dr. Youkhanna for early June. In his place, Gibson delivered an appreciation of Dr. Youkhanna's scholarly contribution to the field. A week later, at an event marking the completion of the Chicago Assyrian Dictionary, Gibson gave an archaeologist's perspective on the CAD. In addition, in March he attended a meeting on the situation of Iraqi academics during war and occupation, sponsored by the Brussels Tribunal held in Ghent, Belgium. He delivered a presentation on the effect on academic life caused by the looting of archaeological museums, universities, and sites. He still serves as the president of The American Academic Research Institute in Iraq, and in that capacity he is currently endeavoring to establish a center in a rented property in Baghdad. He also continues to represent the University of Chicago on the board of the American Institute for Yemeni Studies. In addition, he still serves on the board of the Council of American Overseas Research Centers.

Petra M. Goedegebuure

The basic philosophy that forms the foundation of all **Petra M. Goedegebuure**'s work on the ancient languages of Anatolia — such as Hittite, Luwian, Palaic, and Hattian — is that she takes language as a social phenomenon, in contrast with the equally valid concept of language as a cognitive-biological phenomenon. This is reflected in her approach of combining philology and the cultural background of texts with language typology and functional grammar.

Petra's specific aims are (1) to develop methods for applying modern linguistics to dead languages; (2) to further explore the Anatolian languages at the level of pragmatics, especially information structure and deixis; therefore (3) to arrive at a better understanding of the texts and the communicative goals of the ancient authors.

This year Petra spent most of her time teaching five classes, three in winter (Elementary Hittite II, Language and the Human (a core class co-taught with five other faculty from the departments of Linguistics, NELC, Slavic Languages and Literatures, and Germanic Studies), Readings in Palaic (a research seminar with graduate students in Hittitology), and two in spring (Elementary Hittite III and Hittite Linguistics).

The core class Language and the Human directed Petra toward semiotics, which she then applied to the visual aspects of Hittite culture in the presentation "Anatolian Aniconoclasm: Not Destruction But Deactivation" at the Oriental Institute Post-Doc seminar on Iconoclasm, April 8–9, 2011.

In the Linguistics class Petra explored ergativity, information structure, and aspect from a theoretical linguistic perspective, and asked her students to implement the results on their extinct language of choice. This class relied heavily on Petra's own work on information structure ("The Pragmatic Function Focus in Hittite" presented at the workshop Linguistic Method and Theory and the Languages of the Ancient Near East, April 16, 2010, Oriental Institute; in progress) and ergativity ("Split-ergativity in Anatolian," *Zeitschrift für Assyriologie;* submitted). The study of ergativity is also part of a new book project, *The Core Cases in the Anatolian Languages: Semantics, Syntax, Morphology, Diachrony.* Based on this project Petra was awarded a fellowship from the Franke Institute of the Humanities for 2011–2012.

The following articles were published:

- "The Alignment of Hattian: An Active Language with an Ergative Base," in *Babel und Bibel* 4–5 (2007–08): 949–81.

- "Deictic-emphatic *-i* and the Anatolian Demonstratives," in *Ex Anatolia Lux: Anatolian and Indo-European Studies in Honor of H. Craig Melchert on the Occasion of His Sixty-fifth Birthday*, edited by Ronald Kim, pp. 55–67 (Ann Arbor: Beech Stave Press, 2010).

- "The Luwian Adverbs *zanta* 'Down' and **ānni* 'With, For, Against,'" In *Acts of the 7th International Congress of Hittitology, Çorum, August 25–31, 2008*, edited by Aygül Süel, pp. 299–318 (Ankara: Anit Matbaa, 2010).

- "The Luwian Demonstratives of Place and Manner," in *Luwian and Hittite Studies Presented to J. David Hawkins on the Occasion of his 70th Birthday*, edited by Itamar Singer, pp. 76-94 (Sonia and Marco Nadler Institute of Archaeology Monograph Series 28; Tel Aviv: Emery and Claire Yass Publications in Archaeology, 2010).

Petra also submitted three entries for Blackwell's *Encyclopedia of Ancient History*: "Hattic (Language)," "Labarna," and "Kashka."

Petra furthermore participated in the Chicago Hittite Dictionary Project (see separate report), finishing the lemma *ser* "on top, above, because of, on account of, regarding" (ca. 110 pages).

Gene Gragg

All year long **Gene Gragg** has continued work on the user interface (for paradigm query and manipulation) of the morphological archive project. The latter, with the addition of Semitic and Egyptian, and with forthcoming Berber data, has now been rebaptized as the Afroasiatic Morphological Archive (AAMA, perhaps a more felicitous acronym than the COMA of the former Cushitic-Omotic Morphological Archive). Gene's programmer (Gregg Reynolds) and he are still looking for a "beta release" in fall 2011.

Papers and conferences given in the course of the year reflect for the most part either the content or the structure of the archive:

- Gene gave a paper at the Jagiellonian University in Krakow, November 17, at the invitation of the Polish Academy of Sciences, with the title "Paradigm in Theory and Practice: Towards an Afroasiatic Morphological Archive." A version of that paper was also given on December 9 at a seminar in the Ecole Normale Superieure in Paris.

- "Inflectional Classes and Root Classes in Cushitic," at the 39th North American Conference on Afroasatic Linguistics, University of Texas at Austin, February 12–13.

Work was finished on a chapter, "The Semitic Languages," written in collaboration with Robert Hoberma of the State University of New York, Stony Brook, to be published this fall by Cambridge University Press in *The Afroasiatic Languages*, edited by Zygmunt Frajzyngier of the University of Colorado, Boulder.

————————————

Rebecca Hasselbach

Rebecca Hasselbach worked on several projects during this academic year. One of the main projects consisted of editing a Festschrift for John Huehnergard, her former dissertation advisor, who is a leading expert in the field of comparative Semitics. The editing was done in collaboration with Hasselbach's colleague Naʿama Pat-El from the University of Texas at Austin. The Festschrift contains contributions of twenty-nine scholars working in various fields, including Semitic languages, Hebrew Bible, and even biology. The volume will further include pieces of art by a friend of the honoree. The editing process of the contributions has been completed and the manuscript is currently under review by the Oriental Institute of the University of Chicago.

In addition to the Festschrift, Hasselbach revised her book manuscript on "Grammatical Roles and Relations and the Reconstruction of Case in Semitic," which has been accepted for publication by Harvard Semitic Series.

Another research project Hasselbach has been working on this year is a study on grammatical agreement in Semitic languages. Agreement means features such as adjective-noun or subject-verb agreement, where the adjective or subject shows the same grammatical properties in terms of gender, number, and person-marking as the noun or verb. The individual Semitic languages vary considerably from each other regarding what elements or noun classes take full or partial agreement. The aim of Hasselbach's study is to determine which of the various agreement systems attested in Semitic, if any, represents the original situation of Semitic and to trace the development of agreement systems in the individual Semitic languages.

In addition to these projects, Hasselbach attended the North American Conference on Afroasiatic Linguistics, held in Austin, Texas, in February 2011, where she presented the results of her work on verbal endings in Semitic, which will be published in the Festschrift for John Huehnergard under the title "The Verbal Endings -*u* and -*a*: A Note on Their Functional Derivation." She was further invited to teach a one-week intensive course at the University of Münster (Germany) on the position of Akkadian in Semitic and the methodologies used for the linguistic investigation of Semitic languages. This course was taught at the department of Assyriology in June 2011. During her stay in Münster, Hasselbach gave a public talk on the scholarly history of the field of comparative Semitics entitled "Die semitische Sprachfamilie: Traditionelle Ansätze und Perspektiven."

As a service for the Oriental Institute, Hasselbach further served on the committee for the selection of the annual post-doctoral fellow.

————————————

Janet Johnson

Janet Johnson spent much time during the past year working on the Demotic Dictionary (see separate report), including preparing a brief resume of the history, goals, and status of this project for the winter *Oriental Institute News & Notes* (issue 208). She also continued to work and lecture on topics related to women in Pharaonic and Hellenistic Egypt; her article on "Gender and Marriage in Ancient Egypt" for the conference Ehe als Ernstfall der Geschlechterdifferenz, Herausforderungen für Frau und Mann in kulturellen Symbolsystemen, held in Würzburg, Germany, appeared this year. Also appearing this year was her section on "Self-Identity in Ancient Egypt" for the National Endowment for the Humanities-funded website "Teaching the Middle East: A Resource for Educators," which was prepared through the Oriental Institute Museum Office and which went fully operational this year (see separate report; see http://teachmiddleeast.lib.uchicago.edu/). As a result of this year's special exhibit Visible Language, she turned her attention to the development of writing in ancient Egypt, writing catalog entries on "Egyptian Hieroglyphic Writing," "Egyptian Demotic Script," and a "Demotic Annuity Contract" in the Oriental Institute collection (and the exhibit) for the catalog *Visible Language: Inventions of Writing in the Ancient Middle East and Beyond* and giving a lecture entitled "Origins, Development, and Impact of Writing in Ancient Egypt" for the associated Public Education symposium Inventions of Writing. She sponsored two young Swiss scholars who have Swiss National Science Foundation fellowships to spend three years each here in Chicago researching the development of the ancient Egyptian language. She also served as an "outside reviewer" for cases considering faculty promotion to tenure for institutions both in the United States and abroad. She served on various committees for the Oriental Institute, the Department of Near Eastern Languages and Civilizations, and the Program on the Ancient Mediterranean World in the Department of Classics, as well as serving as a member of the Board of Governors of the American Research Center in Egypt, the American Egyptological professional organization.

––––––––––––––––––

W. Raymond Johnson

This year **W. Raymond Johnson** completed his thirty-third year working in Egypt, his thirty-second full year working for the Epigraphic Survey in Luxor, and his fourteenth season as Chicago House Field Director. On May 5, 2011, Ray presented a lecture entitled "Analysis and Identity: Amenhotep III and Ramses I in the Michael Carlos Museum, Emory University," the Nix Mann Endowed Lecture for 2011 at the Michael C. Carlos Museum, Emory University, Atlanta, Georgia. On June 16, 2011, Ray gave a lecture at the Beverly Hills Women's Club, Los Angeles, and the World Monuments Fund (WMF) entitled "The Epigraphic Survey, Oriental Institute, University of Chicago: Archaeological Field Activities in Luxor, Egypt." He published an article entitled "The New Digital Publication Program of the Oriental Institute and Epigraphic Survey, University of Chicago at Medinet Habu," in *Acts of the International Symposium, The Temples of Millions of Years and the Royal Power at Thebes in the New Kingdom: Science and New Technology Applied to Archaeology*, edited by Christian LeBlanc and Gihane Zaki (Cairo: Supreme Council of Antiquities, 2010). He also contributed an article entitled "A Ptah-Sokar Barque Procession from Memphis," in *Under the Potter's Tree: Studies on Ancient Egypt Presented to Janine Bourriau on the Occasion of Her 70th Birthday*, edited by David Aston, Bettina Bader,

Carla Gallorini, Paul Nicholson, and Sarah Buckingham, pp. 531–40 (Orientalia Lovaniensia Analecta 204; Leuven: Peeters, 2011).

Charles E. Jones

Charles E. Jones continues his association with the Oriental Institute through the Persepolis Fortification Archive Project, and the IraqCrisis Mailing List. He is the editor of the PFA Project weblog (http://persepolistablets.blogspot.com/). At that location you can read news of the project and subscribe to receive updates by e-mail. His article "From the Persepolis Fortification Archive Project, 3: The First Administrative Document Discovered at Persepolis: PT 1971-1," co-authored with Seunghee Yie, appeared early this summer in the open access journal *Achaemenid Research on Texts and Archaeology* (ARTA 2011.003). It is available online (http://www.achemenet.com/bookmark.do?link=arta-contents).

Jones remains the moderator of IraqCrisis, a moderated list for communicating substantive information on cultural property damaged, destroyed, or lost from libraries and museums in Iraq during and after the war in April 2003, and on the worldwide response to the crisis (https://lists.uchicago.edu/web/info/iraqcrisis). While traffic has slowed recently, threats to cultural property in Iraq remain serious more than eight years after the outbreak of war. Subscribers are welcome.

Readers of the Oriental Institute *Annual Report* may be interested also in an initiative Jones has undertaken at the Institute for the Study of the Ancient World in New York: AWOL — The Ancient World Online (http://ancientworldonline.blogspot.com/). AWOL provides a medium for notice and comment on open access material relating to the ancient world, and is an extension of Abzu (http://www.etana.org/abzubib). Abzu, which began at the Oriental Institute Research Archives, has also undergone a face-lift this past year. Abzu is served from Vanderbilt University as a part of ETANA (http://www.etana.org). ETANA is a multi-institutional collaborative project — with the Oriental Institute as a founding member — initiated in August 2000 as an electronic publishing project designed to enhance the study of the history and culture of the ancient Near East.

Anyone who is interested can subscribe to AWOL by e-mail, by means of a feed reader, or on Facebook or Twitter. All are welcome.

Walter Kaegi

Cambridge University Press published **Walter Kaegi**'s hardback book *Muslim Expansion and Byzantine Collapse in North Africa* in November 2010. He published a review of Gill Page's "Being Byzantine," in the *Journal of Interdisciplinary History* 40 (2010): 586–88. He completed two other reviews: *Byzantium and the Arabs in the Sixth Century*, vol. 2, pt. 2, by Irfan Shahid, for the *Journal of Near Eastern Studies;* and *From Hellenism to Islam: Cultural and Linguistic Change in the Roman Near East*, edited by Hannah M. Cotton, Robert C. Hoyland, Jonathan J. Price, and David Wasserstein, for the *Journal of Interdisciplinary History*. He prepared several papers for publication: "Carl Hermann Kraeling: A Reminiscence," to be published in *Pesher Naḥum*, a Festschrift for Norman Golb, in press. He completed his subsection "Empires to Nation-States: Late

Antiquity," for the now posted Oriental Institute National Endowment for the Humanities-funded online project "Teaching the Middle East: A Resource for Educators." He completed revisions for his paper "Seventh-Century Identities: A Reassessment," in preparation for Austrian Academy of Science volume *Visions of Community*, edited by W. Pohl, R. Payne, et al.; the manuscript was revised and corrected and is now in press. It is a revised version of his 2009 paper presented in Vienna. He also prepared and delivered a paper, "Holy War, and the Heraclians," at the conference on Byzantine War Ideology Between Roman Imperial Concept and Christian Religion, University of Vienna, 20 May 2011. He is revising it for publication in the proceedings. He also delivered the following papers at professional meetings: "Reassessing Arnold J. Toynbee, Historian of Byzantium: With an Additional Comment from William H. McNeill" (University of Chicago Workshop on Late Antiquity and Byzantium, 5 October 2010), "Reminiscences of Carl H. Kraeling" (Byzantine Studies Conference, at the annual meeting of the Byzantine Studies Association North America, University of Pennsylvania, 10 October 2010), "The Heraclids and Holy War" (Methodology Seminar, Department of History, University of Kentucky at Lexington, 28 February 2011). He served as a session chair for the post-doctoral seminar Iconoclasm and Text Destruction in the Ancient Near East and Beyond, which was held in Breasted Hall at the Oriental Institute, 9 April 2011. He continued to serve as president of the U.S. National Committee for Byzantine Studies (USNCBS), in which capacity he actively planned for the next International Congress of Byzantine Studies (which meets every five years) that will take place in Sofia, Bulgaria, 19–27 August 2011. He prepared a short paper for the Sofia Congress. He also took much time serving on the Local Arrangements Committee for the Annual Meeting of Byzantine Studies Association of North America (BSANA), which will take place in Chicago, 19–22 October 2011, mostly at De Paul University, but one public lecture and a reception will take place at the Oriental Institute in Breasted Hall on 21 October 2011. He co-authored with Fred Donner a position paper for the Oriental Institute faculty retreat on 29 April at the Gleacher Center, downtown Chicago. He served as a member of the History Department Admissions and Aid Committee and as a member of the University of Chicago Phi Beta Kappa Executive Committee.

Gregory Marouard

Gregory Marouard's year was marked by six archaeological excavations in Egypt, a schedule that was not too much disturbed by the events in the country during the past winter. This first year as research associate in Egyptian archaeology was centered around three principal axes of research:

(1) *Urban and monumental archaeology of the Old and the Middle Kingdoms.* This topic is actually Gregory's main program of research, built around the Tell Edfu Project (directed by N. Moeller; see separate report). He participated:

- As senior archaeologist and assistant director of the Tell Edfu Project at the last field season (October to November 2010). Four months were dedicated to the post-excavation work at the Oriental Institute and was marked by the programming of a new database and the study of an exceptional set of King Khayan's seal impressions. On this last subject, a joint paper with N. Moeller was given at the annual meeting of the American Research Center in Egypt (ARCE), in Chicago, on April 3, 2011. A detailed article on this topic is currently in preparation

- As project director with the collaboration of H. Papazian (University of Copenhagen), he conducted a first reconnaissance survey at the South Edfu Pyramid in order to make a complete map of this last unexcavated provincial pyramid. This work was presented in a paper at this year's ARCE annual meeting and an article is in preparation.

- As collaborator of the Sinki Pyramid Project: in connection to the aforementioned program, a request for a survey authorization by the University of Copenhagen was put together on a similar provincial pyramid in South Abydos in co-direction with H. Papazian.

(2) *The archaeology of pharaonic sites along the Red Sea coast during the Old and the Middle Kingdoms.* Being part of this project since 2002, in collaboration with the French Institute in Cairo (IFAO), the University of Paris - La Sorbonne and the French Foreign Office (MAE), Gregroy participates at the excavations at Ayn Sokhna and Wadi el-Jarf as well as on the extensive Wadi Araba survey. The research aim is to understand the complex phenomenon of royal expeditions which were led to the Sinai and beyond, including an elaborate system of trails, a network of coastal way stations, harbor facilities, and copper or turquoise mining sites along both sides of the Gulf of Suez.

- Gregory participated as archaeologist and ceramicist at the Wadi Araba project, directed by Y. Tristant (Macquarie University, Sydney). This season (December 2010) led to the discovery of a pharaonic track used by donkey caravans during the Old and early Middle Kingdoms. The trail is marked by a complex navigation system consisting of more than seventy visual markers (cairns) and was followed over more than 12.5 km leading to a large copper mining site.

- Acting as senior archaeologist and ceramicist since 2005, he joined the January 2011 season at Ayn Sokhna (co-directed by M. Abd-el-Rhaziq of Suez University, and G. Castel of the IFAO). Significantly curtailed by the Egyptian revolution, the campaign aimed to finish the excavation on an Old Kingdom shipyard area (early Fifth Dynasty) and hoped to start the 3-D mapping of a unique example of a pit used for assembling and/or disassembling boats.

- At Wadi al-Jarf he acted as co-director (with S. Mahfouz of the University of Assiout and P. Tallet of the University of Paris - La Sorbonne). The first season on this exceptional pharaonic harbor site took place in June 2011. This survey and excavation revealed three main areas of interest: an underwater harbor installation preserved in excellent condition (a pier, numerous stone anchors, and complete pottery jars), an area with extensive campsites, and a storage facility consisting of almost thirty galleries (four were excavated this season) in which inscriptions and several boat pieces made of Lebanese cedar have been discovered. The site dates exclusively to the Old Kingdom (end of Fourth–mid-Fifth Dynasties) and can be now considered the oldest sea harbor of Egypt and beyond. Three articles are in preparation to announce this discovery.

(3) *The domestic and urban archaeology of the Late Period and Greco-Roman towns*, which is a research focus related to Gregory's dissertation work (completed in May 2010).

- He is participating as senior archaeologist at the excavations of the settlement site at Buto (directed by P. Ballet of the University of Poitiers). The 2010 season saw the end of a four-year program focusing on a large domestic area dating from the end of the

Persian to the early Ptolemaic period, and a series of pottery kilns dating from the Roman period (Augustus). The 2011 season was a study season in order to prepare the collective monograph and to complete the analysis of the pottery workshop, the first example of sigillata kilns excavated in the Middle East.

- The investigation of the domestic quarter of the early Ptolemaic and Roman town at Tell Edfu, which was started during his doctoral research, is also in progress.

Five of Gregory's articles have been published or submitted this past year:

- "Tell el-Farain 10 – Vorbericht II. Ptolemäisch-römische Zeit," by U. Hartung, P. Ballet, G. Marouard, and others. *Mitteilungen des Deutschen Archäologischen Instituts, Abteilung Kairo* 65 (2009): 133–58.

- "Discovery of the Site of Ayn Sukhna and Initial Excavating Operations," by M. Abd El-Raziq, G. Castel, G. Marouard, and P. Tallet. To be published in the proceedings of the international colloquium The Red Sea in Pharaonic Times: Recent Discoveries along the Red Sea Cost (Cairo, 11–12 January 2009). In press at IFAO.

- "Survey du monastère d'aba Apollô de Baouît: données archéologiques et analyses préliminaires de la céramique et du verre des ermitages 'de la montage,'" by S. Marchand and G. Marouard. To be published in the proceedings of the international colloquium The Egyptian Hermitages during the First Millennium (Cairo, 24–26 January 2009). In press at IFAO.

- "Révision des données archéologiques et architecturales sur les quartiers domestiques et les habitats des fondations et refondations Lagides de la chôra égyptienne," by G. Marouard. To be published in the proceedings of the SFAC colloquium, Greeks and Romans in Egypt (Paris, March 2008). In press at IFAO.

- "Et la Bouto tardive?" by P. Ballet, G. Lecuyot, G. Marouard, M. Pithon, and B. Redon. *Bulletin de l'Institut français d'archéologie orientale* 111 (2011). In press at IFAO.

Carol Meyer

Carol Meyer is delighted to say that the final report on the Bir Umm Fawakhir 1996 and 1997 survey seasons appeared as *Bir Umm Fawakhir 2*, Oriental Institute Communications 30. Checking galleys and page proofs occupied part of winter and spring. Several publications that had been in press for longer or shorter spells also appeared: "Coptus/Coptos" for the *Encyclopedia of Ancient History*; a review of *Antinoupolis I* for the *Bulletin of the American Society of Papyrologists* 47; "Documentation and Conservation of Bir Umm Fawakhir," in *Preserving Egypt's Cultural Heritage*; and "Grinding Stones and Gold Mining at Hosh al-Guruf," in *Gdansk Archaeological Museum and Heritage Protection Fund African Reports* 7. She also presented a paper on "A Ritual Cache from Tell Hamoukar, Syria" at the annual meeting of the American Schools of Oriental Research, in Atlanta, in November 2010. Work continues on the final report on the Bir Umm Fawakhir 1999 excavations and 2001 study season. Only one chapter remains to be drafted, but it is a hefty one, the pottery corpus.

Nadine Moeller

From the beginning of October to mid-December 2010, **Nadine Moeller** directed the annual field season at Tell Edfu in southern Egypt. The new results of this season are described in detail in the *Tell Edfu* project report. In December she participated with Natasha Ayers (PhD candidate at NELC, University of Chicago) at the International Nubian Pottery Workshop, held in Cairo, which had been organized by the Austrian Archaeological Institute. The paper presented during this workshop is currently being prepared for publication. It focuses on the analysis of Nubian pottery from Tell Edfu dating to the late Middle Kingdom and Second Intermediate period.

In February she presented a paper on the latest results from Tell Edfu at the South Suburban Archaeology Society, which was well received. In March she was invited to two study days presenting latest research at Tell Edfu in the United Kingdom, one of which was organized by the Sussex Egyptology Society, at Worthing, and one in London by Ancient World Tours, held at University College.

The exceptional discovery of the seal impressions showing the cartouche of the Hyksos ruler Khayan was presented in collaboration with Gregory Marouard at the annual meeting of the American Research Center in Egypt, which was held in Chicago at the beginning of April. A detailed article about this discovery is currently being prepared by both authors, which will be submitted to the peer-reviewed journal *Egypt and the Levant*.

The substantial article on the results of the 2005–2009 seasons at Tell Edfu has been accepted for publication by the peer-reviewed *Journal of the American Research Center in Egypt* and is currently in press. During the past winter quarter, Nadine was granted a term of leave to focus on her current book project, entitled *The Settlements of Ancient Egypt*. The aim of this monograph is to provide a wide-ranging analysis of different types of settlements, offering a viable model for urbanism that will explain the role of towns and cities in ancient Egyptian civilization. Further work also continues on the Mendes archives with the help of two NELC graduate students, Jessica Henderson and Lindsey Miller. The entire collection of slides will be scanned by the end of the summer. They will then be ready to be stored in the archives of the Oriental Institute.

Robert K. Ritner

On October 6, **Robert K. Ritner** delivered the opening lecture for the Oriental Institute Members' Lecture Series, providing an illustrated synopsis of six centuries of Egyptian history: "The Libyan Anarchy: Egypt and Nubia in the Era from Solomon to Assurbanipal." The event was followed by a book signing for his recent volume of translations from the same era; see Ritner's contribution in the 2009–2010 *Annual Report*. The following month, Ritner provided two lectures for the Museum of Fine Arts, Houston, on the theme "Why Mummify? Egyptian Religion, Medical Theory and the Funerary Arts" (November 19–20). These lectures, which highlighted important and unpublished Houston artifacts, announced Ritner's catalog (in preparation) of the Houston museum's Egyptian collection. Ritner returned to Texas in February to speak for the North Texas Chapter of the American Research Center in Egypt (Dallas, February 12). His lecture, "An American Mummy Tale: The Joseph Smith Papyri," detailed the tragic-comical fate of eleven mummies and several papyri originally found in Thebes in

1831, then toured and sold across America from 1833 until the final four, with their papyri, were purchased by the Mormons in 1835. One of these papyri would be "translated" by Joseph Smith as the "Book of Abraham." Ritner's Dallas lecture was occasioned by his in-press volume of a complete edition of the Joseph Smith papyri; see below.

In April, Ritner participated in the Chicago conference Imagined Beginnings: The Poetics and Politics of Cosmogony, Theogony and Anthropogony in the Ancient World, held at the Franke Institute for the Humanities. His presentation on April 9 surveyed varying cosmologies and myths of origin in "Theogonies and Cosmogonies in Egyptian Ritual." In April and May, he delivered two Harper Lectures for the University of Chicago Alumni Association, speaking on "Ancient Egyptian Magic: Curses and Love Potions" in Oak Park, Illinois (April 28) and Evanston, Illinois (May 12).

Ritner's publications during the academic year included numerous contributions for cross-cultural studies. For the online Oriental Institute Persepolis Fortification Tablets series, he published "Seals with Egyptian Hieroglyphic Inscriptions at Persepolis" with a companion study by Mark Garrison (http://www.achemenet.com/document/2010.002-Garrison&Ritner.pdf). For Richard Steiner's volume on Proto-Canaanite Spells in the Pyramid Texts, Ritner served as a quoted contributor throughout the volume and provided "Foreword: An Egyptological Perspective." Within Earl Leichty's volume on Royal Inscriptions of Esarhaddon, Ritner served as quoted translator for amphora of Takelot III. In addition, he contributed an entry on an archaic "Throwstick" for the Oriental Institute exhibit catalog Before the Pyramids: The Origins of Egyptian Civilization, composed an article "Killing the Image: Killing the Essence" for the seminar Iconoclasm and Text Destruction in the Ancient Near East and Beyond (held opposite his April lecture for the "Cosmogony and Theogony" conference), and published online his study of Egyptian demonology: "An Eternal Curse upon the Reader of These Lines (with Apologies to M. Puig)." Ritner's 2009 Paris lectures were published by the École Pratique des Hautes Études: "Religion de l'Égypte ancienne. Conférences de M. Robert K. Ritner, Directeur d'études invité: Une introduction à la magie dans la religion de l'Égypte antique."

Most importantly, Ritner completed the proofreading for his next monograph, The Joseph Smith Egyptian Papyri: A Complete Edition (P. JS 1–4 and the Hypocephalus of Sheshonq), to be published by the Smith-Pettit Foundation (Salt Lake City). Including a history of the Smith mummies and papyri, comparative transliterations and translations of all the texts, chronological analysis of the documents, and discussions of the historicity of Smith's interpretations of the papyri (including a Mesopotamian perspective offered by Christopher Woods), the volume offers unique, critical insight into a little-known episode of early American "Egyptomania." The book should be available within the coming academic year.

When not lecturing, writing, or proofreading, Ritner served on various committees and taught five courses on Middle Egyptian hieroglyphs, hieratic, and religious texts from the Old Kingdom through the Coptic periods.

Martha T. Roth

I take great pleasure in reporting that the Chicago Assyrian Dictionary Project has come to a successful conclusion (please see separate report). I began working at the Oriental Institute as a post-doctoral researcher on the project in 1979, and the CAD has dominated my scholarly energies for the last thirty-two years. A guide and history, "How We Wrote the Chicago Assyrian Dictionary," appeared this year in the *Journal of Near Eastern Studies* 69 (2010): 1–21.

Meanwhile, I have served as dean of the Division of the Humanities since 2007 and have continued to do research and publish in the area of ancient Mesopotamian legal history. Three articles reassessing categories of personal status were submitted to press in 2010–11: "A Note on *mār awīlim* in the Old Babylonian Law Collections" will appear in the conference volume Dināt mīšarim: *Studien zur Setzung und Legitimation des Rechts im Kodex Hammurapi und im Alten Testament*, a special issue of BZAR; "On Persons in the Old Babylonian Law Collections: The Case of *mār awīlim* in Bodily Injury Provisions" will appear in a volume in honor of our colleague Matthew Stolper; and "Errant Oxen, or: The Goring Ox Redux" will appear in a Festschrift for a dear colleague who (I hope) still is not aware of the volume.

In May 2011, I attended a planning session at the University of Cambridge for the launch of a new comparative ancient law series, for which I will be responsible for the Mesopotamian material. This project will occupy more than a dozen scholars of ancient Greek, Roman, Indian, Chinese, Mesopotamian, and Egyptian legal history for several years to come. I look forward to working with colleagues on this new collaborative project.

Yorke M. Rowan

During July–August 2010, **Yorke M. Rowan** co-directed (with Morag Kersel) the second season of excavations at the Chalcolithic (4500–3600 BC) site of Marj Rabba, in the lower Galilee, Israel (see separate report). The excavations exposed rectilinear stone architecture, possible remains of silos, and evidence for domesticated pigs, sheep, goat, and cattle at the site. In addition, Yorke co-directed (with Gary Rollefson and Morag Kersel) an exploratory survey and recording at the site of Maitland's Mesa in the *badia* of eastern Jordan. A brief article on their work, "Maitland's 'Mesa' Reassessed: A Late Prehistoric Cemetery in the Eastern Badia, Jordan" was published in *Antiquity* (85/327, http://php.york.ac.uk/org/antiquity/projgall. php). The general research project in the eastern desert of Jordan, "Desert Monuments to the Dead: Views of the Early Pastoral Lifeways in Jordan's Eastern Desert," co-authored with Rollefson and Alex Wasse, also appeared in the *American Center for Oriental Research Newsletter* 22/1 (available online at www.acorjordan.org).

Culture, Chronology and the Chalcolithic: Theory and Transition, a volume co-edited with Jaimie Lovell, was published by Oxbow for the Council for British Research in the Levant Supplementary Series and includes an introductory chapter by Rowan and Lovell.

Yorke's review of *The Archaeology of Ritual*, by E. Kyriakidis, appeared in *Near Eastern Archaeology* 73/4 (2010): 254–55.

Yorke participated in a number of conferences during the academic year. In November, at the annual ASOR (American Schools of Oriental Research) meetings in Atlanta, he presented a paper about the Oriental Institute's excavations at Marj Rabba, "Marj Rabba: Excavation of a Chalcolithic Settlement in the Galilee." Also at the ASOR meetings he co-authored a paper with G. Rollefson, A. Wasse, and M. Kersel titled "Mr. Big: Honoring Leaders of Late Prehistoric Pastoral Societies in Jordan's Eastern Badia." In addition, Rollefson, Kersel, and Rowan presented a poster on their research in the eastern desert of Jordan, "Living with the Dead: Mortuary Landscapes in the Badlands of Jordan." Yorke also served as chair at the ASOR meetings for the session "Reports on Current Excavations and Surveys, Non-ASOR Affiliated," and continued with other committee work for ASOR. This year he was elected to the Board of Trustees of the W. F. Albright Institute of Archaeological Research in Jerusalem.

At the annual meetings for the Society for American Archaeology, held in Sacramento, Yorke presented a paper with M. Kersel, titled "Deconstructing the Holy Land: Cultural Heritage, Archaeology, Tourism and the Miniature." Yorke was invited to present a lecture to the Archaeological Institute of American in Milwaukee in May titled, "Death's Dominion during the Chalcolithic Period in the Southern Levant." In addition, he was invited to present a lecture to an avocational archaeology society in Sarasota, Florida, "Death's Dominion: Excavating Religion and Ritual at the End of Prehistory."

With Gil Stein and Abbas Alizadeh, Yorke received a grant from the Wenner-Gren Foundation to organize an international group of scholars for a workshop, Pathways to Power: The Emergence of Political Authority and Hierarchy in the 6th–5th Millennia BC; Near East-Comparative Perspectives, to be held at the Oriental Institute in fall 2011.

Foy Scalf

For the first time in perhaps a decade, an in-class course on the grammar of Middle Egyptian was taught for the Oriental Institute Museum over the winter and fall quarters of 2011. **Foy Scalf** led a dedicated class through eight weeks of an Introduction to Egyptian Hieroglyphs (January 11–March 3), during which the students covered the first eight lessons in James Hoch's *Middle Egyptian Grammar.* Hoch's final eight lessons were completed by a few dedicated souls during Intermediate Egyptian Hieroglyphs (April 14–June 2), thereby giving them a solid foundation in the ancient Egyptian language. The class was a success and Foy continues to meet with a small group of these students to further read Egyptian texts in order to solidify their understanding of Egyptian grammar and expand their cultural knowledge of ancient Egypt.

On July 7, 2010, Foy presented a lecture on "Roman Egypt" for Ancient Egyptian Language, Culture, and History, the Egyptian summer school taught by Rozenn Bailleul-LeSuer at the Oriental Institute. In April, 2011, Chicago hosted the 62nd Meeting of the American Research Center in Egypt at which he presented a paper entitled "Innovation and Tradition: The Placement of Funerary Papyri in Greco-Roman Egypt," describing insights from his dissertation research. In this paper, he argued that distinct changes in how funerary papyri were prepared for burial had ancient parallels among the iconography associated with preparation of the burial equipment.

In addition to ensuring that the Research Archives is well stocked, Foy made strides on several publication projects. He is currently preparing a manuscript for a Festschrift volume on a collection of unpublished Demotic texts on large jar fragments in the Oriental Institute entitled "A Collection of Demotic Votive Texts from the Oriental Institute of the University of Chicago." Although heretofore unidentified, the Demotic texts that adorn these large jars indicate that they were probably once used as sacred ibis votive offerings to Thoth. Another Demotic text from a jar in the Oriental Institute is the subject of his manuscript "An Embalmer's Bowl with Demotic Inscription (OIM 9115)."

Reviews of several volumes have finally appeared over the last year, including Susanne Bickel and Bernard Mathieu (eds.), *D'un monde à l'autre: textes des pyramides et textes des sarcophages*, in *Journal of Near Eastern Studies* 71 (2011); J. Assmann, *Death and Salvation in Ancient Egypt*, in *Journal of Near Eastern Studies* 70 (2011): 124–26; I. Guermeur, *Les cultes d'Amon hors de Thèbes: recherches de géographie religieuse*, in *Journal of Near Eastern Studies* 70 (2011): 126–27.

Andrea Seri

Andrea Seri presented a paper entitled "The Role of Creation in Enūma eliš" at the conference Imagined Beginnings: The Poetics and Politics of Cosmogony, Theogony and Anthropogony in the Ancient World, sponsored by the Center for the Study of Ancient Religions at the University of Chicago, the Midwest Consortium on Ancient Religions, and the Franke Institute for the Humanities. The paper will be published in the volume *Imagined Beginnings: Ancient Cosmogonies, Theogonies and Anthropogonies in the Eastern Mediterranean*, co-edited by Chris Faraone and Andrea Seri. She has also submitted the article "Borrowings to Create Anew: Intertextuality in the Babylonian Poem of 'Creation,'" which will appear in a Festschrift. Andrea published two articles. The first is entitled "Domestic Female Slaves during the Old Babylonian Period," in *Slaves and Households in the Ancient Near East*, edited by L. Culbertson, pp. 49–67 (Oriental Institute Seminars 7; Chicago: The Oriental Institute, 2011). The other article is "Adaptation of Cuneiform to Write Akkadian," in *Visible Language: Inventions of Writing in the Ancient Middle East and Beyond*, edited by Christopher Woods, pp. 85–93 (Oriental Institute Museum Publications 32; Chicago: The Oriental Institute, 2010). She also wrote an entry on the word *naditum* for the *Encyclopaedia of Ancient History* (Wiley-Blackwell) and is currently editing her second book, *The House of Prisoners: State and Slavery in Uruk during the Revolt against Samsu-iluna*, for final submission.

Andrea continues collaborating with the Berkeley Prosopography Services and is preparing electronic editions of all the documents dated to King Rīm-Anum of Uruk to be included in website Oracc (The Open Richly Annotated Cuneiform Corpus, managed by S. Tinney of the University of Pennsylvania, E. Robson of Cambridge University, and N. Veldhuis of the University of California at Berkeley). Andrea has also reviewed articles for the *Journal of Near Eastern Studies*, is one of the members of the Oriental Institute publications committee, and is also an Associate Member (PAMW Affiliate) to the Classics Department of the University of Chicago.

Oğuz Soysal

Oğuz Soysal continued his job with the Chicago Hittite Dictionary (CHD) Project. Much of his time was spent writing articles on words beginning with *tu* and preparing the transliterations of the recent cuneiform editions, *Keilschrifttexte aus Boğazköi* volumes 47, 51, 56, 58, and 60 for the CHD files. His personal research has continued to focus on Hittite history/culture and the Hattian language. Soysal published the following articles in 2010–2011: "Philological Contributions to Hattian — Hittite Religion (II). On the Origin and the Name of the ḫazkarai-women," in *Pax Hethitica: Studies on the Hittites and their Neighbours in Honour of Itamar Singer*, pp. 340–50

(Studien zu den Bogazköy-Texten 51; Wiesbaden: Harrassowitz, 2010), and "Eski Anadolu Toponomisi'nde değişik yorumlara açık bir yapım öğesi hakkında: Hititçe — *aš+ḫapa* '... nehir(i)' ya da Hattice *š(a)ḫap* 'tanrı' ?," in *Acts of the 7th International Congress of Hittitology, Çorum, August 25–31, 2008*, edited by Aygül Süel, volume 2, pp. 783–91 (Ankara: Anıt Matbaa, 2010)

Soysal working on the Bo-texts at the Museum of Ancient Anatolian Civilizations, Ankara, in January 2011

Furthermore, Soysal's long-term cooperation with Dr. Rukiye Akdoğan and Tom Urban brought its fruitful result as the cuneiform publication entitled *Ankara Arkeoloji Müzesinde Bulunan Boğazköy Tabletleri II/ Boğazköy Tablets in the Archaeological Museum of Ankara II* was published by the Oriental Institute in June 2011.

In addition, in winter 2010/2011 Soysal started a new project involved with the unpublished Hittite texts bearing the siglum "Bo," which were transferred from the Staatliches Museum in Berlin to the Museum of Ancient Anatolian Civilizations in Ankara in 1987. After the decision of the Ministry of Culture of the Republic of Turkey in 2010, a new team of Turkish Hittitologists was formed to continue working on the unpublished Bo fragments, wherein Soysal too received an invitation to become a part of that project. The fragments in question are in the number range from Bo 8 to Bo 9736 and they are divided up among twenty-one Hittitologists. Each team member receives about 170 pieces and is primarily obligated to make hand copies of them. Soysal's share includes the range between the numbers Bo 9536 and Bo 9736. In June 2010 he visited the Ankara Museum to check these fragments, which can be utilized as primary source for the works of the Hittite Dictionary Project. To enlarge the material, Soysal also received permission from some of his Turkish colleagues to work on their share of Bo-texts. In winter 2010/2011 and summer 2011 Soysal took digital pictures of about 500 Bo-fragments in the Ankara Museum and started to transliterate the texts, which are to be added to the lexical files of the Hittite Dictionary Project. This would be a great benefit for the Hittite Dictionary Project since the unpublished Bo-texts cannot be used otherwise unless they are cited elsewhere in the secondary literature.

Gil J. Stein

In July–August 2010, **Gil J. Stein** conducted the third field season as American co-director of the Joint Syrian-American excavations at Tell Zeidan, studying the roots of Mesopotamian urbanism in the Ubaid period at this 12.5 ha regional center in the Euphrates river valley. A fuller description of the excavations is presented in this *Annual Report*.

Gil has also continued with the work toward publication of his 1992–1997 excavations at Hacınebi, a fourth-millennium BC Uruk Mesopotamian colony in the Euphrates valley of southeast Turkey. Now that the analyses of the stratigraphy of the site are complete, Dr. Belinda Monahan has been finalizing the typology of local Anatolian and Mesopotamian Uruk ceramic types. Hacınebi has one of the largest stratigraphically excavated ceramic data sets currently available for this time period in the Near East. Once published, Stein hopes that the Hacınebi ceramic sequence can make a significant contribution to the understanding of Uruk Mesopotamia and the world's earliest-known colonial network.

Gil was invited to present a series of lectures and presentations over the past year. On October 6, 2010, he spoke at Harvard University on the topic "Conquest, Colonialism, and Contact: Rethinking Models of Ancient Inter-Regional Interaction." In December, he gave two lectures in Paris at the University of Paris-Nanterre and the Sorbonne (Maison de l'Orient) on the topic of "Complexity, Social Identity, and Inter-Regional Interaction in Ubaid Upper Mesopotamia." On January 26, 2011, in the Yale University Anthropology Department, Gil presented the lecture "Guess Who's Coming to Dinner? Social Identity, Mixed Marriages, and Commensal Politics in an Ancient Mesopotamian Colony." On April 13, Gil presented a lecture at the University of Chicago Interdisciplinary Archaeology Workshop titled "The Emergence of Political Leadership in Sixth–Fifth Millennium Mesopotamia: A Progress Report from Tell Zeidan, Syria."

Gil also gave a number of public outreach lectures. On March 16, he spoke at the Science Café in Evanston, Illinois, on the topic "Archaeology and the Roots of Civilization." On June 15, Gil spoke to a group from the President's Circle of the Chicago Botanic Garden on "The Archaeology of Ancient Fields and Gardens."

Gil has a book chapter in press: "Food Preparation, Social Context, and Ethnicity in a Prehistoric Mesopotamian Colony" in *The Menial Art of Cooking: Archaeological Studies of Cooking and Food Preparation*, edited by Sarah R. Graff and Enrique Rodriguez-Alegria (Boulder: University Press of Colorado).

He is currently working on the publication of preliminary reports from the first three field seasons of excavation at Tell Zeidan, Syria, and is also completing a publication that examines the Persian-period burials from his site of Hacınebi, Turkey.

Matthew W. Stolper

Matthew W. Stolper submitted his presentation, "*Sugirs* of Anshan," for publication in the proceedings of the International Congress on Susa and Elam held at Ghent, Belgium, in December 2009, a meeting that reconvened many who had taken part in a Rencontre Assyriologique International on the same theme twenty years earlier. The paper discussed three texts excavated in the late 1970s at Anshan (Tall-i Malyan), Iran. The texts appear to name two or three previously unheard-of Elamite rulers, but the paper ends in uncertainty about their historical significance. He also submitted a contribution on "The Persian Expedition: The Past and Present of the Oriental Institute's Early Work in Iran," for publication in *Iranian Studies in America*, edited by Erica Ehrenberg and Frank Lewis, to be published for the American Institute of Iranian Studies by Eisenbrauns. The paper reviews the work of the Oriental Institute's Persian Expedition, the last of the great pre-war Oriental Institute field projects, during 1931–1939. The pre-war excavations supervised by Ernst Herzfeld and Erich Schmidt at Persepolis, Tall-i Bakun, Istakhr, and Luristan and the aerial survey initiated by Schmidt live on in postwar Oriental Institute publications and online projects into the present.

Most of Stolper's research effort continues to be devoted to the Persepolis Fortification Archive Project, described elsewhere in this report. Among the results during the past year

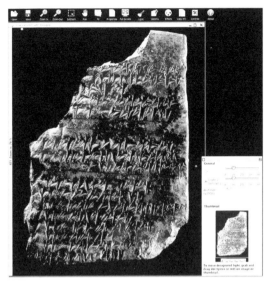

BetterLight (left) and PTM (right) scans of an unpublished Elamite fragment from the Persepolis Fortification Archive. The text uses an Elamite phrase found only once elsewhere, in the great narrative inscription of Darius I at Bisotun, where it describes the death of Cambyses

are "Case in Point: The Persepolis Fortification Archive Project," submitted for publication in *Archaeologies of Text: Archaeology, Technology and Ethics*, the proceedings of a symposium at the Joukowsky Institute at Brown University, edited by Morag Kersel and Matthew Rutz; a paper presented the annual meeting of the American Oriental Society in Chicago that treats new evidence from Fortification texts for the interpretation of a passage in the great Bisotun inscriptions of Darius I, a passage that has been a topic of sharp debate since the first full decipherment of cuneiform scripts more than 140 years ago; and presentations on the contents of the Archive and the methods of the Project to a Smart Museum/Oriental Institute Teacher Workshop, to a minicourse on ancient economies for members and docents, to the Persian Circle, and to a general audience at Illinois Wesleyan University.

Emily Teeter

This was a good year for publications, with the appearance of **Emily Teeter**'s *Baked Clay Figurines and Votive Beds from Medinet Habu* (Oriental Institute Publications 133) and the exhibit catalog *Before the Pyramids: The Origins of Egyptian Civilization* (Oriental Institute Museum Publications 33). *Religion and Ritual in Ancient Egypt* finally appeared from Cambridge University Press, and *Mısır ve Mısırlılar* (the Turkish edition of *Egypt and the Egyptians*) was issued by Arkadaş Publishers in Ankara. A general article about the Before the Pyramids show appeared in *Kmt: A Modern Journal of Ancient Egypt*.

Emily delivered a Harper Lecture in Cleveland on the Visible Language exhibit. She spoke about Meresamun and music and its role in temples at a symposium at the Toledo Art Museum, and she gave another talk on Meresamun to the Seattle Chapter of the American Research Center in Egypt. She lectured for several chapters of the International Women's Association here in Chicago, and she gave a number of gallery talks in conjunction with the Before the Pyramids exhibit.

Emily continues to serve as the president of the American Research Center in Egypt. In October, she and other members of the Board traveled to Egypt to discuss operations. The organization had its annual meeting in Chicago in early April, with a record attendance of 430 people, many of whom came to the Oriental Institute for a tour of the Before the Pyramids and a reception in the Mesopotamian gallery. Independent travels included Beirut and Syria.

Theo van den Hout

This past year marked the last year of **Theo van den Hout**'s first term as chair of the Department of Near Eastern Languages and Civilizations (NELC) and he is looking forward to a sabbatical in 2011–2012. Besides his teaching and work on the Chicago Hittite Dictionary Theo submitted (with the welcome assistance from our Publications Office) in the beginning of the year the final manuscript of 245 Hittite fragments in hand copy with an introductory catalog detailing genres as well as indicating possible duplicates and joins with already known pieces. The resulting book came out in early April (see below). He also wrote three entries for the *Reallexikon der Assyriologie*. Currently he is working on additional and larger entries for the *Reallexikon* and a few short articles.

Since the previous *Annual Report*, a number of publications have appeared in print. First of all the book already mentioned: *Texte aus dem Bezirk des Grossen Tempels X* (Keilschrifttexte aus Boghazköi 59; Berlin: Gebrüder Mann Verlag). In addition there are the following articles: "The Hieroglyphic Luwian Signs L. 255 and 256 and Once Again KARATEPE XI," in *ipamati kistamati pari tumatimis. Luwian and Hittite Studies Presented to J. David Hawkins on the Occasion of His 70th Birthday*, edited by I. Singer, pp. 234–43 (Sonia and Marco Nadler Institute of Archaeology Monograph Series 28; Tel Aviv: Emery and Claire Yass Publications in Archaeology, 2010); "The Rise and Fall of Cuneiform Script in Hittite Anatolia," in *Visible Language: Inventions of Writing in the Ancient Middle East and Beyond*, edited by C. Woods, pp. 99–108, 210–12 (Oriental Institute Museum Publications 32; Chicago: The Oriental Institute, 2010); "Studies in the Hittite Phraseological Construction II. Its Origin," in *Hethitica* 16 (2010) (= Gedenkschrift für Erich Neu), pp. 191–204; "^{LÚ}DUB.SAR.GIŠ = 'clerk'?," *Orientalia* 79 (2010): 255–67 (= Festschrift for Alfonso Archi); "The Written Legacy of the Hittites," in *Insights into Hittite History and Archaeology*, edited by H. Genz and D. P. Mielke, pp. 47–84 (Colloquia Antiqua 2; Leuven-Paris-Walpole: Peeters, 2011).

Two reviews were published: Review of *Die Hethiter*, by Jörg Klinger, in *Die Orientalistische Literaturzeitung* 105 (2010): 430–32, and Review of *Hethitisches Wörterbuch*, Zweite, völlig neubearbeitete Auflage auf der Grundlage der edierten hethitischen Texte, Band III/1: Ḫ, Lieferungen 11–17, by Johannes Friedrich†, Annelies Kammenhuber†, and Inge Hoffmann," in *Kratylos* 55 (2010): 118–24. Finally, Theo wrote a brief article on the CHD entitled "The Chicago Hittite Dictionary — More than just a Dictionary," for *Oriental Institute News & Notes* (issue 208): 9–11.

In September Theo was invited for a lecture at Leiden University, "Recente ideeën over datering van Hethitische teksten en geletterdheid bij de Hethieten" ("Recent Ideas on Hittite Text Dating and Literacy in Hittite Society").

Donald Whitcomb

The summer of 2010 was taken up with **Donald Whitcomb**'s second knee replacement, complicated by a large blood clot. Part of the repair of his leg involved *hirudo* therapy (leeches), which reminded him of traditional medicine in the Middle East (and gave a certain nuance to the motto "Forefront of Medicine"). Happily his recovery was sufficient to take up a variety of projects in the fall. The first was a conference at the Art Institute of Chicago in September on Arthur Upham Pope and Archaeology. This gave him the opportunity to delve into the early history of the Oriental Institute in Iran and the career of Erich Schmidt, one of his heroes and a life-long friend of A. U. Pope. Curiously, Don had met Pope in Shiraz and worked briefly for him as a Peace Corps volunteer, about a year before his death in 1969. A couple of weeks later Don joined a colloquium accompanying the Roads of Arabia exhibition at the Louvre. He presented a paper on the "Hijazi Culture in Early Islamic History"; this is an idea he had been developing for many years, that western Arabia developed a distinctive culture in the first centuries after the beginning of Islam. The idea seemed well received and the director of Antiquities in Saudi Arabia, Dr. Ali al-Ghabban, personally thanked him (but of course most of his evidence drew from al-Ghabban's brilliant field research).

By October Don was teaching Coptic and Islamic Archaeology of Egypt, a useful preparation reviving his understanding of the subject before teaching the course with the Study Abroad program in Cairo. This program was to be a series on Islamic civilization, and his course an interesting mix of two separate subjects, a general introduction to Islamic archaeology and a special focus on Egypt. The idea of teaching Fustat (old Cairo) and other sites, even his old haunt of Quseir al-Qadim on the Red Sea, filled him with pleasure.

At the same time, Don gave a paper for the docents' mini-series on Ancient Economies presenting the *suq*s of the Middle East and culminating with a new shopping mall in Jerusalem. His interest in archaeology in Israel and Palestine was renewed by the visit of Toufik Deadle, a doctoral candidate in the Hebrew University. Toufik has participated in the Tel Aviv University excavations at Khirbet Karak (also known as Beit Yarach and originally an Oriental Institute excavation under Pinhas Delougaz in the 1950s). He is responsible for remains of a *qasr* (palace) and bath of the early Islamic period and had come to see the collections in the Oriental Institute storerooms. Don had a delightful time entertaining him in Chicago, never imagining that a few months later he and his family would visit the Oriental Institute excavations at Khirbet al-Mafjar.

The climax of the year would have to be the beginning of the joint Palestinian-Chicago excavations at Khirbet al-Mafjar (Qasr Hisham). These began on December 15, with a short pause for Christmas in Bethlehem with the hospitality of Iman Saca's family. Iman joined us briefly to initiate a community archaeology program in Jericho, meeting with Hassan Saleh Hussein, the mayor, and Muhammad Hawwash, director of education for the Jericho region. The excavation team included Jihad Yasin, field director and an old friend of Don's from the Aqaba excavations

Pottery reading during the excavations at Khirbet al-Mafjar with the author, his son John, and Awni Shawamra. Recording is being done on an iPad

some fifteen years earlier. Muhammad Ghayyada, Awni Shawamra, and Bassam Helmi participated from the Palestinian side, and Michael Jennings, Enrico Cirelli, and John Whitcomb from Chicago. Details of the season have been sketched in *Oriental Institute News & Notes* (issue 210) and extensive information is now available on our website, www.jerichomafjarproject. org.

Carefully laid plans started to unravel in the spring. First, a conference in Aqaba was canceled, though this had nothing to do with political tensions in Jordan. The turmoil in Cairo prevented the course with the Study Abroad program and the dream of teaching in that country. Rather, Don returned to Chicago in early February and was immediately invited on behalf of the National Geographic Society to participate in a conference at the University of Dhofar in Salalah, southern Oman. Don had done some survey work in Oman in 1975 and wanted to see how this research had fared over the intervening 35+ years; he was pleased and in a way disappointed that this preliminary archaeological study remained key for this region. But this was a first chance to see the great sites along the south coast of Arabia, particularly al-Baleed (now being excavated by Juris Zarins, formerly of the Oriental Institute) and Khor Ruri (an Italian excavation under Alessandra Avanzini, with Alexander Sedov, a wonderful Russian archaeologist whom Don had entertained at the Oriental Institute some years ago). There were stories of civil disturbances in the papers in Salalah, though we were not affected.

In any case, Chicago seemed very quiet and Don settled into working on the results of the Mafjar excavations. He organized a panel for the American Research Center in Egypt in April with papers by Tasha Vorderstrasse, Tanya Treptow, and Choukri Heddouchi, which was well received. This was followed by a panel for the MEHAT (Middle East History and Theory) meeting, also in Chicago, with papers by Tanya, Michael Jennings, and Kristoffer Damgaard. In this latter meeting, Don gave a short presentation on differing perceptions of Khirbet al-Mafjar/Qasr Hisham over the last eighty years. Finally, in June Fred Donner organized a conference on Umayyads in light of his theory of a Believer's movement. Don gave a talk titled "An Archaeology of Muʾawiya," a subject he had long wished to tackle and, happily, it was well received by the historians.

Karen L. Wilson

During the past year, **Karen L. Wilson** continued to work on the final publication of the Oriental Institute excavations at the sites of Nippur and Abu Salabikh in Iraq during the late 1950s and early 1960s. The Nippur Publication Project is sponsored by a grant awarded to McGuire Gibson by the National Endowment for the Humanities and is a joint endeavor undertaken with Robert Biggs, Jean Evans, McGuire Gibson (all University of Chicago), and Richard Zettler (University of Pennsylvania). The project has included the preparation of a digital catalog of finds linked with images of the objects plus the scanning of all negatives and drawings as well as the field records generated by work on the two sites. Karen recently completed preparation of the plates illustrating the pottery for the final publication and has been working with architect Michael K. Hannan of Hannan Architecture and Planning, Ltd., to complete digital plans and elevations for levels 1–21 of the Inanna Temple Sounding. A draft of a final publication covering the results of the excavation of the Inanna Temple at Nippur is planned to be completed by the end of 2012.

In January, Karen gave a presentation on the Inanna Temple pottery sequence in Philadelphia to a graduate seminar on the Early Dynastic period jointly offered by the University of Pennsylvania and Bryn Mawr College.

Karen also continued to serve as research associate and Kish Project coordinator at the Field Museum of Natural History, preparing the final publication of the results of the Joint Field Museum and Oxford University Expedition to Kish in 1923–1933. That publication will include papers presented at a symposium in November 2008 focusing on current research and excavations at the site. Contributions will include studies of the human remains, textual evidence, lithics, animal figurines, and stucco as well as a catalog of the Field Museum holdings from the site.

Karen's book, *Bismaya: Recovering the Lost City of Adab,* which chronicles and presents the results of the University of Chicago's first expedition to Iraq in 1903–1905, is currently in press at the Oriental Institute Publications Office. Her manuscript, *Ancient Mesopotamia, Illustrated with Objects from the Oriental Institute Museum Collections* is also in press and, when published, will serve as the gallery guide to the Edgar and Deborah Jannotta Mesopotamian Gallery.

Christopher Woods

Christopher Woods devoted much of this year to Sumerian writing and the typology of writing systems more broadly, his current major research interest. The year began with September's opening of the special exhibit Visible Language: Inventions of Writing in the Ancient Middle East and Beyond, which he curated with the assistance of Emily Teeter and Geoff Emberling. Visible Language was concerned with the invention of writing from a typological perspective, comparing the Mesopotamian and Egyptian inventions with those documented in China and Mesoamerica, the four "pristine" writing systems. The exhibit — which was accompanied by a comprehensive catalog featuring contributions by a number of Oriental Institute faculty and PhD students — was covered by the *New York Times* and the *Chicago Tribune.* Chris gave talks in connection with the exhibit before the Harvard Club of Chicago, the Caxton Club, and the Oriental Institute membership. Visible Language completed its six-month run in March. The exhibit was inspired by a broader, long-term research project concerned with describing the Sumerian writing system and its development. Much of the groundwork for the project was laid this spring in collaboration with Andréas Stauder, who is planning a similar, diachronic study of Egyptian writing. In May Woods and Stauder participated in the international writing workshop Niltal und Zweistromland: Die Anfänge der Kulturtechnik Schreiben im 4. und frühen 3. Jahrtausend v. Chr. at the University of Bonn, and met with colleagues and potential collaborators in Basel, Zurich, and Geneva. At the annual American Oriental Society meeting in April, Chris presented a paper, "The Morphographic Basis of Sumerian Writing," which describes some of the theoretical underpinnings of the writing project. Chris gave several additional talks of note this year. In March he participated in the Oriental Institute's annual post-doctoral seminar, Iconoclasm and Text Destruction in the Ancient Near East and Beyond, describing the earliest evidence for these acts in Mesopotamian sources. Also in March he delivered the annual ANSHE Lecture at Johns Hopkins. And in June he delivered a lecture at the University of Copenhagen's Center for Canon and Identity Formation.

RESEARCH SUPPORT

COMPUTER LABORATORY

John C. Sanders

The Computer Laboratory lost a friend, its founder, and namesake, when William M. Sumner passed away earlier this year. I also lost a friend and colleague, my former boss, the man who hired me as a research associate to start and manage the Oriental Institute Computer Laboratory back in 1990. Bill's commanding presence in the offices of the Oriental Institute has been absent for many years now, and it hurts to know that he will never again grace its halls. Efforts that started under Bill's auspices, and with his encouragement, however, do carry on within the building, a fitting legacy to a wonderful person and a former director whose vision for the Institute lives on.

Projects

Integrated Database

Bill had a direct connection to the original discussions about the creation of an integrated database (IDB) for all Institute records. Some of those earliest talks took place in Bill's office, from 1990 onward. His passing is unfortunate timing as we are now so close to completion of the first incarnation of the integrated database he and I envisioned. The expected delays when undertaking such an enormous project as the IDB have pushed back our projected spring/summer 2011 rollout date until late 2011 or early 2012. The project is proceeding on track, though, with our first data migration scheduled to start about the time this *Annual Report* is published. This is an exciting time for those of us directly connected with the IDB project; Bill will not share in these moments but he's part of the reason the IDB will soon be launched!

After long hours with either pencil and paper or at a computer screen, Helen McDonald, Susan Allison, and Foy Scalf have designed the customized screen displays for their respective data sets, which will be coded by the KE Software programmers and given to us to test and verify. After that, data migrations will commence, with each of three runs discovering problems that must be fixed before the next run is executed. When the process is finished, several weeks to a month or two later, we will end up with the Institute's Museum Registration and Library catalog data brought into the EMu (Electronic Museum) database system, and displayed on faculty and staff's computer screens according to how Helen, Susan, and Foy designed them. At approximately the same time, the web browser-based portal into these two datasets designed for public use will also be launched.

Electronic Publications Initiative

Once again, this past year saw great progress with the Institute's Electronic Publications Initiative. Twenty-three electronic versions of current or past Institute publications, in Adobe

Portable Document Format (PDF), were made available for free download on the Institute's website. These new downloadable publications pertain to ancient Mesopotamia, Syro-Palestine, and Anatolia, with one Egyptian and one Islamic title. Currently, 298 Oriental Institute publications are available as PDFs. When fully implemented our Electronic Publications Initiative will make accessible all 400+ titles in our Publications Office catalog.

Three new letter volumes (M, P, and ꜣI) for the Chicago Demotic Dictionary Project were finished this past year, converted to Adobe PDFs, and made available for free download on the Institute's website.

The Institute's Electronic Publications Initiative dictates that current and future print publications produced by the Oriental Institute Publications Office are also made available electronically through the Institute's website. I encourage everyone to read that portion of the Publications Office section of this *Annual Report* regarding the status of the Institute's Electronic Publications Initiative, then visit the Catalog of Publications page on our website where you will be able to download these past and current titles of our publications in electronic form:

http://oi.uchicago.edu/research/pubs/catalog/

A list of the volume titles which were processed into digital format and made available to the public on the Institute's website during this past year can be found in the Electronic Resources section of this *Annual Report*.

The Oriental Institute Website

This past year a portion of the electronic publication backlog on our website was eliminated with the addition of all Institute *News & Notes* newsletters from 1999 through 2001, plus the most recent issues from summer and fall 2010, winter 2011, and spring 2011, now all available as PDFs. Select lead articles in *News & Notes* published between 1990 and 1999 remain available on the website, but in HTML format. As time permits over the next year or two these editions will be converted to the Adobe pdf format, along with as many pre-1990 *News & Notes* publications as we can find in our archives.

Donald Whitcomb's new archaeology project, the Jericho Mafjar Project, was added to the Archaeology Research Projects component of the website. These new excavations just underway in the northern areas of Khirbet al-Mafjar, located north of Jericho in the Palestinian territories, will investigate the theory that the site was not just a palace complex, but was instead an incipient Islamic city.

The Tell Edfu Project, under the direction of Nadine Moeller, was added to the Archaeology Research Projects component of the website, providing a brief description of the project's work at the town site of Tell Edfu, several images from their 2009 field season, and a link to the project's independent website.

The Nubia Expedition's archaeological fieldwork in 2008 is detailed in a progress report on the website.

The Epigraphic Survey added an update to the project's homepage with notes and photographs from their eighty-sixth season that ended in April 2010. Alternately, issue 21 of the Survey's *Chicago House Bulletin* (September 2010) was added to the website for download as PDF.

Various types of media presentations were added to our website to present the Oriental Institute Museum's special exhibit Visible Language: Inventions of Writing in the Ancient Middle East and Beyond: an image gallery containing more than fifteen photographs of objects from the exhibit; four YouTube videos showing the evolution of written script over time; and nine audio tours available for free download, so that you can use your own iPod or other MP3 player to listen to Museum staff discuss the exhibition as you view it.

During the past year, two Oriental Institute lectures were made available on our website for viewing as downloadable video presentations: "Exploring the Roots of Mesopotamian Civilization: Excavations at Tell Zeidan, Syria," a lecture by Gil Stein; and "Meluhha: The Indus Civilization and Its Contacts with Mesopotamia," a lecture by Mark Kenoyer.

The Research Archives added their June 2010 through April 2011 Acquisitions Lists to the website, and the Oriental Institute's 2009–2010 *Annual Report* was converted to PDF by the Publications Office and added to the website.

And lastly, several Institute scholars added content to their sections of the Individual Scholarship component of the website: John Brinkman, with his Mesopotamian Directory; six articles by Norman Golb; one article by Robert Ritner; as well as the 2010 dissertation of John Nolan and dissertation proposals by Solange Bumbaugh and Robert R. Tate, all submitted to the Department of Near Eastern Languages and Civilizations, the University of Chicago.

Persepolis Fortification Archive

The Computer Lab continued to stay abreast of the scanning operations, imaging, and recording of the Persepolis Fortification Archive (PFA) tablets throughout the year. Up-to-date information about the project's work is available in the Persepolis Fortification Archive component on the Oriental Institute website. Also, for additional information regarding this project, please read the Persepolis Fortification Archive section of this *Annual Report*, where project director Matthew Stolper outlines in detail the current progress of the scanning and cataloging of these most important ancient texts.

Oriental Institute Terabyte Storage Initiative

As I write this *Annual Report* the Institute's terabyte storage system, the OIA (Oriental Institute Archive), now totals 24.98 terabytes (24,980,000,000,000 bytes). For comparison purposes, a typed, double-spaced, 8½" x 11" paper is roughly 2,000 bytes! Currently, 104 faculty, staff, and research project personnel have access to the OIA for archival storage of computer files and images, as well as for daily computer backup. As more of the Institute's historical records, cards, documents, photographs, and publications are converted to digital format the size of our terabyte storage system will continue to expand. I want to take this opportunity to thank Scott Branting, Robert Tate, Elise MacArthur, and the entire CAMEL staff for their assistance in the maintenance and monitoring of this off-site computer storage space.

Laboratory Equipment/Institute Resources

During the past year, due to the increasing size of several Filemaker databases we host, the underlying hardware for our FileMaker server was switched and computer memory and disk capacity were upgraded to 7 GB and 465 GB, respectively. A similar upgrade was also made to the Institute's FTP server, increasing its disk capacity to 465 GB.

A second dedicated FTP server was established this past year for staff and foreign researchers as they prepare materials for the next series of Oriental Institute Nubian Expedition (OINE) publications. The entire publications project is being coordinated by Bruce Williams. Additional personnel working with material from specific Nubian archaeological sites are as follows: the Kasr el-Wizz component of the project includes Artur Obluski, Alexandros

Tsakos, and Edyta Klimaszewska-Drabot as P.I.s; the Serra-Dorginarti component is split into two parts: for Dorginarti, the P.I. is Lisa Heidorn, for Serra, Bruce Williams is the P.I., collaborating with Nadejda Reshetnikova, a Russian architect, for the architecture study, and Don Whitcomb will be conducting a glazed pottery analysis of the Serra material.

* * * * * * * * * *

For further information concerning the above-mentioned research projects and other electronic resources in general, refer to the What's New page on the Oriental Institute's website, at

http://oi.uchicago.edu/news/

See the *Electronic Resources* section of this *Annual Report* for the complete URL to each of the website resources mentioned in this article.

ELECTRONIC RESOURCES

John C. Sanders

Oriental Institute World-Wide Web Site — New and Developing Resources in 2010–2011

(NOTE: all web addresses below are case-sensitive)

Several Oriental Institute units and projects either updated existing pages or became a new presence on the Institute's website during the past year.

ARCHAEOLOGY: Jericho Mafjar Project

The Oriental Institute announces a new archaeology project, the Jericho Mafjar Project, under the direction of Donald Whitcomb. New excavations just underway in the northern areas of Khirbet al-Mafjar, located north of Jericho in the Palestinian territories, will investigate the theory that the site was not just a palace complex, but was instead an incipient Islamic city.

> https://oi.uchicago.edu/getinvolved/donate/adoptadig/jericho.html
> http://jerichomafjarproject.org/

ARCHAEOLOGY: Nubian Expedition

The Nubia Expedition's archaeological fieldwork in 2008 is detailed in a progress report.

> http://oi.uchicago.edu/research/projects/oine/

ARCHAEOLOGY: Tell Edfu Project

The Tell Edfu Project, under the direction of Nadine Moeller, has created a homepage for the project on the Oriental Institute's website, with a brief description of the project's work at the town site of Tell Edfu, several images from their 2009 field season, and a link to the project's independent website.

> http://oi.uchicago.edu/research/projects/edfu/

MUSEUM: Special Exhibits

An image gallery containing more than fifteen photographs of objects from the Oriental Institute Museum's special exhibit Visible Language: Inventions of Writing in the Ancient Middle East and Beyond, is now available on our website. Additionally, four YouTube videos showing the evolution of written script over time have been added to our Museum's current Special Exhibit page.

> http://oi.uchicago.edu/museum/special/writing/

Nine audio tours of the Oriental Institute Museum's exhibit Visible Language: Inventions of Writing in the Ancient Middle East and Beyond are available for free download, so that you can use your own iPod or other MP3 player to listen to Museum staff discuss the exhibition as you view it.

> http://oi.uchicago.edu/museum/tours/audio.html

ORIENTAL INSTITUTE LECTURES

Two Oriental Institute lectures are now available for viewing as downloadable video presentations: "Exploring the Roots of Mesopotamian Civilization: Excavations at Tell Zeidan, Syria," a lecture by Gil Stein; and "Meluhha: The Indus Civilization and Its Contacts with Mesopotamia," a lecture by Mark Kenoyer.

> https://oi.uchicago.edu/getinvolved/member/events/recordings.html

ORIENTAL INSTITUTE SYMPOSIUM

The 2011 Oriental Institute Symposium, Iconoclasm and Text Destruction in the Ancient Near East and Beyond, April 8–9, 2011.

> http://oi.uchicago.edu/research/symposia/2011.html

PHILOLOGY: Chicago Demotic Dictionary

Chicago Demotic Dictionary publishes letter M.

> http://oi.uchicago.edu/research/pubs/catalog/cdd/

Chicago Demotic Dictionary publishes letter P.

> http://oi.uchicago.edu/research/pubs/catalog/cdd/

Chicago Demotic Dictionary publishes letter ᵓI.

> http://oi.uchicago.edu/research/pubs/catalog/cdd/

PHILOLOGY: Epigraphic Survey

An update to their homepage with notes and photographs from the Epigraphic Survey's eighty-sixth season, which ended in April 2010.

> http://oi.uchicago.edu/research/projects/epi/

The Epigraphic Survey's *Chicago House Bulletin*, issue 21 (September 2010), is available for download as a PDF.

> http://oi.uchicago.edu/pdf/chbXXI.pdf

Updates on the status of the Institute's staff and their work in the area around Luxor, Egypt, as the unrest and protests occurred in Cairo in early 2010.

> http://oi.uchicago.edu/research/projects/epi/#news

PUBLIC EDUCATION DEPARTMENT

Examine x-ray images of a real mummy! Become the archaeologist for a virtual Nubian burial site! Decode inscriptions and learn to write in ancient Middle Eastern scripts! History and archaeology come alive when students discover the Oriental Institute Museum collections with *Ancient Artifacts of the Middle East!*, a new educational DVD about ancient Egypt, Nubia, Mesopotamia, Israel, and Turkey.

> https://oi.uchicago.edu/order/suq/index.html#dvd

Wendy Ennes, associate head of Public Education, was recently invited by EDSITEment to write about the Oriental Institute's new resource, Teaching the Middle East: A Resource for Educators. EDSITEment is a partnership among the National Endowment for the Humanities, Verizon Foundation, and the National Trust for the Humanities and is a proud member of the Thinkfinity Consortium of premier educational websites.

> http://edsitement.neh.gov/teaching-middle-east-new-online-resource-educators#node-21647

PUBLICATIONS OFFICE: Electronic Publications

AS 11. *The Sumerian King List*. By Thorkild Jacobsen. Originally published in 1939.

> http://oi.uchicago.edu/research/pubs/catalog/as/as11.html

AS 16. *Studies in Honor of Benno Landsberger on His Seventy-fifth Birthday, April 21, 1963*. Edited by Hans G. Güterbock and Thorkild Jacobsen. Originally published in 1965.

> http://oi.uchicago.edu/research/pubs/catalog/as/as16.html

CHDS1. *Ankara Arkeoloji Müzesinde bulanan Bogazköy Tabletleri II — Bogazköy Tablets in the Archaeological Museum of Ankara II.* By Rukiye Akdoğan and Oğuz Soysal. 2011.

> http://oi.uchicago.edu/research/pubs/catalog/chds/chds1.html

OIC 4. *The Excavation of Armageddon.* By Clarence S. Fisher. Originally published in 1929.

> http://oi.uchicago.edu/research/pubs/catalog/oic/oic4.html

OIC 9. *New Light from Armageddon: Second Provisional Report (1927-29) on the Excavations at Megiddo in Palestine.* By P. L. O. Guy. Originally published in 1931.

> http://oi.uchicago.edu/research/pubs/catalog/oic/oic9.html

OIMP 32. *Visible Language: Inventions of Writing in the Ancient Middle East and Beyond.* Edited by Christopher Woods. 2010.

> http://oi.uchicago.edu/research/pubs/catalog/oimp/oimp32.html

OIMP 33. *Before the Pyramids: The Origins of Egyptian Civilization.* Edited by Emily Tetter. 2011.

> http://oi.uchicago.edu/research/pubs/catalog/oimp/oimp33.html

OIP 2. *The Annals of Sennacherib.* By Daniel David Luckenbill. Originally published in 1924.

> http://oi.uchicago.edu/research/pubs/catalog/oip/oip2.html

OIP 12. *The Proverbs of Solomon in Sahidic Coptic According to the Chicago Manuscript.* Edited by William H. Worrell. Originally published in 1931.

> http://oi.uchicago.edu/research/pubs/catalog/oip/oip12.html

OIP 26. *Material Remains of the Megiddo Cult.* By Herbert Gordon May. Originally published in 1935.

> http://oi.uchicago.edu/research/pubs/catalog/oip/oip26.html

OIP 32. *The Megiddo Water System.* By Robert S. Lamon. Originally published in 1935.

> http://oi.uchicago.edu/research/pubs/catalog/oip/oip32.html

OIP 33. *Megiddo Tombs.* By P. L. O. Guy. Originally published in 1938.

> http://oi.uchicago.edu/research/pubs/catalog/oip/oip33.html

OIP 52. *The Megiddo Ivories.* By Gordon Loud. Originally published in 1939.

> http://oi.uchicago.edu/research/pubs/catalog/oip/oip52.html

OIP 61. Excavations in the Plain of Antioch 1: *The Earlier Assemblages Phases A-J.* By Robert J. Braidwood and Linda S. Braidwood. Originally published in 1960.

> http://oi.uchicago.edu/research/pubs/catalog/oip/oip61.html

OIP 62. Megiddo 2. *Seasons of 1935-39: Text and Plates.* By Gordon Loud. Originally published in 1948.

> http://oi.uchicago.edu/research/pubs/catalog/oip/oip62.html

OIP 133. *Baked Clay Figurines and Votive Beds from Medinet Habu.* By Emily Teeter. 2010.

> http://oi.uchicago.edu/research/pubs/catalog/oip/oip133.html

OIP 137. Tell Hamoukar 1. *Urbanism and Cultural Landscapes in Northeastern Syria: The Tell Hamoukar Survey, 1999–2001.* Jason A. Ur. 2010.

> http://oi.uchicago.edu/research/pubs/catalog/oip/oip137.html

OIS 7. *Slaves and Households in the Near East.* Edited by Laura Culbertson. 2011.

> http://oi.uchicago.edu/research/pubs/catalog/ois/ois7.html

SAOC 17. *Notes on the Megiddo Pottery of Strata VI–XX.* By Geoffrey M. Shipton. Originally published in 1939.

> http://oi.uchicago.edu/research/pubs/catalog/saoc/saoc17.html

Islamic Bindings and Bookmaking. A Catalogue of an Exhibition in the Oriental Institute Museum, University of Chicago, May 18–August 18, 1981. By Gulnar Bosch, John Carswell, and Guy Petherbridge. Originally published in 1981.

> http://oi.uchicago.edu/research/pubs/catalog/misc/bindings.html

The Assyrian Dictionary of the Oriental Institute of the University of Chicago, Vol. 20: *U and W.* Edited by Martha T. Roth. 2010.

> http://oi.uchicago.edu/research/pubs/catalog/cad/

The Babylonian Genesis: The Story of Creation. By Alexander Heidel. Originally published in 1951.

> http://oi.uchicago.edu/research/pubs/catalog/misc/genesis.html

The Gilgamesh Epic and Old Testament Parallels. By Alexander Heidel. Originally published in 1949.

> http://oi.uchicago.edu/research/pubs/catalog/misc/gilgamesh.html

PUBLICATIONS OFFICE: Oriental Institute Annual Reports

Annual Report 2009–2010

> http://oi.uchicago.edu/research/pubs/ar/09-10/

PUBLICATIONS OFFICE: Oriental Institute News & Notes

The Oriental Institute *News & Notes* for 1999 through 2001, summer and fall 2010, winter 2011, and spring 2011 electronic publications in Adobe PDF format

> http://oi.uchicago.edu/research/pubs/nn/

RESEARCH ARCHIVES

Oriental Institute Research Archives Acquisitions Lists:

> http://oi.uchicago.edu/pdf/AcquisitionsList-June2010.pdf
> http://oi.uchicago.edu/pdf/AcquisitionsList-July2010.pdf
> http://oi.uchicago.edu/pdf/AcquisitionsList-August2010.pdf
> http://oi.uchicago.edu/pdf/AcquisitionsList-September2010.pdf
> http://oi.uchicago.edu/pdf/AcquisitionsList-October2010.pdf
> http://oi.uchicago.edu/pdf/AcquisitionsList-November2010.pdf
> http://oi.uchicago.edu/pdf/AcquisitionsList-December2010.pdf
> http://oi.uchicago.edu/pdf/AcquisitionsList-January2011.pdf
> http://oi.uchicago.edu/pdf/AcquisitionsList-February2011.pdf
> http://oi.uchicago.edu/pdf/AcquisitionsList-March2011.pdf
> http://oi.uchicago.edu/pdf/AcquisitionsList-April2011.pdf

INDIVIDUAL SCHOLARSHIP: Department of Near Eastern Languages and Civilizations Dissertations Online

"Mud Sealings and Fourth Dynasty Administration at Giza," a dissertation presented to the Department of Near Eastern Languages and Civilizations, by John S. Nolan. Department of Near Eastern Languages and Civilizations, The University of Chicago, June 2010.

> http://oi.uchicago.edu/research/library/dissertation/nolan.html

Supplemental data supporting John S. Nolan's dissertation.

> http://oi.uchicago.edu/research/is/scholars/nolan/

INDIVIDUAL SCHOLARSHIP: John Brinkman

2011 version of John A. Brinkman's Mesopotamian Directory

> http://oi.uchicago.edu/pdf/MesDir.pdf

INDIVIDUAL SCHOLARSHIP: Norman Golb

"The Mystery of National Geographic's 'Dead Sea Scrolls Mystery Solved?'"

> http://oi.uchicago.edu/pdf/the_mystery_of_national_geographic_solved.pdf

"The M. H. De Young Memorial Museum (San Francisco) Exhibition of the Dead Sea Scrolls (February 26–May 29, 1994) — A Response"

> http://oi.uchicago.edu/pdf/deyoung_dss_exhibit_1994.pdf

"The 'Qumran Sect' Revindicated?"

> http://oi.uchicago.edu/pdf/qumran_conundrum_2.pdf

"The Rabbinic Master Jacob Tam and Events of the Second Crusade at Reims"
> http://oi.uchicago.edu/pdf/the_rabbinic_master_jacob_tam.pdf

"The Role of Personality in the Transfer of Scientific and Philosophical Knowledge from the Eastern Caliphate Westward."
> http://oi.uchicago.edu/pdf/Role of Personality.pdf

"The Caliph's Favorite — New Light from Manuscript Sources on Hasdai ibn Shaprut of Cordova."
> http://oi.uchicago.edu/pdf/ The Caliph's Favorite.pdf

INDIVIDUAL SCHOLARSHIP: Robert Ritner

"An Eternal Curse upon the Reader of These Lines"
> http://oi.uchicago.edu/pdf/eternal_curse.pdf

INDIVIDUAL SCHOLARSHIP: Dissertation proposal(s) accepted by the Department of Near Eastern Languages and Civilizations, University of Chicago.

Solange Bumbaugh, November 2009: "Meroitic Worship of Isis as Seen through the Graffiti of the Dodecaschoenus"

Robert R. Tate, December 2009: "The Seljuk Caravanserais of Anatolia: A GIScience and Landscape Archaeology Study"

* * * * * * * *

Although Charles Jones is no longer in charge of the Oriental Institute's Research Archives, he still actively maintains several vital electronic resources for ancient Near Eastern studies just as he had done during his tenure in Chicago. Thank you, Chuck, for your continuing service to the field and our faculty, staff, and students.

ABZU: Guide to Resources for the Study of the Ancient Near East Available on the Internet

> http://www.etana.org/abzu

ETANA: Electronic Tools and Ancient Near Eastern Archives – Core Texts

A substantial selection of digitized titles from the collections of the Research Archives has been added to the ETANA Core Texts this year.
> http://www.etana.org/coretexts.shtml

IRAQCRISIS

A moderated list for communicating substantive information on cultural property damaged, destroyed, or lost from libraries and museums in Iraq during and after the war in April 2003, and on the worldwide response to the crisis. A component of the Oriental Institute's response to the cultural heritage crisis in the aftermath of the war in Iraq, this list provides a moderated forum for the distribution of information.

> https://listhost.uchicago.edu/mailman/listinfo/iraqcrisis

————————————

PUBLICATIONS OFFICE

Thomas G. Urban

The full-time staff of the Publications Office remains Thomas G. Urban (managing editor) and Leslie Schramer (editor). Rebecca Cain (assistant editor) began her second year in February. Plamena Pehlivanova and Natalie Whiting have moved on, and we are very fortunate to have hired Jessen O'Brien and Zuhal Kuru as editorial assistants.

The Publications Office continues to provide research support to faculty, research associates, projects, and various Units. For example, we offer assistance to faculty and research associates who are having manuscripts published through outside vendors — we help with font issues, publisher jargon, image preparation, and what authors can reasonably expect from publishers. To Units, the Publications Office provides a range of support, from printing over-sized sheets and answering grammatical questions to, as with the Membership and Development Units, publication of *News & Notes*, *Annual Report*, *Visiting Committee Yearbook*, and miscellaneous postcards, brochures, and posters.

The passing of William Sumner stirs a remembrance: in the early 1990s, the printing schedules of the *Annual Report* and *News & Notes* were too difficult to maintain by the Membership Unit. One day, Sumner walked into the Publications Office with a box under his arm and asked whether the Publications Office could produce the *Annual Report*. I said "yes," and he instructed the office to produce them "from now on." One week later Sumner entered with another box and asked whether the office could produce *News & Notes*. Again, I answered in the affirmative, and Sumner instructed the Publications Office to produce them "from now on." Since these brief conversations, the Publications Office has produced nineteen *Annual Reports* (you're reading the twentieth) and seventy-seven issues of *News & Notes*, and all have appeared on schedule. Looking back twenty years, one appreciates the wisdom Sumner expressed those two memorable days. First, editors trained in the production of ancient Near Eastern works are better suited to the task than business-oriented staff. Second, five deadlines a year has been a stabilizing factor in the Publications Office: we know years in advance when projects are due and are able to work in our many other tasks around them — note the eight new titles published this year.

A couple years ago, the Publications Office became the "storehouse" for materials used by the Post-Doc Scholar, which makes sense because we create the posters, programs, announcements — even the name tags for the seminar — and then produce a book with the seminar papers. We also maintain the manual that is to be updated yearly, making it available as needed. We very much enjoyed working with Natalie May this year.

The print publication of this year's *Annual Report* is once again black and white, but we continue to post a color PDF version online. To view past *Annual Reports* and issues of *News & Notes*, visit the following URL on the Oriental Institute website: http://oi.uchicago.edu/research/pubs

Sales

The David Brown Book Company and Oxbow Books, Ltd., UK, continue to represent the Institute for its book distribution. Although a limited number of titles are available for in-house sales in the Suq shop, please note that all external orders for Institute publications should be addressed to: The David Brown Book Company, P.O. Box 511, Oakville, CT 06779; Telephone Toll Free: 1-800-791-9354; Fax: 1-860-945-9468; E-mail: david.brown.bk.co@snet.net; website: www.oxbowbooks.com.

Information related to the sales and distribution of Oriental Institute titles may be obtained via e-mail:

> oi-publications@uchicago.edu

Electronic Publications

As part of the Oriental Institute's Electronic Publications Initiative, all new titles are simultaneously issued in print and as Adobe Acrobat PDF (Portable Document Format) files delivered through the Internet. Older titles are scanned and saved as .tif and .pdf files, with the latter being posted online, as time and funds permit. This year we had sixteen titles scanned and uploaded to the Internet (see list, below).

The bulk of the older titles have been scanned by Northern MicroGraphics (NMT Corporation, http://normicro.com), located in La Crosse, Wisconsin. For the URLs of the sixteen older titles scanned and uploaded to the Internet this year, as well as the URLs for the new titles, see *Electronic Resources* (previous section, this volume).

This year, the Publications Office began collaboration with Elizabeth Stone of Stony Brook University, who is having several older titles scanned as part of Stony Brook's Archive of Mesopotamian Archaeological Site Reports (AMAR) project. The scanning is being done by the Schoenberg Center for Electronic Text and Image at the University of Pennsylvania.

The scanning of the older titles is nearing completion. Thus far we have had about 230 older titles scanned and uploaded to the Internet. About 121 older titles remain to be scanned.

New Volumes Distributed in Print and Online

1. *The Assyrian Dictionary of the Oriental Institute of the University of Chicago*, Volume 20, Letters U and W. 2010. CAD U and W

2. *Baked Clay Figurines and Votive Beds from Medinet Habu.* By Emily Teeter. 2010. OIP 133

3. *The Chicago House Bulletin.* Edited by W. Raymond Johnson. 2010. CHB 21

4. *The Oriental Institute 2009-2010 Annual Report.* Edited by Gil J. Stein. 2010. AR 2009-2010

5. Tell Hamoukar, Volume 1. *Urbanism and Cultural Landscapes in Northeastern Syria: The Tell Hamoukar Survey, 1999-2001.* By Jason Ur. 2010. OIP 137

6. *Visible Language: Inventions of Writing in the Ancient Middle East and Beyond.* Edited by Christopher Woods. 2010. OIMP 32

7. *Ankara Arkeoloji Müzesinde bulanan Boğazköy Tabletleri II / Boğazköy Tablets in the Archaeological Museum of Ankara II.* By Rukiye Akdoğan and Oğuz Soysal. 2011. CHDS 1

8. *Before the Pyramids: The Origins of Egyptian Civilization.* Edited by Emily Teeter. 2011. OIMP 33

9. *Slaves and Households in the Near East.* Edited by Laura Culbertson. 2011. OIS 7

10-13. *The Oriental Institute News & Notes.* Edited by Maeve Reed. Summer 2010–Spring 2011. NN 206–209

New Volumes Distributed Online

1. *The Demotic Dictionary of the Oriental Institute of the University of Chicago,* Letter P. Edited by Janet H. Johnson. CDD P

2. *The Demotic Dictionary of the Oriental Institute of the University of Chicago,* Letter M. Edited by Janet H. Johnson. CDD M

3. *The Demotic Dictionary of the Oriental Institute of the University of Chicago,* Letter ʾI. Edited by Janet H. Johnson. CDD ʾI

Digital Reprints of Scanned, Older Titles

1. Persepolis 2. *Contents of the Treasury and Other Discoveries.* By Erich F. Schmidt with contributions by Sydney P. Noe, Frederick R. Matson, Lawrence J. Howell, and Louisa Bellinger. Originally published in 1957. OIP 69

2. *The Egyptian Book of the Dead: Documents in the Oriental Institute Museum at the University of Chicago.* Edited by Thomas George Allen. Originally published in 1960. OIP 82

Older Titles Scanned and Uploaded to the Online Publications Catalog

1. *Annals of Sennacherib.* By Daniel David Luckenbill. Originally published in 1924. OIP 2

2. *The Babylonian Genesis: The Story of Creation.* By Alexander Heidel. Originally published in 1951. MISC Genesis

3. Excavations in the Plain of Antioch 1: *The Earlier Assemblages Phases A–J.* By Robert J. Braidwood and Linda S. Braidwood. Originally published in 1960. OIP 61

4. *The Excavation of Armageddon.* By Clarence S. Fisher. Originally published in 1929. OIC 4

5. *The Gilgamesh Epic and Old Testament Parallels.* By Alexander Heidel. Originally published in 1949. MISC Gilgamesh

6. *Islamic Bindings and Bookmaking: A Catalogue of an Exhibition in the Oriental Institute Museum, University of Chicago, May 18–August 18, 1981.* By Gulnar Bosch, John Carswell, and Guy Petherbridge. Originally published in 1981. MISC Bindings

7. *Material Remains of the Megiddo Cult.* By Herbert Gordon May. Originally published in 1935. OIP 26

8. *The Megiddo Ivories.* By Gordon Loud. Originally published in 1939. OIP 52

9. Megiddo 2. *Seasons of 1935–39: Text and Plates.* By Gordon Loud. Originally published in 1948. OIP 62

10. *Megiddo Tombs.* By P. L. O. Guy. Originally published in 1938. OIP 33

11. *The Megiddo Water System.* By Robert S. Lamon. Originally published in 1935. OIP 32

12. *New Light from Armageddon: Second Provisional Report (1927–29) on the Excavations at Megiddo in Palestine.* By P. L. O. Guy. Originally published in 1931. OIC 9

13. *Notes on the Megiddo Pottery of Strata VI–XX.* By Geoffrey M. Shipton. Originally published in 1939. SAOC 17

14. *The Proverbs of Solomon in Sahidic Coptic According to the Chicago Manuscript.* Edited by William H. Worrell. Originally published in 1931. OIP 12

15. *Studies in Honor of Benno Landsberger on His Seventy-fifth Birthday, April 21, 1963.* Edited by Hans G. Güterbock and Thorkild Jacobsen. Originally published in 1965. AS 16

16. *The Sumerian King List.* By Thorkild Jacobsen. Originally published in 1939. AS 11

Volumes in Preparation

1. *Ancient Israel: Cultural Crossroads of the Ancient Near East.* Gabrielle Novacek

2. *Bismaya: Recovering the Lost City of Adab.* Karen L. Wilson

3. *Grammatical Case in the Languages of the Middle East and Europe* (Acts of the International Colloquium Variations, Concurrence et Evolution des Cas dans divers Domaines Linguistiques, Paris, 2–4 April 2007). Edited by Michèle Fruyt, Dennis Pardee, and Michel Mazoyer

4. *The Monumental Complex of King Ahmose at Abydos,* Volume 1: *The Pyramid Temple of Ahmose and Its Environs: Architecture and Decoration.* Stephen P. Harvey

5. *Perspectives on Ptolemaic Thebes.* Edited by Peter F. Dorman and Betsy M. Bryan

6. *Pesher Naḥum: Texts and Studies in Jewish History and Literature from Antiquity through the Middle Ages Presented to Norman Golb.* Edited by Joel L. Kraemer and Michael G. Wechsler, with Fred Donner, Joshua Holo, and Dennis Pardee

———————————

RESEARCH ARCHIVES

Foy Scalf

I have always imagined that paradise will be a kind of library.
— Jorge Luis Borges

Introduction

The recent passing of former Oriental Institute director William Sumner should give us pause, reminding us about the life and legacy of the Institute and its community.[1] With our centennial anniversary quickly approaching, the loss of another distinguished scholar and fundamental personality is certainly more tragic. Much of the history that occurred within our walls will be taken into the beyond by those who experienced it — unless we take steps to preserve and record it, just like the records of the ancient civilizations we study. Current generations would do well to listen closely to the former directors who remain among us as they pass down the intimate history of our fields through stories that rarely find their way into print.

A narrative history of the Oriental Institute has never been written. In 1933, James Henry Breasted published *The Oriental Institute* as volume 12 of the University of Chicago Survey at the request of the survey director.[2] The publication came fortuitously only two years after the opening of the new building on the corner of East 58th Street and South University Avenue. During the opening ceremony Ramond B. Fosdick, a long-time Rockefeller associate, lauded Breasted through an invocation of Emerson, referring to the Institute as "... the lengthened shadow of a man."[3] In *The Oriental Institute*, Breasted magisterially detailed what he called "... the scope, character, and purpose of the Oriental Institute ...," but with only fourteen years since the 1919 foundation, not enough time had elapsed to inspire the sweeping narratives for which Breasted's historical works became renowned.[4]

Since 1933 there have been few attempts to synthesize the history of the Oriental Institute and students have been forced to comb through years of Oriental Institute annual reports and miscellaneous publications in order to pull together the dynamics of interpersonal relationships as well as the impact of the Institute within

William M. Sumner, 1928–2011. Oriental Institute Director, 1989–1997

Groundbreaking ceremony for the Oriental Institute, archival photographic files
apf2-05471, Special Collections Research Center, University of Chicago Library

the larger intellectual world.[5] The illuminating exception is Erica Reiner's *An Adventure of Great Dimension*, which has taken on renewed importance as the Chicago Assyrian Dictionary Project has come to a close.[6] No publication before or since has so opened the doors of the Institute in order to provide glimpses of the personalities inside, their ingeniousness as well as personal shortcomings. It is a rarity to learn so much about the individuals fueling our discipline, those who are generally known only through their printed words and projects.

Although these publications have provided splendid insights into various corners of the world of the Oriental Institute, the passing of a former director and the approaching centennial compel us to reconsider the many important contributions and intellectual impact made over the last 100 years. The significance of such an institution cannot be over emphasized and even today we remain in many ways at the forefront of the field, both in terms of scholarship as evidenced by our many philology and archaeology projects and publications, but also in terms of stewardship as we lead a new generation toward open access by making all Oriental Institute publications available in free digital formats. Over the next eight years, those of us in the Research Archives will not only rigorously work to develop new methods and research tools to better serve our academic and public community, we will also be reflecting about the incredible contributions of past generations that laid the foundation on which we stand. It is that foundation which has made the following goals for 2011–2012 possible.

Goals for 2011-2012

1. Implementation of the Integrated Database

A significant amount of time and energy in 2010–2011 went into the Integrated Database Project. In consultation with John Sanders, Scott Branting, Helen McDonald, and Angela Spinazze, the Research Archives produced a series of documents detailing our current database configuration and the provisional design of the new database relevant to the Research Archives. We are in the process of producing a full data migration map and associated narrative for KE Software engineers to migrate our data into the new system. In addition, we have produced a basic web design template for Alan Takaoka and the University's Information Technology Services (ITS) department for front-end implementation allowing public access to the new Research Archives catalog module with the EMu software client.

While this task has taken an incredible number of hours to complete, there remains an enormous amount of work, the exact size of which is indeterminate and will only be clear once data migration has taken place. There are two major factors that will complicate data migration for the Research Archives: 1) the current database is "flat," that is, it does not have a hierarchy of records indicating that one record belongs to another (e.g., that a journal article belongs to a journal) and 2) the legacy issue of how data has been entered into our database and how it is processed.

The lack of hierarchy in our current system has important implications for database development. In the new system, a hierarchy will govern all our records so that navigation between a journal article and the journal or between a book chapter and the book to which it belongs will be quick and easy. All the records will be "linked" together in parental relationships so users will easily be able to toggle between a record and its "parents" and/or "children." For example, a journal will be the parent of a journal volume which itself will be the parent of a journal article.

Before that hierarchy can be created, however, the data will have to be "cleaned" after migration because of legacy issues. Data currently kept in certain fields in the Research Archives catalog will need to be cut and placed in separate fields within the new client software. This process will be partially automated, but the complex and inconsistent nature of the data means that only a portion of that automation will end successfully. At this point, it is difficult to predict how successful that step will be. Whatever data is not migrated into the appropriate fields will need to be manually copied and pasted into the appropriate fields. For the journals (250,000 records) and serials (32,000 records), we are hopeful that the migration process will result in accurate data mapping. However, that leaves over 100,000 records that will be in need of manual data cleaning, nearly equivalent to re-cataloging all 100,000 records. To complete such a monumental undertaking in a reasonable amount of time, we will need to devote as many people as possible to the task. The major goal for 2011–2012 is the transition, data migration, data clean-up, and website development for implementation of the integrated database software.

2. Installation of Compact Storage in Monograph Suite

The Research Archives has been awarded a budget request for the installation of compact storage in the monograph suite. Initial evaluations will take place throughout the academic year of 2011–2012 with proposed installation in the summer of 2012. Compact storage will allow us to double the amount of shelving space available in the monograph suite, thereby ensuring our continued growth for the next fifteen to twenty years, or 15,000–20,000 additional volumes. Space is ever a premium in the Oriental Institute and the staff of the Research Archives would like to thank Steve Camp and Gil Stein for all their help in making this project a success.

Acquisitions

As predicted in last year's annual report, there was a slight decrease in the number of volumes acquired during 2010–2011. However, acquisitioning efforts have remained strong in the past fiscal year (see table 1). Historically, our acquisition rate can be estimated at 1,000 volumes per year. Our acquisition of 1,012 volumes is a decline by approximately 100–200 volumes from the last two years, during which we acquired nearly 1,200 volumes each year. The decline can be attributed to several factors: an increase in the appearance of costly volumes, an attempt to catch up on two expensive series, and a minor increase in infrastructure costs for the year (increase in labor, repairs to equipment). Despite these declines, the Research Archives continues its commitment to acquire the references crucial to Oriental Institute staff, faculty, students, and Members.

Table 1. Research Archives acquisitions, July 2010–June 2011

Month	Monographs, Series, Pamphlets	Journals	Total
July 2010	62	26	88
August 2010	43	36	79
September 2010	58	39	97
October 2010	128	28	156
November 2010	130	18	148
December 2010	71	33	104
January 2011	46	20	66
February 2011	35	24	59
March 2011	43	25	68
April 2011	45	34	79
May 2011	21	17	38
June 2011	15	15	30
Totals	697	315	1,012
Total Volumes			1,012

Online Catalog

From July 1, 2010, to June 30, 2011, the Research Archives online catalog has grown by 30,000 records, from 360,000 to 390,000 analytic records (see table 2). Although this number has declined (for reasons detailed above) from levels reached during 2007–2009 at the height of our importation of metadata from online database sources, we are still tripling the average number of records added from 2004 levels. With the series and monographs completed, we have turned our attention to cataloging the journals. We currently have several projects on-going, only some of which are reflected in the table below. Over the past year, we have had two volunteers (Roberta Schaffner and Andrea Dudek) working on a comprehensive inventory of our journal collection. This does not add many records to the database because they are not cataloging the individual articles from the journals, but until this project a complete inventory of our collection has not existed. The project is approximately 50 percent completed and once finished it will provide a complete and searchable index of the journal volumes (not articles) in our collection within the library catalog.

Table 2. Catalog records

Year	Number of Catalog Records Added	Total Number of Catalog Records
2010–2011	30,000	390,000
2009–2010	40,000	360,000
2008–2009	63,000	320,000
2007–2008	62,000	257,000
2006–2007	28,000	195,000
—	—	—
2003–2004	10,000	130,000

In addition, we have furthered our project of adding links to individual catalog entries and continue to add links to all online material for newly acquired volumes. As more volumes become available online, our backlist of links to be added grows steadily. Currently, there are over 100,000 links to online material in the catalog, with over 98,000 links to journal articles alone (see table 3). Twenty-five percent of all the records in the database now link to versions available online or copies available for download from our library server.

Table 3. Links to online journal articles

Call Number	Journal	Links	Access
JAOS	Journal of the American Oriental Society	14,690	JSTOR
CBQ	Catholic Biblical Quarterly	11,425	Ebsco
ANT	Antiquity	11,079	Antiquity
AJA	American Journal of Archaeology	10,996	JSTOR/AJA
Syria	Syria	5,657	JSTOR
JNES	Journal of Near Eastern Studies	4,748	JSTOR/JNES
ZPE	Zeitschrift für Papyrologie und Epigraphik	4,619	JSTOR
JEA	Journal of Egyptian Archaeology	4,105	JSTOR
Bib	Biblica	3,510	Open
BASOR	Bulletin of the American School of Oriental Research	3,280	JSTOR
PEQ	Palestine Exploration Quarterly	3,254	Ebsco
ZDMG	Zeitschrift der Deutschen Morgenländischen Gesellschaft	3,219	Open
ZA	Zeitschrift für Assyriologie	2,443	Open
CRAIBL	Académie des inscriptions et belles-lettres. Comptes rendus	2,254	Open
BIAR	Near Eastern Archaeology (formerly Biblical Archaeologist)	2,017	JSTOR
JESHO	Journal of the Economic and Social History of the Orient	1,444	JSTOR
BIFAO	Bulletin de l'Institut Français d'Archéologie Orientale	1,666	Open
JARCE	Journal of the American Research Center in Egypt	1,158	JSTOR
RBL	Review of Biblical Literature	1,084	Open
JCS	Journal of Cuneiform Studies	992	JSTOR
IRQ	Iraq	980	JSTOR
ANS	Anatolian Studies	724	JSTOR
FUB	Forschungen und Berichte	673	JSTOR
IRN	Iran	670	JSTOR
JANES	Journal of the Ancient Near Eastern Society	435	Open
Orj	Orient: Report of the Society for Near Eastern Studies in Japan	369	Open
ARO	Ars Orientalis	315	JSTOR
BSEG	Bulletin: Société d'Egyptologie Geneve	259	Open
KAR	Cahiers de Karnak	89	Open

Table 3. Links to online journal articles (cont.)

Call Number	Journal	Links	Access
BMSEAS	Bristish Museum Studies in Ancient Egypt and Sudan	64	Open
LingAeg	Lingua Aegyptia	47	Open
ARTA	Achaemenid Research on Texts and Archaeology	34	Open
StOr	Studia Orontica	32	Open
CDLJ	Cuneiform Digital Library Journal	29	Open
ENiM	Égypte Nilotique et Méditerranéenne	21	Open
CDLB	Cuneiform Digital Library Bulletin	20	Open
CDLN	Cuneiform Digital Library Notes	13	Open
	Total	98,325	

Resources on the Web

In addition to the online catalog, the Research Archives maintains a series of open access online resources.

Introduction and Guide

http://oi.uchicago.edu/pdf/research_archives_introduction&guide.pdf

An updated introduction and guide to the Research Archives contains a brief history, a guide to the Research Archives collection, and instructions for using the online catalog.

Dissertations

http://oi.uchicago.edu/research/library/dissertation/

With the permission of the authors, the Research Archives provides access to Adobe Portable Document Format (PDF) copies of dissertations completed in the Department of Near Eastern Languages and Civilizations of the University of Chicago. The following were added during the 2009–2010 academic year:

John S. Nolan. "Mud Sealings and Fourth Dynasty Administration at Giza." PhD dissertation. Chicago, 2010.

http://oi.uchicago.edu/research/library/dissertation/nolan.html

Dissertation Proposals

http://oi.uchicago.edu/research/library/dissertation/proposals/

With the permission of the authors, the Research Archives provides access to PDF copies of dissertation proposals completed in the Department of Near Eastern Languages and Civilizations of the University of Chicago. The following were added during the 2009–2010 academic year:

> Solange Bumbaugh. "Meroitic Worship of Isis as Seen through the Graffiti of the Dodecaschoenus." PhD proposal. 2009.

> Tate Paulette. "Magazines, Models, and Artificial Societies: The Archaeology of Grain Storage in Third-Millennium Northern Mesopotamia." PhD proposal. 2007.

> Robert Tate. "The Seljuk Caravanserais of Anatolia: A GIScience and Landscape Archaeology Study." PhD proposal. 2009.

Acquisitions Lists

> http://oi.uchicago.edu/research/library/acquisitions.html

The acquisitions reports of the Research Archives are distributed as PDFs on a monthly basis. This process has been active and continuative since September 2007.

Annual Reports

> http://oi.uchicago.edu/research/library/annualreports.html

Annual reports for the Research Archives are available from 1991 to 2010.

Networking Sites

> http://www.facebook.com/pages/Research-Archives-of-the-Oriental-Institute/153645450792?ref=ts

The Research Archives now maintains an official page on Facebook. Information about recent publications of Oriental Institute scholars or reviews of recent Oriental Institute publications is distributed through this page. Eight hundred fifty-seven fans currently follow the Research Archives through this presence on Facebook.

Monographs

> http://oilib.uchicago.edu

Copies of out-of-copyright monographs have been scanned and are made available as PDFs through links in the online catalog of the Research Archives. As of June 2011, the Research Archives provides access to over 200 volumes. A selection of recent additions follows:

> E. Douglas van Buren. *The Fauna of Ancient Mesopotamia as Represented in Art.* Analecta Orientalia 18. Rome: Pontificium Institutm Biblicum, 1939.

> Georges Dossin. *Correspondance de Šamši-Addu et de ses fils.* Archives Royales de Mari 1. Paris: Imprimerie Nationale, 1950.

> Charles-F. Jean. *Lettres Diverses.* Archives Royales de Mari 2. Paris: Imprimerie Nationale, 1950.

> J. R. Kupper. *Correspondance de Kibri-Dagan, Gouverneur de Terqa.* Archives Royales de Mari 3. Paris: Imprimerie Nationale, 1950.

> N. Schneider. *Die Götternamen von Ur III.* Analecta Orientalia 19. Rome: Pontificium Institutum Biblicum, 1939.

Adopt-a-Journal

http://oi.uchicago.edu/research/library/adopt-a-journal.html

The Research Archives has launched an "Adopt-a-Journal" campaign in order to increase support for the Research Archives. Donors are recognized through personalized book plates made in their honor and placed in volumes of their choosing. The following volumes were adopted on behalf of the Research Archives during the past year:

Between the Cataracts (Proceedings of the 11th Conference for Nubian Studies. Warsaw University, 27 August–2 September 2006), Part 2, Fascicle 1: *Session Papers.* Warsaw: Warsaw University Press, 2010.

Adopter: Andrea Dudek

Between the Cataracts (Proceedings of the 11th Conference for Nubian Studies. Warsaw University, 27 August–2 September 2006), Part 2, Fascicle 2: *Session Papers.* Warsaw: Warsaw University Press, 2010.

Adopter: Andrea Dudek

Francesca Rochberg. *In the Path of the Moon: Babylonian Celestial Divination and Its Legacy.* Studies in Ancient Magic and Divination 6. Leiden: Brill, 2010.

Adopter: Joan Fortune

Hermann Knuf, Christian Leitz, and Daniel von Recklinghausen (eds.). *Honi soit qui mal y pense. Studien zum pharaonischen, griechisch-römischen und spätantiken Ägypten zu Ehren von Heinz-Josef Thissen.* Orientalia Lovaniensia Analecta 194. Leuven: Peeters, 2010.

Adopter: Joan Fortune

Visitors

The Research Archives is a popular place for visiting scholars and we have had the pleasure to accommodate the research trips of many individuals, including (in alphabetical order): Amar Annus, Richard Averbeck, Nicole Brisch, A. J. Cave, Günter Dreyer, Stephen Durchslag, Jack Green, Wouter Henkelman, Isaac Kalimi, Sandra Knudsen, Jacob Lauinger, Natalie May, Adam Miglio, Cynthia Miller-Naude, Nora al Naim, John Nielsen, Stephanie Rost, Tsubasa Sakamoto, Seth Sanders, JoAnn Scurlock, Julie Stauder, Andréas Stauder, Susan Steffen and students from Elmhurst College, Jessica deVega, Joan Westenholz, and Magnus Widell.

Acknowledgments

The heart of the Research Archives beats through collaboration and relationships with many individuals and institutions. I remain thankful for the support continually received from my predecessors Chuck Jones and Magnus Widell. The Oriental Institute community also plays a very important part in our successes. Tom Urban and Leslie Schramer in the Oriental Institute Publications Office have been most gracious in aiding our exchange relationships. Likewise, Chris Woods, Kathleen Mineck, and Drew Baumann of the *Journal of Near Eastern Studies* continue to make it possible for us to acquire volumes we would otherwise lack. I would like to further acknowledge here the generous donations and help from the following (in alphabetical order): Abbas Alizadeh, Steve Camp, Fred Donner, Andrea Dudek, Geoff Emberling, Joan Fortune, Mary Louise Jackowicz, Martha Roth, Gil Stein, Emily Teeter, Donald Whitcomb, and Bruce Williams.

As always, it would be impossible to accomplish what we have without the blood, sweat, and (hopefully few) tears shed by the Research Archives staff. NELC graduate student Laura Holzweg continued what has become a lengthy service to the Research Archives, performing a variety of duties including cataloging journals and new acquisitions, data clean-up, and she helps dearly with the messy problem of Arabic language publications. With her lightning speed cataloging skills, Jill Waller, an undergraduate at the University moving into her senior year, may have produced the most new records while cataloging new acquisitions and retrospective journals. Monique Vincent, another NELC graduate student, made tremendous strides in the retrospective cataloging of journals before moving on to focus on her PhD studies. I would like to thank them for all their help, hard work, dependability, and collegiality.

Although we don't pay them, volunteers for the Research Archives have become increasingly important over the last year. During 2010–2011, Volunteer Ray Broms scanned fifty-nine volumes from the Research Archives collection. These PDF copies are now hosted on the Research Archives server and can be accessed through links in the online catalog, bringing the total number of volumes accessible in this fashion to 200. Stephanie Duran spent many hours cataloging articles from *Archaeology Magazine*. Roberta Schaffner and Andrea Dudek are working on a comprehensive inventory of our journal collection. Without them, the Research Archives would suffer, and we appreciate them greatly.

Notes

[1] An obituary by William Harms appeared in the University of Chicago news on July 12, 2011, and was accessed here: http://news.uchicago.edu/article/2011/07/12/william-sumner-director-emeritus-oriental-institute-1928-2011.

[2] James Henry Breasted. *The Oriental Institute*. Chicago: University of Chicago Press, 1933. This followed his publication of "The Oriental Institute of the University of Chicago: A Beginning and a Program," *American Journal of Semitic Languages and Literatures* 38/4 (1922): 233–328, reprinted as volume 1 of the series Oriental Institute Communications.

[3] *Addresses Delivered at the Dedication and Opening of the New Oriental Institute Building, December 5, 1931*, reprinted from the University Record for January 6, 1932. The quote references Ralph Waldo Emerson's essay "Self-Reliance," published in 1841.

[4] For example, Ralph A. Habas reviewed Breasted's *The Dawn of Conscience* (New York: Charles Scribner's Sons, 1933) for the *Jewish Quarterly Review* 25/2 (1934): 153–54, stating: "Dr. Breasted uses his remarkable literary gifts to the hilt and livens up his materials with illustrations and allusions closely related to our own life and thinking. It is refreshing indeed to find a distinguished and scholarly work studded with brisk references to current phenomena like Tammany Hall, the Eighteenth Amendment, Technocracy, H. L. Mencken, Al Capone, Spengler, the Radio and the Depression of 1933. This reviewer can think of few first-rank historians in the Oriental field who can handle words as neatly and effortlessly as Dr. Breasted. Few of our popularizers, moreover, can boast of a more serviceable style. Only two or three times does the author slip up in the present work and let his rhetoric get the best of him, as when he uses old-maidish expressions like 'Father Man' and 'the Delectable Mountains'; but the lapses in question are not serious." In *Art World* 3/4 (1918): 337, *Breasted's Ancient Times: A History of the Early World* (Boston: Ginn & Company, 1916) is described as "… a model text-book of the sort, in which the curious student can never complain of dryness of style or that impression of lack of proportion which is often made by able and excellent works that deal with kindred subjects."

[5] There are many publications devoted to specific episodes in the history of the Oriental Institute, for example, Geoff Emberling (ed.), *Pioneers to the Past: American Archaeologists in the Middle East, 1919-1920*, Oriental Institute Museum Publications 30 (Chicago: The Oriental Institute, 2010), but few of them attempt to place the people and contributions of the Oriental Institute within a discussion of the impact in the broader intellectual world.

[6] Erica Reiner, *An Adventure of Great Dimension: The Launching of the Chicago Assyrian Dictionary* (Philadelphia: American Philosophical Society, 2002). The final volume of the dictionary appeared in 2010 as *The Assyrian Dictionary of the Oriental Institute of the University of Chicago*, Volume 20, Letters U and W (Chicago: The Oriental Institute, 2010). The completion of the dictionary was memorialized by Martha T. Roth, "How We Wrote the Chicago Assyrian Dictionary," *Journal of Near Eastern Studies* 69/1 (April 2010): 1–21, who relied partially on the "oral legacy" of long-time editor Erica Reiner.

TABLET COLLECTION

Andrew Dix

During the past year the Tablet Room hosted a dozen scholars from around the world who visited to work on cuneiform texts in the Oriental Institute's Tablet Collection. Nicole Brisch of Cambridge University, Richard Zettler, a University of Chicago graduate and currently professor of archaeology at the University of Pennsylvania, and Christine Proust of the Institut Méditerranéen de Recherches Avancées in Marseille, each conducted a research project on tablets excavated at Nippur by the Oriental Institute. Aage Westenholz of the University of Copenhagen visited to study the Early Dynastic and Old Akkadian tablets in the Tablet Collection. Lance Allred of the Cuneiform Digital Library Initiative, based at the University of California, Los Angeles, scanned published tablets from the collection, which will be made available online. Digital photographs of tablets, made possible by funds from the James Henry Breasted Society, allowed scholars not able to physically visit Chicago to study texts housed in the Oriental Institute.

Greg Gibson, on behalf of the heirs of Joseph W. Gibson, recently donated seven tablets to the Tablet Collection. Walter Farber, Oriental Institute professor of Assyriology and curator of the Tablet Collection, and Gertrud Farber, Oriental Institute research associate, are collaborating to publish the tablets, one of which will shortly appear on display in the Oriental Institute Museum.

MUSEUM

The Museum continues to be a hub of frenetic activity with special exhibits, improvements to the galleries, archives, and storage areas, the implementation of conservation grants, loans in and out, accommodating visiting researchers, filling photo orders, and record sales at the Suq. Details of the activities of each section of the Museum are found in the following pages.

In contrast to the continuity of the Museum's programs and activities, we regret to report a major change: the departure of Chief Curator Geoff Emberling, in mid-October 2010. The Museum prospered and matured under Geoff's leadership. He completed the reinstallation of the permanent galleries and then instituted the special exhibits program, overseeing nine exhibits over his six-year tenure at the museum. Under his guidance, the special exhibits matured as procedures for their review and implementation were established. The exhibits became more complex and professional, with exhaustive and attractive catalogs and, more recently, with audio guides and interactive components. Working in partnership with Director Gil Stein, Geoff led the Museum forward on the adoption of an integrated database that will change the way the entire Oriental Institute will work, conduct research, and interact with scholars and the public. It was a very important six years for the Museum. We all wish Geoff the very best in the next phase of his career.

By the time this report is published, we will have welcomed Jack Green, formerly of the Ashmolean Museum, University of Oxford, as our new chief curator. The Museum staff looks forward to working with Jack on the many aspects of Museum operations and exhibits.

SPECIAL EXHIBITS

Emily Teeter

In the period covered by this report, three special exhibits were presented in the Doris Holleb Family Gallery for Special Exhibits: Pioneers to the Past (closed August 29, 2010); Visible Language: Inventions of Writing in the Ancient Middle East and Beyond (September 28, 2010, to March 6, 2011), and Before the Pyramids: The Origins of Egyptian Civilization (opened March 29, and will close on December 31, 2011). For details of the Pioneers show, see the 2009–2010 *Annual Report*, pages 166–68.

The Visible Language exhibit was a perfect way to share the more recent research on the origins of writing. Sumerologist and Oriental Institute Associate Professor Christopher Woods was the curator, assisted by Oya Topçuoğlu, Elise MacArthur, Geoff Emberling, and myself. A major theme of the exhibit was the current theory that there are four pristine writing systems originating in Mesopotamia, Egypt, China, and Mesoamerica, and that all other scripts were derived from these four. Another important message amplifying that theme was that the perceived similarities between the Sumerian and Egyptian writing systems are not due to diffusion, but rather to the fact that early scripts inherently share certain

Figure 1. View of the Visible Language exhibit. Photo by Anna Ressman

features. A third point was that writing in Egypt, which traditionally has been viewed as a later development than writing in Mesopotamia, is in fact contemporary with it — both scripts appearing around 3200 BC. It was an exhibit that, as I told many visitors, proved that everything we had learned in school was now obsolete. And that is why our special exhibits matter.

The show was very complex, and ultimately it included 105 objects, including loans from the Vorderasiatisches Museum Berlin, Yale, the Semitic Museum of Harvard University, the Art Institute of Chicago, and the Smart Museum of Art. Among the loans were a fine eleventh-century BC *gui* (bronze grain vessel), Chinese oracle bones, and a Mayan cylinder stone incised with hieroglyphs. The to-ing and fro-ing of the couriers, and arranging their travel, lodging, and per diems, kept our registrar Helen McDonald even busier than usual.

The installation (fig. 1), designed by Brian Zimerle and Erik Lindahl, posed its own challenges with so many small objects with almost a seemingly inverse relationship between size and importance. Among the smallest artifacts were the Uruk IV tablets from Berlin, perhaps the earliest writing from Mesopotamia, and a tiny numerical tag from tomb U-j at Abydos. The judicious use of diagrams (fig. 2) allowed visitors to appreciate these gems.

A fun and useful feature was the overhead projection of (the hands of) Ray Johnson painting hieroglyphs on papyrus and Theo van den Hout incising Hittite cuneiform on a clay tablet (view at: http://www.youtube.com/watch?v=LoqavHDlKZ0). Theo and Foy Scalf made brief films discussing scribes and writing in Anatolia and Egypt, respectively (now at: http://www.youtube.com/watch?v=LoqavHDlKZ0 and http://www.youtube.com/watch?v=HuzoE0qod9g). These very popular films were shown on an interactive kiosk in the gallery and they were watched by more than a thousand others on YouTube. One of the most popular features was the development of alphabetic signs designed by Tom James (http://www.youtube.com/watch?v=XPzQWYlRmXE&feature=relmfu), that showed an Egyptian hieroglyph gradually morphing into a Greek letter. The exhibit had an audio guide produced by Tiffany Salone of Chicago Media Initiatives Group. Thanks to Tom James for loading the files and images onto our iPods and to the Suq for handling iPod rentals. That audio (along with others) can be downloaded at: http://oi.uchicago.edu/museum/tours/audio.html.

The Visible Language catalog, edited by Chris Woods, proved to be a substantial resource because many of the essays reflect the most current state of knowledge of the origins of writing and the nature of early scripts. Anna Ressman handled the huge photo request with aplomb and efficiency, and Tom Urban and Leslie Schramer, aided by other Oriental Institute staff members, transformed the very complicated manuscript and images into a beautiful book with a striking cover that was designed by Dianne Hanau-Strain. The catalog continues to sell very briskly, and the 1,500 copies we printed are almost sold out.

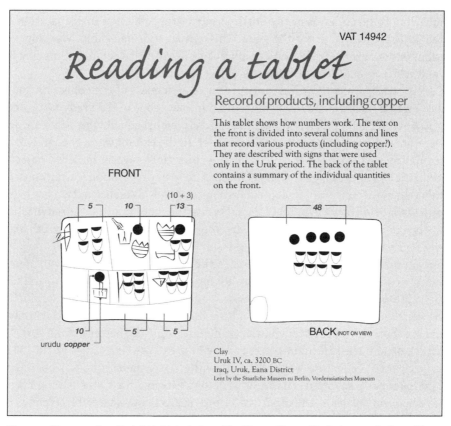

Figure 2. Diagram of an Uruk IV tablet, designed by Dianne Hanau-Strain in consultation with Chris Woods and Geoff Emberling

The Visible Language show received a huge amount of favorable press coverage, including the *New York Times* (see separate *Publicity* report). Attendance and sales at the Suq were up markedly as a result. Denise Browning, manager of the Suq, who is often the eyes and ears for the Museum concerning visitors' reactions to our exhibits, reported that she repeatedly heard positive comments about the show and how much our visitors enjoyed the challenging nature of the material.

In July 2010, the Museum advisory group, consisting of Randy Adamsick, Nathan Mason, Angela Adams, Molly Woulfe, Beverly Serrell, Matt Matcuk, Dianne Hanau-Strain, Mike Shea, and Patty McNamara, met with Geoff, Emily, Carole Krucoff, and Wendy Ennes to review the early plans for the show. After it opened, most of the same group convened to critique it, making very valuable comments about its structure and presentation.

We are grateful to the funders of this important exhibit: Exelon Corporation, the Women's Board of the University of Chicago, the T. Kimball Brooker Foundation, Judy and David Harris, the Rhoades Foundation, Catherine Moore, the Rita Picken Memorial Fund, Mary and Charles Shea in memory of Rita Picken, Toni Smith, and Anna White. We have to raise the funds for each exhibit, and your support is appreciated and essential for the success of our exhibits program.

We had the luxury of several years of preparation for Before the Pyramids: The Origins of Egyptian Civilization (March 29–December 31, 2011). In early 2009, Museum Assistant Noelle Timbart and Assistant Registrar Susan Alison implemented a project originated by

Geoff Emberling to take photos of the entire Predynastic collection in preparation for the integrated database as well as for the show. This was an enormous help. Working with the registration lists of objects, I could pull up photos from my office computer, making it much quicker and easier to make the preliminary object selection.

The decision to do this show was motivated by the richness of our collection and by the desire to showcase the tremendous advances in our knowledge of the Predynastic and Early Dynastic periods in Egypt. Much of the new research is published in highly academic journals and is therefore not accessible to the general reader, so the exhibit was a good way to convey new information to a wide audience. As for the collection, several hundred objects were exhibited in the old Egyptian gallery that closed in 1996 in preparation for the construction and installation of the new climate-control systems, and only a small selection are in the new Joseph and Mary Grimshaw Egyptian Gallery. Most of the more than 3,000 Predynastic–Early Dynastic objects in our collection had, to my knowledge, never been exhibited, making it even more imperative to show a selection of them to the public.

The main message that is carried through the exhibit is that the roots of so much of later Egyptian culture — the idea of a (semi-)divine king, polytheism, offering and funerary cults, the representation of the human form — all began more than 500 years before the pyramids were built. The show was divided into six sections: Introduction to the Predynastic; Petrie and the Discovery of the Predynastic; Predynastic Culture (pottery, stonework, lithics); Predynastic Religion; The Rise of the State; and the Power of the First Kings. About 130 objects from the permanent collection were in the show (fig. 3). A major coup was borrowing two seminal pieces of early Egyptian art: the Battlefield Palette and the statue of King Khasekhem from the Ashmolean Museum, University of Oxford. Loans require a lot of staff time and they have significant costs, but these two objects really "made" the show.

The input of the advisory group proved to be especially valuable for this exhibit. I presented them with what I thought was a well-reasoned show with the title "Before the Pharaohs," which they rapidly and very gently persuaded me was not quite the correct approach. Many of their comments were taken into account, resulting in a much stronger, clearer show.

As we did for the Visible Language show, we printed all graphics in-house on the CAMEL Lab's 44-inch ink-jet color printer. This gave Brian much more flexibility to print what he

Figure 3. View of the exhibit Before the Pyramids. Photo by Anna Ressman

wanted, when he wanted, and to do more test prints of large graphics. Completely new to this show was Brian's redesign of the object labels, which traditionally have been card style, printed in-house in black ink on tinted paper. For this show, he ganged object labels into a continuous strip along the case's label rail. This had a lot of advantages: it was much cleaner in appearance, the type could be in color,

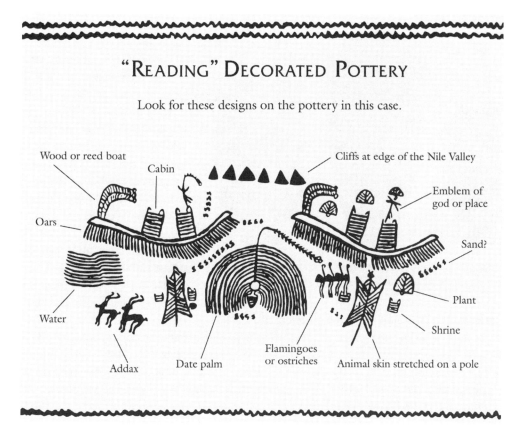

"READING" DECORATED POTTERY

Look for these designs on the pottery in this case.

Wood or reed boat — Cabin — Cliffs at edge of the Nile Valley — Emblem of god or place — Oars — Sand? — Water — Plant — Shrine — Addax — Date palm — Flamingoes or ostriches — Animal skin stretched on a pole

Figure 4. Label from Before the Pyramids, *deciphering decoration on Naqada II pottery. Designed by Brian Zimerle*

and color images could be added alongside the text. Brian incorporated elements of design from Predynastic pottery along the label rail (as well as in the borders of the main text panels). The contrast of the slightly colored background to the terra-cotta-color type greatly increased legibility (fig. 4).

A grant from the Antiquities Endowment Fund of the American Research Center in Egypt allowed Associate Conservator Alison Whyte to test samples from the objects with the scanning electron microscope (see the *Conservation* report).

Like many of our exhibit catalogs, *Before the Pyramids* has proved to be a valuable resource that can, and will, stand separately from the show. There is no other publication on Predynastic and Early Dynastic Egypt that is as up to date, comprehensive, and well illustrated. Twenty-two authors contributed essays and catalog entries. Anna took absolutely beautiful photos of the material. It is very rare for archaeological material to get the full studio treatment, and the results are dazzling (fig. 5). I am confident that these images will be requested by publishers for years to come. Brian Zimerle designed the very handsome catalog cover, and Tom Urban, Leslie Schramer, and Rebecca Cain of our Publications Office turned the massive amount of material into an attractive and user-friendly publication. Each of these Museum publications demands several months of intense work on the part of the Publications staff. It is clear that one of the keys to the success of our special exhibits catalogs is that the work is done in-house, allowing for the immediate resolution of issues that come up in the design of the book. Otherwise it would be impossible for us to produce these publications on such a tight schedule.

Figure 5. Example of Anna Ressman's photographs of three basalt vessels (ca. 4000 BC) for the exhibit catalog

Longtime Egypt enthusiasts and Oriental Institute supporters Tom and Linda Heagy were major benefactors of the show. They invited a select group of their friends to a pre-opening dinner in the Museum galleries. Additional funding came from Exelon and the Antiquities Endowment Fund of the American Research Center in Egypt.

We were delighted that Before the Pyramids was voted Best Chicago Museum Exhibit of 2011 in a poll conducted by the *Chicago Reader*. The exhibit Pioneers to the Past won the same award in 2010.

The pace and rhythm of the special exhibits program and staff is not apparent to visitors, but there is very little downtime between shows as we move ahead with final object selection and the cycle that fully involves the curator(s), registrars, conservators, preparators, designers, Public Education Office, the membership coordinator, and events planner. The efficiency of the final stages of planning and installation have been improved over the last few exhibits thanks to Erik's procedure in which objects are brought case by case to his studio and laid out (fig. 6). This allows us to verify the case size and arrangement. Decks and mounts can be built well in advance of the opening of the show and stored in the Prep Shop. Once the fabric has arrived, the case decks are covered and the objects fitted with their mounts. Then, the artifacts are removed and returned to transit storage until the show is ready to be installed, at which time the empty cases with their mounts are moved to the gallery and the objects placed in their mounts. Once the closing date of an exhibit has come, it is shocking how rapidly all traces of years of effort by so many people disappear. Erik, Brian, Tom, and the conservators and registrars swoop into the gallery, and within a day or two the exhibit has vanished.

Figure 6. Erik Lindahl in his studio laying out cases for the Before the Pyramids exhibit. Photo by Tom James

The planning of special exhibits doesn't let up with such a small museum staff. In June, we were already working hard on the next exhibit, Picturing the Past: Imaging and Imagining the Ancient Middle East, curated by Jack Green, John Larson, and myself; and also on Birds in Ancient Egypt, curated by doctoral candidate Rozenn Bailleul-LeSuer. The theme for the show following Birds awaits Jack's input. As you can see from last year's report (p. 169), changes do happen over a year. The Predynastic show has been extended through the end of the year to allow more time for Jack to get settled, and the show on Ceramic Arts of the Ancient Middle East that was to be curated by Geoff Emberling was taken off the schedule to be replaced by Picturing the Past.

We hope that you find our special exhibits to be engaging and that they provide an incentive for you to visit our galleries often.

Current and Upcoming Exhibits (*some titles and dates are tentative*)

Before the Pyramids: The Origins of Egyptian Civilization
March 29–December 31, 2011

Picturing the Past: Imaging and Imagining the Ancient Middle East
February 5–September 2, 2012

Birds in Ancient Egypt
October 7, 2012, closing date to be established

PUBLICITY AND MARKETING
Emily Teeter and Thomas James

The press continues to show an interest in our research and special exhibits. On the research front, the completion of the Chicago Assyrian Dictionary hit the press all over the world with comments by editor Martha Roth online and in print, including the *New York Times*, and a June 20 segment on WBEZ's *Worldview*. The ongoing Persepolis Fortification Archive Project also garnered press throughout the year. Other stories highlighted Don Whitcomb's excavation near Jericho and Yorke Rowan's work in the eastern Badia in Jordan.

On the museum front, the special exhibits continue to generate additional publicity for the Institute overall. Even late in its run, Pioneers to the Past was featured on *Worldview*, with Geoff Emberling and Orit Bashkin. The Visible Language show was featured in the *New York Times*, the *Chicago Tribune, Time Out Chicago*, and the *University of Chicago Magazine*. For Before the Pyramids, the *Chicago Tribune* had fun covering the arrival of the statue of King Khasekhem from the Ashmolean Museum, University of Oxford, entitling the story "The King is in the Building!" Another story on the show appeared in *Time Out Chicago*. The same publication listed Emily as being one of Chicago's important "Culture Curators," which is an acknowledgment of the growing awareness of our special exhibits program. We continue, now so many years on, to be grateful to William Harms of the University's Communications Office for all his help coordinating media coverage and successfully pitching stories to major outlets.

We continued our efforts to connect with destination management companies to encourage them to include the Oriental Institute in their itineraries. We worked with the Chicago Convention and Tourism Bureau (CCTB) on a number of events. One was a May 4 familiarization tour for "top domestic tour operators." This was a "speed dating"-style sales pitch at McCormick Place, where Emily met with domestic and international tour operators and told them why their clients would be interested in visiting the Oriental Institute and spending a day in Hyde Park. The next day, the group came to the Oriental Institute for a tour. One can always extol the wonders of the Oriental Institute, but there is no substitute for seeing the museum galleries themselves. We have already had a few tour groups sent by professional tour packagers.

The CCTB and the city are jointly trying to attract in-bound Chinese visitors to Chicago, and CCTB staff suggested that we might try offering Mandarin-language resources. William Harms cleverly used the Chinese objects in the Visible Language exhibit as an incentive for a press conference at the Oriental Institute on October 28 that was attended by local Chinese media and staff of the CCTB. We introduced an audio tour of highlights of the collection in Mandarin and a press release for the exhibit, both of which were translated by volunteer Siwei Wang. The story was carried in Chinese-language media, including the *World Journal*. On May 16, we hosted another group of ten members of in-bound tour operators and media from China seeking to develop more Chinese tourism in Chicago.

The Mandarin initiative coincided with our Department of Public Programs initiative to translate museum resources into Spanish (see *Public Education: Interactive Learning and the Middle East*).

On April 8, eight writers attending the annual convention of the Midwest Travel Writers Association visited us through the agency of the Chicago Office of Tourism and Culture. As a result, we have had several syndicated stories about the Oriental Institute, including the heavily syndicated "Chicago Travel Tips: Five Things You Shouldn't Miss" (we were number one!).

On May 1, in our effort to reach other audiences, we partnered with HyPa (Hyde Park Alliance for Arts and Culture) to have a special Sunday-morning program for registrants of Art Chicago. In other miscellaneous promotions aimed at increasing our number of visitors, Suq Manager Denise Browning arranged for a one-time 15 percent discount in our shop for top donors to WTTW and WYYC. In October, as for the last many years, we had a table at Spotlight on Chicago, a city-sponsored showcase of cultural attractions.

We now budget for paid advertising for all our fully funded special exhibits. For Visible Language, we ran spots on WBEZ, printed rack cards, and placed an ad in the *Hyde Park Herald*. We also experimented with other promotions, including two ads along the bottom edge of the "Play" section of the *Chicago Tribune* and placement in their online edition (fig. 7). These "sold" the overall experience of the Oriental Institute with an inset on the Visible Language exhibit. Ads for the show also appeared on CTA buses.

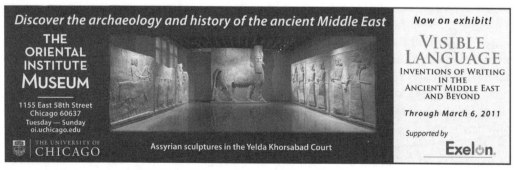

Figure 7. Ad that appeared in the Chicago Tribune, *designed by Brian Zimerle*

Our advertising strategy for the Before the Pyramids exhibit is similar but less extensive, with rack cards (designed by Rachel Yung; fig. 8), WBEZ spots, and an ad in the *Hyde Park Herald*. In the next fiscal year we will ramp up contact, with street-pole banners and ads in the *New York Times* and *Pioneer Press*. A persistent problem, not unique to us, is evaluating the effectiveness of our paid advertising.

Last year, Membership Coordinator Maeve Reed and Chief Curator Geoff Emberling attended a symposium that resulted in an Arts Engagement Exchange Implementation Grant for a Qualitative Audience Research study focusing on developing a greater understanding of our audience. The study was conducted by Slover-Linett Strategies. The questions addressed "Experiences at the Museum," "Membership" and "Visions for the Future." For more information, please see the *Marketing* section of the Membership report. The study was based on the experiences of two groups. The first, "potential" visitors who had never before been to the Oriental Institute were asked to record their impressions of their initial visit. The second was made up of people who have visited us numerous times. Maeve, Carole, and Emily observed the focus groups in action at the National Opinion Research Center (NORC) on November 16.

The study concluded that the primary motivations for people to come for an initial visit are public programming and the exhibits, both of which were also cited as encouraging repeat visits. "Relative ignorance" of the Oriental Institute, our southern location, and lack of parking are still barriers to increasing our visitorship. Positive comments included that the visitors "see the present though new eyes" after their visit, that they "take away new facts and new perspectives," and that many of them enjoy the "tranquil, highly introspective experience" of our galleries. The study concluded that our "visitors are not clamoring for wholesale changes to the museum," in fact there was concern expressed that "whatever changes they make, they need to preserve that [character] because that's what makes this place unique," and "whatever steps the museum takes next, it should stay true to its singular strengths." Things that can be improved include, of course, parking, but also the audio guide hardware (many visitors had difficulty with the iPods). Overall, there were not too many surprises, but to see the comments presented in an organized fashion was very helpful. Generally, we seem to be doing most things right, but we continue to struggle with our location, the unclear message that our name gives to those unfamiliar with us, and parking — all of which seem to prevent us from dramatic increases in the number of visitors. However, these limitations are tempered by the push that our Public

Figure 8. *Rack card for Before the Pyramids, designed by Rachel Yung*

Education Department is making for web-based courses and lectures and the Institute's move to the integrated database that will ultimately make it possible for anyone, anywhere, to view our collection. We need to keep in mind that due to our Internet presence our audience is broader than the people who walk through our museum galleries — it is in fact global.

New Media

Each generation has its own technological jump that in some way changes the game when it comes to communication. The Oriental Institute's founder, James Henry Breasted, communicated primarily through the postal service — and we're lucky to have copies of many of his letters. He also would send a telegram if time were of the essence. During Breasted's lifetime he saw some of the most significant advances in communications technology with the rise of radio, telephone, and television. We are now in the middle of a second great metamorphosis of communications. In the communications world, newspapers, radio, and television are one-way streets. Even the World Wide Web has been, until recently, a fairly non-interactive place. Over the past couple of years, however, we've seen an increasing number of ways in which we can directly interact with the world over the Internet. These "new media" outlets, such as Facebook, have become too big to ignore — in March 2010, Facebook edged out Google to become the most visited site on the Internet, accounting for more than 7 percent of all Internet traffic. The interactive web has blossomed into a place where it is easy to follow people or institutions on Twitter, subscribe to blogs, or become a friend or fan on Facebook. In addition to the official Oriental Institute webpage and the *E-Tablet*, our monthly e-newsletter (fig. 9), we have recently begun to try to expand the way we communicate with our Members and the world at large through new media by creating a presence on Facebook (fig. 10) and Twitter (fig. 11), and by blogging (fig. 12).

The main Oriental Institute presence on Facebook is in the form of our official Oriental Institute page (http://bit.ly/OI-Facebook). If you haven't seen it, we hope you'll visit soon. You can visit whether you're a member of Facebook or not – but if you are a member of

Figure 9. The April 2010 edition of the E-Tablet

Figure 10. The Oriental Institute page on Facebook

Figure 11. The Oriental Institute Twitter page   Figure 12. James Henry Breasted's Blog

Facebook, we'd love it if you became a fan! We're using Facebook to pose questions, announce events, share photographs and videos, and compile links to news stories about the Oriental Institute and our ongoing research. The Research Archives also has a page on Facebook, and we encourage you to check it out as well (http://bit.ly/OI-Archives).

The vision we have for the Oriental Institute Twitter page (http://twitter.com/ oimuseum/) is a place where we can share not only the things that we're doing here at the Oriental Institute, but as a place to share all noteworthy news to those who are interested in Near Eastern studies. We'd really appreciate your feedback on our new Twitter page — follow us and send us an @ message over Twitter with your suggestions on how to improve.

One of the greatest things about these new media sites that they all easily connect to one another: all Facebook status updates automatically go out as tweets on our Twitter page not long afterward, and Breasted Blog posts are automatically announced on Facebook and Twitter. This makes it easy for us to reach multiple audiences and to keep everyone informed.

In the future we may branch out into other forms of new media. We're working on a Flickr account, where we'll be able to show people a lot more of what we have in our photographic collection. The newest emerging site seems to be Foursquare, the location-based social-networking site, and we haven't yet decided how or if we're going to use this new offering. Be sure though, that as additional new media outlets and networks come to market, we'll look into them and see if they fit our mission.

We hope you'll take a moment and visit us online:

- The Oriental Institute's page on Facebook: http://bit.ly/OI-Facebook
- The Research Archives' page on Facebook: http://bit.ly/OI-Archives
- Oriental Institute Twitter page: http://twitter.com/oimuseum/
- The Oriental Institute Web page: http://oi.uchicago.edu

Subscribe to the *E-Tablet*, our monthly e-newsletter for Members and friends of the Oriental Institute, by filling out the subscription form at the bottom of the Oriental Institute home page (http://oi.uchicago.edu) with your name and e-mail address.

Not a Facebook or Twitter member? You can still view the Oriental Institute's pages on Facebook and Twitter without signing up. If you are interested in joining Facebook and Twitter, visit www.facebook.com or www.twitter.com.

REGISTRATION

Helen McDonald and Susan Allison

Last summer the University signed a contract with the KE company to buy its museum specific database software program EMu (Electronic Museum) for the Oriental Institute. This purchase is the first stage in the Integrated Database project (IDB) that will take in all the Museum databases and also some from the rest of the Oriental Institute. The first two groups of records to be moved into EMu will be Museum Registration's object databases and the library catalog of the Research Archives. Much of our time this year has been spent preparing for this move. As part of our preparations we looked at the existing templates of other museums that use KE EMu, including the Field Museum and the University of Pennsylvania Museum of Archaeology and Anthropology. We decided that Penn's was closest to what we needed for Museum Registration and set about working out modifications that we would need for the design to accommodate our present data and a few new fields that would be useful. Now that we have agreed on the design of the parts of the database that will take our present data, it is up to KE to build it for us. At some point in the next few months we will present KE with our data mapping document that lists all the fields in our current databases and the destination fields in the new KE database, and they will load our data in for the first time. There will then be a period of examination and modification after which the data will be reloaded and this process will be repeated for a third time at which point we hope that any glitches will have been ironed out and our data will be in the correct fields. While we wait for KE to build the database, we are continuing with the data cleanup that we have been engaged in for the last year or so. We would like to thank Tom James and George Sundell, who have met with Registration every week to work through all the terms in the materials and classification fields to agree on a broad and a specific term for each material and object type. As a result we have built thesauri for these fields and have edited our present database with standardized specific terms.

We are nearing the end of the 2009–2011 Institute of Museum and Library Services (IMLS) re-housing grant and received our last delivery of cabinets in January of this year. We have re-housed and registered all the material from the Nubian sites of Qasr el-Wizz (nearly 3,000 pieces, mostly sherds) and those in the Bab Kalabsha area (just under 550 sherds and stone fragments), as well as re-housing the remaining Egyptian and Nubian registered stone material (over 150 objects) and thirty-three large Megiddo jars. To fulfill the terms of the grant we have forty-five large Nubian pots left to unpack and re-house and will complete this in the next month. A total of 3,377 digital images have been taken of the re-housed material. We have also registered and re-housed 600 Nubian sherds from sites like Qustul and Ballana that somehow escaped being registered earlier. We expect the Nubian collection to be a focus of research as publications on the sites of Dorginarti, Serra, and Qasr el-Wizz will be in preparation during the next few years as Lisa Heidorn, Bruce Williams, and Artur Obluski work on their respective material.

We have continued to re-assemble a selection of sherds and other material to form the basis of a teaching collection for faculty members to use. So far, over 7,500 sherds have been identified and moved, many of them newly registered. In the next month or so we will be ready to send out lists of the new teaching collection material to members of faculty to see if we have found most of what they hope to use and consult with them as to what else might be added. We expect to keep adding to this collection for at least another year and then intermittently as appropriate.

On October 25 we held a Behind the Scenes with Museum Registration event for Oriental Institute Members. The evening began with a short talk in Breasted Hall on the different aspects of the job of registrar. Tables with recently registered material and volunteers to talk about what was being registered, how, and why, were set up in the Edgar and Deborah Jannotta Mesopotamian Gallery. Janet Helman talked to Members about the site of Tall i-Ghazir or Geser (Iran) and the registration of the sherds in preparation for the publication. Jim Sopranos presided over Aegean and Cypriot sherds registered for the teaching collection. Lisa Heidorn manned a table of Nubian material registered as part of the IMLS re-housing grant, and Courtney Jacobson talked about some drawers of Egyptian sherds from Helene Kantor's personal teaching collection (now part of our new teaching collection). Four backstage tours of our storage areas were conducted during the evening by the registrars and our student museum assistant. Food and drink was provided in the Robert and Deborah Aliber Persian Gallery.

Outgoing loans included a loan of Egyptian material to the Toledo Museum of Art that went out in October. Bronze projectile points made their second trip out to Argonne Labs for analysis in November in the company of Laura D'Alessandro. Uruk-period sherds from the Robert McC. Adams Warka and Akkad surveys were sent out to Leah Minc (Oregon State University) for Neutron activation analysis in late summer 2010 and returned promptly in March 2011. Two Egyptian tomb statuettes (OIM nos. E10625 and E10627) went to the Roemer und Pelizaeus Museum (Hildesheim, Germany) for an exhibit on Giza that marked the Museum's centenary in March and will return in late August.

A number of longer-term loans came back to us. These included sixty Egyptian objects that had been at Wheaton College since 1948. This loan was packed by Conservation and Preparation and came back in November. In October Laura D'Alessandro, Erik Lindahl, and Helen McDonald traveled to Salem, Massachusetts, to spend a week packing a long-term study loan of objects from the site of Semna South (Sudan) and driving it back to Chicago. The site was excavated by Professor Louis Žabkar and since his passing his widow Joan Žabkar has continued work on the publication. A collection of sherds, nearly two thousand fragile clay sealings and metal objects, beads, and a variety of textile and leather fragments are now back here and in the process of being registered (650 done so far). Other returning loans included two pots from the Tut cache that had been loaned to the Metropolitan Museum of Art (New York) and a stone horned altar from Megiddo that was out on loan to the Jewish Museum (New York); these returned in October and May respectively.

As to incoming loans, five were associated with the Visible Language exhibit. These included early tablets from the Vorderasiatische Museum Berlin and the Yale Babylonian collection; inscribed material from the Harvard Semitic Museum; Chinese oracle bones from the Smart Museum, and a Chinese bronze vessel and a Mayan stone from the Art Institute of Chicago. Registration liaised with couriers, shippers, and arts brokers; booked some of the courier accommodation and arranged courier per diems. The same thing happened in reverse in March when the exhibit was dismantled. For the next temporary exhibit, Before the Pyramids, a major loan of the statue of King Khasekhem and a piece of the Battlefield Palette came in from the Ashmolean Museum (Oxford) that opened at the end of March. Both this loan and the Berlin tablet loan required entries in the Federal Register to allow a court to grant immunity from seizure if such a claim is made against them during the period of the loan. The entry in the Federal Register requires an application to the Department of State made by the registrar and we are glad that in both cases the objects received entries in the Federal Register.

Registration has also played its part in other Museum-wide projects such as the re-doing of labels in the Mesopotamian gallery and the Khorsabad Relief Fragment Project. The latter is to register, re-house, clean, and photograph all our reliefs from Khorsabad and make them available for study and has been running for the last couple of summers. We have also helped with the new metals survey and re-housing grant by removing extraneous material from the metals room and the small objects store (the latter is to become a temporary photo studio dedicated to metals photography). Along with other Museum staff members, the registrars have attended disaster-planning workshops at the Newberry Library and the Chicago History Museum as we all work toward updating our own disaster plan.

The Registration Department has moved or inventoried just over 24,000 objects this year (a total of some 30,000 object movements). Over 3,100 were the subject of research of all kinds and 1,861 objects were used in teaching and training. Nearly 600 objects were moved for either photography or drawing. Just over 6,500 were inventoried or had their locations updated. Over 6,000 objects were registered, mostly relating to the current re-housing grant and the development of the teaching collection. A further 3,000 objects were re-housed. Nearly 5,200 bag labels were printed for newly registered objects or inventoried objects whose labels were inadequate. Over 460 objects were moved for temporary exhibits that were installed, dismantled, or in preparation this year. Over 120 objects were moved relating to loans or while being considered for loans of various sorts.

It has been another busy year for visiting researchers.

- Parts of the Amuq publication project have been winding down slowly. James Osborne made a final visit in September to finish work on the Tayinat pottery. Marina Pucci and Lynn Dodd made visits relating to the Chatal Höyük and Tell Judaidah publications. Courtney Jacobson finished the sherd drawing for Chatal Höyük and Dan Mahoney has continued to work on the recording of sherds from Judaidah. For the second time we lent fifty-five bronze projectile points dating to the Iron Age from the Amuq sites, Megiddo, and Persepolis to Argonne Labs for x-ray fluorescence and x-ray diffraction analysis with high energy synchrotron radiation. The principal investigators of this project are Lynn Dodd, Heather Snow, and Liz Friedman. Last summer Professor Günter Hölbl spent a month studying and photographing Amuq scarabs for the three publications and has now submitted his reports for Chatal Höyük and Tell Tayinat. Angela Altenhofen completed the illustrations of the Chatal Höyük objects.

- Hülya Calışkan Akgül ("La Sapienza," Rome/Yüzüncü Yıl University, Turkey) visited for the month of January to study red/black burnished pottery from Alishar Höyük.
- Annalies Bleecker (Dordrechet, the Netherlands) visited in May to study our Egyptian first dynasty labels.
- In November, Taufik Deadle visited from the Palestinian Autonomous Area to study Islamic pottery from Khirbet Kerak.
- Günter Dreyer visited in February and again in May to study 300 Egyptian predynastic objects from Abydos, particularly those from the tomb of Djer.
- Faiza Drici (University Charles de Gaulle-Lille III, France) came for a fortnight in June to study a selection of Nubian weapons and related equipment such as quivers and finger looses for her dissertation.
- Henning Franzmeier (Freie University, Berlin) came to study the objects from W. F. Petrie's excavations at Sedment for his thesis and a publication.
- Meg Gundlach and Kenneth Griffin (Swansea University, Wales) studied Twenty-fifth Dynasty stone shabtis from Thebes for a week in January.
- Abdul Ameer Hamdani (Iraqi Antiquities Service/State University of New York, Stony Brook) visited in January and studied sherds from Robert McC. Adams' Akkad survey.
- Carolin Jauss (Freie University, Berlin) came for a month this spring to make a study of use-wear analysis of over 430 ceramic vessels from the Diyala and Chogha Mish, as part of her dissertation research.
- Shannon Martino came in July to study clay human figurines from Alishar.

The collections continue to be used for teaching and research by Oriental Institute staff, NELC faculty, and students. Users include the following:

- Angela Altenhofen has continued to draw seal impressions for the Diyala project, among other illustration projects.
- Natasha Ayers borrowed a drawer of Mendes sherds to use to teach sherd drawing.
- A selection of Egyptian pots were laid out in Registration for the class of high school students taught at the Oriental Institute this summer by Rozenn Bailleul-LeSuer, with the assistance of Natasha Ayers, for the ceramics section of the course.
- Throughout the year, Rozenn Bailleul-LeSuer has studied objects relating to the planned special exhibit on the Birds of Ancient Egypt that is scheduled for autumn 2012.
- Kathryn Bandy has begun to study some of the Oriental Institute hieratic ostraca as comparanda for the ostraca from current excavations at Tell Edfu.
- Clemens Reichel visited and photographed a selection of Diyala sealings and tablets. Larry Lissak has continued to photograph a variety of Diyala objects for the Diyala online database project.
- Robert Ritner used a number of heart scarabs for the Beginning Hieroglyphs class, and the inscribed jar OIM E13945 for a class on hieratic.
- Sam Speigel has been working through the Mannheimer collection of coins (mostly classical) identifying them and providing us with catalog information on them.
- Bruce Williams has continued work on the Serra material for a forthcoming OINE volume (no. 11).

- Karen Wilson has continued working on a publication of the pottery from the Inanna temple sounding at Nippur with Mac Gibson, Richard Zettler, Jean Evans, and others.

These accomplishments have been made possible by the capable and efficient efforts of our student museum assistant Courtney Jacobson, with the assistance of a wonderful group of volunteers and interns, including Janet Helman, Ila Patlogan, Matthew Sawina, Daila Shefner, Toni Smith, Jim Sopranos, George Sundell, Leslie Warmus, and (periodically) Gretel Braidwood and Raymond Tindel. The volunteers have altogether contributed over a thousand hours of their time to Museum Registration and we are grateful for all their help. In June, Courtney Jacobson retired as student museum assistant after five years in the job, during which time she registered over 12,400 objects. Her care with object handling, careful record keeping, and cheerful demeanor has been appreciated in Registration and she will be much missed.

ARCHIVES

John A. Larson

As of December 2010, John Larson has served as Museum Archivist for thirty years.

Photographic Services

The income from photographic image sales and reproduction fees enables us to purchase archival supplies and equipment for the Archives and for Photography. Between July 1, 2010, and June 30, 2011, we processed seventy-two orders, with thirty-six being paid, for a total of $8,410.00. Thomas R. James, assisted by Michael Camp and Lise Truex, prepared the paperwork and handled all the other details that are involved in processing the requests that we received for Oriental Institute proprietary images and reproduction permissions during the past year.

There are now 91,728 records in the photo database, with information from photo catalog cards having been added by Greg Brown, Patrick Chew, Gerard Dougher, Ginger Emery, Ami Huang, Aram Sarkisian, and Derek Walker — an increase of 11,000 records. We have also removed about 7,500 duplicate records from the photo database. There are a total of 48,177 photo catalog cards in the photo database now, with 32,372 negative cards and 4,762 slide cards.

Archives

Visiting scholars during fiscal year 2010/2011 included Jeffrey Abt, John M. Adams, Hulya Akgul, Lindsay Allen, Corrado Alvaro, Flora Anthony, Pedro Azara, Lydia Carr, William Carruthers, Petr Charvát, Adina Hoffmann, Albert Imperial, Yuka Kadoi, Matt Kohlstedt, Marc Marin, Shannon Martino, Jeffrey Spurr, and Avi Winitzer. In July 2010, Shannon Martino of the University of Pennsylvania arrived to do a study of figurines from Alishar Hüyük, Turkey. September was a particularly busy month, with Matt Kohlstedt of George Washington University working from September 7 to 10 on a study of John A. Wilson's contacts with

Middle Easterners in the 1920s and 1930s; Lindsay Allen of King's College, London, returning on September 13–14 to continue her research on Persepolis; John M. Adams coming in on September 15 to discuss Theodore Montgomery Davis for a forthcoming biography; Jeffrey Abt on September 16 to put the finishing touches on his biography of James Henry Breasted, which is due out this autumn; and William Carruthers who investigated several Egyptologists on September 21. On October 14, Lydia Carr came to do research on Anna (Nina) Macpherson Davies and her ancient Egyptian facsimile paintings. From November 15 to 19, William Carruthers returned. On December 6, 2010, Petr Charvát of the Archaeological Institute, Academy of Sciences of the Czech Republic, looked at the documentation for Tell Al-Ubaid, Iraq. Hulya Akgul came from the University of Rome to do a study of East Anatolian red-black burnished ware from Alishar Hüyük on January 12, 2001. On March 3, 2011, Jeffrey Spurr came to look at our collection of nineteenth century photographs of Iran by Antoine Sevruguin. Corrado Alvaro arrived on March 8 to look at our holdings of photographs for Arslantepe/ Malatya, Turkey. On March 15, Avi Winitzer looked at the Papers of A. Leo Oppenheim for a biography, and on March 31, Flora Anthony came to investigate some Theban Tomb paintings from Egypt. In early April, Yuka Kadoi from the Art Institute of Chicago came to do research on Arthur Upham Pope for the papers of a recent symposium. Pedro Azara, together with Albert Imperial and Marc Marin, arrived on May 31 to look at photographs of Eridu, Lagash, Ur, and Warka in southern Iraq for a forthcoming exhibit in Spain. On June 8, 2011, Adina Hoffmann came to do research on the origins of the Rockefeller Museum in Jerusalem. From within our own Oriental Institute community, Abbas Alizadeh, Rozenn Bailleul-LeSuer, John A. Brinkman, Justine James, Megaera Callisto Lorenz, Martha Roth, Randy Shonkweiler,

Figure 13. Musicians playing rababa. Drawing by Douglas Champion

Emily Teeter, Bruce Williams, and Karen L. Wilson have conducted research using Archival materials. We would especially like to thank Tom James for his tireless assistance in the ongoing operation of the Archives.

Recent Acquisitions

On November 3, 2010, the last installment of Douglas Champion's drawings of Chicago House staff arrived (fig. 13). Mr. Champion was an artist with the Epigraphic Survey from 1947 until 1958. In 2001, he donated eight sketches and watercolors of Egyptian house staff to the Archives. The recent gift brings the total to twenty. This is a most welcome addition to the Archives, as it provides a glimpse of life in Luxor in the 1950s.

Volunteers and Student Assistants

The following people have contributed their time as Archives volunteers during fiscal year 2010–2011 and have made it possible for us to continue a number of projects in the Oriental Institute Archives that would not have been possible without their generous assistance: Jean Fincher, Peggy Grant, Sandra Jacobsohn, Robert Wagner, and Carole Yoshida. We are grateful to have benefited from the help of these dedicated volunteers, and we thank them here for all of their efforts on behalf of the Archives.

Adrienne Frie, Manuel Alex Moya, Stephanie O'Brien, and Andrew Rutledge worked on the compact-storage project (see below) through the summer and early autumn of 2010. Archivist John Larson has also been assisted in the Oriental Institute Archives during this academic year by Near Eastern Languages and Civilizations (NELC) graduate student Jessica Henderson and by Master of Arts Program in the Social Sciences (MAPSS) graduate students Patrick Chew, Gerard Dougher, Aram Sarkisian, and Derek Walker. Elizabeth Wolfson, who has worked past summers for John in the Archives (2008) and Helen McDonald in Museum Registration (2009), returned in June to work on the Archives compact-storage project for the summer of 2010.

Archives Compact-Storage Project

Beginning in June 2010, we started moving the archives collections back into our newly remodeled space. This process continued until the end of August 2010, and we re-opened the Oriental Institute Archives for research appointments after Labor Day, on Tuesday, September 7, 2010. During the summer of 2011, we will be moving the oversize materials into the new mapcases.

The overall appearance of the Oriental Institute Archives storage room has changed dramatically during the past six months. We now have more than 1,050 new shelves and fifty additional mapcase drawers for oversize materials. The compact-storage shelves are mounted on carriages set on tracks, which enable us to take the greatest possible advantage of our available floor space. Our previously existing installation of sixty-five shelves for our collection of boxed black-and-white large-format negatives has been moved to a new location, and we have also moved four mapcase cabinets, which contain a total of 160 drawers.

The successful implementation of the Oriental Institute Archives compact-storage project would not have been possible without the hard work and cooperation of a large number of individuals and teams. On behalf of the Archives, John Larson would like to record our thanks to Gil Stein and Steve Camp for submitting the original proposal to the University of Chicago's Capital Projects Committee; to the members of the Capital Projects Committee for approving and funding the project; to the Capital Project Delivery section of the Facilities Services department, especially Denise Davis and Richard Bumstead; to Andy Cobb of the Facilities Services department; to Mark Cheng and Jonathan Estanislao of MDC Architects, PC, Streamwood, Illinois; to Mike Dawson, Rick Dasko, and their installation team at Bradford Systems Corporation, Bensenville, Illinois; to Thomas Fawcett, Shaun Gray, and their team at 360 Contractors; to Carlos and the guys at Hogan and Son Movers and Storage, Chicago; to Susan Allison, Laura D'Alessandro, Brian Zimerle, Thomas James, Erik Lindahl, Helen McDonald, and Alison Whyte, all of the Oriental Institute Museum staff; and to Carla Hosein and D'Ann Condes of Oriental Institute Administration.

———————————

CONSERVATION

Laura D'Alessandro

This was an exciting year for the Conservation Lab as we welcomed two new conservators to our staff. In March, Simona Cristanetti joined the Oriental Institute staff as contract conservator for our Metals Survey and Re-houseing Project, which is funded by the National Endowment for the Humanities (NEH). Simona, a graduate of the Winterthur/University of Delaware graduate conservation training program, came to us after five years at the National Gallery of Art in Washington, DC. She will be surveying all the metals in our collection — over 11,000 objects. An important component of the project will be the use of the scanning electron microscope to identify metals that are difficult to correctly identify by visual examination alone. Simona and her cadre of conservation volunteers will then re-house the collection in archival packing materials and new, custom-designed Delta Designs cabinets. Another component of the project involves the photography of the collection by Anna Ressman and her assistants as it is re-housed. All this was made possible by a generous grant from the NEH Sustaining Cultural Heritage Collections program.

Robyn Haynie joined the staff in May as our Parsa-funded Persepolis tablet conservator. Robyn is a graduate of the University College London graduate conservation training program and came to us from a stint at the National Museums of Scotland. Both conservators hit the ground running and jumped right into their respective projects. Within days, Simona was busy setting up an electronic version of the survey form that will be used to record the condition of the objects within the metal collection. Matt Stolper and his team started bringing Persepolis tablets to the lab as soon as Robyn arrived. She's been buried under tablets ever since.

Alison Whyte received a well-deserved promotion to associate conservator this year. Alison started at the Oriental Institute in 2001 as a Getty post-graduate fellow and became a contract conservator for the Khorsabad Relief Fragment Project after her Getty-funded year was completed. In 2005, Alison was hired as the assistant conservator and took responsibility for a wide range of projects. Her professionalism and ongoing commitment to the Oriental Institute have contributed to the success of the Conservation Laboratory.

Simona Cristanetti, NEH-funded Metals Survey and Re-housing Project conservator

Robyn Haynie cleaning a Persepolis Fortification tablet in the Conservation Laboratory

Alison's year has been an active one. She continued to serve as the lead conservator for the special exhibits program, starting off with Visible Language followed by Before the Pyramids. Picturing the Past is her current focus, and because a conservator's job is never done, she has already begun treatment of objects scheduled for exhibit in the fall of 2012. In addition to her work on special exhibits, Alison has been in charge of conservation's duties for the Khorsabad Relief Fragment Project. She has also worked on the several loans that went out this past year, an activity that is so important to the collegial relationship that the Oriental Institute has with museums around the world. Alison also carried out a variety of analyses over the year, including the identification of pigments on slate palettes in the Before the Pyramids exhibit. Her contribution was included in the catalog for the exhibit *Before the Pyramids: The Origins of Egyptian Civilization*, edited by Emily Teeter (OIMP 33). Finally, Alison also participated in the Kerkenes Dağ excavations, where she devised and implemented a new relative humidity storage system for actively corroding iron artifacts and assisted in the conservation and installation of monumental stone artifacts in the Yozgat museum.

The Laboratory staff also continued work on a project to identify organic residues on Egyptian pottery from the site of Deir el-Bahri at Thebes, dating to the Middle Kingdom and New Kingdom periods (ca. 2080 to 1070 BC). We began collaboration with the Department of Chemistry and Physics at Chicago State University, under the direction of Bob LeSeur, associate professor. Bob is the husband of one of our graduate students, Rozenn LeSeur. Bob arranged an independent research project with one of his senior students to begin the analysis of one of the residues. To kick off this collaboration, I presented a seminar to the Department of Chemistry and Physics on the collections of the Oriental Institute and some of the recent analyses that have been carried out here. Alison and I have been working with Bob's student Rachel Durham on some of the background information that she needed. Her work has helped move the project forward, but there is still much to be done.

In January, the Conservation Laboratory hosted French researchers J. Bianca Jackson and Julien Labaune from the Louvre and the Institut de la Lumière Extrême (ILE), who are using terahertz energy to examine and image ancient materials. Bianca and Julien brought the terahertz equipment with them from France. The delicate and expensive equipment required its own seat on the plane. This is a particularly exciting project because the terahertz energy is non-destructive and, if successful, will ultimately provide another analytical technique that can be used to study and characterize cultural materials.

In keeping with our heavy research orientation this year, the Conservation Laboratory served as the site for a demonstration by Bruker of their portable FT-IR (Fourier Transform Infrared)

Alison Whyte making an Escal bag for microclimate storage of an iron band found at Kerkenes (iron band in foreground)

equipment, the ALPHA. Conservators from the Field Museum of Natural History and the Chicago History Museum spent the day as the Bruker representative demonstrated the capabilities of this device to non-destructively analyze organic materials.

As we did last year, we hosted four Iraqis from the Field Museum's program for two weeks. This year's group was made up of two archaeologists and two conservators. As in past years, we welcomed the opportunity to meet and interact with our Iraqi colleagues. It was also a wonderful opportunity to get updates on our friends from previous years and learn about the changes that have been taking place within the cultural heritage world.

And we cannot talk about the past year without mentioning our wonderful volunteers. Both last year and this year we have been fortunate to have been assisted in the Conservation Laboratory by conservation pre-program interns. These interns are preparing to apply to graduate conservation programs and the entry requirements call for a significant number of hours of conservation laboratory experience. They have worked on projects as diverse as the Khorsabad Relief Fragment Project and the NEH-funded Metals Survey and Re-housing Project: Kristen Gillette, Jen Hunt Johnson, Amy Lukas, and Nicole Pizzini.

PREP SHOP

Erik Lindahl

Over the 2010–2011 fiscal year the Oriental Institute Exhibition Preparation and Design Workshop (commonly known as the Prep Shop) has been a hive of activity. It has been involved in the planning and execution of a range of projects such as the special exhibit program as well as other projects relating to gallery maintenance, publicity, collections management, research projects, the search for a new chief curator, assisting with special events, and also dealing with facilities-related issues.

It was a very exciting year in the Marshall and Doris Holleb Family Special Exhibits Gallery. In August Pioneers to the Past was put away. In September the exhibit Visible Language: Inventions of Writing in the Ancient Middle East and Beyond opened. After the opening of Visible Language, the exhibits team began serious work on the design of Before the Pyramids, a special exhibit that opened in March 2011. We are now preparing for the next two exhibits, tentatively titled Picturing the Past and Birds in Ancient Egypt.

The Visible Language exhibit was a great opportunity to bring together scholars and material from around the world to create an exciting show on a topic that has had many recent developments. The Prep Shop especially enjoyed working with our colleagues from several loaning institutions to create a densely informative exhibit.

Before the Pyramids was an exciting show to put together. It is loaded with artifacts that are not only informative but are also beautiful art objects. This is the second exhibit that was designed and produced almost entirely in-house and it is looking like a success.

If everything goes well, the Birds in Ancient Egypt exhibit is going to be a new height for the exhibits team. It is going to have a strong multimedia component as well as many beautiful objects. Currently we are planning on having a very large projection in the gallery.

Following are some of the improvements we have made to the permanent galleries. Along with Assistant Curator of Digital Collections Tom James, PhD candidate Kathryn Hansen, and volunteer Sue Geschwender, we continued with the Edgar and Deborah Jannotta Mesopotamian Gallery re-labeling project. Brian Zimerle worked with Public Education to create bilingual signage for the Polk Brothers Foundation-funded computer kiosks.

In the fall, Laura D'Alessandro, Helen McDonald, and Erik Lindahl made a trip to Salem, Massachusetts, to collect a long-outstanding study loan of Nubian material from Joan Žabkar. It was a long, productive, and exciting trip. The team drove in a van from Chicago to Salem. The material and staff made it back to Chicago without incident and in better condition than expected.

During the last year, Brian Zimerle has been doing the bulk of our graphic design for Museum exhibits as well as designing advertisements for CTA buses and newspapers, the Oriental Institute Gala program, and outdoor signage for the Oriental Institute. He also designed Before the Pyramids-themed tote bags for the Suq.

The Museum staff has continued working with Research Associate Eleanor Guralnick to catalog, photograph, and eventually publish all the Oriental Institute's Khorsabad relief fragments. The Museum staff expects their portion of this project to be completed by next year.

The Prep Shop also contributed to the success of the Oriental Institute Gala in preparing the galleries for the event. Also Brian Zimerle contributed a reproduction of a predynastic vessel and Erik Lindahl contributed the design of a personal display to the various auctions at the Gala.

The Oriental Institute has been preparing for an upgrade to its fire alarm system. There will be construction activity in the Museum galleries and storage areas starting in the next fiscal year. To prepare for this, the Oriental Institute staff — including the Prep Shop — has been meeting with all parties involved to make sure this project can be completed as quickly and smoothly as possible.

Overall it has been an exciting year in the Prep Shop. We look forward to the next.

SUQ

Denise Browning

This was a very good year for the Suq with our net sales up 24 percent over last year's sales. The Visible Language special exhibit was very popular and we ended up selling 419 catalogs! The other items we developed for the exhibit also did well; we sold 1,270 note cards of five different images from the collection, and 240 mugs that depicted all the different languages in the exhibit. We had special mugs and vases hand thrown by master potters in Wisconsin to resemble the Egyptian Black-Topped Ware, and Brian Zimerle designed a great tote bag with the line drawings from the Egyptian D-Ware pottery.

Our excellent docents were kept busy with many questions from Suq customers. Thanks to Ray Broms, Judy Bell-Qualls, Peggy Grant, Jane Meloy, and Norma van der Meulen. Plus, Norma designed and strung some beautiful necklaces for the Suq this year! We were very lucky to have our student staff. Megaera Lorenz took charge of the online and mail orders besides helping in the store. Niebel Atiyeh was excellent, as was Stephanie Ruggles, who came at the end of the year. Mathew Hess helped in the office by pricing, displaying, and storing literally thousands of items for the Suq. Florence Ovadia and Jane Meloy worked on Mondays to keep our displays beautiful and interesting for our customers.

Many thanks to all those who helped make this such an outstanding year. We look forward to the exciting exhibits that are coming in this next year.

PHOTOGRAPHY

Anna R. Ressman

The past year has been, as always, an extremely busy and productive year for the Photography Department. It was our great fortune to have two dedicated, experienced, and talented assistants, both of whom were instrumental in the completion of two of the largest projects undertaken to date. Kevin Duong, a graduate of the MAPSS program in political science and a digital photography assistant for the 2009–2010 school year, was an excellent and extremely reliable assistant during the summer of 2010. His skills grew to the point where he was able to run many Khorsabad large fragment shoots on his own in July and August of 2010. In September of 2010, Kevin Bryce Lowry, a current anthropology PhD candidate and 2008 MAPSS graduate, returned as the only digital photography assistant for the 2010–2011 year. He was in training for the entire school year to become an assistant photographer for a grant-funded project to re-house the objects in the metals storage room beginning in the fall of 2011. Thanks to some very hard work, extra-curricular study, and dedication on her part, Kathryn Hansen, a MAPSS graduate and digital photography assistant for the 2009–2010 school year, trained under me to learn the technical requirements of archaeological photography while in the field and was hired as the dig photographer for the summer 2010 season with Gil Stein at Tell Zeidan.

Work began in September 2010 on the catalog for the special exhibit Before the Pyramids: The Origins of Egyptian Civilization, which is open from March through December 2011. This exhibit catalog was the most extensive to date in terms of new photography. It generated new images of 138 objects in the Oriental Institute collections, 128 of those as solo object photographs, twelve new contextual group images which included fifty-seven objects in total, ten of which were not photographed as solo objects. The photography in the catalog was very well received, and garnered a flattering review in the Summer 2011 issue of the magazine *KMT: A Modern Journal of Ancient Egypt*. An article about Before the Pyramids in the same magazine issue included fourteen color photographs from the exhibit catalog. In addition to this, five images from the catalog were published in *Time Out Chicago* and on the corresponding website.

Photographs from prior exhibits continued to be published beyond the time frame covered in the *Annual Report* for 2009–2010. Images from Visible Language: Inventions of Writing in the Ancient Middle East and Beyond were published in print and online in various *Time Out Chicago* issues, as well as in the *Chicago Tribune* and the *Chicago Sun Times*. The publication *Saudi Aramco World* also published photographs from the Visible Language special exhibit catalog in the September/October 2010 issue. In addition, a number of photographs of Egyptian objects were published in Emily Teeter's latest book, *Religion and Ritual in Ancient Egypt*, published in June 2011 by Cambridge University Press.

After an extended break due to special exhibit catalog photography, new photography work resumed on the upcoming Nubia Gallery highlights book. To date, 144 Nubian objects have been photographed individually, many of which had never been photographed before. These objects come from various periods of history, including A Group, C Group, New Kingdom, Napatan, Meroitic, X Group, and X Group Kalabsha. In the coming months, photography of Christian-era objects and contextual group object images from various eras will be completed.

In addition to working on these publications, the Photography Department continued work on the Khorsabad Relief Fragment Project during the summer and fall of 2010. Work on this project resumed in June of 2011. Numerous requests for photography were fulfilled for work outside the Oriental Institute, as well as for various research projects originating inside the Institute. Preparations have been underway for the Photography Department to begin the imaging involved in the effort to re-house the objects in the metals storage room. A major upgrade of departmental computer hardware was begun in the spring of this year and will continue throughout the year. This will give us the ability to keep up with the technological demands of evolving digital-imaging software while maintaining fiscal responsibility with available funds. The photography studio also got an upgrade with a new work station that adds flexibility and a technically accurate way to view and manage color while utilizing a tethered imaging setup.

Overall, it has been a fruitful and exciting year for the Photography Department. Major publications were completed, digital photography assistants were some of the most successfully trained to date, numerous images helped to advertise the hard work and scholarly pursuits of the Oriental Institute, additional needed upgrades were acquired, and another book highlighting a collection of the Museum is near completion. Once again, it was a great year working with all of the wonderful people at the Oriental Institute.

PUBLIC EDUCATION

Carole Krucoff

Introduction

Public Education's first full year as its own unit within the Oriental Institute has been marked by exciting growth and innovation, both in the structure and operation of our department and the educational services we are providing on site and online. Working together as one department, Education and Volunteer Program staff are collaborating in new and rewarding ways with Oriental Institute faculty, staff, and students, as well as with the wider university community. Read on to see how our joint efforts this past year attracted 6,870 adult, youth, and family visitors — a record-breaking number — to our public programs, and how major grant-funded initiatives have enabled us to reach nearly one million online visitors with web-based educational services for teachers, students, and families. Then see how both the Institute and the community are benefitting from the invaluable public and behind-the-scenes services provided by our Volunteer Program.

Adult Education

Presenting rich and meaningful adult education programs to serve longtime friends and engage new audiences is central to the mission of Public Education. This year we collaborated closely with faculty, graduate students, and museum staff to develop a wide range of courses, workshops, symposia, and special events (fig. 1). These programs attracted over 2,400 adults of all ages and backgrounds who were eager to broaden their understanding of the ancient Middle East and its connections to the modern world.

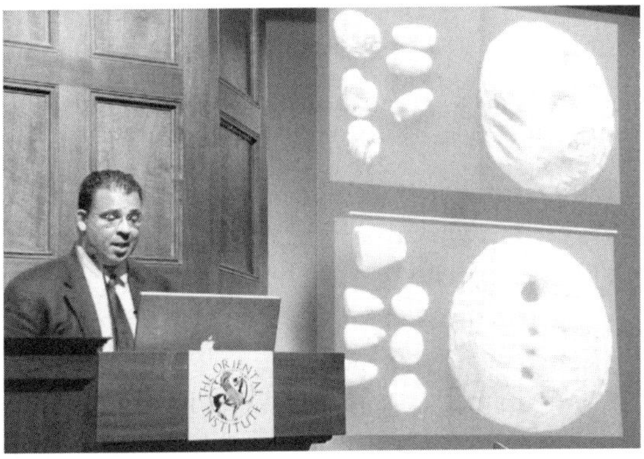

Figure 1. Christopher Woods, Associate Professor of Sumerology, shares recent research at the "Inventions of Writing" symposium. Woods is also a member of the new Faculty Working Group for Public Education. Photo by Wendy Ennes

Courses

Many of our on-campus adult-education courses are offered in collaboration with the University of Chicago's Graham School of General Studies. This year our joint multi-session courses included:

- Sex, Drugs, and Rock and Roll: A Lively Introduction to the Ancient Near East, which was team-taught by Katharyn Hanson and Eudora Struble
- Images for Eternity: An Introduction to Ancient Egyptian Art, taught by Rozenn Bailleul-LeSuer

- An Introduction to Ancient Egyptian Hieroglyphs, and Intermediate Ancient Egyptian Hieroglyphs, both taught by Foy Scalf
- Iran Past and Present, taught by Tobin Hartnell
- The Splendors of Assyria: History and Culture of an Ancient Empire, taught by Vincent J. van Exel

In addition to on-campus courses we offered three distance-learning opportunities. Hieroglyphs by Mail, a sixteen-week correspondence course, was taught by Andrew Baumann and Mary Szabady. Mary also taught Intermediate Ancient Egyptian Hieroglyphs by Mail, a follow-up to the introductory course.

Figure 2. Terry Friedman, Wendy Ennes, and Kate Grossman visit the Mesopotamian Gallery to discuss production of materials on ancient Mesopotamia for docent training and online adult education.
Photo by Carole Krucoff

Our third distance-learning course is a prime example of ways new collaborations with Oriental Institute faculty and students are helping us enhance our educational programming. For the last several years we offered Cuneiform by Mail, a course that introduced the cuneiform writing system using Akkadian vocabulary from the first millennium BC. This year, Christopher Woods, associate professor of Sumerology, suggested that since Sumerian was one of the languages for which cuneiform was likely created, we might want to change the focus of Cuneiform by Mail to provide an introduction to Sumerian. Under Woods guidance, graduate students Monica Crews and Seunghee Yie developed and are now instructing students nationwide with a course curriculum that provides a rich introduction to the Sumerian language, culture, and script.

The success of our distance learning courses has inspired another innovative collaboration based on two important needs. First is the desire many of our distance-learning students have expressed for adult education courses to be offered online, including courses that focus on ancient Mesopotamia, today's Iraq. Second is the need for an expanded and updated training manual section on ancient Mesopotamia as a resource for our volunteer docents. Wendy Ennes, associate head of Public Education, Terry Friedman, volunteer services associate, and Kate Grossman, PhD candidate in Near Eastern art and archaeology, who has special interest in ancient Mesopotamia, have joined together in a research project that is producing material to meet both these needs (fig. 2).

Each of these three people bring special expertise to the project. As part of the process that has made Public Education its own unit with the Oriental Institute, two advanced graduate students are now on our staff as content specialists. Megaera Lorenz, PhD candidate in Egyptology, has joined us, and Kate Grossman is also with us as a content specialist. Using her in-depth knowledge of ancient Mesopotamian history and culture, Kate is developing content for inclusion in the docent training manual and for a new online course on Mesopotamia. Terry is working with Kate to ensure the material meets our docents' needs, and Wendy, who holds a Master Online Teaching Certification from the University of Illinois, is shaping the ways text, images, captions, and interactive discussion will be presented online.

The training manual and online course material will receive a final review by another group of new partners, the faculty members who are now serving as the Faculty Working Group for Public Education. Fred Donner, professor of Near Eastern history, is the group's chairman. Donald Whitcomb, associate professor (research associate) of Islamic and medieval archaeology, and Christopher Woods, associate professor of Sumerology, are also members. As our new collaborators, the Faculty Working Group will advise, review, and act as a sounding board for development of materials and innovative new programs and edit content where needed to ensure academic accuracy.

We look forward to partnering with the Faculty Working Group, especially in regard to adult education online. In tandem with developing the online course on ancient Mesopotamia, Wendy and graduate student Jane Messah — whose skills and support have been invaluable — are creating an online module designed to train Oriental Institute graduate students in best practices for online teaching. Once trained, these students will be able to create and then offer an array of distance learning courses similar in variety to those offered on campus. The involvement of the Faculty Working Group will ensure the highest standards of range, content, and quality for these learning experiences, holding great promise for eventual expansion of Oriental Institute outreach to lifelong learners across the nation and around the world.

Special Adult Education Events

Along with exciting new developments in courses for a lifelong learning, we offered a broad spectrum of single-session adult education events throughout the year. Many highlighted the museum's special exhibits and featured presentations by Oriental Institute faculty, museum staff, and students. During the summer we presented three programs in conjunction with Pioneers to the Past: American Archaeologists in the Middle East: 1919–1920, which showcased Oriental Institute founder James Henry Breasted's historic travels to obtain ancient Middle Eastern art and artifacts. "Egypt in Chicago," an Oriental Institute/Art Institute Field trip led by Emily Teeter, special exhibits coordinator, and Lucas Livingston, Art Institute assistant director of museum programs, offered an insider's view on how Breasted's travels led

to the creation of Chicago's three major ancient Egyptian collections. "Who Owns the Past: An Exploration of Archaeology, Politics, and Cultural Heritage" was offered in partnership with the Road Scholar organization (previously called Elderhostel). Former chief curator Geoff Emberling and Emily Teeter were the presenters for this special program. The event also included docent-led tours of the Egyptian Gallery (fig. 3), and a buffet luncheon at the Quadrangle Club. The final Pioneers to Past program featured a tour of the exhibit with Museum Archivist John Larson who discussed Breasted's Middle East travels and behind-the-scenes information in the archival collections that bring those journeys to life.

Figure 3. Docent Deloris Sanders leads a tour for Road Scholar (formerly Elderhostel) highlighting the special exhibit, Pioneers to the Past: American Archaeologists in the Middle East: 1919–1920. Photo by Carole Krucoff

Figure 4. Theo van den Hout introduces the "Inventions of Writing" symposium held in conjunction with the Visible Language special exhibit. Photo by Wendy Ennes

Visible Language: The Invention of Writing in the Ancient Middle East and Beyond, inspired several programs in conjunction with this special exhibit. "Inventions of Writing" a half-day symposium, explored how the latest research shows that writing was invented not just once but separately in four distinct times and places — ancient Mesopotamia, Egypt, China, and Mesoamerica. The program featured speakers from the Oriental Institute as well as guest lecturers; all fielded numerous questions from the audience during a lively panel discussion after the individual presentations. Speakers from the Oriental Institute included Theo van den Hout, professor of Hittite and Anatolian languages, executive editor of the Chicago Hittite Dictionary Project, and chairman of the Department of Near Eastern Languages and Civilizations (fig. 4); Christopher Woods, associate professor of Sumerology and curator of the exhibit; Janet Johnson, Morton D. Hull Distinguished Service Professor of Egyptology; and Joseph Lam, PhD candidate in Semitic languages. Guest speakers included Edward Shaughnessy, Lorraine J. and Herrlee G. Creel Distinguished Service Professor in Early Chinese Studies, University of Chicago, and Joel Palka, associate professor, anthropology and Latin American studies, University of Illinois at Chicago.

"Cuneiform 101," a special workshop led by Kathleen Mineck, PhD candidate in cuneiform studies and Hittitology and managing editor of the *Journal of Near Eastern Studies*, offered a unique approach to Visible Language programming. After a slide lecture on the development of the cuneiform script, Kathleen gave everyone a hands-on lesson in producing the script, followed by a museum tour to examine how cuneiform script was used for a variety of languages all across the ancient Middle East.

Reading the Past, a professional development program for teachers, was another innovative Visible Language program. Offered in conjunction with the University of Chicago's Smart Museum of Art and supported by the upcoming Reva and David Logan Center for the Arts, this program featured the exciting stories told by sixth-century Chinese art on view at the Smart Museum and the Persepolis Fortification Archives clay tablets stored at the Oriental Institute. Jointly planned by Wendy Ennes, Kristy Peterson, Smart Museum education director, and Julie Marie Lemon of the Logan Center, the program included a Smart Museum tour led by Peterson,

Figure 5. Matthew Stolper explains how 3-D digital technology is changing the ways we conduct research during "Reading the Past," a professional development program for teachers co-sponsored by the Smart Museum of Art and the University's of Chicago's upcoming Logan Center for the Arts. Photo by Wendy Ennes

a reception and visit to Visible Language at the Oriental Institute, and a presentation by Matthew Stolper, John A. Wilson Professor of Assyriology and director of the Persepolis Fortification Archives Project, who explained how 3-D digital technology is changing the way we conduct research and understand the past (fig. 5). Gallery talks by Curator Christopher Woods in the fall and by Emily Teeter in winter rounded out our Visible Language programming.

Figure 6. Günter Dryer (left) clarifies a point as Emily Teeter (center) and Renée Friedman (right) listen during their panel discussion for The Scorpion King program. Photo by Wendy Ennes

In the spring we presented *The Scorpion King*, an exclusive film screening and discussion session in conjunction with the special exhibit Before the Pyramids: The Origins of Egyptian Civilization. This National Geographic film featured world-famous archaeologists who shared discoveries on the earliest era of ancient Egyptian civilization. Breasted Hall was filled to near capacity with visitors who came for the screening and panel discussion with two of the eminent scholars who appeared in the film. The panel, moderated by Emily Teeter, curator of Before the Pyramids, included Günter Dryer, director of excavations for the German Archaeological Institute at Abydos, and Renée Friedman, Heagy Research Curator of Early Egypt at the British Museum and director of the expedition at Hierakonpolis (fig. 6). Both shared their experiences during the making of the film and their discovery of early developments that are among the most important in the history of humankind. We thank Oriental Institute Visiting Committee member Tom Heagy and his wife, Linda, for their support, which enabled us to offer this special event free of charge for everyone.

Two gallery tours of Before the Pyramids led by Emily Teeter also drew large audiences. The first focused on the special exhibit; the second highlighted Before the Pyramids followed by a tour of the Egyptian Gallery to trace the rise of one of the ancient world's most powerful civilizations.

Other special programs also drew large audiences this past year. Hosting concerts as part of the annual Hyde Park Jazz Festival continues to attract hundreds of new visitors to the Oriental Institute. This year the Charlie Johnson Quartet delighted the crowd in Breasted Hall with great jazz and a dash of funk and blues. Flutist Steve Flowers (fig. 7) and keyboard artist Roger Harris filled every chair in the Persian Gallery for two concerts in that magnificent setting. All told, these programs attracted nearly 500 visitors, many of whom had never been to the Oriental Institute. Most asked to be signed up for the *E-Tablet* and are now regularly receiving event and membership information.

Figure 7. An ancient Persian sculpture from Persepolis smiles down on flutist Steve Flowers during his Hyde Park Jazz Festival performance at the Oriental Institute. Photo by Marc Monaghan

The U.S. premiere of Incredible Isfahan, a major new production from internationally acclaimed Iranian documentary filmmaker Farzin Rezaein, brought another large audience of new visitors to the Oriental Institute. After introducing the film, which uses contemporary views combined with dazzling computer images of the Persian city of Isfahan (fig. 8), Rezaein joined everyone for a signing of the film's companion book and a reception featuring Persian cuisine catered by Masouleh Restaurant. This special event was co-sponsored by the University's Center for Middle Eastern Studies.

Our free Sunday afternoon screenings of documentary and feature films on the ancient Middle East, shown in Breasted Hall, continue to attract media and community interest. We celebrated Women's History Month in March with a screening of the 1963 version of Cleopatra starring Elizabeth Taylor (fig. 9), presenting the latest, re-mastered version of this Oscar-winner on the big screen, as it was meant to be seen.

Outreach and Partnerships with the University Community

Collaboration with departments and organizations on campus to serve the University of Chicago and the wider community became an important focus of Public Education outreach this year. Two special collaborative events took place this fall when the University of Chicago joined with the citywide Humanities Festival for a full day of programming in Hyde Park. Two of the festival's thirteen events were hosted and publicized by the Oriental Institute. In conjunction with the festival's theme of The Body, one event was "A Mummy Comes to Life." This program, organized by Emily Teeter, spotlighted our ancient Egyptian mummy Meresamun

and featured a talk by Emily on Meresamun's personal and professional life. The event also included presentations by Dr. Michael Vannier, professor of radiology at the University of Chicago, who showed the results of the latest CT scanning of Meresamun, and by forensic artist Joshua Harker, who demonstrated how he used the CT data to reconstruct Meresamun's physical appearance. Breasted Hall also hosted a program on "Studying the Body," a history of medicine presented by the University of Chicago's library.

For the University's own Humanities Day, Fred Donner drew an overflow crowd to Breasted Hall with a lecture on his recent book Muhammad and the Believers: At the Origins of Islam. Our docents also led two sold-out Humanities Day tours of the museum.

Outreach to University of Chicago students also took center stage for us. We joined with Morris Fred of the University of Chicago's Master of Arts in the Social Sciences (MAPSS) program to manage this year's recruitment and placement of MAPSS students as Oriental Institute interns. We hosted an orientation program and reception attended by eighty students who heard various staff members describe the internship opportunities available in their departments. We then

Figure 8. Poster for the Oriental Institute screening of Incredible Isfahan, which was the U.S. premiere showing of the latest major production by Iranian documentary filmmaker Farzin Rezaein

directed the formal applications we received to the appropriate staff and faculty so that interviews could be arranged. The process resulted in placement of twenty-two MAPSS interns all across the Oriental Institute, with ten coming to our own department to provide the invaluable support you will see described throughout this report (fig. 10). Later in the fall, we received a letter from John MacAloon, director of the MAPSS program, who wrote to tell us how pleased he was to have this extensive collaboration with the Oriental Institute, which he called "our most valued inter-unit relationship."

Figure 9. Filmgoers at our Sunday film series enjoyed a spectacular cinema epic when we screened the 1963 version of Cleopatra during Women's History Month in March

We joined with the Oriental Institute Membership Office for additional outreach to students. As part of the University of Chicago's Arts Pass program, the Oriental Institute began offering free memberships to all University students in May 2010. In September, Membership Coordinator Maeve Reed and Education Programs Associate Jessica Caracci joined together to build awareness of the Oriental Institute and its student membership program during New Student Orientation Week. They distributed materials at student resource fairs all across campus, ran information booths at several of these events, and they developed, publicized, and arranged for a new students' museum tour and reception focusing on "Treasures of the Oriental Institute." These outreach efforts brought us hundreds of new student members. Later in the year, Jessica joined with Maeve to offer student members "Tell Night" — a simulated archaeological dig in the Kipper Family Archaeology Discovery Center managed by Public Education. We all agree that this new membership program is key to building student awareness of the Oriental Institute, making us an integral part of the student and campus experience.

Major Initiatives for Teachers and Students

Empowering teachers to enrich student learning through meaningful study of ancient civilization is also central to the mission of Public Education. Grant-funded support is the vital foundation that enables us to provide innovative and in-depth on site and online learning experiences for teachers and their students. This year we completed two major grant-funded multi-year initiatives and received support for two new projects. All are helping us reach teachers and students in ways that will be meaningful and beneficial well into the future.

Figure 10. Intern Samuel Crenshaw, who provided vital office management and Kipper Family Archaeology Center assistance for Public Education, was among the many MAPSS students who contributed invaluable support to the Oriental Institute this year. Photo by Terry Friedman.

Teaching the Middle East: A Resource for Educators

A prime way to serve teachers and their students is to draw upon the Oriental Institute's scholarly expertise, renowned collections, and online capabilities. This year nearly one million visitors were attracted to the online educational outreach programs we have already made available on the Institute's website. These include Ancient Mesopotamia: This History, Our History, the Teacher Resource Center, and Kids Corner, which features a unique interactive on mummification in ancient Egypt.

Teaching the Middle East: A Resource for Educators is our newest online educational initiative. Funded by the National Endowment for the Humanities (NEH), this large-scale, web-based project was developed by the Institute in collaboration with two University of Chicago partners — the Center for Middle Eastern Studies (CMES) and the eCUIP Digital Library Project.

Teaching the Middle East was designed with the needs of educators in mind. In our outreach work with local high school teachers, both the Oriental Institute and CMES have often heard how difficult it can be to unravel complex historical and current events in the Middle East and link those events to the required curriculum. World history teachers across the United States face the same instructional challenges.

Teaching the Middle East directly addresses these challenges. Launched in December 2010 after three years of development, the project's website provides teachers of ancient and modern Middle Eastern history and cultures with in-depth, reliable, and accessible online resources that draw upon the best in humanities scholarship to help build student understanding of the ancient and contemporary Middle East (fig 11).

The Teaching the Middle East website contains eighteen learning modules that focus on major topics of Middle Eastern history and culture. Each module is organized following the same blueprint. Scholarly essays introduce the themes, concepts and ideas for each topic; Framing the Issues discusses key concepts in greater depth; Examining Stereotypes considers timely, often controversial issues; Image Resource Banks offer copyright free visuals for educational use; Learning Resources provides ready access to maps, books, websites, interactives, and more. Classroom Connections provides teacher-developed lesson plans that directly connect all module materials to curriculum.

Such an extraordinarily rich and diverse educational resource involved a host of contributors. The essays as well as in-depth discussion of key issues and stereotypes were prepared by fourteen University of Chicago scholars whose expertise ensure the resource provides the best in academic research. Contributors include:

- Orit Bashkin, assistant professor of modern Middle Eastern history
- Fred M. Donner, professor of Near Eastern history
- Geoff Emberling, former chief curator, Oriental Institute Museum
- Janet H. Johnson, Morton D. Hull Distinguished Service Professor of Egyptology
- Wadad Kadi, The Avalon Foundation Distinguished Service Professor Emerita of Islamic Studies
- Walter E. Kaegi, professor of history
- Jennie Myers, Oriental Institute research associate
- Michael Sells, John Henry Barrows Professor of Islamic History and Literature
- Holly Shissler, associate professor of Ottoman and Turkish history

- Gil J. Stein, professor of Near Eastern archaeology and director, Oriental Institute
- Martin Stokes, fellow of St. John's College, Oxford University
- Matthew W. Stolper, John A. Wilson Professor of Assyriology
- Christopher Woods, associate professor of Sumerology
- John F. Woods, professor of Iranian and Central Asian history and Near Eastern languages and civilizations

Orit Bashkin, Geoff Emberling, and Gil Stein served as the project's Faculty Review Committee.

The Classroom Connections sections of each module were developed by eight accomplished high school educators from across the metropolitan area who served as Teaching the Middle East's advisory board. These educators, whose feedback and ideas were invaluable, created the discussion questions and thirty-six classroom lesson plans that are key teaching and learning tools for each module. Advisors included Farhat Khan, Roosevelt High School; Maryhelen Matejevic, Mount Carmel High School; Blake Noel, Bronzeville Scholastic Institute; Lisa Perez, Department of Libraries, Chicago Public Schools; Peter Scheidler and Mike Shea, both of Kenwood Academy; Laura Wangerin, Latin School of Chicago; and Howard Wright, Hinsdale South High School.

A complex, multi-year and many-layered initiative, Teaching the Middle East needed a dedicated, creative, and visionary project director. Wendy Ennes, Associate Head of Public Education, was the driving force of Teaching the Middle East; her organizational abilities and guidance were central to the project from the time she developed the successful grant proposal in 2007 to the moment the resource was launched. Wendy arranged for and facilitated meetings with faculty and teacher advisors; handled all budgetary concerns and reports; and served as liaison to the National Endowment for the Humanities. She also supervised the work of Department of Near Eastern Languages and Civilizations and CMES graduate students and other student interns who researched and provided links to web resources and helped edit essays and lesson plans. In addition, she worked closely with colleagues from the Institute and our partners on campus. Leslie Schramer of the Institute's Publication Office copy edited each module with care and precision. Alex Barna, outreach coordinator for CMES, played a key role in facilitating completion of faculty essays; Steven Lane of eCUIP designed the handsome and highly user-friendly website; and Julia Brazas, director of the University of Chicago's WebDocent project, served as professional evaluator. All told, Wendy managed the workflow of forty-five people over the entire project.

Since its launch, Teaching the Middle East: A Resource for Educators has been attracting nationwide attention. Wendy has written two articles on the project; one was fea-

Figure 11. Homepage for the NEH Teaching the Middle East: A Resource for Educators website. Design by Steven Lane, eCUIP Digital Library Project, The University of Chicago Library

tured on EDSITEment, the NEH website for educators, and one appeared in the Spring 2011 issue of The Middle Ground Journal, published online by the National Middle School Association. Wendy has also spoken about the project at educator meetings throughout Chicago and she has been invited to speak at the annual meeting of the National Conference for the Social Studies when it convenes this fall in Washington, D.C.

Teaching the Middle East has been an extraordinary partnership that combined the expertise of scholars, teachers, public programs specialists, and technology professionals. As Wendy herself describes it, our common aim has been to help teachers and their students discover the great currents of continuity and change throughout Middle Eastern history, and to contradict the stereotypes that sometimes cloud our perception of this region. Teaching the Middle East seeks to offer new ways of seeing and understanding how our shared human concerns cross oceans, cultures, and time.

Interactive Learning and the Middle East: Serving Schools and the Latino Community

Over the past several years, the generosity of the Polk Bros. Foundation has enabled us to reach underserved school and family audiences in a wide variety of significant ways. These include the creation of award-winning curriculum materials on the ancient Middle East for classroom use, the creation of Family Activity Cards in English and Spanish to engage families with key objects on view in the museum, and the development of interactive computer kiosks that are now available throughout the museum's galleries. Most recently, the Foundation awarded us support for Interactive Learning and the Middle East: Serving Schools and the Latino Community. Begun in 2008, this initiative, which was designed to help us serve the city of Chicago's growing Latino community, had four major goals:

1. Transform our interactive computer kiosks from an English-only to a bilingual English/Spanish format so that Spanish-speaking as well as English-speaking families could take full advantage of these educational museum experiences

2. Partner with a panel of educators representing a cross-section of schools and student needs to transform our computer interactives into a curriculum-related DVD in English and Spanish that would enrich state-mandated study of ancient civilizations and as well as technology instruction

3. Build increased awareness among Latino families about the rich resources available to them at the Oriental Institute

4. Build awareness of the new DVDs as a highly effective educational resource for Chicago's educational community, as well as for educators across the nation and Spanish-speaking communities worldwide.

Over the past three years, this project has drawn upon the talents and creativity of a broad range of educators, translators, multi-media specialists, and marketers. The Herculean task of creating a Spanish-language version for the materials that accompany our computer interactives was accomplished over the first year and half, led by Wendy Ennes as project manager and by Catherine Dueñas, volunteer services associate, whose fluency in Spanish has been crucial to the entire initiative. All of our other translators are listed in previous annual reports.

During the translation phase we also turned our attention to ways our computer interactives could most effectively be transformed in a curriculum-related DVD, which would move these resources beyond the museum's walls and into the classroom. An advisory board of five Chicago Public School (CPS) educators worked with Wendy on shaping the format of the DVD and they created a rich array of curriculum-based lesson plans related to the ancient Middle Eastern content of our computer interactives. The board's members all had in-depth experience in teaching ancient civilizations and also represented a broad cross-section of the CPS community. Board members included Joanne Groshek, teacher of special needs students; Ninfa Flores, bilingual education instructor; Stephanie Pearson-Davis, teacher of at-risk students; Jeffrey Sadoff, teacher of gifted students; and Mary Cobb, former computer education instructor. The educational expertise of these teachers is reflected in the excellence of the lessons they developed, which is important assurance that the DVD will enhance and enrich classroom learning.

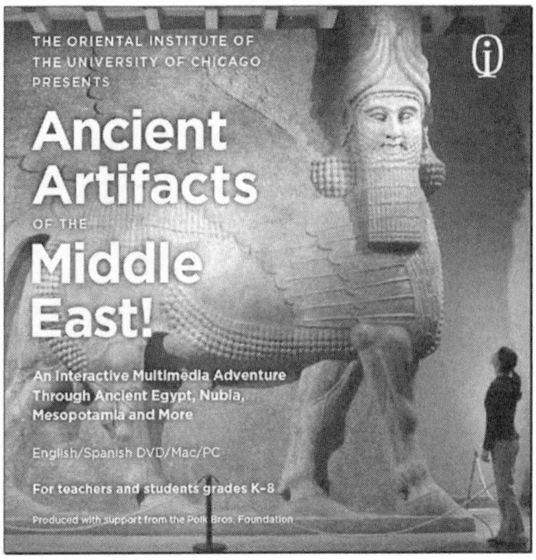

Figure 12. Ancient Artifacts of the Middle East! — an interactive, curriculum-related DVD in English and Spanish developed with support from the Polk Bros. Foundation — is designed to enrich K-8 classroom study of ancient civilizations, as well as technology instruction and bilingual education. Cover design by Wendy Ennes

In last developmental phase of Interactive Learning and Ancient Middle East, Wendy Ennes assumed the role of multi-media specialist and focused her attention on the time-and-labor-intensive process of integrating both written and spoken Spanish-language materials into the software programming and the kiosks in the museum. Only then could she turn to the production of the DVDs. Wendy completed both crucial aspects of the project this year and we were ready to focus on our final goals — building awareness about the bilingual services available at the Oriental Institute and also awareness of the new DVDs — entitled *Ancient Artifacts of the Middle East!* (fig. 12).

Our awareness campaign took two approaches. The first, for the museum, is called "Every Day is Family Day at the Oriental Institute." At the suggestion of staff at the Chicago Public Libraries (CPL) and the Metropolitan Library System (MLS) we created brightly colored bilingual posters and thousands of bilingual bookmarks announcing this theme. CPL then distributed the posters and bookmarks to all of its seventy-two branches and the materials are also in place at eighty-eight branches of the MLS.

Mariel Gruszko, a MAPSS intern who worked with us this year, took charge of this library project along with several other aspects of "Every Day is Family Day." Fluent in Spanish and experienced in community outreach, Mariel made contact with Latino student groups on the University of Chicago campus to spread the word about our bilingual resources. She also worked with William Harms of the University's News and Information office on an outreach campaign to the Spanish-language media to determine what would be the most effective approaches for developing an ongoing relationship with them. In addition, she wrote an *Informacíon en Español* page for the Oriental Institute website, making descriptions of all our bilingual services available to Latino website visitors. Finally, she edited both the Spanish and English text for a new bilingual Oriental Institute lobby sign. Designed by Preparator Brian Zimerle, this sign was created in order to make all Spanish-speaking, as well as English-speaking, families feel welcome at the Oriental Institute (fig. 13).

Figure 13. This new lobby sign, designed by Preparator Brian Zimerle as part of our outreach initiative to the Latino community, was created to welcome Spanish-speaking as well as English-speaking families to the Oriental Institute

Mariel also joined us to in January to help host a special Educator Open House (fig. 14) that launched and distributed the new DVD free of charge to every teacher who attended. Since that time we have been working with the CPS Department of Libraries and Information Services and the CPS Office of Language and Cultural Education to join us in promoting this new educational resource. The DVD is also on sale for a modest price at the Suq, and it is featured on Suq's webpage, promoting it to all the local, regional, national and international educators who visit our website annually.

Our entire department is grateful for the long-standing support of the Polk Bros. Foundation, and we take great pride in the outcomes of Interactive Learning and the Ancient Near East. This project has enabled us to make the Oriental Institute a more welcoming environment for Chicago's Latino community and to provide educators with a unique bilingual resource that we believe will enrich teaching and learning about the ancient world for years to come.

The ACCESS Project

Along with completion of two major projects, Public Education began an exiting new initiative this year in collaboration with the Oriental Institute's Center for Middle Eastern Landscapes (CAMEL). Funded by the Lloyd A. Fry Foundation, the name of this initiative is ArcGIS Cross-Curricular Education for Sixth Grade Students (ACCESS). CAMEL uses ArcGIS, a suite of standard Geographic Information Systems. for analysis of Middle Eastern landscapes, which can reveal the imprint of thousands of years of human activity. The ACCESS project is designed to demonstrate that ArcGIS can also be used to change and enrich the ways middle school educators teach required social studies and science content.

ACCESS is modeled after an earlier Oriental Institute outreach initiative with middle school teachers from Claremont Math and Science Academy, a CPS school whose students come from an underserved community on the city's southwest side. In a unique collaboration led by Wendy Ennes and Scott Branting, assistant professor and director of CAMEL, the Claremont teachers received a brief professional development course on how landscape analysis using geo-spatial technologies can impact and guide

Figure 14. MAPSS intern Mariel Gruszko (left), provides teachers with classroom and museum resources in English and Spanish at an Educator's Open House supported by the Polk Bros. Foundation.
Photo by Carole Krucoff

archaeological study of the past. The teachers then helped CAMEL staff customize the ArcGIS software and exercises into lessons for use by their sixth grade students. CAMEL and Oriental Institute staff joined the Claremont staff to teach these lessons, which successfully engaged the students in using distributional analysis to discover the buried location of a rare golden medallion. The outcome of this pilot project showed us that middle school students can master highly sophisticated research processes if they are presented in ways that appeal to their interests and are taught jointly by experts in science and technology, public education specialists, and middle school teaching professionals.

Built on the foundation of the Claremont pilot, ACCESS is expanding both the process and the project team. Dr. John Loehr, CPS K–12 director of science, and Martin Moe, K–12 director of social science, have become new partners. They are helping us recruit three underserved schools where principals and teachers are eager to access new tools and ways of teaching science and social science to engage a variety of learning styles and student needs (fig. 15). There is great need for these new tools and methods. Loehr and Moe have told us that 95 percent of CPS middle school students enter high school unprepared for science and that new approaches such as the use of ArcGIS are crucial, since CPS students struggle to work with data, form hypotheses and understand the relationship between cause and effect.

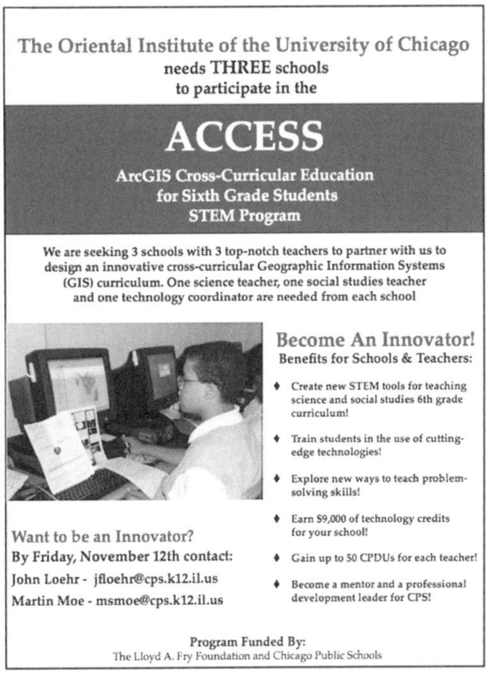

Based upon this understanding of teacher and student needs, Wendy has been working with CAMEL staff to create an in-depth professional development program that will train teachers to focus on student learning through study of GIS. This real world technology can inspire students' development of critical intellectual and practical skills in both science and social science, as well as increase their employability in today's world.

The curriculum of the Ancient Landscapes course that is taught at the University of Chicago by CAMEL staff is the foundation for the ACCESS

Figure 15. Recruitment flyer for ACCESS, our new ArcGis Cross-Curricular Education for Sixth Grade Students program supported by the Lloyd A. Fry Foundation. Flyer design by Wendy Ennes

professional development program. This school year, Tiana Peyer-Peireira and Xander Piper, MAPSS interns interested in science teaching and learning, joined the project and began to clarify and edit the content of the Ancient Landscapes course. Their goal was to make this material more accessible to an audience of teachers unfamiliar with ArcGIS. After months of intensive work, Xander and Tiana left us at the end of the school year, and Allison Hegel, an intern from the University's Jeff Metcalf Fellows Program, joined the project. With her strong educational design skills, Alison is shaping the labs into their final form.

Recruitment of teachers and their involvement in professional development is scheduled for this fall. Throughout their training, the teachers will be asked to transform the content they are learning into lessons designed to meet the needs and interests of their students.

The effectiveness of the teacher training, as well the learning outcomes for students, will be evaluated by Dr. Jonathan Margolin of Learning Point Associates, who has already begun to draft evaluation tools.

We believe the ACCESS project is a model that can help transform the ways CPS educators teach and study by providing real-world teaching and learning resources. Follow our progress in next year's annual report.

The Museums and the Public Schools Project

The Museums and the Public Schools (MAPS) project is a ten-year partnership between selected museums in the city and more than twenty Chicago Public Elementary Schools. This year, the Oriental Institute was invited to join the MAPS project, becoming part of an initiative that also includes the Art Institute of Chicago, Chicago Children's Museum, Chicago History Museum, DuSable Museum of African-American History, National Museum of Mexican Art, and the Peggy Notebart Nature Museum.

The goal of the MAPS program is to create a lasting impact on teaching and learning by integrating museum resources into the educational process of participating schools through sustained museum/school partnerships throughout the academic year. The partnership process begins with each museum offering a professional development workshop for all the schools taking part in the project. Then the schools apply to the museums they wish to work with as partners. Each museum is encouraged to select three schools from among the applicants so that a strong, year-long relationship of outreach visits to the schools as well as visits to the museum can be established and maintained.

Lauren Wojnarowski, who holds a master's degree in historical administration from Eastern Illinois University, joined our department as MAPS program coordinator, a position supported by funding from CPS. Lauren had been an intern at the Oriental Institute in 2009 as part of requirements to earn her master's degree. The excellence of her work, especially with schoolchildren, as well as her familiarity with our educational resources, made her the ideal candidate for the coordinator's position.

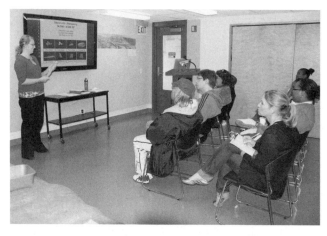

Figure 16. Lauren Wojnarowski, Coordinator for our Museums and the Public Schools (MAPS) partnership with city schools, leads a workshop introducing teachers to Oriental Institute educational resources and services, including programming in the Kipper Family Archaeology Discovery Center (KADC). Photo by Wendy Ennes

Working under Wendy's Ennes' supervision, Lauren developed and presented a professional development workshop for participating MAPS schools. The workshop introduced teachers to the Oriental Institute's resources and school programming (fig. 16). Because of their strong interest in the Oriental Institute and its content connection to their curriculum, Lauren chose Johnnie Coleman Academy, Kanoon Magnet School, and McCutcheon Elementary School as our three MAPS partners.

Over the course of the school year, Lauren visited each school to have planning sessions with teachers and principals; distribute Oriental Institute curriculum materials; set schedules for school outreach and museum visits; and teach classroom lessons using reproduction artifacts, images; and other museum materials. She also prepared the students for their museum visits, which included guided gallery tours as well as a hands-on dig experience in the Kipper Family Archaeology Discovery Center (KADC), the Oriental Institute's simulated excavation site (fig. 17).

Figure 17. Students from Johnnie Coleman Academy, one of our MAPS partner schools, excavate, record, and analyze discoveries during their KADC experience at the Oriental Institute. Photo by Carole Krucoff

While many of our grant-funded programs enable us to provide extraordinary resources and learning experiences for teachers, the MAPS program is unique in that it focuses on bringing museum educators into the classroom to work side-by-side with teachers, joining with them to integrate museum resources and field trips directly into the classroom curriculum. We look forward to an ongoing relationship with the MAPS program and the meaningful partnerships it encourages between the Oriental Institute and the Chicago Public Schools.

The Kipper Family Archaeology Discovery Center

The Kipper Family Archaeology Discovery Center (KADC) is a simulated archaeological dig that recreates an ancient Middle Eastern excavation site. Designed to be a hands-on learning laboratory, the KADC engages students in thinking like scientists as they uncover, record, and analyze their finds in the simulated site. Then they discover how ancient artifacts go "from ground to gallery" on a docent-led tour of the museum.

The KADC served 750 and middle school students and their teachers this past year. Participants came from the city and suburbs and ranged from gifted students to those with special needs. In addition, support from the MAPS program, described above, enabled us to provide bus transportation and fund all costs of the complete KADC experience for our three partner schools (fig. 18).

Jessica Caracci, education programs associate, became KADC Coordinator in 2008 and her management was integral to the program's development and success. Along with publicizing the program and scheduling all school visits to the KADC, this past year Jessica recruited, trained, and supervised three graduate students from the

Figure 18. On a recent visit to the Oriental Institute, major KADC supporter Barbara Kipper (left) joined Morris Fred and Gil Stein to commend MAPS partner teacher Shevinna Sims from Johnnie Coleman Academy for her excellent work in preparing students for their KADC experience. Photo by Carole Krucoff

Figure 19. "Dad, look what I found." A
father and son team up to excavate
and record their discoveries during a
KADC program for families as part of
the Neighborhood Adventure Series
sponsored by the Chicago Office of
Tourism. Photo by Jessica Caracci

MAPSS program — Matthew Nunnelley, Marissa Stevens, and Cathleen Stone — to serve as KADC facilitators. They were joined by Erica Griffin, Oriental Institute volunteer. Kendra Grimmett, a student in the University of Chicago's Art Department, returned as a facilitator for a second year and joined Jessica in training the new recruits. Jessica also invited Katharyn Hanson and Eudora Struble, PhD candidates in the Department of Near Eastern Languages and Civilizations, to provide special insights on archaeology and the reproduction artifacts in the KADC tell during the facilitators' training.

Along with its service to schools, the KADC has become the springboard for development of programs to provide new learning experiences for youth and families. This past year, Jessica collaborated with the Chicago Office of Tourism to offer a KADC program for families as part of the city's Neighborhood Adventure Series (fig. 19). This program sold-out almost as soon as it was announced. Jessica also included excavation sessions during our annual children's summer day camps offered with the Lill Street Art Center. And she worked with MAPSS intern Sam Crenshaw, along with KADC facilitators Erica Griffin and Matthew Nunnelley, to provide a special excavation and pottery reconstruction program for Boy Scouts to earn their Archaeology Badge (fig. 20).

University of Chicago students enjoyed the KADC this past year when Public Education and Membership hosted a special hands-on dig for student members during an evening event that quickly filled to capacity. A more formal learning experience took place when students enrolled in the University's Anthropology of Museums course taught by Morris Fred came to experience the simulated dig. They then joined Gil Stein to discuss the unique educational environment of the KADC and its role within the setting of a renowned archaeological museum and research institution.

The success of all these programs validates Jessica Caracci's vision for the KADC. After being with the Oriental Institute for over five years, Jessica left us this spring. Among her many contributions, she gave us the foundation for development of an array of KADC programs that can provide diverse audiences with meaningful learning experiences for many years to come.

Figure 20. Boy Scouts from Troop 28 intently
engage in reconstructing pottery during a
KADC program to earn their Archaeology
Badge. Photo by Carole Krucoff

Youth and Family Programming

Public Education presented longtime favorites as well as new initiatives for youth and families this past year, nearly all in collaboration with local or citywide partners. Several programs used off site outreach formats to reach new audiences, while other events took place at the Oriental Institute to serve old friends and attract new visitors.

Outreach Programs

This past summer was our busiest outreach season. For the thirteenth straight year we traveled to the Lill Street Art Center on the city's north side for "Be an Ancient Egyptian Artist," a week-long day camp for children ages eight to twelve that fills to capacity every time it's offered. Teaching artists Agnes Sohn and Meg Peterson took part in two week-long sessions of the camp; each included a visit to the Oriental Institute, where the campers took part in a KADC excavation and art-making session led by

Figure 21. Docent Carole Yoshida helps a mother and child make an ancient Egyptian-style "book" at the 57th Street Children's Art Fair. Photo by Carole Krucoff

Agnes, Kendra Grimmett, and former facilitator Sarah Brophy.

In August we ventured out to Millennium Park for a Family Fun Festival sponsored by Chicago's Department of Cultural Affairs. More than 1,000 parents and children gathered under the big festival tent to enjoy music, games, and the opportunity to "get up close and personal" with our reproduction mummy, who came with us and became a star of the show. Erica Griffin, Kendra Grimmett, and Jessica Caracci introduced our mummy and invited everyone to visit the real mummies on view at the Oriental Institute. In September we took part in the 57th Street Children's Book Fair, where docent Carole Yoshida invited children and their parents to make and take home a scroll that became their own ancient Egyptian-style "book" (fig. 21). All these events help introduce the Oriental Institute to local and citywide audiences.

Two special outreach programs helped us share information about all of the bilingual services we now have available at the Oriental Institute. After hearing about our new services, the Pilsen Neighbors Community Council invited us to take part in *Fiesta del Sol*, their annual summer festival for the city's Latino community. Catherine Dueñas, volunteer services associate, organized the activities and arranged for the staffing of our Fiesta del Sol booth. Erica Griffin, summer intern Lauren Horn, and docent Semra Prescott joined Cathy to paint children's faces with ancient Egyptian-style symbols and offer everyone samples of our bilingual family activity cards, discount coupons for the Suq, and directions on how to find the Oriental Institute (fig. 22).

Later in the year we took part in *Día del Niño*, a spring celebration for the Latino community hosted by Chicago's National Museum of Mexican Art. Catherine

Figure 22. Visitors to the Oriental Institute booth at Fiesta del Sol were welcomed with smiles and greetings in Spanish by (L-R) interns Lauren Horn and Erica Griffin, Volunteer Services Associate Catherine Dueñas, and docent Semra Prescott. Photo by Carole Krucoff

Figure 23. MAPSS intern Abigail Abisinito helps visitors make origami pyramids during the Día del Niño family festival organized by the National Museum of Mexican Art. Photo by Carole Krucoff

and Semra, along with MAPSS interns Abigail Abisinito and Mariel Grusko, staffed the Oriental Institute booth. While all are fluent in Spanish, it was impossible for them to speak to the several thousand people who attended *Día del Niño*. However, more than 750 visitors lined up at our table to fold origami pyramids (fig. 23) and learn about the Oriental Institute, which was new to almost everyone our staff encountered. All received samples of our bilingual materials and information about our Spanish-language website, as well as special invitations to visit the Oriental Institute and enjoy a free museum audio-tour in either English or Spanish. We hope these outreach programs, along with our marketing campaign to the Spanish-language press, will bring us many new Latino visitors.

At the Museum

The KADC was the site of a family event this past year — the sold-out Neighborhood Adventures program. And visitors to the museum took home 13,480 of our bilingual Family Activity Cards, a 14 percent increase over last year. But once again it was mummies who took center stage with the family audience when we hosted our annual "Mummies Night" in October. This pre-Halloween event, which was offered in conjunction with the citywide celebration of "Chicagoween," featured a "tomb-full" of activities led by docents and interns. These ranged from a "Guess the Mummy Lollipops" contest to dressing up in costumes from "King Tut's Closet" (fig. 24), and from folding origami pyramids, bats, and frogs to treasure hunts in the Egyptian Gallery. This year, the Membership and Education Offices joined together to present "Mummies Night" and for the first time a modest admission fee was charged, with free admission as a special benefit for Oriental Institute members (fig. 25). While attendance was somewhat less than in years past, "Mummies Night" attracted over 300 children and their families, and the admission fees covered all the event's costs.

Figure 24. Adults as well as children enjoyed dressing up in items from "King Tut's Closet" during Mummies Night, our annual pre-Halloween celebration for families. Photo by Wendy Ennes

In February we presented "The Magic Carpet: Stories, Songs, and the Art of Writing," a family program in conjunction with the Visible Language special exhibit. Funded by the Illinois Arts Council, this event, which included hands-on activities and gallery treasure hunts, featured master storyteller Judith Heineman and musician Daniel Marcotte in an interactive performance that explored how writing began. Then the performers invited children onto the stage in Breasted Hall to bring tales from ancient Egypt and Mesopotamia to life. Even though this program took place in the midst of an historic Chicago blizzard, 120 people came to "The Magic Carpet," and many parents told us how grateful they were to have such a special mid-winter event for families.

Behind the Scenes

Looking back on all that has been accomplished this past year, I'd like to say how much Public Education appreciates the on-going interest, expertise, and support of faculty, staff, and students, many of whom are

Figure 25. Education Programs Associate Jessica Caracci, dressed as a cowgirl, and Membership Coordinator Maeve Reed, a friendly pirate, greeted guests and sold admission tickets for Mummies Night. This year's pre-Halloween celebration was co-sponsored by Public Education and Membership. Photo by Wendy Ennes

mentioned in this report. Special thanks go to Gil Stein, director of the Oriental Institute, and Steve Camp, executive director, who guided and encouraged us throughout the first year as our own unit. Additional thanks go to Kate Grossman and Megaera Lorenz, our new graduate student content advisors. Kate's work on volunteer training and on-line course materials development has been invaluable. Megaera has been equally helpful in re-shaping the content of our on site adult education programming to reflect the latest Oriental institute research, an outcome that will be visible in our fall programming. She is also adding depth to the upcoming training sessions for new KADC facilitators.

Our sincere appreciation goes to the family events and special programs volunteers who worked with us this past year. All our special programming for adults, families, and the university community could not have taken place without the time and talents of these dedicated people (fig. 26). A record of all their names appears in the Volunteer section of this report.

Wendy Ennes, associate head of Public Education, is central to every aspect of the department. Her leadership in all our major grant-funded initiatives for teachers, students, and families is evident throughout this report. Wendy's strong strategic planning skills and goal-setting abilities have also been vital to new initiatives during our first year as an independent Oriental Institute unit. A prime example is her leadership in moving our adult education programming into the online realm, which holds such great promise for outreach to life-long learners nation-wide and around the world.

Wendy's vision and drive, along with her grant-writing abilities, project-man-

Figure 26. Docents Gabriele Correa da Silva and Katje Lehmann stand ready and waiting to meet children and their parents at Mummies Night. Gabriele and Katja were among the many volunteers who contributed their time and talents to special programs and family events this past year. Photo by Wendy Ennes

Figure 27. Children learn KADC excavation techniques from facilitators Kendra Grimmett and Matthew Nunnelley. They were among the corps of interns who aided us in countless ways this past year. Photo by Carole Krucoff

agement skills and online expertise, also make her a major asset to the Institute as a whole. She supports a wide range of Institute and museum initiatives, from participating on the New Media Committee and the museum's Community Focus Group panel to her work on the Institute's Integrated Database (IDB) project, a long-term initiative to link the many computerized databases throughout the institute. Wendy is managing a pilot program funded by grant from the Institute of Museum and Library Services to develop and test a user-friendly front end, or online portal, to the IDB. The accessibility of this portal is key to successful use of the IBD by academic researchers and the general public.

Wendy would be among the first to acknowledge the invaluable role that our department's sixteen MAPSS and volunteer interns have played this past year. Many have already been mentioned in this report, but their major contributions as members of our team deserve recognition here. Jane Messah is working with Wendy on the writing and editing, as well as development of technological aspects, for the upcoming online course on ancient Mesopotamia and the online training course for graduate students. Tiana Peyer-Peireira, Xander Piper, and Allison Hegel have provided crucial editorial support for the ACCESS project. Matthew Nunnelley, Marissa Stevens, and Cathleen Stone, along with Erica Griffin, did outstanding work as KADC facilitators. Kendra Grimmett made vital contributions as KADC trainer and facilitator, as well presenter and coordinator for special adult and family programs (fig. 27). Caitlin Wyler provided research and programmatic support in her second year as a summer intern. Abigail Abisinito provided invaluable assistance with marketing and public relations as well as office management, and her Spanish language skills were key for our outreach to the Latino community. Along with planning and taking part in *Día del Niño*, she translated into Spanish all the main label text from the Before the Pyramids so that this special exhibit could become accessible to Spanish-speaking visitors. Huiying Chen translated the Before the Pyramids labels into Chinese as part of a Chicago Convention and Tourism Bureau outreach program for visitors from China. She also helped plan and evaluate several of our major public programs, including the "Invention of Language" symposium, "The Scorpion King" event, and "The Magic Carpet." Interns Rachel Kornfield, Mariah-Grooms Garcia, and Susan Weaver made major contributions to the Volunteer program; their work is described in the Volunteer section of this report.

MAPSS intern Samuel Crenshaw merits special mention here. Throughout the fall and winter he worked alongside Jessica Caracci to provide essential office management and KADC support. When Jessica left the Oriental Institute in the spring, he stepped in to assume the multi-faceted role of education programs associate, doing a superbly professional job until he graduated from the MAPSS program in June.

Jessica Caracci's many contributions to the success of Oriental Institute public programming are visible throughout this report. With us since 2005, her professionalism and grace brought her the respect and admiration of the volunteers, faculty, and staff who had the pleasure to work with her. Along with her outstanding leadership as coordinator of the KADC, her organizational skills were evident in all she did to make our group tour program run smoothly and efficiently. Her administrative abilities and creativity were also central to the success of our programs for adults, youth, and families, and her marketing and public relations skills were key to our increases in program participation. Jessica left her position as education programs associate to pursue her life-long dream of becoming a pastry chef. We appreciate all her efforts as a valued member of our team, and we wish her the very best of success in her new career.

In June, Kathryn ("Kat") Silverstein joined us to become our new education programs associate. Kat holds a MA in education from the University of New Hampshire, a BFA from the University of Michigan, and she has a broad range of experience with cultural and arts institutions in Chicago. We welcome her aboard and look forward to working with her!

The following section presents the many achievements of the Volunteer Program, supervised by Volunteer Services Associates Terry Friedman and Catherine Dueñas, our extraordinarily talented and dedicated colleagues. This year our collegial relationship became even closer as we all collaborated with faculty, staff, students, and volunteers to shape and present new outreach programming for the public. Read on to see how the Institute and the community have benefitted from the work of our remarkable volunteers, and all that Terry and Catherine have helped them accomplish.

———————————

VOLUNTEER PROGRAM

Catherine Dueñas and Terry Friedman

2010–2011 Volunteer Program

This year the Volunteer Program celebrated a benchmark in its history, the forty-fifth anniversary of its founding. With age comes maturity and resilience, both of which have been clearly demonstrated by the program's ability to evolve and change throughout the decades to meet the demands and opportunities of the twenty-first century.

The Oriental Institute Volunteer Program was created in 1966 by Robert McCormick Adams, the Institute's director at that time. Although its mission has been modified over the years, it was Adams' intention to create a program to provide guided tours that would make the museum's scholarly gallery displays more accessible to schools and the general public. The program's original mission, to provide training for a cadre of volunteers (known as museum docents) who would give tours to visitors of all ages, continues to be our guiding principle to this day. Serving as the first docent coordinator, Carolyn Livingood was instrumental in helping develop the educational component of the program as well as recruiting candidates for its first Docent Training class. Throughout the decades, the program has been able to retain its unique character by offering rich educational opportunities that challenged and inspired its members while upholding the highest standards. It is truly the volunteers' intellectual curiosity coupled with a deep sense of camaraderie and loyalty that is at the core of what has defined, sustained, and paved the way for the program's historic longevity.

Tour Program

> The museum is a gem, but Docents are needed to interpret the displays, especially to younger visitors. To be sure, the artifacts are well chosen and charmingly displayed, but it is the human voice, explaining and describing, which gives emphasis to what the eyes see.

> — Ida Depencier, member of the first Docent Training class
> in 1966, from "Reflections of A Volunteer Docent,"
> Oriental Institute News & Notes, April 1974.

Docents play a critical role in a visitor's museum experience as the above insightful quote from the late Ida Depencier describes.

As the public face of the museum, docents help to interpret the collection while serving as goodwill ambassadors. Whether with school students, religious groups, community organizations, or senior citizens, the Oriental Institute Museum Docents are eager to share their knowledge and pride for the museum's collection. During the fiscal year 2010–2011, we are pleased to announce that 5,198 visitors enjoyed the advantage of a docent-led tour, while 4,827 visitors chose the self-guided option. This gives us a total of 10,025 visitors.

Tracking Trends (It's All in the Numbers)

Following the progress from last year's efforts, we continued to refine our systems for tracking statistical information regarding museum tours and visitors. This year we have focused on collecting more detailed information on the different visiting groups, to ensure the accuracy of the data, and making periodic attendance reports readily available to our colleagues throughout the museum. After validating the accuracy of previously collected data, we began the process of transferring our multi-year data set into a new program with a user-friendly format and increased functionality. This process was a year-long endeavor that will allow us to efficiently generate summary statistics and graphical representations of emerging trends and patterns. Our efforts have already yielded useful information about the changing demographic characteristics of our visitors. We expect that our improved database system will continue to facilitate in-depth analyses of our tour programs in the coming months and years. It was through the tireless efforts of Rachel Kornfield, our Master of Arts Program in the Social Sciences (MAPSS) 2010–2011 intern, that this project reached its current level of sophistication and relevance. The process was time consuming and tedious, but the end result will help internal and external office communication run with a new level of efficiency. We want to thank Erica Griffin for her assistance during the early stages of this project, Sue Geshwender, who was instrumental in helping us conceptualize and implement all stages of this project, and Steve Camp for his guidance and support as we moved through each phase.

Visitor Trends Over Time

By focusing our attention on tour data, we were able to extract very significant information concerning visitor trends over time. Despite an uncertain economy, we were pleased that numbers for this fiscal year 2010–2011 revealed a 4% increase over last year in the total number of visitors participating in tours. This year we had 10,025 visitors who participated in 314 tours. This growth in part reflects a dramatic jump in the number of school and youth groups visiting the museum, a 9% increase since the 2008–2009 fiscal year. We have seen a

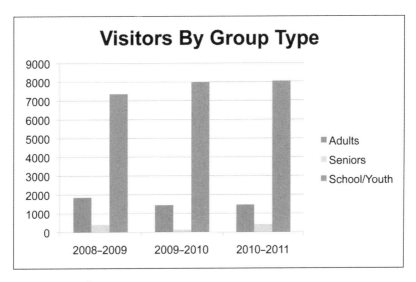

Figure 1. Visitors by group type

particular increase in high school and elementary school group attendance.

In figure 1, our tour participants over the past three years are broken down into the following categories: adult, senior, and school/youth visitors. In the current fiscal year, 15% of visitors were adults, 4% were seniors, 80% were school/youth group members, and 1% were non-specified. Despite overall increases in our tour numbers this year, we have noted that adult tours have not increased at the same rate as our school/youth tours. To increase adult tour and senior group attendance, we are developing a more effective marketing strategy to attract these groups to our museum. We feel that through more detailed analysis, we will be able to reinvigorate this specific group's attendance and find areas for improvement and possible expansion.

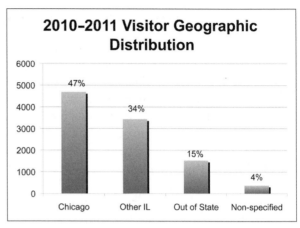

Figure 2. 2010–2011 visitor geographic distribution

Geographic Distribution

We were surprised to discover that a decrease in the number of out-of-state visitors over the past three years has been met by a 36% increase in our Chicago-area tour participants. The geographic breakdown of our tour participants for the 2010–2011 fiscal year is represented in figure 2. As you can see, 47% of our visitors were from Chicago, 34% were from the rest of Illinois, 15% were from out of state, and 4% were non-specified.

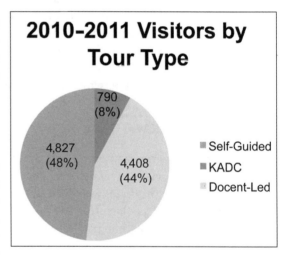

Figure 3. 2010–2011 visitors by tour type

Types of Tours

In figure 3, our tour participants are broken down by tour type. Consistent with prior years, our tours for the 2010–2011 fiscal year were divided between guided and self-guided options. As you can see, 4,827 (48%) opted for self-guided tours, 790 (8%) participated in a Kipper Family Archaeology Discovery Center (KADC) program, and 4,408 (44%) participated in a stand-alone docent-led tour. We are pleased that the tour numbers this past fiscal year revealed our program's continuing strength in delivering quality tours to local schools as well as to other community groups from within and outside Illinois.

Fall 2010 Mini-Series

Ancient Economies: The Consumer Report

Building on the success of the fall mini-series the past two years, we were proud to present another program to provide docents and volunteers the opportunity to examine a particular topic in greater depth. Over the course of five Saturdays, interesting lectures were given by Yorke Rowan, Gil Stein, Emanuel Mayer, Don Whitcomb, and Matt Stolper as part of our fall 2010 mini-series on Ancient Economies: The Consumer Report. All who attended were thrilled with the opportunity to participate in such an intellectually enriching program. These presentations and the discussions that followed helped us understand the connections between the economic realities of the ancient world and those of our own time. We thank our lecturers for sharing their wealth of knowledge and years of research with us.

The entire event was filmed by Chicago Media Initiatives Group. We look forward to including the DVD of this mini-series in our permanent library of training materials. We were pleased this year to have partnered with the University of Chicago Alumni Association who generously assisted with underwriting a portion of the costs associated with the production of the DVDs. We are proud that these taped lectures will be available to the University of Chicago Alumni as part of the Minds on Line series.

Revision of Training Materials

Persian Gallery

In September, we were pleased to announce the completion of the revised Persian Gallery Training Manual, which became available for distribution to the volunteers. We are certain that it will become an extremely valuable resource to help current and future docents understand and appreciate the history and culture of this fascinating region.

Our thanks and appreciation to Abbas Alizadeh and Don Whitcomb for their vision and determination in producing such an outstanding Docent Training Guide for the Robert and Deborah Aliber Persian Gallery. We also want to express our appreciation to Suzan Bazargan for her meticulous editing of the manuscript, and to Alice Brown, our MAPSS (2009–2010) intern, for scanning, compiling, and reformatting the Persian section as well as the entire Docent Training Manual over the course of her internship.

We would also like to acknowledge the many contributions of the following individuals, who helped make this project possible: Tom James, Tom Urban, Karen L. Wilson, and Natalie Whiting.

The official unveiling of the new Persian Training Manual took place on Saturday, September 11. Abbas Alizadeh conducted a brilliant introductory session for the docents and volunteers about these materials. His PowerPoint presentation and discussion gave us a fresh perspective on how to utilize this information to enhance our understanding of the gallery and to integrate these ideas into our tours.

Mesopotamian Gallery

In January, focusing on the Edgar and Deborah Jannotta Mesopotamian Gallery, we began the second phase of the revision of the Volunteer Training Manual. Under the leadership and guidance of Kathryn Grossman, PhD candidate in Mesopotamian archaeology, work began on the rewriting of the Mesopotamian materials. Kate, who has served as content specialist, brought much enthusiasm to this project. Her efforts will introduce new and revised sections for the Volunteer Training Manual. We look forward to the project's completion.

A Faculty Working Group is assisting Kate in the process of vetting and writing recommendations concerning the content and accuracy of the Mesopotamian section of the Training Manual. The Faculty Working Group was created by Gil Stein in June 2011 as part of an initiative to ensure that the materials produced by and distributed through the Public Education Department maintain the highest standards of academic accuracy while remaining interesting and engaging to the general public. We are honored to have our academic colleagues Fred Donner, Don Whitcomb, and Chris Woods be a part of this important process, and look forward to working with them.

Volunteer Recognition

December Volunteer Day

December Volunteer Day has become an annual tradition when docents, faculty, staff, and volunteers gather to enjoy a festive holiday celebration together. This popular event includes a guest speaker, the introduction of new volunteers, and the Volunteer Recognition Ceremony. The program concludes with a lovely holiday luncheon at the Quadrangle Club. This year's special event took place on Monday, December 6, in Breasted Hall.

The program officially began as Steve Camp, executive director of the Oriental Institute, gave the volunteers a museum update and afterward addressed some of their concerns.

The program continued with our guest speaker David Schloen, who gave an outstanding presentation on "Highlights from the Recent Excavations at Zincirli." His fascinating lecture brought to life this large-scale Iron Age city in southeastern Turkey and the many discoveries that are helping to reshape our knowledge of the history of this region.

Following David's talk, the program continued with an introduction of the individuals who joined the Volunteer Program in 2010:

Volunteers of 2010–2011

Tim Agra	Erica Griffin	Katharine Marsden
Rebecca Bailey	Ruth Guth	Sarah Means
Eugenia Briceno	Abigail Harms	Jean Nye
Paul Burton	Mary Louise Jackowitz	Elizabeth Penny-O'Brien
Clark Godinez	Paul Johnson	Roberta Schaffner
	Katja Lehmann	

MAPSS 2010–2011 Intern

Rachel Kornfield

2010 Recognition Award Recipients

This year seventeen people were recognized for their years of volunteer service to the Oriental Institute.

Award recipients were divided into two categories: active volunteers, those who participate on a routine basis, and emeritus volunteers, those who have not been as active in recent years, but who still remain involved and a part of the Oriental Institute community.

Active Volunteers

5 Years	10 Years	15 Years
Doug Baldwin	Joe Diamond	Pat McLaughlin
Gaby Cohen	Dario Giacomoni	
Andrea Dudek	Nancy Patterson	
Margaret Manteufel	Semra Prescott	
	Joy Schochet	
	George Sundell	

20 Years	25 Years	35 Years
Nancy Baum	Christel Betz	Teresa Hintzke

Emeritus Volunteers

30 Years	35 Years
Debbie Aliber	Maria "Ria" Ahlstrom (deceased)
	Pat Hume
	JoAnn Putz

Docent Library

Through the Docent Library, volunteers have access to an extensive lending library of books and materials on all topics relating to the ancient Near East. Head Librarian Margaret Foorman meticulously oversees the collection, managing acquisitions and circulation. The Docent Library eagerly accepts donations from faculty, staff, and volunteers; Margaret highlights these new additions to the library regularly in *The Volunteer Voice*. New materials are also purchased directly for the program with funds raised at the annual book sale, held in conjunction with December Volunteer Day. This year, our annual book sale raised over $100 for the Docent Library. Many thanks to Margaret for her hard work and resourcefulness.

The Docent Library also serves as a volunteer lounge. The room bustles every day as staff and volunteers use the space to socialize, look over training materials, and get caught up on Oriental Institute news. We thank all the generous donors who have consistently replenished the sweets and treats that so many of us enjoy regularly.

Volunteer Days

The Volunteer Program is committed to providing meaningful, ongoing educational opportunities for docents and volunteers. These events and programs provide a stimulating learning environment for volunteers to explore personal scholarly interests while also developing informative and up-to-date tours. The 2010–2011 season featured many successful programs. We wish to thank Abbas Alizadeh, W. Ray Johnson, Gil Stein, Emily Teeter, and Chris Woods for contributing their time and expertise to these educationally enriching programs.

Volunteer Training and Management

Docent Captain System

The Docent Captain System is a key component to the success of the Tour Program and provides the critical synergy between the Public Education's administrative staff and museum docents. Each captain is responsible for scheduling docent staffing on a specific day of the week as well as supervising their team of docents, with whom they communicate via weekly e-mail reminders. Captains also mentor and guide new docents in training, giving them the support they need to become successful and confident museum guides.

Throughout the year, several docent captains encouraged their groups to organize informal study sessions that focused on the development of special-interest tour topics. These sessions helped docents enhance their own knowledge of specific areas of the collection while sharing creative approaches for engaging audiences with interactive touring methods.

We extend our thanks and appreciation to the following captains and co-captains for their hard work and dedication throughout this past year: Doug Baldwin, Noel Brusman, Myllicent Buchanan, Gabriele DaSilva, Dennis Kelley, Stuart Kleven, Larry Lissak, Lo Luong Lo, Demetria Nanos, Stephen Ritzel, Lucie Sandel, Deloris Sanders, Hilda Schlatter, and Carole Yoshida. Their attention to detail and organizational skills allows the Docent Program to run smoothly and efficiently.

This year the Volunteer Program was saddened to announce the retirement of two longtime captains, Sunday Co-Captain Teresa Hintzke and Saturday afternoon Co-Captain Lo Luong Lo. We thank them for their leadership and support throughout the years.

Connecting a Community of Volunteers

Volunteer Voice

The monthly newsletter, The Volunteer Voice, is an important communication tool that connects the many volunteers, faculty and staff working at the Oriental Institute. The newsletter publicizes upcoming educational events and volunteer opportunities, chronicles important happenings from the past month, and disseminates important new information. The Volunteer Voice is sent out to all docents, faculty, staff, and volunteers by e-mail, or via the United States Postal Service.

Volunteer Directory

Continuing her hard work updating the volunteer databases that she began last year, museum docent and faculty assistant Sue Geshwender still contributes many hours, helping the office become more sophisticated with its use of technology. We were pleased that this past December, the second edition of the Volunteer directory was ready for widespread distribution. Thank you, Sue, for your continued support and help with this ongoing project. Your efforts help us stay connected.

Volunteer Fairs

In October we were invited to attend a Volunteer Fair sponsored by the Little Brothers – Friends of the Elderly. It was a wonderful chance to promote volunteer opportunities at the Oriental Institute and to find out about volunteering options at other nonprofit organizations throughout the Chicago metropolitan area.

Interns

We were fortunate to work with an outstanding group of interns this past year. Rachel Kornfield was our 2010–2011 MAPSS intern throughout the entire academic year and for a portion of the summer. During the winter quarter Moriah Grooms-Garcia moved from her role as museum docent to that of intern. These young women were responsible for numerous administrative tasks, special projects, and the implementation and maintenance of statistical database systems. Their many contributions helped to support and enrich the Volunteer Program's ongoing operations and new initiatives.

We were also delighted to have intern Susan Jones from Wheaton College join us for the 2011 summer. She has helped us on a number of challenging projects over the summer months.

We want to express our sincere thanks to all three interns who have assisted in the production of this year's annual report. Their valuable contributions to its content and its editing process have been deeply appreciated.

Public Education Staff

We would also like to thank our Public Education Department colleagues for their ongoing support and astute advice throughout this past year: Jessica Caracci, Education Programs Associate; Wendy Ennes, associate head of Public Education, Educational Technology and Innovation; and Carole Krucoff, head of Public Education. In our shared office space, filled with activity and many projects, their sense of humor and collaborative spirit foster a collegial and productive working environment.

A special note of thanks to Education Programs Associate Jessica Caracci, whose outstanding organization and communication skills are at the very core of the tour program's success. Her patience and friendly demeanor are truly appreciated by everyone with whom she works. Sadly, Jessica left her position at the end of March to pursue her life-long dream of becoming a pastry chef. We wish her every success in her new career. In June, Kathryn Silverstein joined the Public Education staff to serve as the new Education Programs Associate. We look forward to working with her and welcome her aboard!

In Memoriam

This year the Volunteer Program and Oriental Institute lost two devoted friends and supporters, Maria Ahlstrom and Bernadine Basile. These individuals epitomized the essence of a volunteer, sharing their unique talents and skills in order to further the goals and mission of the Oriental Institute. We are so thankful for their many years of service and dedication and will miss them greatly.

Reflections

The forty-fifth year of the Volunteer Program has witnessed the continued efforts of a lively team of volunteers and interns who are dedicated to making the history and culture of the ancient Near East alive and engaging to museum visitors of all ages. It has been a year of milestones and new initiatives. While many technological advances have taken the program to new levels of efficiency and accessibility, it is the volunteers themselves who continue to hold on to many of the traditions that make this program unique. Although each person's motivation to join the volunteer corps may be different, the common denominator that unites them is their love of learning and their eagerness to contribute their time and talents to help enrich the Institute's mission and goals.

It is hard to imagine that the Volunteer Program has reached such a significant milestone in its history. Forty-five years, in terms of archaeological time, is very brief, yet for the Volunteer Program it is a landmark event, one that we reflect upon with great pride and a deep sense of accomplishment.

We are so fortune to have three members from the first training class in 1966 who are still actively involved with the Institute and the Volunteer Program: Cissy Haas, Carlotta Maher, and O. J. Sopranos. Their years of service truly exemplify a long-standing tradition of commitment and dedication — a legacy that holds true to this day.

We thank all volunteers past, present, and future for their enthusiasm, intellectual curiosity, and loyalty throughout these past forty-five years. They form a unique community of dedicated individuals whose passion for learning and pride in the Institute's work and the museum's collection are the cornerstones of the program's success and historic longevity.

We are pleased to announce that volunteers donated 9,168 hours of their time to the Oriental Institute and the museum this past fiscal year. Kudos for a job well done!

Advisors to the Volunteer Program

Carlotta Maher	Peggy Grant	Janet Helman

Interns

MAPSS Intern 2010–2011	Winter/Spring 2011	Summer 2011
Rachel Kornfield	Moriah Grooms-Garcia	Susan Jones

We are proud to announce that twenty-two people joined the Volunteer Program this past fiscal year (July 1, 2010–June 30, 2011)

Class of 2010–2011

Tim Agra	Abigail Harms	Elizabeth Penny-O'Brien
Melissa Bellah	Mary Louise Jackowitz	Noah Rapel
Mervyn Berenie	Alfia Lambert	Nancy Rose
Paul Burton	Debra Mack	Roberta Schaffner
Clark Godinez	Marilyn Murray	Dee Spiech
Erica Griffin	Karina Meza	Robert Threatte
Ruth Guth	Srila Nayak	James Wolfgang
	Jean Nye	

Docent Advisory Committee (Executive Board)

Joe Diamond	Dennis Kelley	Mary Shea

Museum Docents (Active)

John Aldrin	Erica Griffin	Mary O'Shea
Dennis Bailey	Moriah Grooms-Garcia	Nancy Patterson
Douglas Baldwin	Debby Halpern	Kitty Picken
Nancy Baum	Janet Helman	Stephen Ritzel

Museum Docents (Active) (cont.)

Suzan Bazargan	Lee Herbst	Nancy Rose
Christel Betz	Teresa Hintzke	Gerladine Rowden
Rebecca Binkley-Albright	Mark Hirsch	Lucie Sandel
Noel Brusman	Morton Jaffe	Deloris Sanders
Myllicent Buchanan	Paul Johnson	Ljubica Sarenac
Roberta Buchanan	Dennis Kelley	Hilda Schlatter
Gabriella Cohen	Stuart Kleven	Joy Schochet
Susan Cossack	Panagiotis (Pete) Koutsouris	Anne Schumacher
Joan Curry	Alfia Lambert	Mary Shea
Gabriele DaSilva	Larry Lissak	Daila Shefner
John DeWerd	Lo Luong Lo	Mae Simon
Joe Diamond	Debra Mack	Toni Smith
Djanie Edwards	Paul Mallory	Dee Spiech
Jean Fincher	Margaret Manteufel	Mari Terman
Mary Finn	Sherry McGuire	Karen Terras
Margaret Foorman	Kathy Mineck	Craig Tews
Barbara Freidell	Marilyn Murray	James Tillapaugh
Sue Geshwender	Demetria Nanos	Siwei Wang
Dario Giacomoni	Jean Nye	Ronald Wideman
Bill and Terry Gillespie	Daniel O'Connell	Inge Winer
Clark Godinez	Mary O'Connell	James Wolfgang
Anita Greenberg	Elizabeth Penny-O'Brien	Carole Yoshida
Ira Hardman	Semra Prescott	Agnes Zellner

Outreach Volunteers

Andy Buncis	Bettie Dwinell	Larry Lissak
Janet Calkins	Bill and Terry Gillespie	Margaret Manteufel
Joan Curry	Ira Hardman	Demetria Nanos
Joe Diamond	Panagiotis (Pete) Koutsouris	Carole Yoshida

Volunteers Emeritus

Debbie Aliber	Joan Friedmann	Masako Matsumoto
Maria Ahlstrom (deceased)	Carol Green	Robert McGiness
Muriel Brauer	Cissy Haas	Roy Miller
Charlotte Collier	Alice James	Muriel Nerad
Erl Dordal	Mary Jo Khuri	Patrick Regnery
Mary D'Ouville	Betsy Kremers	Janet Russell
Bettie Dwinell	Nina Longley	Elizabeth Spiegel
	Jo Lucas	

Affiliated Volunteers
(not active, but still part of the Oriental Institute community)

Sylwia Aldrin	David Giba	Alice Mulberry
Bernadine Basile (deceased)	Marda Gross	Donald Payne
Andrew Buncis	Janet Kessler	Pramerudee Townsend
Davis Covill	Henriette Klawans	Arveal Turner
	Pat McLaughlin	

Camel Lab Volunteers

Alexander Elwyn   Peter Fiske   Larry Lissak   Craig Tews

Conservation Lab Volunteers

Kristen Gillette   Jen Johnson   Amy Lukas   Nicole Pizzini

Chicago House Volunteers

Andrea Dudek   Joan Fortune

Diyala Project Volunteers

Larry Lissak   George Sundell

Galilee Pre-History Project Volunteers

Robyn Dubicz   Abigail Harms   Roberta Schaffner

Hacinebi Project Volunteer

Irene Glasner

Nippur Project Volunteer

Karen Terras

Museum Volunteers

Abigail Abisinito   Huiying Chen   Siwei Wang   Mariel Gruszko

Registration Work Study Volunteer

Courtney Jacobson, Museum Assistant

Volunteers

Janet Helman   Daila Shefner   Jim Sopranos
Ila Patlogan   Toni Smith   Leslie Warmus (MAPSS student)
Matthew Sawina   Sam Speigel (numistmatist)

Professor Brinkman's Volunteer

James Torpy

Demotic Dictionary Volunteer

Larry Lissak

Museum Archives Volunteers

Jean Fincher   Sandra Jacobsohn   Robert Wagner
Peggy Grant   Carole Yoshida

Research Archives Volunteers

Ray Broms   Andrea Dudek   Stephanie Duran   Roberta Schaffner

Suq Volunteers

Barbara Storms-Baird	Ray Broms	Jane Melroy
John Baird	Peggy Grant	Erin Mukwaya
Judy Bell-Qualls		Norma van der Meulen

NELC Graduate Students

Adrienne Frie	Manuel Alex Moya	Andrew Rutledge
Jessica Henderson	Stephanie O'Brien	Elizabeth Wolfson

MAPSS Graduate Students

Patrick Chew	Gerard Dougher	Derek Walker	Aram Sarkisian

Tall-e Geser Project Volunteer
Janet Helman

Kipper Family Archaeology Discovery Center (KADC) Volunteer
Erica Griffin

Strategic Planning Volunteer
Shel Newman

2011 Gala Volunteers

Rebecca Bailey	Terry Friedman	Adam Lubin
Karin Christiaens	Bill Gillespie	Jean Nye
D'Ann Condes	Terry Gillespie	Mariana Perlinac
Gabriele Correa da Silva	Emma Harper	Maeve Reed
Kristen Derby	Anna Hill	Rebecca Silverman
Cathy Dueñas	Tom James	Craig Tews
Wendy Ennes		Meghan Winston

2011 Gala Committee

Andrea Dudek	Sue Geshwender	Debby Halpern
Margaret Foorman		Mari Terman

Family Events and Special Programs Volunteers

Abigail Abisinito	Sue Geshwender	Demetria Nanos
Rebecca Binkely-Albright	Bill Gillespie	Jean Nye
Doug Baldwin	Terry Gillespie	Semra Prescott
Christel Betz	Erica Griffin	Stephen Ritzel
Noel Brusman	Mariel Gruszko	Lucie Sandel
Huiying Chen	Mark Hirsch	Deloris Sanders
D'Ann Condes	Lauren Horn	Mary Shea
Kristin Cooper	Dennis Kelley	Hilda Schlatter
Gabriele DaSilva	Stuart Kleven	Mae Simon
John DeWerd	Panagiotis (Pete) Koutsouris	Toni Smith
Jean Fincher	Katja Lehmann	Craig Tews
Dario Giacomoni	Lo Luong Lo	John Whitcomb
Moriah Grooms-Garcia	Mary O'Connell	Carole Yoshida
	Kathy Mineck	

2010-2011 Volunteer Program Photo Gallery

This year's Volunteer Recognition ceremony took place on December 6th in Breasted Hall. Before leaving for lunch at the Quadrangle Club, the award recipients posed for a group picture. Top row left to right: Margaret Manteufel, Semra Prescott, JoAnn Putz, Doug Baldwin, George Sundell, Nancy Baum, Gaby Cohen, and Joy Schochet. Bottom row: Cathy Dueñas, Andrea Dudek, Teresa Hintzke, Christel Betz, Dario Giacomoni, Joe Diamond, and Terry Friedman. Photo by Craig Tews

Volunteers gathered on September 29th to hear an introductory lecture on the new special exhibit Visible Language: The Invention of Writing in the Ancient Middle East and Beyond. Christopher Woods, exhibition curator, gave an excellent overview of its content and the artifacts that would be on display. Photo by Terry Friedman

2010–2011 Volunteer Program Photo Gallery

Our thanks to all five presenters who helped make the fall 2010 mini-series, Ancient Economies:
The Consumer Report, a great success: Gil Stein (top left), Yorke Rowan (top right),

Emanuel Mayer (bottom left), Don Whitcomb (bottom center), and Matt Stolper (bottom right).

Screen shots by Tom James, from video taken by Chicago Media Initiatives Group

2010–2011 Volunteer Program Photo Gallery

In October we attended a city-wide Volunteer Fair at Little Brothers – Friends of the Elderly. It was a great opportunity to meet new people and to professionally network with other nonprofit organizations. Cathy Dueñas enjoyed telling many of the participants about the Oriental Institute. Photo by Terry Friedman

Our summer 2011 intern was Susan Jones from Wheaton College. She spent the summer working on evaluating and updating the KADC program as well as doing a phone survey of guided tour groups and other miscellaneous tasks. Photo by Terry Friedman

Rachel Kornfield was our MAPSS 2010–2011 intern. Rachel was instrumental in updating our database systems, developing information tables, and creating graphs. Her patience and expertise was greatly appreciated by all with whom she worked. Photo by Terry Friedman

2010–2011 VOLUNTEER PROGRAM PHOTO GALLERY

This past January, Kate Grossman, PhD candidate in Mesopotamian archaeology, began the rewriting of the Mesopotamian Training Materials. Kate's dedication to this research project and serving as its content specialist will yield an outstanding new and revised section to the Volunteer Training Manual. Photo by Terry Friedman

Teresa Hintzke receiving her Recognition Award for thirty-five years of service at the Volunteer Recognition ceremony. Photo by Craig Tews

Moriah Grooms-Garcia moved from her role as a museum docent to serving as an intern during the winter and spring quarters. Photo by Terry Friedman

Camaraderie and Conversation at the Annual Holiday Luncheon:
A Photo Gallery

Members of the Thursday docent team paused for a moment to pose for a photograph during the Volunteer Recognition Luncheon at the Quadrangle Club. From left to right: Noel Brusman, Hilda Schlatter, and Ira Hardman. Photo by Craig Tews

Some of the Wednesday docents, as well as Registrar Helen McDonald, enjoyed the food and good time at the Volunteer Recognition Luncheon in December. From left to right: Gabriella Cohen, Deloris Sanders, Suzan Bazargan, and Oriental Institute Registrar Helen McDonald. Photo by Craig Tews

Camaraderie and Conversation at the Annual Holiday Luncheon: A Photo Gallery

Docents socializing while enjoying the Volunteer Recognition Luncheon in December. From left to right: Debby Halpern, Daila Schefner, and Ila Patlogan. Photo by Craig Tews

Joe Diamond and three teachers from James Hart School sitting together and enjoying the Volunteer Recognition Luncheon in December. From left to right: Shirley Watkins, Gail Huizinga, and Sue Johnson are seated with Joe Diamond. Photo by Craig Tews

2009-2010 Volunteer Program Photo Gallery

Due to technical difficulties, some of the photographs from the 2009–2010 *Annual Report* were inadvertently omitted from the printed and bound version distributed to all Oriental Institute Members. We apologize for this omission, but we are pleased to be able to include them in this year's report.

Presenters for the fall 2009 mini-series Creation Myths gathered on November 5, 2009, to answer questions from the audience in a final panel discussion. Seated from left to right are Foy Scalf, Andrea Seri, Theo van den Hout, and Margaret Mitchell. Photo by Cathy Dueñas

2009–2010 Volunteer Program Photo Gallery

Interns' contributions are crucial for the enrichment of the Volunteer Program's ongoing operations and initiatives. Alice Brown, 2009 MAPSS intern, works hard to update and edit the new digitized version of the volunteer training manual. Photo by Terry Friedman

Former MAPSS intern Karina Chavarria continues her work with the Volunteer Program, compiling and tracking past visitor statistics. Karina has also played an integral role in a new project that was launched this summer and is aimed at expanding our resources to Chicago's Spanish-speaking communities. Photo by Terry Friedman

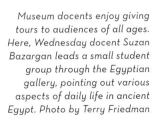

Museum docents enjoy giving tours to audiences of all ages. Here, Wednesday docent Suzan Bazargan leads a small student group through the Egyptian gallery, pointing out various aspects of daily life in ancient Egypt. Photo by Terry Friedman

2009–2010 Volunteer Program Photo Gallery

Mari Terman, another Wednesday docent, explains ancient Egyptian games to an interested group of young students from the LaSalle Academy. Photo by Terry Friedman

A large project undertaken by the Volunteer Program this past year was to replace the current Persian chapter of the Volunteer Training Manual. Here, Suzan Bazargan and Senior Research Associate Abbas Alizadeh rewrite the old chapters in order to present this material in a more concise manner. Photo by Terry Friedman

MAPSS Intern Alice Brown also played an important role in the Persian chapter rewrite. She is working here with Abbas Alizadeh and Suzan Bazargan to further edit changes. Photo by Terry Friedman

2009–2010 Volunteer Program Photo Gallery

Education Programs Associate Jessica Caracci and intern Melanna Kallionakis instruct a visiting group from the LaSalle Academy on proper excavation technique in the KADC. Photo by Terry Friedman

A group of students from the Millennium School in Homewood-Flossmoor got to be kings and queens for a day during one of the school outreach programs. Photo by Terry Friedman

Girls from the Millennium School were able to dress in ancient Egyptian-style attire during these highly interactive outreach programs. Photo by Terry Friedman

2009–2010 VOLUNTEER PROGRAM PHOTO GALLERY

The boys at the Millennium School enjoyed trying on traditional pharaonic costumes as part of the outreach program. Photo by Terry Friedman

The volunteers that participated in the outreach program to the Millennium School in Homewood-Flossmoor sit down for a nice lunch with Volunteer Service Coordinators Terry Friedman (at head of table, top) and Catherine Dueñas (at head of table, left). Photos by Cathy Dueñas and Terry Friedman

Old Persian

Babylonian   Elamite

DEVELOPMENT AND MEMBERSHIP

Overleaf: Ornamental peg with inscription of Darius I (522–486 BC), the founder of Persepolis: "Knobbed peg of precious stone (or lapis lazuli) made in the house of Darius the King." The upper line is in Old Persian, in Old Persian writing; the lower line has the Babylonian and Elamite versions, in two variants of Mesopotamian cuneiform writing. OIM A29808B. Blue frit. Iran, Persepolis, Southeast Palace. Achaemenid period, reign of Darius I, 522–486 BC. 7.9 x 12.4 cm. After Matthew W. Stolper, "61. Ornamental Peg with Trilingual Text," in Visible Language: Inventions of Writing in the Ancient Middle East and Beyond, *edited by Christopher Woods, no. 61, p. 96 (Oriental Institute Museum Publications 32; Chicago: The Oriental Institute, 2010). Photo by Anna Ressman*

DEVELOPMENT AND MEMBERSHIP

DEVELOPMENT

Steven Camp

Oriental Institute supporters have once again helped us move forward on a number of key projects during a tough economic period. As the chart below shows, we received $2,329,446 in gifts to the Institute during the past fiscal year. This was an 11.4% increase from the previous period. As a result, we were able to offer continued support for unique special exhibits, seven nationally recognized and ongoing excavation projects across the Middle East, and the record of tablets belonging to the Persepolis Fortification Archive. We were also able to fund the launch of the first ever joint Palestinian-American archaeological excavation, located at Jericho in the Palestinian territories. We were also very fortunate to receive multiple research grants throughout the year, including continued support from the Women's Board of the University of Chicago, multiple grants from the National Endowment for the Humanities (NEH), the Andrew W. Mellon Foundation, the American Research Center in Egypt (ARCE), the Institute of Museum and Library Services (IMLS), the PARSA Community Foundation, the Exelon Foundation, and the Wenner Gren Foundation. Our development staffing also changed during the year as we replace Rebecca Silverman, who transitioned into a new position at the University's Court Theatre in June.

Once again, our success could not have been achieved without the loyal support of all our Members and Donors. On behalf of all of us at the Oriental Institute, thank you for joining as partners in discovery.

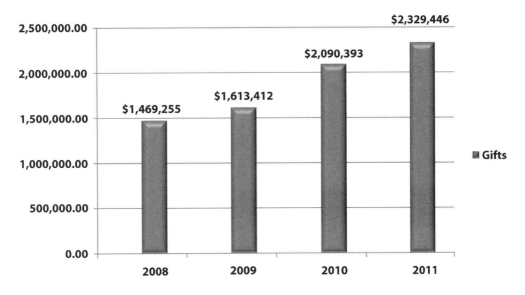

Oriental Institute fund-raising 2008-2011

VISITING COMMITTEE

The Oriental Institute Visiting Committee 2010–2011

Harvey B. Plotnick, Chair

Marilynn Alsdorf
Dr. Kathleen G. Beavis
Guity Nashat Becker
Gretel Braidwood*
Andrea M. Dudek
Emily Huggins Fine
Dr. Marjorie M. Fisher
Margaret E. Foorman
Joan S. Fortune
Isak V. Gerson
Nancy H. Gerson
Margaret H. Grant
Lewis S. Gruber
Misty S. Gruber
Howard G. Haas
Deborah G. Halpern
Thomas C. Heagy*
Janet W. Helman*

Dr. Arthur L. Herbst*
Doris B. Holleb*
Neil J. King
Daniel A. Lindley, Jr.
Lucia Woods Lindley
Jill Carlotta Maher*
John W. McCarter, Jr.
Kathleen Picken
Crennan M. Ray
John W. Rowe*
Robert G. Schloerb
Lois M. Schwartz*
O. J. Sopranos*
Mari D. Terman
Dr. Walter H. A. Vandaele
Anna M. White
Nicole S. Williams

* denotes Life Member

MEMBERSHIP

Maeve Reed

Publications

With the assistance of the Publications Office, the Membership Office continues to publish *News & Notes*, the quarterly Members' magazine. The fall 2010 issue (no. 207) featured an in-depth preview of the special exhibit Visible Language: Inventions of Writing in the Ancient Middle East and Beyond, as well as the annual Chicago House Bulletin. Winter 2010 (no. 208) highlighted the Institute's three main dictionary projects, the Chicago Assyrian Dictionary, Chicago Demotic Dictionary, and Chicago Hittite Dictionary. In spring 2011 (no. 209), the magazine provided Members with a preview of the special exhibit Before the Pyramids: The Origins of Egyptian Civilization. Finally, in summer 2010 (no. 210) Members were treated to a report of the first season of excavation at the Institute's newest field project, the Jericho Mafjar Project, in the West Bank. Additionally, *News & Notes* honored the following Members and donors for their support of the Oriental Institute:

- Fall 2010: The University of Chicago Women's Board
- Winter 2011: O. J. (Jim) Sopranos, Harvey Plotnick, and Janet Helman
- Spring 2011: Tom and Linda Heagy, Debby and Ned Jannotta, and the 2010 Volunteer Recognition Award Recipients (for a full listing of recipients, please see the *Volunteer* section of this annual report)
- Summer 2011: The Oriental Institute Visiting Committee

The Membership Office is greatly appreciative of the Publications Office for their hard work and guidance in producing *News & Notes*, as well as to all the authors and staff contributors who provide exciting and engaging articles and program notices each quarter for our Members.

Since October of 2009, the Membership Office has been publishing the *E-Tablet*, our e-newsletter, with great success. Almost 7,000 friends and supporters of the Oriental Institute receive the *E-Tablet*, which keeps them up to date with news, events, and announcements. The *E-Tablet* is published on the first Tuesday of every month and is free to the public. To sign up for the *E-Tablet*, visit our website (http://oi.uchicago.edu) and click on "Subscribe to our e-newsletter" at the bottom of the page.

In addition to the *E-Tablet*, the Membership Office has been involved in launching and maintaining several New Media profiles and sites with the assistance of the New Media Working Group (Maeve Reed, Thomas James, John Sanders, and Wendy Ennes). Members are encouraged to follow the Oriental Institute on Twitter, visit the Oriental Institute page on Facebook, our channel on YouTube, and our website to interact with and learn more about the Oriental Institute and our online community. For a complete report of New Media efforts, please see the *Museum* section of this annual report.

Marketing

With the support and assistance of Emily Teeter and Carole Krucoff, the Membership Office has participated in a grant-funded study to conduct membership and visitor research to better understand the various audiences we serve as a museum and research institute. In January and February of 2011, seven long-term Members agreed to participate in an in-depth phone interview administered by Slover-Linett Strategies, an audience research and planning group. The qualitative results of these interviews are invaluable in that they provide insight into both motivations for why Members initially join the Institute, and why they become long-term Members and supporters. Results indicate that Members are intrigued by our research and field projects, are life-time learners, and view membership communication vehicles (*News & Notes*, the *E-Tablet*, and the *Annual Report*) as well-organized and valuable resources to stay up to date on Institute news while strengthening their connection to the Institute's mission. For more information, please see the *Publicity and Marketing* section of the Museum's report.

Student Memberships

As part of the University of Chicago's Art Pass program the Oriental Institute began offering free membership to all University students in May 2010. As of June 2011, the Institute had over 600 University of Chicago student members, more than any other campus organization. To manage this new and rapidly growing program, the Membership Office hired two incredibly talented graduate student interns, Brittany Wheeler and Emily Pavell. Through partnerships with the Office of Publication and the Museum, the Membership Office was able to host several successful student member events throughout the year:

- Treasures of the Oriental Institute (September 2010) — a tour of the Museum for new college students as part of OI Week activities (co-sponsored by Public Education, Museum, and Volunteer Program)
- Study at the OI (December 2010 and March and June 2011) — quarterly, late-night study hall hosted in the Museum galleries
- Tell Night (February 2011) — fantasy archaeology camp and learning opportunity in the Kipper Family Archaeology Discovery Center (co-sponsored by the KADC and Public Education)
- Indy Film Fest (April 2011) — month-long film festival featuring all four of the Indiana Jones films in Breasted Hall, with an introduction by Yorke Rowan and Morag Kersel

In total, we hosted over 1,000 university students at the Institute during the academic year through these special events and programs. The student membership program aims to increase student awareness of the Oriental Institute, make the Oriental Institute an integral part of the student and campus experience at the University, and become active participant in student events.

Events

Members enjoyed a wide variety of events in 2010–2011:

- Members' Preview — Visible Language: Inventions of Writing in the Ancient Middle East and Beyond (September 27, 2010)
- Associate Members' Event — Behind Closed Doors: An Evening with Oriental Institute Registrars (November 8, 2010)
- James Henry Breasted Society Event — Records of Their Time: Chinese Bronzes at the Art Institute and the Invention of Writing (December 1, 2011)
- Members' Preview — Before the Pyramids: The Origins of Egyptian Civilization (March 28, 2011)

For in-depth information on the above events, please see the *Special Events* section of this annual report.

In addition to Members' Events, Oriental Institute Members enjoyed a comprehensive Members' Lecture Series in 2010–2011, with topics ranging from the Sasanian Empire to the ritual of artifact and relic collecting in the Holy Land:

- The Libyan Anarchy: Egypt and Nubia in the Era from Solomon to Assurbanipal — Robert K. Ritner (October 2010)
- Towards a Better Understanding of Amarna: Recent Research in the City and Its Main Cemetery — Barry Kemp (November 2010); co-sponsored by the American Research Center in Egypt
- *Ab Urbe Condita*: Early Cities at Hamoukar during the Chalcolithic and Early Bronze Age — Clemens Reichel (December, 2010)
- Visible Language: The Earliest Writing Systems — Christopher Woods (January, 2011)
- Ozymandias in Ararat: The Cities of the Near East's Least-Known Great Monarch — Paul Zimansky (February 2011); co-sponsored by the Archaeological Institute of America
- The Rise and Fall of Kerkenes Dağ — Scott Branting (March 2011)
- Sasanian Iran: The Other Great Empire of Late Antiquity — Touraj Daryaee (April 2011)
- The Lure of the Relic: Collecting the Holy Land — Morag Kersel (May 2011)
- Dr. Donny George Youkhanna: One Scholar's Contribution to Mesopotamian Archaeology — McGuire Gibson (June 2011); co-sponsored by Oriental Institute Director Gil J. Stein and the Oriental Institute Museum

A very special thank-you is in order for all of our lecturers, co-sponsors, and Members for making the 2010–2011 Members' Lecture Series the best-attended series in four years. The Oriental Institute Members' Lecture Series aims to bring a varied selection of the most recent work and scholarship on the ancient Middle East to our Members and the local community. We look forward to an exciting and dynamic lecture line-up for the 2011–2012 series, which beings in October 2011.

Members' Events would not be possible without the hard work of many dedicated Oriental Institute staff members and volunteers, and the Membership Office is thankful for all their assistance with a very successful 2010–2011 events season.

Travel

In the past year the Oriental Institute offered two travel programs to the Middle East. In October 2010 Yorke Rowan escorted eight travelers to Israel in the travel program The Holy Land: Heritage of Humanity. This travel program provided a comprehensive look at Israel, from prehistoric burial sites to the modern-day architecture of Tel Aviv, and included a private tour of Marj Rabba, the Oriental Institute's newest excavation in Israel. Unfortunately, due to political unrest in Egypt in the winter and spring of 2011, Robert K. Ritner's sold-out March 2011 travel program, The Wonders of Ancient Egypt, had to be canceled. Thankfully, registration for a 2012 tour of the same name and itinerary is currently underway. In addition to canceling our March 2011 Egypt tour, we also had to cancel our September 2011 tour, In the Footsteps of the Hittites: Turkey and Syria, as political unrest and violence continues to plague Syria. We hope to be able to reschedule this tour, led by Theo van den Hout, in the near future. In addition to our March 2012 Egypt tour, we are excited to announce a unique tour opportunity in collaboration with the Archaeological Institute of America, the Explorers Club, and Zeghram Travel. Voyage through the Red Sea: Jordan, Egypt, Saudi Arabia, Sudan & Eritera will be led by Oriental Institute Research Associate Emily Teeter along with other expert lecturers, and will explore an astounding array of archeological sites along the Red Sea. Travelers will cruise the sea aboard the comfortably elegant *Clipper Odyssey*. The tour is scheduled to depart on November 6, 2011; registration for this program is currently ongoing.

Oriental Institute travel programs are unique in that our passengers experience exclusive site visits and on-site learning privileges not enjoyed by other institutions or travel groups. Our Members learn directly from some of the most eminent scholars in the world, at sites the Oriental Institute has been working on and researching for almost a century. For more information on Oriental Institute travel programs, contact the Membership Office at oi-membership@uchicago.edu or visit our website at http://oi.uchicago.edu/getinvolved/member/travel.html.

Administrative Notes and Benefits

In order to provide an easier way to identify and understand membership benefits and levels, the Membership Office designed this reference chart for benefits in the spring of 2011 (see opposite). Beginning in the fall of 2011, this chart will replace bulleted lists and descriptions of benefits currently found on membership renewal notices, the Institute's website, and all other membership materials.

This year, there were three staffing changes for the Membership Office. In July 2011, longtime Development Gifts Assistant Meredyth Syneed (AB '10) left the office to pursue her PhD in anthropology at the University of California, Berkeley. In March 2011, Bethany Page Bouldin (AB '11) graduated from the College with a degree in history and immediately took a position at the Chicago Botanical Gardens as a customer call center coordinator. Following Bethany's departure, Emma Harper (MA '12) joined the office in March 2011 as the new membership programs assistant and has been doing an excellent job managing the membership database, hosting events, and responding to Members' questions and inquiries.

Oriental Institute Members' Benefits	Individual	Family	Associate	Breasted Society Patrons	Breasted Society Director's Circle
	$50	$75	$100+	$1000+	$2500+
Complimentary Museum admission	•	•	•	•	•
Member Card	•	•	•	•	•
10% Suq discount and free audio tour rental	•	•	•	•	•
News & Notes magazine and E-Tablet newsletter	•	•	•	•	•
Invitation to Members' events and lectures	•	•	•	•	•
Discounts on programs, courses, and symposia	•	•	•	•	•
Access to the Research Archives	•	•	•	•	•
Travel Program brochures	•	•	•	•	•
The Oriental Institute Annual Report	•	•	•	•	•
20% off Journal of Near Eastern Studies	•	•	•	•	•
Access to the Oriental Institute Volunteer Program	•	•	•	•	•
2nd Member Card		•	•	•	•
Complimentary admission for children under 18		•	•	•	•
Discounts on birthday party rentals		•	•	•	•
Discounts on family programs		•	•	•	•
Invitations to Associates' events			•	•	•
Reciprocal privileges to 400+ museums			•	•	•
Recognition in the Annual Report			•	•	•
Invitation to the Oriental Institute Gala			•	•	•
Invitations to Breasted Society events				•	•
Invitations to VIP dinners with faculty				•	•
Use of the Oriental Institute for private functions					•
One complimentary exhibit catalog per year					•

SPECIAL EVENTS

Meghan A. Winston

The 2010–2011 event schedule was an exciting one for the Oriental Institute! We welcomed over 800 guests through a variety of events, including two Members' previews, an Iranian film premiere, and a dictionary completion celebration. We also welcomed many different groups, including the American Research Center in Egypt, the American Oriental Society, and the Women's Board of the University of Chicago. It was truly a pleasure to host our Members and donors, who make the work we do here possible.

Visible Language Members' Preview

On September 27, 216 Oriental Institute Members enjoyed an exclusive preview of Visible Language: Inventions of Writing in the Ancient Middle East and Beyond, a special exhibit showcasing some of the earliest writing systems in the world.

After Gil J. Stein, director of the Oriental Institute, welcomed all guests, Geoff Emberling, research associate and chief curator of the Oriental Institute Museum, introduced Chris Woods, associate professor of Sumerian, as the guest curator of our newest exhibit. During his talk, Woods helped Members understand the origins of written language through ancient cuneiform tablets, hieroglyphics, and Chinese characters.

Following Woods' lecture, guests were invited to tour the exhibit and to enjoy a reception with food from Amazing Edibles Catering in the Edgar and Deborah Jannotta Mesopotamian Gallery. Members enjoyed delectable hors d'oeuvres in addition to a special expansion of the Suq, which featured specially ordered merchandise and autographed copies of exhibit catalogs.

A special thank-you goes out to Steve Camp, Chris Woods, Geoff Emberling, Emily Teeter, Maeve Reed, Erik Lindahl, and Adam Lubin for all they did to ensure the night's success.

Behind Closed Doors: An Evening with Oriental Institute Registrars

On November 8, we invited forty-one Associate Members to join us for cocktails, hors d'oeuvres, and a behind-the-scenes look at Oriental Institute Registration. Beginning at 6:00 PM, guests were treated to a twenty-minute presentation by Helen McDonald, Oriental Institute registrar, regarding the registration process as a whole.

Following the presentation, guests broke into smaller groups and took exclusive tours of the registration and organic storage areas. As part of this special evening, we invited registration volunteers Jim Sopranos, Janet Helman, and Lisa Heidorn to showcase the different projects on which they have worked, which were on display at different stations situated throughout the Edgar and Deborah Jannotta Mesopotamian Gallery. All food for the evening was provided by Occasions Chicago Catering.

A special thank-you goes out to Maeve Reed, Helen McDonald, Jim Sopranos, Janet Helman, Lisa Heidorn, and all others who ensured the night's success.

Records of Their Time — A James Henry Breasted Society Event

On December 1, thirty-seven James Henry Breasted Society Members met at the Art Institute of Chicago for a personalized tour of the special exhibit Ancient Chinese Bronzes from the Shouyang Studio: The Katherine and George Fan Collection. After a greeting from James Cuno, president of the Art Institute of Chicago, the tour, lead by Visible Language curator Christopher Woods and University of Chicago professor Edward Shaughnessy, covered the ancient Chinese bronzes, which highlighted the historical and technical elements of China's most prized cultural possession — its writing system. Following the tour, guests enjoyed cocktails, hors d'oeuvres, and a seated dinner at the nearby University Club. The menu for the evening included duck spring rolls, lobster bisque, grilled chicken breast, and a citrus cheesecake.

A special thanks goes out to everyone involved who ensured the night's success.

Before the Pyramids Members' Preview

On March 28, 210 Oriental Institute Members enjoyed an exclusive preview of Before the Pyramids: The Origins of Egyptian Civilization, a special exhibit showcasing hieroglyphic writing, architecture, and the origins of kingship — some of the most fundamental aspects of ancient Egyptian civilization.

After Gil J. Stein, director of the Oriental Institute, welcomed all guests, Geoff Emberling, former research associate and chief curator of the Oriental Institute Museum, introduced Emily Teeter, research associate, as the guest curator of our newest exhibit. During her talk, Teeter helped Members understand the Predynastic and Early Dynastic periods of Egypt through a discussion of ancient pottery, statues, and palettes.

Following Teeter's lecture, guests were invited to tour the exhibit and to enjoy a reception with food provided by Amazing Edibles Catering in the Edgar and Deborah Jannotta Mesopotamian Gallery. Members enjoyed delectable hors d'oeuvres in addition to a special expansion of the Suq, which featured specially ordered merchandise and autographed copies of exhibit catalogs.

A special thank-you goes out to Steve Camp, Emily Teeter, Maeve Reed, Erik Lindahl, Brian Zimerle, and Adam Lubin for all they did to ensure the night's success.

2011 Post-Doctoral Seminar — Iconoclasm and Text Destruction in the Ancient Near East and Beyond

From April 8 to 9, the Oriental Institute welcomed fourteen scholars from various universities spanning North America and Europe for its annual post-doctoral seminar. Participants who arrived on Thursday night were treated to a dinner at the University's own Quadrangle Club.

On Friday evening, various Oriental Institute professors, in addition to conference participants, attended a small reception for our guests in the Edgar and Deborah Jannotta Mesopotamian Gallery followed by a trip to Chicago's Chinatown, where attendees dined on dumplings, wonton soup, Mongolian chicken, and other delicious dishes.

To round out the weekend, we enjoyed one last session of papers as well as a pizza lunch. A special thanks goes out to Mariana Perlinac and Natalie May for all they did to ensure the weekend's success.

Incredible Isfahan Film Premiere

On April 27, the Oriental Institute invited 250 Members and friends to witness the premiere of *Incredible Isfahan: Discovering Persia's Past*, brought to us by Iranian documentary film-maker and director Farzin Rezaeian. After an introduction by Professor John Woods of the University of Chicago's Department of Near Eastern Languages and Civilizations, guests took in the first public screening of the film. Afterwards, guests enjoyed an elaborate northern Iranian dinner provided by Masouleh restaurant. Fare included beef and chicken kabobs, multiple salads, and other Middle Eastern delicacies.

A special thanks goes out to Carole Krucoff and Abbas Alizadeh for all of their hard work.

Feast with the Pharaohs: The 2011 Oriental Institute Gala

On May 2, the Oriental Institute invited 240 guests to feast with the pharaohs as it celebrated its 92nd year with an ancient Egyptian-themed, black-tie gala. As guests arrived, they mingled, enjoyed cocktails and hors d'oeuvres, and bid on a plethora of silent-auction items in the Edgar and Deborah Jannotta Mesopotamian Gallery.

Afterwards, attendees convened in Breasted Hall to listen to a presentation by Gil J. Stein, director of the Oriental Institute. The highlight was the presentation of the James Henry Breasted Medallion to O. J. Sopranos, longtime Member, donor, and friend of the Oriental Institute. After the medal ceremony, attendees also enjoyed a slideshow honoring all five emeritus Oriental Institute directors — Robert McC. Adams, John Brinkman, Janet Johnson, Bill Sumner, and Gene Gragg — and their various contributions to the Oriental Institute.

Following the presentation, guests participated in a live auction in Breasted Hall. Auction items included a catered dinner for ten in the Oriental Institute Museum galleries with University of Chicago paleontologist Paul Sereno, and a retrofitted museum case customized by Oriental Institute preparator Erik Lindahl. During dinner in the Museum galleries, guests enjoyed an elegant plated dinner, including filet mignon and lemon soufflé cake, served by Calihan Catering, Inc. Throughout the evening, guests were entertained by Environmental Encroachment, an acting troupe whose members dressed as a belly dancer, a pharaoh, a pharaoh's attendant, and a variety of other Egyptian personalities. Finally, to complement our Ancient Egyptian feast, guests were given individually wrapped chocolate pharaohs as favors.

Special thanks goes out to everyone who worked tirelessly to ensure the evening's perfection. A particularly special thank-you is extended to the Gala committee — Deborah Halpern, Andrea Dudek, Margaret Foorman, Mari Terman, and Susan Geshwender — without whom this event would not have happened.

Donny George Memorial

On June 1, the Oriental Institute hosted 200 Members and friends of the Chicago Assyrian community in celebration of the life of Donny George Youkhanna, Iraqi Assyrian archaeologist, anthropologist, and scholar. Beginning at 7:00 PM, guests listened to a lecture given by McGuire Gibson, professor of Mesopotamian archaeology and director of the Oriental Institute expedition to Nippur, Iraq. After the lecture, guests joined Gil J. Stein, director of the Oriental Institute, in the Edgar and Deborah Jannotta Mesopotamian Gallery to dedicate and exhibit case to Dr. Youkhanna. Attendees also enjoyed and array of cocktails and hors

2011 ORIENTAL INSTITUTE GALA PHOTO GALLERY

Guest check in and receive their BidPals to participate in the silent auction

Caterers and performers wearing Egyptian costumes and headdresses entertained guests with dancing, juggling, and music

University of Chicago President Robert Zimmer

Gil Stein delivering a presentation honoring emeritus directors of the Oriental Institute

2011 ORIENTAL INSTITUTE GALA PHOTO GALLERY

Gil Stein presenting the Breasted Medallion to O. J. Sopranos

Breasted Medallion recipients past and present: (left to right) Carlotta Maher, Margaret Grant, O. J. Sopranos, and Janet Helman

2011 Oriental Institute Gala Photo Gallery

Guests enjoying dinner in the Yelda Khorsabad Court of the Oriental Institute Museum: (counterclockwise from left) Janet Johnson, Greg Mueller, Betty Mueller, Don Whitcomb, Nicole Suzann Williams, Todd Schwebel, Liliana Lark, and Lawrence Becker

Clockwise from top left: Thomas and Linda Heagy with Ray Johnson and Jay Heidel; floral arrangement by Plants Alive and place settings provided by Calihan Catering, Inc.; Gala attendees Oriental Institute Visiting Committee Chair Harvey Plotnick, Todd Schwebel, and Lawrence Becker; Scott Branting, Morag Kersel, and Yorke Rowan

d'oeuvres provided by Amazing Edibles Catering, including chilled beef and chicken skewers, summer pasta salad, and mini cupcakes.

Chicago Assyrian Dictionary Celebration

On June 6, we celebrated the completion of the Chicago Assyrian Dictionary, which took ninety years to complete. The first part of the day-long event featured a symposium, in which scholars from various American and European universities recounted their experiences in working collaboratively to create the dictionary. After the symposium portion, guests enjoyed a reception in the Edgar and Deborah Jannotta Mesopotamian Gallery featuring a light hors d'oeuvres artfully presented by Amazing Edibles Catering.

———————————

HONOR ROLL OF DONORS AND MEMBERS

* THE JAMES HENRY BREASTED SOCIETY *

Named for the founder of the Oriental Institute, the James Henry Breasted Society is an elite group of donors whose contributions are vital for the support of major research programs, as well as the day-to-day operation of the Oriental Institute. Patrons of the James Henry Breasted Society contribute $1,000–$2,499 annually, while we welcome donors of $2,500 or more into the Director's Circle.

DIRECTOR'S CIRCLE
$50,000 and Above

Alwin Clemens Carus Mineral Trust, Dickinson, North Dakota
The Andrew W. Mellon Foundation, New York, New York
Col. & Mrs. William T. Bennett, Palm Harbor, Florida
Exelon Corporation, Chicago, Illinois
Mr. & Mrs. Thomas C. Heagy, Chicago, Illinois
Lloyd A. Fry Foundation, Chicago, Illinois
Mr. Joseph Neubauer & Ms. Jeanette Lerman-Neubauer, Philadelphia, Pennsylvania
Friends of the Oriental Institute
Parsa Community Foundation, Redwood City, California
Mrs. Elizabeth & Mr. Harvey B. Plotnick, Chicago, Illinois
Dr. & Mrs. Arnold L. Tanis, Fernandina Beach, Florida

$25,000–$49,000

American Research Center in Egypt, Inc., Atlanta, Georgia
Mr. & Mrs. Robert A. Helman, Chicago, Illinois
Mr. Piers Litherland, Hong Kong, China
Mr. & Mrs. John W. Rowe, Chicago, Illinois
The Revival Fund, Detroit, Michigan
The Women's Board of the University of Chicago, Chicago, Illinois

$10,000–$24,999

Anonymous
Mr. Eric & Ms. Andrea Soros Colombel, New York, New York
Ms. Aimee Leigh Drolet & Mr. Peter E. Rossi, Beverly Hills, California
Fidelity Brokerage Services, LLC, Cincinnati, Ohio
Mr. & Mrs. Lewis S. Gruber, Chicago, Illinois
Mrs. Barbara Kipper, Chicago, Illinois
Michael & Patricia Klowden, Santa Monica, California
Mr. Frank L. & Ms. Maureen L. Kovacs, Corte Madera, California
National Philanthropic Trust, DAF, Jenkintown, Pennsylvania
Mr. & Mrs. Roger R. Nelson, Chicago, Illinois
Mrs. Maurice D. Schwartz, Los Angeles, California

$10,000–$24,999 (cont.)

Toni S. Smith, Chicago, Illinois
Mr. & Mrs. O. J. Sopranos, Winnetka, Illinois
Wenner-Gren Foundation, New York, New York

$5,000–$9,999

Ms. Jennifer Aliber, Lexington, Massachusetts
Mr. & Mrs. Michael A. Aliber, Kensington, South Africa
Professor & Mrs. Robert Z. Aliber, Hanover, New Hampshire
Mr. & Mrs. Gary S. Becker, Chicago, Illinois
Ms. Catherine Novotny Brehm, Chicago, Illinois
Mrs. Mary G. & Mr. Curtiss T. Brennan, Santa Fe, New Mexico
Ms. Andrea M. Dudek, Orland Park, Illinois
Mr. & Mrs. John Francis Duffy, Morrisville, Vermont
Estate of Mr. Chester D. Tripp, Chicago, Illinois
Fidelity Charity Gift Fund, Boston, Massachusetts
Mr. & Mrs. James L. Foorman, Winnetka, Illinois
Mrs. Nancy H. & Mr. Isak V. Gerson, Chicago, Illinois
Mr. & Mrs. Robert M. Grant, Randolph, New Hampshire
Mr. Byron & Ms. Maryann L. Gregory, Wilmette, Illinois
Mr. & Mrs. Howard G. Haas, Glencoe, Illinois
Mrs. Deborah G. & Mr. Philip Halpern, Chicago, Illinois
Mrs. Marjorie H. Buchanan Kiewit, Chestnut Hill, Massachusetts
Mrs. Linda Noe Laine, New York, New York
Lucia Woods Lindley & Daniel A. Lindley, Jr., Evanston, Illinois
Mrs. Barbara Mertz, Frederick, Maryland
Mr. & Mrs. James B. Nicholson, Detroit, Michigan
Mr. & Mrs. Robert Parrillo, Chicago, Illinois
Mr. & Mrs. Norman J. Rubash, Evanston, Illinois
Ms. Roberta Schaffner, Chicago, Illinois
Mr. & Mrs. Robert G. Schloerb, Chicago, Illinois
Mr. & Mrs. H. Warren Siegel, San Juan Capistrano, California
Dr. & Mrs. Francis H. Straus II, Chicago, Illinois
Ms. Jean P. Stremmel, Winnetka, Illinois
Mr. & Mrs. Robert Wagner, Chicago, Illinois
Ms. Helen Wentz, Lansing, Michigan

$2,500–$4,999

AHI International Corporation, Rosemont, Illinois
Mr. & Mrs. Norman R. Bobins, Chicago, Illinois
Distant Horizons, Long Beach, California
Exxon Mobil Foundation, Houston, Texas
Far Horizons Archaological and Cultural Trips, Inc., San Anselmo, California
Mrs. Mary L. & Mr. Richard Gray, Chicago, Illinois
Mr. & Mrs. Dietrich M. Gross, Wilmette, Illinois
Mr. Howard E. Hallengren, New York, New York
Iran Heritage Foundation, London, United Kingdom
Mr. & Mrs. Edgar D. Jannotta, Chicago, Illinois

$2,500–$4,999 (cont.)

Dr. Donald S. Whitcomb & Dr. Janet H. Johnson, Chicago, Illinois
Mr. William K. Kellogg III, Chicago, Illinois
Mr. Jack A. Koefoot, Evanston, Illinois
Mr. & Mrs. David W. Maher, Chicago, Illinois
Mr. & Mrs. John W. McCarter, Jr., Chicago, Illinois
Museum Tours, Inc., Littleton, Colorado
Nuveen Benevolent Trust, Chicago, Illinois
Ms. Kathleen Picken, Chicago, Illinois
Miss M. Kate Pitcairn, Kempton, Pennsylvania
R. Crusoe & Son, Chicago, Illinois
Mrs. Crennan M. Ray, Santa Fe, New Mexico
Dr. Miriam Reitz, Chicago, Illinois
Mr. & Mrs. Thomas J. Schnitzer, Chicago, Illinois
Mr. Richard Henry Beal & Ms. Jo Ann Scurlock, Chicago, Illinois
Secchia Family Foundation, Grand Rapids, Michigan
Dr. Coleman R. Seskind, Chicago, Illinois
Seven Wonders Travel, Grayslake, Illinois
Ms. Helen Shin, New York, New York
Greater Kansas City Community Foundation & Affiliates, Kansas City, Missouri
Raymond D. Tindel & Gretel Braidwood, Earlysville, Virginia
Dr. & Mrs. Walter H. A. Vandaele, Washington, DC
Ms. Anna M. White, Terre Haute, Indiana
Mr. George M. Whitesides & Ms. Barbara Breasted Whitesides, Newton, Massachusetts
Ms. Nicole Suzann Williams & Mr. Lawrence Becker, Glencoe, Illinois
Dr. & Mrs. Sharukin Yelda, Chicago, Illinois

$1,000–$2,499

Gail H. Adele, Moscow, Idaho
Mr. & Mrs. Stanley N. Allan, Chicago, Illinois
Mr. John J. Barbie, Chicago, Illinois
Mr. & Mrs. Cameron Brown, Lake Forest, Illinois
Mr. Quigley Bruning, New York, New York
Ms. Heidi & Mr. Steven H. Camp, Chicago, Illinois
Ms. Ruth E. Campbell, Winnetka, Illinois
Mr. & Mrs. Bruce S. Chelberg, Chicago, Illinois
Mr. John L. Crary, San Mateo, California
Ms. Katharine P. & Mr. Peter H. Darrow, Brooklyn, New York
Mr. & Mrs. Terry D. Diamond, Chicago, Illinois
Mr. & Mrs. E. Bruce Dunn, Chicago, Illinois
Ms. Margaret Hart Edwards & Mr. William T. Espey, Lafayette, California
Ms. Joan S. Fortune, New York, New York
Mr. & Mrs. James J. Glasser, Chicago, Illinois
Ms. Louise Grunwald, New York, New York
Mr. & Mrs. Walter M. Guterbock, Hermiston, Oregon
Mr. Andrew Nourse & Ms. Patty A. Hardy, Woodside, California
Dr. & Mrs. Arthur L. Herbst, Tucson, Arizona
Dr. & Mrs. David C. Hess, Downers Grove, Illinois
Ms. Doris B. Holleb, Chicago, Illinois

$1,000–$2,499 (cont.)

Illinois Institute of Technology, Chicago, Illinois
Dr. Joseph W. & Dr. Rebecca R. Jarabak, Hinsdale, Illinois
Mrs. Christine S. & Mr. Waheeb N. Kamil, Westfield, New Jersey
Mr. & Mrs. Michael L. Keiser, Chicago, Illinois
Ms. Polly Kelly, Pinehurst, North Carolina
Eleanor Kilgour, Chapel Hill, North Carolina
Mr. & Mrs. Neil J. King, Chicago, Illinois
Joseph T. Lach, PhD, & Ms. Carol C. Albertson, Evanston, Illinois
Mr. Marvin H. & Ms. Isabel Leibowitz, Aventura, Florida
Mr. & Mrs. Barry L. MacLean, Mettawa, Illinois
MacLean-Fogg Company, Inc., Mundelein, Illinois
Dr. John C. & Mrs. Christine G. Michael, Wilmette, Illinois
Mr. & Mrs. William L. Morrison, Chicago, Illinois
Mostafa Family Charitable Lead Trust, Pasadena, California
Muchnic Foundation, Atchison, Kansas
Ms. Virginia O'Neill, Chicago, Illinois
Mr. Donald Oster, London, United Kingdom
Ms. Joan Hunt Parks, Chicago, Illinois
Dr. & Mrs. Harlan R. Peterjohn, Bay Village, Ohio
Dr. Audrius Vaclovas Plioplys & Dr. Sigita Plioplys, Chicago, Illinois
Dr. Erl Dordal & Ms. Dorothy K. Powers, Atlanta, Georgia
Mrs. Annabelle L. & Mr. Laurance M. Redway, Washington, DC
Mr. & Mrs. Patrick Regnery, Burr Ridge, Illinois
Louise Lee Reid, Chicago, Illinois
Renaissance Charitable Foundation, Inc., Indianapolis, Indiana
Mr. Thomas F. Rosenbaum & Ms. Katherine Faber, Wilmette, Illinois
Ms. Frances F. Rowan, Reston, Virginia
Mr. & Mrs. Harold Sanders, Chicago, Illinois
Schwab Charitable Fund, San Francisco, California
Mrs. Charlotte Mailliard Shultz & Honorable George P. Shultz, San Francisco, California
Dr. Norman Solhkhah, Lincolnwood, Illinois
St. Lucas Charitable Foundation, Burr Ridge, Illinois
Mr. Matthew W. Stolper, Chicago, Illinois
Mrs. Harriet Augustus Swanson, Mount Vernon, Iowa
Dr. David M. & Mrs. Mari D. Terman, Wilmette, Illinois
Ms. Karen M. Terras, Chicago, Illinois
The Diamond Family Foundation, Chicago, Illinois
Mr. Thomas G. & Ms. Mary Christine Urban, Chicago, Illinois
Mr. Michael VanDusen, Houston, Texas
Mr. Kent Weeks, Old Lyme, Connecticut
Alexander Weintraub, Newton Center, Massachusetts
Ms. Annette & Mr. Daniel Youngberg, Albany, Oregon
Mr. & Mrs. Howard O. Zumsteg, Jr., San Francisco, California

$500–$999

Abbott Laboratories Employee Giving, Princeton, New Jersey
Adventures in Lifelong Learning, Kenosha, Wisconsin
Thomas G. Akers, PhD, & Dr. Ann B. Akers, New Orleans, Louisiana

$500–$999 (cont.)

Mr. & Mrs. Walter Alexander, Geneva, Illinois
Ascot Shopping Center, Prospect Heights, Illinois
Mr. Gregory D. S. Anderson & Ms. Mary R. Bachvarova, Salem, Oregon
Mr. & Mrs. John Batchelor, Fernandina Beach, Florida
Ms. Judith Baxter & Mr. Stephen Smith, Oak Park, Illinois
Dr. Vallo Benjamin, New York, New York
Mr. & Mrs. Charles E. Bidwell, Chicago, Illinois
Mr. Steven Anthony Clark & Ms. Janet L. Raymond, Oak Lawn, Illinois
Ms. Cheryl Crane, Tinley Park, Illinois
Mrs. Bettie Dwinell, Chicago, Illinois
Mr. S. Cody & Ms. Deborah Engle, Chicago, Illinois
Mr. Wolfgang Frye, Phoenix, Arizona
Mr. John R. & Dorothy Hannon Gardner, Chicago, Illinois
Mr. & Mrs. John S. Garvin, Winnetka, Illinois
Mr. Matthew W. Dickie & Ms. Elizabeth R. Gebhard, Glenfarg, United Kingdom
Mr. Kevin S. & Ms. Susan Geshwender, Barrington, Illinois
Mr. & Mrs. Sidney A. Guralnick, Chicago, Illinois
Mr. Collier Hands, Lovell, Maine
Herbst Family Foundation, Chicago, Illinois
Mr. & Mrs. Scott E. Hertenstein, Cary, North Carolina
Mr. Mark Samuel Hoplamazian & Ms. Rachel DeYoung Kohler, Chicago, Illinois
Mr. John H. Kelly, Conyers, Georgia
Professor Adrian R. Kerr & Mrs. Louise H. Kerr, Fort Myers, Florida
Shelley Korshak, MD, & Mr. Laurence A. Sode, Chicago, Illinois
Mr. Richard Kron & Mrs. Deborah A. Bekken, Chicago, Illinois
Mr. & Mrs. John D. Lewis, Milwaukee, Wisconsin
Mr. & Mrs. Michael D. Lockhart, Rembert, South Carolina
Ms. Deborah Long, Bellevue, Washington
Mrs. Gail Pinc McClain, Chicago, Illinois
Mr. Robert Ralph Moeller & Ms. Lois Patricia Moeller, Evanston, Illinois
Ms. Vivian B. Morales, Saint Paul, Minnesota
Ms. Betty L. Perkins, Los Alamos, New Mexico
Mr. Philip J. Perry & Ms. Elizabeth Cheney Perry, McLean, Virginia
Mr. & Mrs. James M. Ratcliffe, Chicago, Illinois
Mr. Percy Mwanzia Wegmann & Ms. Karen M. Rexford, Austin, Texas
Mr. Robert J. Robertson, Forest Hills, New York
Mr. John W. & Ms. Nancy Kimball Robinson, Northfield, Illinois
Dr. Randi Rubovits-Seitz, Washington, DC
Dr. Bonnie M. Sampsell, Chapel Hill, North Carolina
Mr. Hal Stewart Scott & Mrs. Joanna Scott, Cambridge, Massachusetts
Mr. & Mrs. Clyde Curry Smith, PhD, River Falls, Wisconsin
St. Jude Medical, Inc., St. Paul, Minnesota
Mr. & Mrs. Solon A. Stone, Sherwood, Oregon
Mr. Rexford K. Stone & Ms. Selma Stoorman, Surprise, Arizona
Trans Union Corporation, Chicago, Illinois
University of Wisconsin at Madison, Madison, Wisconsin
Mr. & Mrs. Douglas R. White, Taneytown, Maryland
Wilderness Travel, Berkeley, California
Mr. Charles Mack Wills, Jr., East Palatka, Florida

$500–$999 (cont.)

Mr. Robert I. Wilson, Peoria, Illinois
Dr. & Mrs. Jerome A. Winer, Chicago, Illinois
Wolf Point Shopping Center, Wheeling, Illinois
Ms. Debra F. Yates, Chicago, Illinois
Mrs. George B. Young, Chicago, Illinois

$250–$499

Ms. Karen AbuZayd, Chicago, Illinois
Mrs. Geraldine Smithwick Alvarez, Burr Ridge, Illinois
Mr. & Mrs. Edward Anders, Burlingame, California
Dr. Thomas W. Andrews, Hinsdale, Illinois
Mrs. Julie Antelman, Santa Barbara, California
Miss Janice V. Bacchi, San Diego, California
Mr. Kevin Francis Rock & Ms. Cynthia A. Bates, Evanston, Illinois
Ms. Susan Bedingham, Covington, Washington
Mr. & Mrs. Mark Bergner, Chicago, Illinois
Ms. Julia A. Beringer, Western Springs, Illinois
Mr. Michael Dean Brandt & Mrs. Janet Brandt, Madison, Wisconsin
Dr. Martin P. Buchheim & Dr. Cynthia Jurisson, Chicago, Illinois
Mr. Bruce P. Burbage, Venice, Florida
Christ Church of Oak Brook, Oak Brook, Illinois
Christian Oriental Research Center, Eichstätt, Germany
Congregation Sukkat Shalom, Wilmette, Illinois
Mr. Timothy John & Ms. Cecila Crowhurst, New York, New York
The Honorable Barbara F. Currie, Chicago, Illinois
Mr. & Mrs. Nirmal Singh Dhesi, Santa Rosa, California
Mr. Irving L. Diamond & Ms. Dorothy J. Speidel, Wilmette, Illinois
Ms. Mary E. Dimperio, Washington, DC
Mr. Michael Dorner, St. Paul, Minnesota
Mr. Gregory G. & Mrs. Susan P. Drinan, Wheaton, Illinois
Ecclesia Sancti Petri, Chicago, Illinois
Ms. Ann R. Esse, Sioux Falls, South Dakota
Mr. William A. Farone & Ms. Cynthia H. O'Douohue, Irvine, California
Mr. Barry Fitzpatrick, West Midlands, United Kingdom
Dr. Samuel Ethan Fox, Chicago, Illinois
Mrs. Eleanor B. Frew, Flossmoor, Illinois
Ms. Patty Gerstenblith & Rabbi Samuel Gordon, Wilmette, Illinois
Mr. & Mrs. Gene B. Gragg, Chicago, Illinois
Francis P. Green, Bloomington, Illinois
Ms. Dianne S. Haines, Naperville, Illinois
Ms. Ednalyn Hansen, Chicago, Illinois
Mrs. Lucy H. & Mr. Richard S. Harwood, Colorado Springs, Colorado
Mr. Edward Day Hatcher & Ms. Valerie Hoffman Hatcher, Morris, Illinois
Mr. Robert F. Hendrickson, Princeton, New Jersey
Ms. Patricia A. & Mr. Stephen L. Holst, Westport, Massachusetts
Mr. Paul & Ms. Linda Houdek, Berwyn, Illinois
Mr. & Mrs. Roger David Isaacs, Glencoe, Illinois
Mrs. Sandra Jacobsohn, Chicago, Illinois

$250–$499 (cont.)

Richard E. & Marie T. Jones, Wilmette, Illinois

Professor Gerald E. Kadish, Binghamton, New York

Dr. John Sobolski & Dr. Zara Khodjasteh, Chicago, Illinois

Mr. Stuart Kleven & Ms. Andrea Pogwizd, Bensenville, Illinois

Irmgard Kilb Koehler, MD, Chicago, Illinois

Mr. & Mrs. Martin J. Kozak, Wilmette, Illinois

Mr. Bernard L. Krawczyk, Chicago, Illinois

Mr. Peter Lacovara, Atlanta, Georgia

Mrs. Elisabeth F. Lanzl, Chicago, Illinois

Mr. & Mrs. William J. Lawlor III, Chicago, Illinois

Mr. Richard Lee, Holland, Pennsylvania

Mrs. Frances M. & Mr. Jacob B. LeVine, Teaneck, New Jersey

Mr. Ronald G. Lindenberg & Ljubica Sarenac, Chicago, Illinois

Mr. Donald Allen Link & Mrs. June Link, Princeton, New Jersey

Dr. & Mrs. John M. Livingood, Bethesda, Maryland

Ms. Johanna W. Lucas, Chicago, Illinois

Mr. Daniel R. Malecki, Kensington, California

Ms. Glennda Susan Marsh-Letts, Springwood, Australia

Ms. Susanne Mathewson, Chicago, Illinois

Mr. Raymond McBride, Chicago, Illinois

Mr. R. Darrell Bock & Ms. Renee Marie Menegaz-Bock, Chicago, Illinois

Ms. Holly J. Mulvey, Evanston, Illinois

Mary Jane Myers, Los Angeles, California

Dawn Clark Netsch, Chicago, Illinois

Mr. & Mrs. John P. Nielsen, Lombard, Illinois

Mr. Larry Paragano, Basking Ridge, New Jersey

Mr. J. Richard & Mrs. Martha Pine, Rockville, Maryland

Ms. Genevieve Plamondon, Telluride, Colorado

Mrs. Semra Prescott, Chicago, Illinois

Ms. Anne N. Rorimer, Chicago, Illinois

Mr. & Mrs. John Eric Schaal, Burr Ridge, Illinois

Mrs. Lawrence J. Scheff, Chicago, Illinois

Mr. Todd D. H. Schwebel & Mr. Thomas C. Driscoll III, Chicago, Illinois

Prof. Dr. Esther Segel & Prof. Dr. Ralph Segel, Wilmette, Illinois

Mr. & Mrs. Jason Bakwin Selch, Chicago, Illinois

Mrs. Daila Shefner, Chicago, Illinois

Mr. Peter & Ms. Phyllis Shellko, Chesterland, Ohio

Mr. & Mrs. Louis J. Skidmore, Jr., Houston, Texas

Dr. Benjamin A. & Mrs. Radiah A. Smith-Donald, Chicago, Illinois

Mr. Kent D. Sternitzke, Fort Worth, Texas

James Swinerton, Chicago, Illinois

Ms. Betsy Teeter, San Francisco, California

Mr. Joseph Daniel Cain & Ms. Emily Teeter, Chicago, Illinois

Mr. & Mrs. Lester G. Telser, Chicago, Illinois

The Chicago Community Trust, Chicago, Illinois

The Martin Companies, Houston, Texas

Dr. Robert Y. Turner, Haverford, Pennsylvania

Mr. & Mrs. Russell H. Tuttle, Chicago, Illinois

Ms. Mary Valsa & Mr. Warren Valsa, Chicago, Illinois

Mr. & Mrs. Karl H. Velde, Jr., Lake Forest, Illinois
Mr. John Vinci, Chicago, Illinois
Mr. & Mrs. Edward F. Wente, Chicago, Illinois
Mr. & Mrs. Wayne L. White, Rockport, Texas
Mr. Thomas K. Yoder, Chicago, Illinois
Mr. Franklin J. & Mrs. Sandra T. Zieve, Midlothian, Virginia

$100–$249

Mr. D. M. & Ms. Mary C. Abadi, Iowa City, Iowa
Mr. Daniel L. Ables, Scottsdale, Arizona
Mr. Matthew J. Adams, State College, Pennsylvania
Dr. Charles Martin Adelman, Cedar Falls, Iowa
Mrs. Elizabeth M. Adkins, Chicago, Illinois
Mr. & Mrs. John C. Aldrin, Gurnee, Illinois
Philip Alexander, Winnetka, Illinois
Mr. & Mrs. James P. Allen, Providence, Rhode Island
Mr. & Mrs. Brian Robert Alm, Rock Island, Illinois
Ms. Salwa Alwattar, Bannockburn, Illinois
Andrews University, Berrien Springs, Michigan
Ms. Mary A. Anton & Mr. Paul M. Barron, Chicago, Illinois
Ms. Nissa Applequist, Chicago, Illinois
Mr. Edward H. Ashment, Manteca, California
Robert Atkins, Evanston, Illinois
Roger Atkinson & Janet Arey, Riverside, California
Ayco Charitable Foundation, Albany, New York
Doris Ayres, Chicago, Illinois
Mr. Douglas Baldwin, Arlington Heights, Illinois
Ms. Priscilla Bath, Trenton, New Jersey
Mr. Douglas Baum & Mrs. Lynne M. Wait, Homewood, Illinois
Barry Baumgardner, Dunnellon, Florida
Mr. John M. Beal, Chicago, Illinois
Ms. Barbara Bell, Cambridge, Massachusetts
Mr. Frederick N. Bates & Dr. Ellen J. Benjamin, Chicago, Illinois
Mr. & Mrs. John F. Benjamin, Jupiter, Florida
Dr. & Mrs. Richard W. Benjamin, North Augusta, South Carolina
Ms. Catherine Bennett, Des Moines, Iowa
Mr. Clive Davies & Ms. Phoebe Bennett, Arlington, Virginia
Mr. & Mrs. Thomas H. Bennett, New York, New York
Mr. Larry & Ms. Zaida Bergmann, Fairfax, Virginia
Ms. Julie L. & Mr. Lawrence J. Bernstein, Chicago, Illinois
Bethlehem Lutheran Church, West Dundee, Illinois
Ms. Margaret L. & Mr. Matthew D. Blake, Singer Island, Florida
Mr. Edward C. Blau, Alexandria, Virginia
Mr. & Mrs. Merill Blau, Highland Park, Illinois
Mr. Alan & Ms. Mary Alyce Blum, Chicago, Illinois
Glenn F. Boas, DDS, Lake Forest, Illinois
Mr. & Mrs. Norman M. Bradburn, Arlington, Virginia
Mr. James Thomas Bradbury III, Knoxville, Tennessee
Mrs. Jerald C. Brauer, Chicago, Illinois

$100–$249 (cont.)

Mr. James Henry Breasted III, Carbondale, Colorado

Mr. Bob Brier, Bronx, New York

Mrs. Lita H. Brody, Chicago, Illinois

Mr. Hugh K. & Ms. Jane M. Brower, Winnetka, Illinois

Ms. Margaret R. Brown, Washington, DC

Mr. Stephen Hayze Brown, Jr., Chicago, Illinois

Ms. Marilyn A. Brusherd, Sugar Grove, Illinois

Ms. M. Kennedy Buchanan, Chicago, Illinois

Ms. Romie & Mr. T. J. Bullock, Chicago, Illinois

Mr. Salvatore Calomino & Mr. James L. Zychowicz, Chicago, Illinois

Calvin College, Grand Rapids, Michigan

Allan C. Campbell, MD, Peoria, Illinois

Cardinal Stritch University, Milwaukee, Wisconsin

Ms. Cinthya Carrillo, Chicago, Illinois

Mr. Afsar M. Cave, San Francisco, California

Mr. John L. Cella, Jr., & Ms. Laura Prail, Chicago, Illinois

Ms. Chamberlain, Houston, Texas

Charitable Flex Fund, Paramus, New Jersey

Mr. Charles A. Chesbro, Missoula, Montana

Dr. Mary Chuman & Dr. Charles Chuman, Chesterton, Indiana

Mr. Heinke K. Clark & Mr. Jacques M. Beckers, Kirkland, Washington

Mrs. Zdzislawa Coleman, Chicago, Illinois

Ms. Cynthia Green Colin, New York, New York

Ms. Jane Comiskey, Chicago, Illinois

Mr. Courtney B. Conte, Santa Monica, California

Mr. Richard L. & Ms. Sally W. Cook, Sherman Oaks, California

Mr. Jason Cordero, Tea Tree Gully, Australia

Mr. & Mrs. Edward T. Cotham, Jr., Houston, Texas

Dorothy & David Crabb, Chicago, Illinois

Mrs. Caroline P. Cracraft, Chicago, Illinois

Mr. David E. Craig, Tallahassee, Florida

Mr. Robert Crawford, Chicago, Illinois

Dr. Eugene D. Cruz-Uribe & Dr. Kathryn Cruz-Uribe, Marina, California

Ms. Helen M. Cunningham, Arlington Heights, Illinois

Ronald E. Curran DBA Carefree Tours, Galena, Illinois

Mr. Edwin L. Currey, Jr., Napa, California

Ms. Agnes Dale Hooper, Madison, Tennessee

Ms. Barbara Wilson D'Andrea, Wainscott, New York

Mr. Robert A. Koos & Ms. Diane L. Dau-Koos, Kenosha, Wisconsin

Ms. Rebecca Davidson, Chicago, Illinois

Mr. Claude Davis, Hillsborough, North Carolina

John M. Davis, MD, & Ms. Deborah J. Davis, Chicago, Illinois

Mr. & Mrs. Mark D. Dawson, Chicago, Illinois

Ms. Maybrit S. De Miranda, Rancho Palos Verdes, California

Mr. Leoti de Vries-Mostert, Waarle, Netherlands

Ms. Catherine Deans-Barrett, Corrales, New Mexico

Mrs. Quinn E. Delaney, Winnetka, Illinois

Mr. Kevin M. Dent, White Sands Missile Range, New Mexico

Mr. Tom & Mrs. Ursula Digman, Elgin, Illinois

$100–$249 (cont.)

Ms. Patricia Dihel & Mr. Glen Wilson, Third Lake, Illinois

Ms. Betsy & Mr. J. Kane Ditto, Jackson, Mississippi

Mr. Peter FitzGerald Dorman & Ms. Kathryn Dorman, New York, New York

Dr. James & Mrs. Sara L. Downey, Chicago, Illinois

Ms. Elizabeth Zenick Dudley, East Boothbay, Maine

Mrs. Rose B. Dyrud, Chicago, Illinois

Mr. Robert Dyson, Essex, New York

Mr. Robert Eager, Washington, DC

Mr. Christopher Boebel & Ms. Glenna Eaves, Chicago, Illinois

Mr. C. David Eeles, Columbus, Ohio

Sidney & Sondra Berman Epstein, Chicago, Illinois

Dr. & Mrs. Richard Evans, Chicago, Illinois

Ms. Elizabeth A. Byrnes & Mr. Barton L. Faber, Paradise Valley, Arizona

Hazel S. Fackler, Chicago, Illinois

Mr. & Mrs. Eugene F. Fama, Chicago, Illinois

Ms. Mary G. Finn, Chicago, Illinois

Mr. & Mrs. John H. Fisher, River Forest, Illinois

Mr. James L. Padgett & Ms. Rosanne Fitko, Lake Forest, Illinois

Mr. John Fletcher & Ms. Margaret C. Kingsland, Missoula, Montana

Dr. Michael S. Flom, Boynton Beach, Florida

Ms. Marie-Anne & Mr. Michael Fogel, Oakland, California

Ms. Carol L. & Mr. Scott M. Forsythe, Forest Park, Illinois

Mr. John L. Foster, Chicago, Illinois

Leila M. Foster, JD, PhD, Evanston, Illinois

Mr. & Mrs. Charles J. Fraas, Jr., Jefferson City, Missouri

Mr. & Mrs. Paul E. Freehling, Chicago, Illinois

Mr. Kere Frey, Chicago, Illinois

Mr. & Mrs. Charles Barry Friedman, Chicago, Illinois

Friendship Village, Schaumburg, Illinois

Mr. Robert C. Gaffaney, Algonquin, Illinois

Mr. Gregory J. Gajda, Mount Prospect, Illinois

Mr. W. Randall Garr & Ms. Laura Kalman, Goleta, California

Dr. Francois Pierre Gaudard, Chicago, Illinois

Mr. Ted & Ms. Hildegard H. Geiger, Lake Villa, Illinois

Mr. & Mrs. Thomas J. Gillespie, Chicago, Illinois

Mr. Lyle Gillman, Bloomingdale, Illinois

Mr. John & Ms. Janet B. Gills, Elmhurst, Illinois

Mr. Gary Glassman, Providence, Rhode Island

Glenbard North High School Activity Fund, Carol Stream, Illinois

Mr. Jerome Godinich, Jr., Houston, Texas

Rev. Raymond Goehring, Lansing, Michigan

Mr. & Mrs. William H. Gofen, Chicago, Illinois

Mr. & Mrs. Howard Goldberg, Chicago, Illinois

Mrs. Betty Goldiamond, Chicago, Illinois

Mrs. Ethel F. Goldsmith, Chicago, Illinois

Dr. Helen T. Goldstein, Iowa City, Iowa

Mr. John Goldstein, Chicago, Illinois

Mr. & Mrs. Frederick J. Graboske, Rockville, Maryland

Mr. & Mrs. Charles W. Graham, Camden, Maine

$100–$249 (cont.)

Ms. Jean Grant, Chicago, Illinois
Mr. & Mrs. David Gratner, Sulphur Springs, Indiana
Mrs. Barbara S. Graves, Olympia Fields, Illinois
Mr. Donald M. Green, Coral Gables, Florida
Dr. & Mrs. Nathaniel D. Greenberg, Wilmette, Illinois
Dr. Joseph Adams Greene & Mrs. Eileen Caves, Belmont, Massachusetts
Dr. & Mrs. Samuel Greengus, Cincinnati, Ohio
Ms. Ann Marie Gromme, Edina, Minnesota
Mr. Kenneth Gross, Downers Grove, Illinois
Ms. Carolyn & John P. Guhin, Pierre, South Dakota
Dr. & Mrs. Clifford W. Gurney, Gainsville, Florida
Mr. & Mrs. Joseph R. Gyulay, Panama City, Florida
Ms. Barbara J. Hall, Chicago, Illinois
Mr. Joel L. Handelman & Ms. Sarah R. Wolff, Chicago, Illinois
Dr. Lowell Kent Handy & Ms. Erica Lynn Treesh, Des Plaines, Illinois
Mrs. Theresa Hannah, Glenview, Illinois
Dr. W. Benson Harer, Seattle, Washington
Mr. Bill & Mrs. Myra Harms, Grayslake, Illinois
Mr. Mitchell Harrison & Mrs. Donna Mitchell, Chicago, Illinois
Ms. Mary Jo & Mr. James B. Hartle, Santa Barbara, California
Dr. & Mrs. Robert Haselkorn, Chicago, Illinois
Ms. Patricia Hautzinger, Nampa, Idaho
Ms. Lynne Pettler Heckman & Mr. James J. Heckman, Chicago, Illinois
Mr. Matthew Hedman, Ithaca, New York
Dr. & Mrs. H. Lawrence Helfer, Pittsford, New York
Mr. Gilbert B. & Ms. Laura N. Heller, Denver, Colorado
Mrs. Ariel Herrmann, New York, New York
Ms. Hedda Hess, Chicago, Illinois
Mr. & Mrs. Roger H. Hildebrand, Chicago, Illinois
Mr. Ronald L. Hills & Mrs. Suzanna C. Hills, Saratoga, California
Mrs. Mary P. Hines, Winnetka, Illinois
Mr. & Mrs. Marshall Hoke, New London, New Hampshire
Mr. John W. Holt III & Mrs. Mary R. Holt, Naperville, Illinois
Ms. Jayne Honeck, Streamwood, Illinois
Mr. John C. Hook, McLean, Virginia
Mr. Kurt Peters & Ms. Elizabeth Hopp-Peters, Evanston, Illinois
Ms. Marcia Howell, Portland, Maine
Mr. Richard Huff, Oak Park, Illinois
Mr. Herbert B. Huffmon, Madison, New Jersey
Ms. Lyric M. Hughes-Hale, Winnetka, Illinois
Ms. Ann R. Israel, Highland Park, Illinois
Ms. Mary L. Jackowicz, Chicago, Illinois
Mrs. Angela C. & Mr. George Thomas Jacobi, Milwaukee, Wisconsin
Ms. Caroline C. January, New York, New York
Mr. Erwin Jaumann, Gaithersburg, Maryland
Mr. Thomas Jedele & Dr. Nancy J. Skon Jedele, Laurel, Maryland
Chris Jensen, Downers Grove, Illinois
Ms. Kate L. Bensen & Mr. C. Richard Johnson, Chicago, Illinois
Mr. Mark E. & Ms. Kelly Johnson, Tinley Park, Illinois

$100–$249 (cont.)

Mr. James R. Johnston, Port Richey, Florida
Mr. Charles E. Jones & Ms. Alexandra Alice O'Brien, New York, New York
Justin J. Tedrowe, Downers Grove, Illinois
Ms. Loretta A. Kahn, Evanston, Illinois
Drs. Michael & Maureen Kaplan, Lexington, Massachusetts
Mr. Larry Katkin, Fairbanks, Alaska
Mr. Stephen Katz, Chicago, Illinois
Mr. John A. Kelly, Jr., & Mrs. Joyce J. Kelly, Winnetka, Illinois
Ms. Janet Zell Kessler, Chicago, Illinois
Ms. Mary C. Kilmon, West Bath, Maine
Mr. Joe Klug, Chesterton, Indiana
Mr. Gregory Gene Knight, Eagle, Idaho
Mr. & Mrs. William J. Knight, South Bend, Indiana
Mrs. Annie A. Kohl, Media, Pennsylvania
Mr. Martin Krasnitz & Ms. Betsy Levin, Chicago, Illinois
Mr. Donald W. & Mrs. Jane F. Krejci, Monte Sereno, California
Mr. Paul R. Kressin & Ms. Kay Lee, Oak Park, Illinois
Ms. Lottie J. Krzywda, Chicago, Illinois
Mr. & Mrs. James Kulikauskas, Arlington Heights, Illinois
Mr. Arthur Yuan Ao Kuo, Cerritos, California
Lane Tech High School, Chicago, Illinois
Mr. & Mrs. Charles Larmore, Providence, Rhode Island
Mr. John Lawrence, Chicago, Illinois
Mr. John K. Lawrence, Ann Arbor, Michigan
Mr. Mark Lehner, Milton, Massachusetts
Ms. Sara Leonard, Beverly Shores, Indiana
Dr. & Mrs. Leonard Henry Lesko, Seekonk, Massachusetts
Jill & John Levi, Chicago, Illinois
Mr. & Mrs. Josef B. Levi, Chicago, Illinois
Mr. & Mrs. Bernard Leviton, Chicago, Illinois
Prof. Saul Levmore & Ms. Julie Roin, Chicago, Illinois
Mrs. Diane & Mr. Michael Levy, Chicago, Illinois
Mr. Lixing & Ms. Shannon Li, Chicago, Illinois
Mr. Robert B. Lifton & Mrs. Carol Rosofsky, Chicago, Illinois
Mr. Paul S. Linsay & Ms. Roni A. Lipton, Newton, Massachusetts
Mr. Robert Lipman, Evanston, Illinois
Ms. Donna M. Lipsky, Seattle, Washington
Mr. Alfred R. Lipton & Ms. Kathleen Roseborough, Glencoe, Illinois
Ms. Janet & Mr. Laurence Lissak, Lombard, Illinois
Nina A. Longley, Park Forest, Illinois
Mrs. Helen Lowell, Cheadle Hume, United Kingdom
Mr. & Mrs. Philip R. Luhmann, Chicago, Illinois
Mr. James Lunt & Ms. Jeanne Mullen, Berkeley, California
Ms. Corinne M. Lyon, Chicago, Illinois
Mr. George MacDonald, Largo, Florida
Ms. Maria Danae Mandis, Chicago, Illinois
Carole Mangrem, MD, Clarksdale, Mississippi
Dr. L. Mantell & Dr. J. Mantell, New York, New York
Ms. Masako I. Matsumoto, Napa, California

$100–$249 (cont.)

Ms. Eva C. May, New Rochelle, New York

Mr. William McCuskey, Los Angeles, California

Ms. Helen McDonald, Chicago, Illinois

Mr. Glen V. McIntyre, Kingfisher, Oklahoma

McMaster-Carr Supply Company, Elmhurst, Illinois

Mr. Richard H. Meadow, Canton, Massachusetts

Mr. Richard L. Means, Kalamazoo, Michigan

Mrs. Mila Maria Meeker, Chicago, Illinois

Mr. Dimitri Meeks, Saint Clement de Rivere, France,

Mr. Bob & Ms. Pat Meier, Tampa, Florida

Sarah Meisels, Wheaton, Illinois

Mr. & Mrs. George E. Mendenhall, Ann Arbor, Michigan

Dr. Carol Meyer & Mr. Robert K. Smither, Hinsdale, Illinois

Dr. Ronald Michael, MD, Bourbonnais, Illinois

Mr. Neil C. Miller, Jr., Tucson, Arizona

Dr. William K. Miller, Duluth, Minnesota

Mr. A. Patrick Papas & The Honorable Martha A. Mills, Chicago, Illinois

Mr. & Mrs. D. Read Moffett, Chatham, Massachusetts

Ms. Marian H. Morgan, Cape Elizabeth, Maine

Ms. Shirley A. Morningstar, Los Angeles, California

Mrs. Barbara B. & Mr. John H. Morrison, Evanston, Illinois

Vivian Mosby, Woodland, Washington

Mr. Charles H. Mottier, Chicago, Illinois

Mrs. George & Mr. George E. Moulton, Overland Park, Kansas

Mr. Henry Moy, Idabel, Oklahoma

Ms. Maureen Mullen, Greenfield, Wisconsin

Mr. & Mrs. Douglas G. Murray, Santa Barbara, California

Mr. David E. Muschler & Ms. Ann L. Becker, Chicago, Illinois

Mr. & Mrs. Dan K. Myers, Coon Rapids, Minnesota

Mr. & Mrs. Stanley F. Myers, Hanover, New Hampshire

Ms. Demetria D. Nanos, Chicago, Illinois

Mrs. Linda Thoren Neal & Mr. Phil C. Neal, Chicago, Illinois

New Trier Extension, Northfield, Illinois

Mr. Dale George Niewoehner, Rugby, North Dakota

Mr. & Mrs. Timothy Michael Nolan, Palos Park, Illinois

Dr. Edward Brovarski & Mrs. Del Nord, Brookline, Massachusetts

Ms. Karen Nordheim, Chicago, Illinois

Ms. Karen Norrell, Ben Lomond, California

Norwottock Charitable Trust, Chicago, Illinois

Mr. & Mrs. Khalil Noujaim, Granville, Massachusetts

Mr. & Mrs. James H. Nye, Chicago, Illinois

Mr. Craig O'Brien, Downers Grove, Illinois

Dorinda J. Oliver, New York, New York

Mr. Gary M. Ossewaarde, Chicago, Illinois

Ms. Carol E. & Mr. Clinton W. Owen, Chula Vista, California

Ms. Martha Padilla, Sanland, California

Ms. Malgorzata Palka, Mokena, Illinois

Mr. Nazario Paragano, Basking Ridge, New Jersey

Mr. S. Courtenay Wright & Ms. Sara N. Paretsky, Chicago, Illinois

$100–$249 (cont.)

Kisoon & Moonyoung Park, Chicago, Illinois
Erika O. Parker, MD, Chicago, Illinois
Ms. Lois J. Parker, Reno, Nevada
Mr. Bob Partridge, Knutsford, United Kingdom
Mr. & Mrs. Thomas G. Patterson, Chicago, Illinois
Mr. Mark R. Pattis, Highland Park, Illinois
Mr. Peter & Ms. Carolyn Pereira, Chicago, Illinois
Mr. & Mrs. Michael Perlow, Chicago, Illinois
Mr. & Mrs. Norman Perman, Chicago, Illinois
Mr. Jeffrey Peters, Saint Paul, Minnesota
Ms. Rita Petretti, Kenosha, Wisconsin
Ms. Gloria C. Phares & Mr. Richard Dannay, New York, New York
Ms. Mari Philipsborn, Chicago, Illinois
Dr. Peter Anthony Piccione, PhD, & Ms. Myrna Lane, Johns Island, South Carolina
Ms. Joan G. Pings, Chapel Hill, North Carolina
Mr. Jeffrey C. & Mrs. Yvonne L. Pommervile, Scottsdale, Arizona
Dr. Barbara A. Porter, Aman, Jordan
Mr. Cameron Poulter, Chicago, Illinois
Mr. & Mrs. Richard H. Prins, Chicago, Illinois
Mr. & Mrs. Joseph A. Putz, Palos Heights, Illinois
Mr. Robert Pyle, Greenville, Delaware
Mr. Jeff McCarthy & Ms. Jane Quinn, Chicago, Illinois
Ms. Xue Y. Fung & Mr. David E. Reese, Chicago, Illinois
Mr. Clemens D. Reichel, PhD, Toronto, Canada
Mr. & Mrs. David R. Reynolds, Oak Park, Illinois
Ms. Ruth M. O'Brien & Prof. Stuart A. Rice, Chicago, Illinois
Mr. Dean F. Richardson, Pittsburgh, Pennsylvania
Mr. & Mrs. George G. Rinder, Burr Ridge, Illinois
Ronald Allan Ferguson, MD, & Ms. Agnes Ann Roach, Gurnee, Illinois
Karen Robinson, Saint Paul, Minnesota
Mr. Douglass F. Rohrman, Kenilworth, Illinois
Mrs. Leona Zweig Rosenberg, Chicago, Illinois
Mr. & Mrs. Martin Rosenstein, Santa Monica, California
Mr. Gregg Alan Rubinstein & Ms. Andrea Christine Blackburn, Washington, DC
Ms. Anne Rugh, Portland, Maine
Ms. Maria A. Rull, Brasilia, Brazil
Ms. Margaret Rutledge, Costa Mesa, California
Mr. & Mrs. Patrick G. Ryan, Chicago, Illinois
Mr. Mazin Fuad Safar & Mr. Michal Safar, Chicago, Illinois
Ms. Hilda Schlatter & Mr. Paul Sakol, Oak Park, Illinois
Mr. Dan Saltzman, Portland, Oregon
Mr. & Mrs. John Sanders, Chicago, Illinois
Mr. Peter Sargon, Chicago, Illinois
Ms. Lynne F. & Mr. Ralph Arthur Schatz, Chicago, Illinois
Mr. Paul Benjamin Schechter & Ms Naomi Reshotko, Denver, Colorado
Dr. & Mrs. Rolf G. Scherman, MD, Greenbrae, California
Mr. & Mrs. Timothy J. Schilling, Hammond, Indiana
Ms. Erika L. Schmidt, Ottawa, Illinois
Mr. Kirk Lee Schmink, Chicago, Illinois

$100–$249 (cont.)

Frank & Karen Schneider, Chicago, Illinois

Mr. Jonathan Green & Ms. Joy Schochet, Chicago, Illinois

Dr. Hans & Ms. Karin Schreiber, Chicago, Illinois

Ms. Lillian H. Schwartz, Chicago, Illinois

Ms. Alice Sgourakis, Oakland, California

Dr. Michael Sha, Carmel, Indiana

Mr. & Mrs. R. Chelsa Sharp, Limestone, Tennessee

Mr. Robert M. & Mrs. Tatiana A. Shelbourne, Washington, DC

Ms. Emma Shelton & Ms. Florence Kate Millar, Bethesda, Maryland

Mrs. Junia Shlaustas, Chicago, Illinois

Mr. Howard A. Shuman, Chicago, Illinois

Mr. George Shuttic, Washington, DC

Ms. Lois B. Siegel, Chicago, Illinois

Mrs. Adele Smith Simmons & Mr. John Simmons, Chicago, Illinois

Mrs. Diana & Mr. Robert Simon, Chicago, Illinois

Mr. Henno Simonlatser, Oakland, California

Professor W. Kelly Simpson, Katonah, New York

Ms. Ruth A. Singer, New York, New York

Mr. Michael A. Sisinger & Ms. Judith E. Waggoner, Columbus, Ohio

Dr. & Mrs. Henry D. Slosser, Pasadena, California

Mr. & Mrs. Kenneth Small, Irvine, California

Mr. Allen R. Smart, Chicago, Illinois

Mr. Douglas C. & Mrs. Teresa A. Smith, Calgary, Canada

Amelia Smithers, Gentiliano, Switzerland

Mr. & Mrs. Hugo F. Sonnenschein, Chicago, Illinois

Mr. Stephen C. Sperry, Litchfield, Minnesota

Mr. David A. Spetrino, Wilmington, North Carolina

Mr. Robert S. Spinelli, Chicago, Illinois

Mr. James & Mrs. Carol M. Springer, Washington, DC

Ms. H. A. Stelmach, Evanston, Illinois

Mrs. Phyllis Mazer Sternau, New York, New York

Mr. Stephen M. & Mrs. Virginia Stigler, Chicago, Illinois

Ms. Patricia Stoll, Wood Dale, Illinois

Mr. Gary David Strandlund & Ms. Jessica Jones, Batavia, Illinois

Dr. Jonathan Blake Strauss, Chicago, Illinois

Mr. & Mrs. Harold Stringer, Garland, Texas

Mr. George R. Sundell, Wheaton, Illinois

Reverend Darrell A. Sutton, Red Cloud, Nebraska

Mrs. Peggy Lewis Sweesy, San Diego, California

Mrs. Faye E. Takeuchi, Vancouver, Canada

Mrs. John Tatum, Oxford, Mississippi

Mr. Michael Tausch, Vancouver, Washington

The Malcolm Gibbs Foundation, Inc., New York, New York

Mr. & Mrs. Randolph Frank Thomas, Chicago, Illinois

Miss Kristin Thompson, Madison, Wisconsin

Mr. Charles E. Thonney, Torrance, California

Janet Todaro-Stubbs, PhD, Marblehead, Massachusetts

Mr. Gilbert D. Totten, Chicago, Illinois

Mr. & Mrs. John E. Townsend, Winnetka, Illinois

$100–$249 (cont.)

Mrs. Harriet M. Turk, Joliet, Illinois

U.S. Bancorp Foundation, Minneapolis, Minnesota

Mr. Sugihiko Uchida, Niigata, Japan

Ms. Lidwina Hout-Hui & Mr. Theo van den Hout, Chicago, Illinois

Ms. Annelize van der Ryst, Johannesburg, South Africa

Mr. Zsolt Vasaros, Budapest, Hungary

Ms. Eva von Dassow, Saint Paul, Minnesota

Dr. Kelvin Ward, Chicago, Illinois

Mr. Richard A. Watson & Professor Patty Jo Watson, Missoula, Montana

Mr. LeRoy Weber, Jr., Rio Vista, California

Mr. Johannes & Ms. Julia R. Weertman, Evanston, Illinois

Ms. Eileen & Mr. Tom Wehrheim, Oak Park, Illinois

Mr. & Mrs. J. Marshall Wellborn, New York, New York

Mr. Vic Whitmore, Boise, Idaho

Mrs. Joan V. & Mr. Raymond J. Wielgos, La Grange, Illinois

Ms. Elizabeth B. Wier, Naperville, Illinois

Dr. Katherine Wier, Chicago, Illinois

Mr. Ralph E. Wiggen, Los Angeles, California

Mrs. Audrey J. & Mr. David H. Wilson, Tucson, Arizona

Mr. & Mrs. R. Douglas Wilson, Annapolis, Maryland

Dr. Wendall W. Wilson, Victoria, Texas

Professor Robert C. Hunt & Professor Irene J. Winter, Cambridge, Massachusetts

Mrs. Grace W. Wolf, Chicago, Illinois

Ms. Ann S. Wolff, Winnetka, Illinois

Ms. Bette & Mr. James Wolfgang, Naperville, Illinois

Ms. Lorien Yonker, Chicago, Illinois

Ms. Carole Y. Yoshida, Orland Park, Illinois

Ms. Robin Young, La Habra, California

Mrs. Agnes Zellner, Chicago, Illinois

Mr. J. Raymond Zimmer, Charleston, South Carolina

Mr. Marvin Zonis & Ms. Lucy L. Salenger, Chicago, Illinois

We are grateful to the 1,014 Donors, Members, and Friends who contributed more than $47,000 in the form of gifts of up to $100 in 2010–2011. Due to space limitations, we are unable to list all our Friends-level donors in this volume; a special thanks to our Members and Donors for their support.

FACULTY AND STAFF

FACULTY AND STAFF OF THE ORIENTAL INSTITUTE

July 1, 2010–June 30, 2011

EMERITUS FACULTY

Lanny Bell, Associate Professor Emeritus of Egyptology

Robert D. Biggs, Professor Emeritus of Assyriology
r-biggs@uchicago.edu, 702-9540

John A. Brinkman, Charles H. Swift Distinguished Service Professor Emeritus
of Mesopotamian History
j-brinkman@uchicago.edu, 702-9545

Miguel Civil, Professor Emeritus of Sumerology
m-civil@uchicago.edu, 702-9542

Peter F. Dorman, Professor Emeritus of Egyptology
p-dorman@uchicago.edu

Gene B. Gragg, Professor Emeritus of Near Eastern Languages
g-gragg@uchicago.edu, 702-9511

Harry A. Hoffner, Jr., John A. Wilson Professor Emeritus of Hittitology & Co-editor
of Chicago Hittite Dictionary Project
hitt@uchicago.edu, 702-9551

William M. Sumner†, Professor Emeritus of Archaeology

Edward F. Wente, Professor Emeritus of Egyptology
e-wente@uchicago.edu, 702-9539

FACULTY

Fred M. Donner, Professor of Near Eastern History
f-donner@uchicago.edu, 702-9544

Walter T. Farber, Professor of Assyriology
w-farber@uchicago.edu, 702-9546

McGuire Gibson, Professor of Mesopotamian Archaeology
m-gibson@uchicago.edu, 702-9525

Petra Goedegebuure, Assistant Professor of Hittitology
pgoedegebuure@uchicago.edu, 702-9550

Norman Golb, Ludwig Rosenberger Professor in Jewish History and Civilization
n-golb@uchicago.edu, 702-9526

Rebecca Hasselbach, Assistant Professor of Comparative Semitics
hasselb@uchicago.edu, 834-3290

Janet H. Johnson, Morton D. Hull Distinguished Service Professor of Egyptology &
Editor of Chicago Demotic Dictionary Project
j-johnson@uchicago.edu, 702-9530

Walter E. Kaegi, Professor of Byzantine-Islamic Studies
kwal@uchicago.edu, 702-8346, 702-8397

Nadine Moeller, Assistant Professor of Egyptian Archaeology
nmoeller@uchicago.edu, 834-9761

Dennis G. Pardee, Henry Crown Professor of Hebrew Studies
d-pardee@uchicago.edu, 702-9541

Seth Richardson, Assistant Professor of Ancient Near Eastern History
seth1@uchicago.edu, 702-9552

Robert K. Ritner, Professor of Egyptology
r-ritner@uchicago.edu, 702-9547

Martha T. Roth, Chauncey S. Boucher Distinguished Service Professor of Assyriology, Director
& Editor-in-charge of Chicago Assyrian Dictionary Project and Dean of the Division of the
Humanities
nroth@uchicago.edu, 702-9551

David Schloen, Associate Professor of Syro-Palestinian Archaeology
d-schloen@uchicago.edu, 702-1382

Andrea Seri, Assistant Professor of Assyriology
aseri@uchicago.edu, 702-0131

Gil J. Stein, Professor of Near Eastern Archaeology & Director of the Oriental Institute
gstein@uchicago.edu, 702-4098

Matthew W. Stolper, John A. Wilson Professor of Assyriology, Director, Persepolis Fortification
Archive Project
m-stolper@uchicago.edu, 702-9553

Theo P. J. van den Hout, Professor of Hittite and Anatolian Languages,
Executive Editor of Chicago Hittite Dictionary Project, & Chairman of the Department of
Near Eastern Languages and Civilizations
tvdhout@uchicago.edu, 834-4688, 702-9527

Christopher Woods, Associate Professor of Sumerology & Editor of the *Journal of Near Eastern
Studies*
woods@uchicago.edu, 834-8560

K. Aslıhan Yener, Associate Professor of Archaeology
a-yener@uchicago.edu, 702-0568

RESEARCH ASSOCIATES

Abbas Alizadeh, Senior Research Associate, Iranian Prehistoric Project
a-alizadeh@uchicago.edu, 702-9531

Annalisa Azzoni, Research Associate, Persepolis Fortification Archive Project
annalisa.azzoni@vanderbilt.net

Richard H. Beal, Senior Research Associate, Chicago Hittite Dictionary Project
r-beal@uchicago.edu, 702-9527

Scott Branting, Research Associate (Assistant Professor) & Director, Center for Ancient Middle Eastern Landscapes (CAMEL)
branting@uchicago.edu, 834-1152

Stuart Creason, Research Associate, Syriac Manuscript Project
s-creason@uchicago.edu, 834-8348

Geoff Emberling, Research Associate & Chief Curator (until 9/30/10)

Jean Evans, Research Associate, Nippur Project

Gertrud Farber, Research Associate, Sumerian Lexicon Project
g-farber@uchicago.edu, 702-9548

Amir Sumaka'i Fink, Research Associate, Zincirli Project
asumakai@uchicago.edu

John L. Foster†, Research Associate, Egyptian Poetry

Mark Garrison, Research Associate, Persepolis Fortification Archive Project
mgarriso@trinity.edu

François Gaudard, Research Associate, Chicago Demotic Dictionary Project
fgaudard@uchicago.edu, 702-9528

Ronald Gorny, Research Associate, Alishar Regional Project
rlg2@uchicago.edu, 702-8624

Eleanor Guralnick, Research Associate, Khorsabad Project
guralnick@uchicago.edu

Wouter Henkelman, Research Associate, Persepolis Fortification Archive

Thomas A. Holland, Research Associate, Tell es-Sweyhat Project
t-holland@uchicago.edu

Carrie Hritz, Research Associate, Zeidan Project, Girsu Project

W. Raymond Johnson, Research Associate (Associate Professor) & Field Director, Epigraphic Survey
wr-johnson@uchicago.edu, 834-4355

Charles E. Jones, Research Associate
cejo@uchicago.edu

Morag Kersel, Research Associate, Galilee Prehistory Project

Mark Lehner, Research Associate, Giza Plateau Mapping Project
MarkLehner@aol.com

Lec Maj, Research Associate, Persepolis Fortification Archive Project
lec@uchicago.edu

Gregory Marouard, Research Associate, Tell Edfu Project
marouardg@uchicago.edu, 834-4270

J. Brett McClain, Research Associate & Senior Epigrapher, Epigraphic Survey
jbmcclai@uchicago.edu, 702-9524

Carol Meyer, Research Associate, Bir Umm Fawakhir Project
c-meyer@uchicago.edu

Rana Özbal, Research Associate, Tell Kurdu Project

Hratch Papazian, Research Associate

Marina Pucci, Research Associate, Chatal Höyük Publication Project

Clemens D. Reichel, Senior Research Associate, Diyala Project
cdreiche@uchicago.edu, 416-586-7938

Yorke Rowan, Research Associate, Ancient Studies and Director, Galilee Prehistory Project
ymrowan@uchicago.edu, 702-0086

Abdul-Massih Saadi, Research Associate, Syriac Manuscript Initiative
asaadi@nd.edu, (574) 631-8419

Moain Sadeq, Research Associate
msadeq@uchicago.edu

John C. Sanders, Senior Research Associate & Head, Computer Laboratory
jc-sanders@uchicago.edu, 702-0989

Seth Sanders, Research Associate, West Semitic Political Lexicon

Oğuz Soysal, Senior Research Associate, Chicago Hittite Dictionary Project
o-soysal@uchicago.edu, 702-3644

Benjamin Studevent-Hickman, Research Associate
benjaminsh@yahoo.com

Geoffrey D. Summers, Research Associate, Kerkenes Project
summers@metu.edu.tr

Emily Teeter, Research Associate & Special Exhibits Coordinator
eteeter@uchicago.edu, 702-1062

Raymond Tindel, Research Associate
r-tindel@uchicago.edu

Donald Whitcomb, Research Associate (Associate Professor) of Islamic and Medieval Archaeology
d-whitcomb@uchicago.edu, 702-9530

Magnus Widell, Research Associate
widell@uchicago.edu

Tony Wilkinson, Research Associate, MASS Project
t.j.wilkinson@durham.ac.uk

Bruce Williams, Research Associate
    Bbwillia@uchicago.edu, 702-3686

Karen L. Wilson, Research Associate
    k-wilson@uchicago.edu

Richard Zettler, Research Associate
    rzettler@sas.upenn.edu

STAFF

Keli Alberts, Artist, Epigraphic Survey
    kelialberts@hotmail.com

Susan Allison, Assistant Registrar, Museum
    srallison@uchicago.edu, 702-9518

Alain Arnaudiès, Digital Archives Database, Epigraphic Survey
    arnaudies@laposte.net

Emmanuelle Arnaudiès, Digital Archives Database, Epigraphic Survey
    emmanuellearnaudies@free.fr

Denise Browning, Manager, Suq
    d-browning1@uchicago.edu, 702-9509

Marie Bryan, Librarian, Epigraphic Survey
    mebryan@usa.net, 702-9524

Steven Camp, Executive Director
    shcamp@uchicago.edu, 702-1404

Dennis Campbell, Research Project Professional, Persepolis Fortification Archive Project
    drcampbell@uchicago.edu, 702-5249

Jessica Caracci, Education Programs Associate, Public Education (until 3/31/11)

D'Ann Condes, Financial Management Assistant
    dcondes@uchicago.edu, 834-0451

Simona Cristanetti, Contract Conservator, Museum (from 3/7/11)
    cristanetti@uchicago.edu, 702-9519

Laura Culbertson, Postdoctoral Scholar (until 8/31/10)

Laura D'Alessandro, Head, Conservation Laboratory, Museum
    lada@uchicago.edu, 702-9519

Margaret De Jong, Artist, Epigraphic Survey
    mdejong98ch@hotmail.com, 702-9524

Christina Di Cerbo, Epigrapher, Epigraphic Survey
    tinadicerbo@hotmail.com, 702-9524

Catherine Dueñas, Volunteer Programs Associate, Public Education
    cjduenas@uchicago.edu , 702-1845

Virginia Emery, Epigrapher, Epigraphic Survey
vlemery@uchicago.edu, 702-9524

Wendy Ennes, Associate Head, Public Education
wennes@uchicago.edu, 834-7606

Terry Friedman, Volunteer Programs Associate, Public Education
et-friedman@uchicago.edu, 702-1845

Christian Greco, Epigrapher, Epigraphic Survey
christian.greco@usa.net

Samir Guindy, Administrator, Epigraphic Survey
samsgu1952@hotmail.com

Lotfi Hassan, Conservator, Epigraphic Survey
hslotfi@yahoo.it, 702-9524

Robyn Haynie, Contract Conservator, Museum (from 5/2/11)
rhaynie@uchicago.edu, 702-9519

James B. Heidel, Architect, Epigraphic Survey
jbheidel@gmail.com, 702-9524

Anait Helmholz, Library Assistant, Epigraphic Survey
anaith@succeed.net

Frank Helmholz, Mason, Epigraphic Survey
frankhel@succeed.net

Jason Herrmann, Research Project Professional, Persepolis Fortification Archive Project (from
10/6/10)
herrmann@uchicago.edu

Carla Hosein, Financial Manager
cchosein@uchicago.edu, 834-9886

Thomas James, Assistant Curator of Digital Collections, Museum
trjames@uchicago.edu, 834-8950

Helen Jacquet, Egyptologist Consultant, Epigraphic Survey
jeanhelka@aol.com, 702-9524

Jean Jacquet, Architect Consultant, Epigraphic Survey
jeanhelka@aol.com, 702-9524

Richard Jasnow, Epigrapher Consultant, Epigraphic Survey
rjasnow@jhu.edu, 702-9524

Hiroko Kariya, Conservator, Epigraphic Survey
hkariya@aol.com, 702-9524

Jen Kimpton, Epigrapher, Epigraphic Survey
jenkimpton@hotmail.com, 702-9524

Yarko Kobylecky, Photographer, Epigraphic Survey
museumphoto@hotmail.com, 702-9524

Carole Krucoff, Head, Public Education
c-krucoff@uchicago.edu, 702-9507

John Larson, Museum Archivist, Museum
ja-larson@uchicago.edu, 702-9924

Susan Lezon, Photo Archivist and Photographer, Epigraphic Survey
suelezon@gmail.com, 702-9524

Erik Lindahl, Gallery Preparator, Museum
lindahl@uchicago.edu, 702-9516

Adam Lubin, Security and Visitor Services Supervisor
alubin@uchicago.edu, 702-5112

Jill Carlotta Maher, Assistant to the Director of the Epigraphic Survey
jillcarlottamaher@yahoo.com, 702-9524

Samwell Maher, Assistant Administrator, Epigraphic Survey
samwellmaher@yahoo.com, 702-9524

Natalia Naomi May, Postdoctoral Scholar (from 9/1/10)
natalmay@uchicago.edu, 702-2589

Helen McDonald, Registrar, Museum
helenmcd@uchicago.edu, 702-9518

Kathleen R. Mineck, Managing Editor, Journal of Near Eastern Studies
kmineck@uchicago.edu, 702-9592

Clinton Moyer, Research Project Professional, Persepolis Fortification Archive Project (until 6/21/11)

Susan Osgood, Artist, Epigraphic Survey
sittsu@sover.net, 702-9524

Safinaz Ouri, Finance Manager, Epigraphic Survey (until 3/31/11)

Mariana Perlinac, Assistant to the Director
oi-administration@uchicago.edu, 834-8098

Conor Power, Structural Engineer, Epigraphic Survey
conorpower@msn.com, 702-9524

Miller Prosser, Research Project Professional, Persepolis Fortification Archive Project (from 6/9/11)
m-prosser@uchicago.edu

Maeve Reed, Membership Coordinator
oi-membership@uchicago.edu, 834-9777

Anna Ressman, Head of Photography, Museum
annaressman@uchicago.edu, 702-9517

Essam el Sayed, Senior Accountant, Epigraphic Survey (from 4/1/11)
essam_nados, 702-9524

Foy Scalf, Head of Research Archives
scalffd@uchicago.edu, 702-9537

Sandra Schloen, Database Analyst, Chicago Hittite Dictionary Project, & Persepolis Fortification Archive Project
sschloen@uchicago.edu

Julia Schmied, Blockyard and Archives Assistant, Epigraphic Survey
julisch@citromail.hu, 702-9524

Leslie Schramer, Editor, Publications Office
leslie@uchicago.edu, 702-5967

Rebecca Silverman, Development Associate (until 5/31/11)

Kathryn Silverstein, Education Programs Associate, Public Education (from 6/9/11)
ksilverstein@uchicago.edu, 702-9507

Elinor Smith, Photo Archives Registrar, Epigraphic Survey
elliesmith26@yahoo.com, 702-9524

Karen Terras, Research Project Professional, Nippur Project (until 6/30/11)

Thomas Urban, Managing Editor, Publications Office
t-urban@uchicago.edu, 702-5967

Krisztián Vértes, Artist, Epigraphic Survey
euergetes@freemail.hu, 702-9524

Alison Whyte, Associate Conservator, Conservation Laboratory, Museum
aawhyte@uchicago.edu, 702-9519

Meghan Winston, Assistant Director of Development for Special Events
meghanwinston@uchicago.edu, 834-9775

Brian Zimerle, Preparator
zimerle@uchicago.edu, 702-9516

NOTES

INFORMATION

The Oriental Institute
1155 East 58th Street
Chicago, Illinois 60637

Museum gallery hours:
    Tuesday and Thursday to Saturday 10:00 AM–6:00 PM
    Wednesday 10:00 AM–8:30 PM
    Sunday 12:00 NOON–6:00 PM

Telephone Numbers (Area Code 773) and Electronic Addresses

Administrative Office, oi-administration@uchicago.edu, 702-9514
Archaeology Laboratory, 702-1407
Executive Director, 702-1404
Assyrian Dictionary Project, 702-9551
Computer Laboratory, 702-0989
Conservation Laboratory, 702-9519
Department of Near Eastern Languages and Civilizations, 702-9512
Demotic Dictionary Project, 702-9528
Development Office, 834-9775
Director's Office, 834-8098
Epigraphic Survey, 702-9524
Facsimile, 702-9853
Hittite Dictionary Project, 702-9543
Journal of Near Eastern Studies, 702-9592
Membership Office, oi-membership@uchicago.edu, 702-9513
Museum Archives, 702-9520
Museum Information, 702-9520
Museum Office, oi-museum@uchicago.edu, 702-9520
Museum Registration, 702-9518
Public Education, oi-education@uchicago.edu, 702-9507
Publications Editorial Office, oi-publications@uchicago.edu, 702-5967
Research Archives, 702-9537
Security, 702-9522
Suq Gift and Book Shop, 702-9510
Suq Office, 702-9509
Volunteer Guides, 702-1845

World-Wide Web Address

oi.uchicago.edu